Science for Humanism

In the eighteenth century, the pre-modern Judeo-Greco-Christian problem of freedom and determinism is transformed by Kant into the modern problem of the freedom of human agency in the natural and cultural worlds of deterministic structures; it is this version of the freedom and determinism issue which centers the Science and Humanism debates, and thus marks the history of the social sciences.

Anthony Giddens is credited with providing the new vocabulary of "structure" and "agency" in order to formulate the problem of freedom and determinism in those terms, thus making this formulation fruitful. In this book, Charles R. Varela proposes that Kant originally formulated this problem, and makes a series of wide-ranging and groundbreaking observations based on Kant's metaphysics of realism which enables Varela to propose a solution to the structure/agency problem.

Subjects revisited in this book include:

- "Giddens's Call"
- The stalemate of the social and psychological sciences
- The determinist tradition of modern science
- Postmodernism

This breadth of themes, drawn together by Varela with his work on Kant, fully realizes Giddens's principle that human agency is a real causal force. It is Kant's conception of causal power that is the causal force that Giddens's has called for.

Science For Humanism: The Recovery of Human Agency will be of particular interest to students of humanism and therefore realism, Kant, and Giddens.

Charles R. Varela was a professor of psychology and sociology for 37 years at Union County College, Cranford, New Jersey. As a research associate in the Department of Anthropology at the University of Illinois, he is engaged in writing papers and books for the scholarly community and is electively involved in graduate seminars on social and anthropological theory.

Ontological Investigations

Other Books in the Series:

From One "Empire" to the Next
Radha D'Souza

Science for Humanism

The recovery of human agency

Charles R. Varela

Routledge
Taylor & Francis Group

LONDON AND NEW YORK

First published 2009
by Routledge
2 Park Square, Milton Park, Abingdon, Oxon OX14 4RN

Simultaneously published in the USA and Canada
by Routledge
270 Madison Avenue, New York, NY 10016

Routledge is an imprint of the Taylor & Francis Group, an informa business

© 2009 Charles R. Varela

Typeset in Times New Roman
by Taylor & Francis Books
Printed and bound in Great Britain by
CPI Antony Rowe, Chippenham, Wiltshire

British Library Cataloguing in Publication Data
A catalogue record for this book is available from the British Library

Library of Congress Cataloging in Publication Data
Varela, Charles.
    Science for humanism : the recovery of human agency / Charles R.
Varela.
        p. cm.
    [etc.]
    1. Humanism. 2. Agent (Philosophy) I. Title.
    B821.V37 2009
    128'.4–dc22
    2008034972

ISBN 0-415-48182-1 (hbk)
ISBN 0-415-48520-7 (pbk)
ISBN 0-203-88227-X (ebk)

ISBN 978-0-415-48182-3 (hbk)
ISBN 978-0-415-48520-3 (pbk)
ISBN 978-0-203-88227-6 (ebk)

The spirit only becomes free at the point where it ceases to be invoked as a support

Franz Kafka

Contents

Preface

Since the 1970s, a growing number of social scientists informed by realist philosophies of science have come to believe that they have therefore moved into a time "After Postmodernism" (Lopez and Potter 2001). What especially marks this historical movement is the opening up of a new encounter between Science and Humanism. While the old encounter was between Positivism and Humanism, the new one is between science as the realist practice that it is, and the social sciences as – quite naturally – a humanist enterprise. This unprecedented encounter is informed by Humanism's proper regard for preserving the ontological integrity of human being. My focus on ontology (metaphysics) stems from the Science/Humanism problem of establishing the reality of human freedom against the standard view that determinism threatens it. Generally, I maintain that the way in which the reality of human freedom can be legitimately established is by formulating a theory of human cultural practice that provides ontologically adequate conceptions of human agency, embodiment, discourse, and particularly, that those conceptions should emerge from their interconnections in human social action.

Underwriting the above humanist metaphysical concern, and its conceptual ambitions from the standpoint of a realist view of natural science, is the following new understanding of the social sciences: ontology is the deep business of scientific theory, and thus the regard for the ontology of human being is a legitimate theoretical interest for social scientists so informed. It is this understanding that creates the possibility of naturalism in the social sciences. The crucial lesson of Rom Harré's philosophy of scientific realism for the social sciences identifies what I am after, and Roy Bhaskar's elegant understanding of it is captured in this paraphrase: in the desire to be a science in the same sense, but not in the same way, as the natural sciences, the social sciences should pursue the precision of meaning and not the accuracy of measurement. It is Harrean realism that informs us that the accuracy of measurement is an unrealistic dogma of positivist social science in its *experimental* research ambitions. It also shows us that the precision of meaning is the best that can be achieved in social science in the theoretical work that informs its *naturalistic* research endeavors. Thus, from this realist perspective on rigor and its relevance to the social sciences I can decisively define my scientific ontological interest: the aim to establish the reality of human freedom by virtue of attaining an ontological conception of human agency, is to be seen as an instance of the pursuit of the precision of meaning. In this book, *Science For Humanism: the Recovery of Human Agency*, my theoretical interest is to show that science, properly conceived as a realist practice, promotes the recovery of human agency from the alleged fact of deterministic structures that supposedly threaten the very possibility of our agency. In this special way, science, not positivism, can be *for* humanism, in the latter's commitment to preserving the ontological integrity of human being; especially in its freedom.

The proper regard for the ontological reality of the freedom of human being that I am arguing a realist science makes possible, is the best that such a New Humanism can now offer those social scientists who understand Marshall Sahlins's (1982) correct insistence that the social sciences should be interested in the problem of freedom and determinism as a matter of course. In reference to the New Humanism, and, because of it, Foucault's attempt to discredit Humanism by virtue of the historical variability of its substantive commitments, just cannot be taken seriously any longer; certainly not from the standpoint of the work of his last period when seen from the perspective of his paper, "What is Enlightenment?" There, Foucault returns to Kant in order to reclaim a notion of human agency, on Baudelaire's terms, to inform his (Foucault's) version of his work as a Kantian critical project. However, Foucault's return results in a reclamation of agency that is in principle the same as the traditional humanist return to Kant, in order to *rescue* human agency from the natural and human worlds of alleged deterministic structures. Reclaiming or rescuing human agency in this manner simply amounts to its affirmation as a subjective truth in the terms of a belief in, or the experience of, human agency. However, such an affirmation is an antidote, rather than an answer to, the ontological question of whether it is the case that a deterministic natural world is incapable of providing a ground for a conception of the agency of physical particulars, and hence for a conception of the agency of human persons. While Foucault perpetuated the standard terms of the Science (as positivism) and Humanism debate on human agency with, wittingly or unwittingly, an earlier theory of discourse determinism, I will elsewhere show that his later work clearly reveals him to be struggling to overcome that earlier mistake. And not without some impressive success in reference to the structure and agency problem.

In referring to the irreconcilable conflict between Science (as positivism) and Humanism that centers around the traditional idea of human agency as a reality *outside* of the natural world of determinism, the structure and agency problem has, on the one hand, set up Science (as positivism) to be *against* Humanism in the name of its commitment to determinism. On the other hand, the conflict has set up Humanism to be involved in some form of a *defiance* of Science in the name of its commitment to freedom. The upshot is that the humanist rescue, or its anti-humanist reclamation, pays the price of being unable to provide any cogent conception of human agency as a *real causal force* with respect to the worlds of nature and culture. As a direct result, the cardinal thesis that drives *Science For Humanism* is that *there can be no viable theory of human agency without a cogent ontological conception of human agency as a real causal force.* Thanks to the foundational work of Rom Harré and Roy Bhaskar in the philosophy of scientific realism, Russell Keat, importantly, and Peter T. Manicas, especially, have articulated for us the philosophical and historical mistake of conflating science and positivism. As a direct consequence of the achievement, we have been granted an insight into the inner sanctum of the Science and Humanism debate at issue. And that is, that the failure of the strategy of rescuing freedom from nature is the case only within the confines of the traditional Science and Humanism encounter wherein both sides tacitly assume that science is a positivist practice. The absolutely critical point is that positivism is rooted in Humean empiricism, which substitutes correlation (regularity or constant conjunction) for causality (causal power), and hence prescribes a metaphysic of nature which is devoid of *any* kind of real causal forces, whether physical, biological, or indeed human. Hence, Nietzsche never got it quite right: it is not that God is dead, it is that nature is dead – without agency – and so the very idea of God – the supreme agent – is impossible. In reference to Nietzsche's story, therefore, there is no God, in the first place, to kill. This is no surprise, for, given the supremacy of Hume's legacy, which Nietzsche and just about everybody else took for granted, Nietzsche never understood causality, and so he never understood science, to begin with. But of course, as a closet and most treacherous realist, Freud did, and then improperly assigned the status of supreme agency to the unconscious and not the person.

It is exactly on this question of the ontological viability of the humanist idea of human agency that Anthony Giddens's work turns out to be of fundamental importance for this book. In *New Rules of Sociological Method* (1976) and *Central Problems in Social Theory* (1979) Giddens appears to have been the first to have transformed the traditional problem of freedom and determinism (tucked away in the Parsonian vocabulary of system and voluntarism) into the late modern problem of structure and agency. As a matter of historical fact, however, I argue that Giddens has, without quite realizing it, rediscovered Kant's original formulation of the problem of deterministic structures and embodied human agency that centers the three *Critiques.*

In my reading, with what amounts to an implied claim to a new kind of Humanism, Giddens's ultimate concern with preserving the ontological integrity of human being can now be appreciated as aiming to establish the reality of human agency in a natural world of other kinds of agency. In other words, in declaring that human agency is to be understood as a species of a non-Humean causality in nature, Giddens refers to it as an "agent causality."

Here, exactly, we have Giddens's key idea: the threat of determinism to human freedom can be set to one side in favor of the deeper (originally Kantian) thesis that freedom itself is a form of determinism that is to be understood, anew. Giddens has openly admitted that, since he does not know how to fulfill the requirement of a causally grounded concept of human agency, consequently he can only make this ontological claim dogmatically. *The goal of this book is to realize Giddens's dogmatic principle that human agency is a real causal force.*

This significant principle and the call for its realization is exactly what Mestrovic (1998) has completely missed in his otherwise reasonable, although traditionally speaking, quite expected, critique of Giddens's theory of agency. Mestrovic dismisses it as being nothing more than an overemphasis on rationality, and therefore, he insists, seriously omits human passion and irrationality. But of course in this ontologically uncritical reemphasis on human passion and irrationality we are up against, once more, the Freudian trick of using the unconscious to ground human irrationality. Thus we have been returned to the paradigm instance of the problem of structure and agency: the loss of human agency in the deterministic structure of the (psychological, social, cultural, linguistic) unconscious. While Mestrovic abandons us to this problem, once more, a proper understanding of Giddens's version of it opens up a way to address it fruitfully.

My proposal for answering what I shall refer to as "Giddens's Call," is the following: *instead of employing the traditional humanist strategy of returning to Kant in order to rescue human agency from the natural world, a New Humanism directs us instead to return to Kant for the purpose of recovering natural agency from the physical world, which then enables us to recover human agency from a new understanding of Kant's theory of freedom for the cultural world.* Inspired by the *purpose* of Foucault's return to Kant, but *informed* instead by Giddens's Call, my return to Kant for the recovery of agency is directed by the philosophy of scientific realism that has been presented first and foremost in the work of Rom Harré, and then of course, Roy Bhaskar. In the case of Harré, his systematic work on the conceptions of causal powers and plausibility is of paramount importance here, while Bhaskar's breakthrough insight into the fallacy of the very idea of determinism is fundamental to my endeavor. Furthermore, the recovery of human agency is exactly what Harré's Kantian-centered theory of personal being (1984) and Roy Bhaskar's Kantian-informed theory of human agency (1979) presume, but do not provide.

Charles (Carlos) R. Varela
December 2008

Acknowledgements

I want to especially thank Rom Harré for his tireless and excellent reading and re-reading of the manuscript, and his spot-on suggestions to improve the clarity and directness of the thematic structure of the discussion. In this regard, I also want to thank Douglas Porpora for his sympathetic reading of the manuscript. To my dear friend and colleague, Alejandro Lugo, I thank him for his absolute belief in the value of *Science For Humanism: The Recovery of Human Agency*. To my "brother" Larry Ferrara, I thank him for his extraordinary appreciation of this work; an appreciation that never sacrificed the demand for excellence. And Andy Tuck, what can I say, but thanks for your readings. Last, but never least, I thank my partner, friend, and colleague, Brenda Farnell, for her most intelligent support of this work and always, her keen understanding of what I am doing.

Part I
Science for Humanism

1 Historical context
Humanism and Giddens's Call

Introduction

During the last 40 years of the twentieth century the decline of various positivist philosophies of science was accompanied by a rise in a variety of realist philosophies of science (contrary to Skinner 1990: 5–6, 1–20). This realist turn is evidenced in the works of Jerrold L. Aronson (1984, 1995), Roy Bhaskar (1975 [1998]), Mario Bunge (1979 [1959], 1996), Rom Harré (1970, 1975, 1986, 1993), Stephen Mumford (1998), and William A. Wallace (1974, 1996). At the margins of the social sciences with the 1970s and since, this new development worked its way into the philosophy of social science and thus promoted a quiet and modest pursuit of the possibility of naturalism in the social sciences. This was initially reflected in the work of Margaret Archer (1995, 1996 [1988], 2000), Roy Bhaskar (1979,1991), Rom Harré (1979, 1984, 1991), Russell Keat and John Urry (1975), Peter T. Manicas (1987, 2006), and John Shotter (1993). There are three major results of the realist turn that I will be briefly dealing with here in order to bring out both the historical context that justifies *Science for Humanism: the Recovery of Human Agency,* and the theoretical framework that promotes it.

In my judgment, there has been a particular result of the shift to scientific realism in the social sciences that is of cardinal importance: the reopening of the Science and Humanism debate on the ontology of human being, especially with respect to its key problem of freedom and determinism. In the second half of twentieth-century social science that problem has gone through two critical formulations: while Parsons's vocabulary of "(social) system and (individual) voluntarism" dominated the three decades from the 1950s to the 1970s, the last 25 years of the twentieth century witnessed its transformation into Giddens's new vocabulary of "(social) structure and agency." As we will now see, the realist turn in the philosophy of science is presupposed by the sociological problem of *social* structure and human agency, and that very fact encourages the move to *generalize it to be the problem of deterministic structures and human agency.*

In each of the social sciences their respective theoretical interests have given us the traditional structures of the psychological, the social, and the cultural. I now want to propose that the theoretical thread that connects these three structures into a fundamental metaphysical problem is based on the non-traditional structures of biology and language. Biology can then be understood as resolving into two internally related concepts: the organism and the body; and language can also be understood as resolving into two internally related concepts: practices and discourse. The second somatic revolution in the social scientific theorizing of embodiment that stems from the combined work of Drid Williams, Brenda Farnell, and Charles Varela leads to the proposal that biology and language can be assimilated under the key concept of dynamically embodied discursive practices (Farnell and Varela 2008 in press; Williams 1982: 161–82). Hence, I can now assert that the general problem of structure(s) and agency can be given an enriched formulation: *the problem of deterministic structures and dynamically embodied discursive agency.*

In this book, my interest is restricted to the fundamental problem of deterministic structure and human agency. For the sake of convenience, although he never presented it, as far as I know, with this generalization and enrichment in mind, I will refer to this new formulation simply as Giddens's problem of structure and agency.

The realist turn and the problem of structure and agency, furthermore, are connected in what I will refer to as Giddens's Call. The "Call" is articulated in the *New Rules of Sociological Method* (1976: 91): a viable theory of structuration is in need of a suitable realist philosophy of science in order to ground its concept of human agency in a concept of "agent causality." Particularly important for this book's interest is the understanding that there is a specific implication in Giddens's theory of structuration: any prospect of a solution to the structure and agency problem will take the form of an answer to that "Call."

The second result of the realist turn is an examination of the phenomenological theory of freedom that threads together the philosophical work of Wilhelm Dilthey, Edmund Husserl, Martin Heidegger, Jean-Paul Sartre, and Maurice Merleau-Ponty from the perspective of Giddens's Call. This theory of freedom in all of its varieties has been of great importance, for it has informed and fueled the Humanist revolt against Science in the social sciences in the three decades that spanned the 1950s to the 1970s. The use of Giddens's perspective allows us to discover that the theory of phenomenological freedom turns out to be, itself, the crucial reason for the demise of the Science and Humanism debate as we entered the 1980s. *In other words, the death of traditional Humanism in the social sciences must be laid at the doorstep of the phenomenological tradition.* To see this clearly, the key theorist here is Merleau-Ponty: his representative theory of freedom openly addresses the structure and agency problem, and in doing so, human freedom is, technically speaking, actually being cast as the "power of agency." However, in Merleau-Ponty's traditional phenomenological denial of science that was his signature to the very end, it will be shown that this concept of freedom as a power of agency is thus deprived of any possibility of being correctly grounded in a concept of "agent causality." Thus, this particular effort to rescue freedom from determinism is fatally limited to being a defiance of determinism by the theoretically ineffective act of merely affirming freedom. Here, precisely, is the very reason why the phenomenological theory of freedom leads to the death of traditional Humanism. And yet, Merleau-Ponty's theory of agency as a "power" can be given a new lease of life if it is simply addressed in terms of the entire metaphysical context of Giddens's problem of structure and agency. Indeed, I now want to propose that this entire context of the problem of structure and agency, the call to ground agency in "agent causality," and the turn to scientific realism that the call implies, is indeed the emergence of a New Humanism in the social sciences.

The third major result will be an examination of both the Postmodernism of Knowledge and its complementary, the Postmodern Philosophy of Science (Best and Kellner 2003: 285–88; Giddens 1979; Harré 1998: 353–77; Newton 1997: 8–44). The two Postmodernisms together make up a serious challenge to the view taken here, that structure and agency is a genuine problem, and thus is open to possible solutions under the auspices of a suitable realist philosophy of science. The challenge to this view from the Postmodernism of Knowledge is found in Jacques Derrida's theory of language and in Jean Baudrillard's theory of hyper-reality. Specifically, it is an implication of Derrida's theory that human freedom is to be identified with the spontaneous structural activity of human language that constitutes a reality wholly unto itself. Thus, the world of natural causation is not a problem for human freedom because the latter is imprisoned in the solipsism of the lived life of human language. The other challenge from the Postmodernism of Knowledge in the case of Jean Baudrillard goes one step further. His outright banishment of "reality" and the "social" seems to eliminate both "structure" and "agency" as possible problems. For, the implication is that there is no natural reality for there to be any problem of deterministic structures, and there is no social reality for there to be any issue of human agency. But there is another similar but deeper challenge to taking seriously Giddens's problem and its possible solution that issues from the Postmodernism of the philosophy of science.

Harré's analysis of the idea of science in the works of Nelson Goodman, Richard Rorty, Bruno Latour, and Ian Hacking, indicates that they converge, however unwittingly, on a common outcome: the delegitimation of the rational and empirical authority of natural science. The concept of nature, the sovereign pillar of Western theological, philosophical, and scientific realism, is exclusively reduced to being the social construction of the scientific cultural community. And as a direct consequence, science itself thus is taken to be just another community that of course arbitrarily privileges its ontological beliefs. From such a standpoint, the problem of deterministic structures and the freedom of human agency is an artifact of a radical social constructionism. In short, there can be no such problem.

The three major results of the realist turn in the social sciences are here intimately connected: the reopening of the Science and Humanism debate promotes the question as to the possible relevance of the phenomenological tradition and the two Postmodernisms to the advancement of social scientific theory, specifically with respect to the prospect of a solution to Giddens's problem of structure and agency. The answer that I will present is that a fatal inadequacy in the theory of phenomenological freedom and in the two Postmodernisms of Knowledge justifies the conclusion that they are irrelevant to the new Science and Humanism debate concerning the problem of structure and agency. Thus, in consequence, I am afforded the opportunity to take the Science and Humanism debate seriously, and, under the auspices of Giddens's New Humanism, to present an answer to his Call: *the recovery of human agency.*

Humanism in defiance of science: Kant, Dilthey, and Heidegger

Throughout the modern history of the encounter of Science and Humanism the debate on the problem of freedom and determinism has been based on this theme: *in its idea that determinism is the reality behind the appearance of freedom Science is against Humanism; in its affirmation of freedom in defiance of that determinism Humanism is against Science.* The theme is underwritten by the following principle: since the natural and human worlds are constituted by a metaphysic (ontology) of deterministic structures, there can be no metaphysical space for the grounding of natural agency in the physical world nor human agency in the cultural world. In the *Critique of Pure Reason* (1781) and in the *Critique of Practical Reason* (1788), Kant proposed a two-world (or two-story) solution as a way out of this predicament with respect to human freedom: within the metaphysical framework of scientific naturalism, freedom is to be located in the noumenal realm and determinism is to be located in the phenomenal realm (Allison 1990, 1995). The metaphysical character of Kant's two-world solution, however, poses a serious problem, to which Pistorius, Dilthey, and Heidegger have given us three complementary interpretations. In 1794 Herman Andreas Pistorius famously articulated this problem, which, today, Henry E. Allison informs us is still accepted in modern philosophy as the essence of the difficulty of Kant's theory of freedom (Allison Ibid: 29).

> I readily confess that this double character of man, these *two I's in the single subject,* are for me, in spite of all the explanations which Kant and his students have given it, particularly with respect to the resolution of the well known antinomy of freedom, the most *obscure* and *incomprehensible* in the entire critical philosophy
>
> (Allison 1990: 29, emphasis provided)

Pistorius's specific reference to the resolution of the antinomy of freedom is the actual site of the problem, to be sure. However, he is, nevertheless, crucially vague concerning the specific issue of the perplexity of the two "I's" in the third antinomy. For now, this perplexity can be quickly indicated in a single statement when Kant says that, "Reason in its causality is not subject to any conditions of appearance or time" (Kant1985a: A 556 B 584). It must be precisely noted that in *this* statement Kant does *not* actually say that freedom as reason is a causal act that is "not in time," but that it is "not subject to any conditions of ... time." For now, this difference, and it will be shown to be a significant difference, will be set to one side; I will, then, treat this issue according to the received or traditional view in the history of philosophy. In that history, Kant's theory of freedom is a revolutionary response to the Judeo-Greco-Christian traditional theory of *Transcendent* freedom: a *spiritual* power that is a reality *neither in time nor in space.* This, technically, is the root of the commonsense version of this theory referred to as freedom of the will; in short, free will. Thus, in the case of Kantian theory the issue of freedom can be stated as follows. When human subjects are considered to be in the phenomenal realm (the first "I") and therefore are in space and *in time,* they are thus under the conditions of determinism: hence freedom is impossible; nevertheless, when those same subjects are considered to be in the noumenal realm (the second "I") and are *not in time,* they are in consequence under the conditions of freedom: hence freedom is possible. Concerning the distinction between phenomenal determinism and noumenal freedom, it is important to observe, as the quote clearly reveals, that Kant actually took the distinction to be a reference to two types of causality: for the former, the "causality of nature," for the latter, the "causality of (or through) freedom." Kant thus provided us with a two-world theory of the problem of freedom and determinism, which has been interpreted as giving us a special and specific solution to that problem: *the possibility of freedom is a matter of rescuing freedom from the phenomenal world by locating it not in the spiritual but in the noumenal world.*

It is in this strict sense of the location of freedom in reference to space and time that Kantian freedom and religious freedom can be precisely differentiated: the former is transcendental but not transcendent, whereas the latter is transcendent but not transcendental. Furthermore, ontologically speaking, transcendental freedom is thus situated in the metaphysical space of naturalism, and so, of course, transcendent freedom is situated in the metaphysical space of supernaturalism. Ultimately, therefore, the Kantian theory of freedom is integral to his Copernican Revolution in philosophy, as the latter is located within the context of the Scientific Revolution.

Dilthey: noumenal to phenomenological

In the late nineteenth century Dilthey's revolt against Kant's theory of freedom, I contend, was precisely a revolt against (let us now say) the Pistorius issue of the atemporality of freedom (as clarified above); and this can be seen in the following three quotes from Dilthey's *Introduction to the Human*

Sciences (1989). The important point to pick out here is that Dilthey gives us a three-part conception of human agency, or what he in fact calls an "efficacy of the will" – *"power," "temporality," and "dynamic embodiment"* (Farnell and Varela 2008).

Power

Here we only want to emphasize what we find in our own *lived experience,* namely, that the will can direct our representations and set our limbs in motion, and that it has this capacity *even when it is not exercising it.* Indeed, in the event of an external restraint, *this capacity can be immobilized* by a similar or greater force, *but is nevertheless felt as present.* Thus we grasp the representation of an *effectuating capacity (or a power)* which precedes the particular effective act; particular voluntary acts and deeds flow from a sort of *reservoir of effective force* [thus a power]. ... [a] productive force.

(Dilthey Ibid: 20–21, my emphasis)

Temporality

It is much more difficult to conceive the ideality of time than that of space, since time is just as much the form of inner lived experience [of the efficacy of the will] as of outer processes [constituted by the efficacies of other wills and physical and biological entities]. The increase in the intensity of attention or the feeling of pain is given as reflexive awareness. It is contained in every reflexive awareness of our vitality, and, since consciousness of the state and experienced vitality exist undifferentiated here, it is nonsense to place an appearance between consciousness and vitality, which are, after all, totally undifferentiated. [We can therefore say that] *Duration, succession in time, is a psychic state rooted in the nature of consciousness, which manifests itself in terms of acts [i.e. of perception and/or the will].* It is our consciousness that imparts this property of itself to the process.

(Dilthey Ibid: 382, 385, my emphasis)

Dynamic embodiment

The attempt by idealists to reduce this fact [of the efficacy of the will] to a mere representational concept of efficacy and resistance produces an intellectualist illusion. ... *The will's experiential content as given in reflexive awareness lies in the relation between efficacy and resistance.* ... [Which is to say that] the will becomes reflexively aware of that which is outside of itself and which exerts resistance in the form of something that impinges on it. [*Therefore,*] *the sense of touch is the primary sense that guarantees thinghood (reality, materiality).* It is characteristic of the sense of touch that through it an object and a state of the subject are felt simultaneously. ... *The kinesthetic feeling is nothing other than the reflexive awareness [immediate experience not reflective and thus representational awareness]* of the strength and direction of an impulse of the will toward movement.

(Dilthey Ibid: 356, my emphasis)

For Dilthey, as he shows us above, the alternative to Kant's noumenal or atemporal freedom is phenomenological freedom, that is the *freedom that is internal to human lived experience.* Thus, as it should be, dynamically embodied freedom *is* temporal, "since time ... is the form of inner lived experience." The Pistorius perplexity of the two I's is, presumably, resolved: the subject is now in space and always in time. Nevertheless, Dilthey has left us with a new perplexity: the subject and its freedom may well be "in time," but the subject is in a phenomenological "region" and thus, somehow, not "in" the phenomenal realm? But, as "next door neighbors," so to speak, how is freedom rescued from phenomenal determinism by locating it in the phenomenological region of human being?

Heidegger: the two causalities problem

What should now be brought out in reference to the Kant/Dilthey legacy are two themes of cardinal importance for this discussion. First of all, in his very important study of Kant's theory of freedom, *The Essence of Human Freedom* (2005), Heidegger has identified a crucial question intrinsic to that theory that has been either unnoticed or implicitly dismissed by Dilthey (the question, not Heidegger) in his justified revolt against the idea of what Heidegger refers to as the "extra-temporal" theory of freedom (Heidegger Ibid: 164–65). Heidegger is raising a question with regard to Kant's distinction between the two causalities under the auspices of his, Heidegger's, ontology of "Being" in "Time" (Heidegger 1962). And from that standpoint he comments that,

Kant's view that the intelligible causality of freedom runs parallel to, but independently of, natural causation raises the additional problem of explaining *how man can unite both types of causality* (XXXI).

(quoted in Wood 2000: 75, emphasis provided)

In light of Heidegger's question, Dilthey's resort to the phenomenological alternative to noumenal freedom certainly begs a next question that is implied by that alternative. What would be required in order to "unite both types of causality" and thus, in effect, nullify Dilthey's alternative? This brings us directly to the second and related theme.

There is an overlooked deep consensus between Kant's concept of "causality of freedom" and what can now be called Dilthey's the "power of freedom" (in place of "efficacy of the will"), and it is, I contend, something very much like Giddens's idea of "agent causality." And this of course suggests that there is a connection of some importance between Kant and Giddens on the issue of agency. It comes to this: Giddens's Call for a concept of "agent causality" in reference to the need for a concept of human agency can, I believe, be understood to be, more fundamentally, a call for an answer to Heidegger's question. And it is quite a different answer than that which Heidegger himself gives in his study of Kant's theory of freedom (Heidegger 2005: 205–8). Heidegger's answer stems from a metaphysics of (the) "Being" (of beings) rather than a metaphysics of the "powers" of beings (or "agent causality") (Heidegger Ibid). Since I will show that for the prospect of recovering human agency the latter metaphysic and not the former is exactly right, I must therefore give a formulation of Giddens's position.

Giddens's Call

The context of Giddens's discussion is the proposal that a thesis of the personal agency of human beings presupposes that "reasons are causes" (1993 [1976]: 91). The issue involved in this presupposition is that there are two counter-claims concerning it: "reasons" and "causes" *are and are not* internally related. The conclusion for Giddens is that, most importantly, which claim is to be chosen depends on which notion of causality is going to be adopted: "*agent* causality" or "*event* causality." Giddens's Call is articulated in this context.

> I think that it would be true to say that most of the contributions to the debate [on causality and reasons] have been made ... within the framework of Humean Causality. A detailed discussion ... is impossible ... [in this] ... study, and here I shall dogmatically assert the need for an account of *agent causality*, according to which causality does not presuppose "law" of invariant connection ... but rather (1) the necessary connection between cause and effect, and (2) the idea of causal efficacy. The action is caused by an agent's reflexive monitoring of his or her intentions in relation to both wants and appreciation of the demands of the "outer" world, supplies a sufficient explication of freedom of conduct for the needs of this study; *I therefore do not oppose freedom to causality, but rather "agent causality" to "event causality." Determinism* in the social sciences, then refers to any theoretical scheme which *reduces human action solely to "event causality."*
>
> (Giddens Ibid: 91–92, emphasis supplied)

Note that Giddens's thesis that human conduct is free specifies the concepts of, first of all, "person" and "agency" for the idea of "personal agency": a *person* as a "knowledgeable actor" – one is enabled to *use reasons as causes of action*; and second of all, "agency" and "efficacy" for the idea of the "efficacy of agency" – *a person is enabled* to use "reasons" as causes of action (Giddens 1984: 345–46). And also note the following: the concept of personal agency demands a concept of "agent causality" so that the "efficacy" of agency is taken to be "causal"; now, this is explicitly opposed to treating personal agency according to the tradition of "free will," in which case "efficacy" is assigned instead to the "will." There is a subtle point here: the implicit idea of "power" should no longer be exclusively identified with the tradition of "free will." For, in the traditional case indicated above, "power" is not a reference to "causality" in nature but to "causality" in some "other-worldly" spiritual ontology. The link between the two is that the realist theory of "causal powers" accounts for the fact that "agent causality" is a "this-worldly" "causal efficacy" rather than an "other-worldly" spiritual "causal efficacy." For the sake of clarity, we can refer to the traditional case of free will as the transcendent (other-worldly) theory of freedom and the Giddens case of personal agency as an immanent (this-worldly) theory of freedom. And since, as it will be shown in Chapter 3, Jean-Jacques Rousseau explicitly formulated the idea of free will in transcendent terms, I will from this point on refer to free-will theory as *Rousseau's transcendent theory of freedom.* The implication of all this is of paramount importance in this book: in being transcendental, *Kant's theory of freedom is a "supersensible" and thus not a "supernatural" dimension of the human subject.*

Kant and Giddens: internal connection

We are now in a position to note the direct evidence for the Kant/Giddens connection here in reference to the "subtle point" concerning the location of the "power" of personal agency. That evidence is found in this comment of Kant's.

> What has always so greatly embarrassed *speculative* reason in dealing with the question of freedom of the will, is its strictly *transcendental* [not transcendent] aspect. The problem, properly viewed, is solely this: whether we must admit a *power* of *spontaneously* beginning a series of successive things or states.
>
> (Kant 1985a: A449 B477, emphasis is also mine)

Heidegger approvingly saw this clearly when, in using this quote, he declares that for Kant the problem of freedom "does not relate specifically to will-governed or spiritual being. ... It is by no means the case that Kant posits being-free as ... essentially spiritual. ... " (Heidegger Ibid: 150). Now, although in this quote Kant did not in fact italicize "power," I did, there is every reason to suppose that he is to be taken seriously on this score. In the following quote (and note that it and the one above are from the first *Critique*) it is clear that he means to indicate that the "absolute spontaneity," which is the freedom through causality to begin something anew, is indeed underwritten by the idea of "power."

> It is possible to admit present things, substances, which have the power of acting out of freedom.
>
> (Kant 1985a: A 450, B 478)

Once more, the issue is the location of that power, and here Kant is deeply ambivalent and of course problematic: although the "power" of agency is not transcendent, nor is it clearly immanent, it is noumenal. Thus, overall, we have four distinctions: *Rousseauan freedom, transcendent; Kantian freedom, transcendental; Diltheyan freedom, immanental but phenomenological; and Giddensian freedom, immanental but not phenomenological.* Kant and Giddens are connected in their theories of freedom only with respect to the idea that freedom is an "agent causality" and not with respect to the location of the "power" of that causality. And together, their theories imply that neither transcendent nor phenomenological freedom is acceptable.

Kant, Dilthey, and Giddens

In view of the above discussion, Kant, Dilthey, and Giddens are significantly connected in their various notions that are underwriting their theories of human freedom: *"causality of freedom," "power of freedom," "personal agent,"* respectively. Certain implications of the relation of Kant and Dilthey to Giddens in reference to the Science against Humanism debate in the history of the social sciences can now be worked out. The implications have to do with two historical facts concerning the social sciences with their emergence and development at least since the late eighteenth century: the institutionalization of a belief that involves the conflation of natural science and positivism, and the consequent institutionalization of a belief regarding the relationship between causality and agency. The implication of the institutionalization of this conflation is that any metaphysical talk of causality, in reference to either physical or human particulars, is being snuffed out. Of course, as we will see later, that is historically what happened with the developing hegemony of the positivist conception of science as we moved from Hume to Comte to Mill to Ernst Mach, and of course on to Logical Positivism/Logical Empiricism.

The standard belief regarding causality and agency that comes to be institutionalized in the history of the social sciences that is given with the conflation of science with positivism is this: the idea that *determinism is agent-less in being causal, and the idea that freedom is a-causal in being agentive.* Thus, *causality and agency are presumed to be metaphysical opposites.* But now it is particularly important to remind ourselves that it is the case that Dilthey has perpetuated this standard belief. For, the suggestion that Dilthey's temporal and embodied freedom is a conception of "agent causality" is true enough, as the quotations give definitive testimony. *However, Dilthey's remarkable achievement for that time was seriously compromised by his damning dismissal of the realism of science.* Having adopted the positivist standpoint that was hegemonic in his day, Dilthey is therefore absolutely sure that any idea of such unobservables as "substance" and "causality," as well as "atom," "force," and "gravitation," etc., are, as he says, "the phantoms of metaphysics," that thus can only be "heuristic construction(s)" in science (Makkreel and Rodi Ibid: 217, 192–206, 207–40). And then he goes further with a view that Heidegger is to take on later and fully exploit in his fundamental ontology of Being.

> Since the rise of the mechanistic conception of nature, literature has preserved the great *feeling of life in nature, which is mysterious and inaccessible to explanation*. Similarly, poetry everywhere protects the content of lived experience which *cannot be conceptualized*, so that *what is experienced will vanish in the analytic operations of science*.
>
> (Dilthey Ibid: 206, my emphasis)

Dilthey, on the one hand, has relegitimated the positivist dogma that agency is to be associated only with "subjects" and causality is to be associated only with "objects," and on the other, he has perpetuated the defiant Romantic/ Humanist dogma that consists in the mystification of the ground of human freedom or agency in some alleged phenomenological region that is certainly in the natural world, but yet is apart from the phenomenal region that constitutes the rest of the world.

At this juncture, stepping back, what we should especially emphasize is that the foregoing discussion brings a crucial issue to the fore: despite the fact that the theories of freedom of both Kant and Dilthey link agency with causality, in their own way they then make it impossible to ground human agency in the causality of the phenomenal world. Apparently from within the natural world, Kant carves out the noumenal realm for a conception of transcendental freedom, and again from within the natural world, Dilthey carves out the realm of "lived experience" for a conception of "phenomenological" freedom. Furthermore, in both theories, human agency and phenomenal determinism have been radically segregated: in Kant's theory, the Great Gap between the noumenal and the phenomenal; in Dilthey's theory, the mystical gap between the phenomenological and the phenomenal. And, as I have already indicated, what is gaining prominence throughout the nineteenth century and is about to virtually totally obscure the Kant/Dilthey legacy with the turn of the twentieth century in the social sciences, is the belief that causality and agency are metaphysical opposites. Thus, what has happened is that *the association of causality with and not against agency in the theories of Kant and Dilthey is never actually noticed, and thus never articulated*. After all, of all people, Giddens (in his published writings on the issue) has not recognized that the idea of "agent causality" was anticipated, first by Kant, and then again, but a bit more clearly, by Dilthey, in their respective conceptions of freedom.

On the eve of the twentieth century the traditional debate between Science and Humanism began to crystallize from out of the traditions of Kant and

Dilthey. *Humanism now was in possession of what had become the two stan-dard safe havens of the noumenal and the phenomenological with which to rescue freedom from the determinism of a Hull in psychology or a Freud in psychoanalysis, a Marx or a Durkheim in sociology, and a Kroeber or a White or a Levi-Strauss in anthropology.* Freedom then, in the Humanist tradition of the defiance of science, is to be rescued from nature for human beings and their social life in culture. In view of this history of the Science and Humanism debate on the topic of human agency, a thesis of the recov-ery of agency from the natural world, in order to then recover human agency from Kant's theory of freedom for the cultural world, is an impossible one to conceive of. What is required for such a thesis to be conceivable is that Humanism must get beyond its antagonistic encounter with science. As we will now see, in the second half of the twentieth century this required the death of traditional Humanism and the emergence of a New Humanism.

Science and Humanism: traditional encounter

In "Notes from Underground" part I, Dostoevsky dramatically anticipated what, in the first half of the twentieth century, was to become the stance of a defiant spirit of Humanism in its encounter with science in European philo-sophy. Under its influence, as I will specify below, that spirit was of cardinal importance for the neo-Humanist revolt of the social sciences in the 1960s (Hughes 1964; Toulmin 1990).

> Can I have been constructed simply to come to the conclusion that all my construction is a cheat? Can this be the whole purpose? I do not believe it. ... Good heavens, gentlemen, what sort of free will is left when we come to tabulation and arithmetic, when it will all be a case of twice two make four? Twice two makes four without my will. As if free will meant that!
>
> (Dostoevsky in Kaufman 1977: 76, 80)

In specific reference to what looks like Dostoevsky's anti-scientific declara-tion in the defense of human freedom, there have actually been two pro-grammatic statements with regard to the emergence and development of what now must be acknowledged to be the two faces of twentieth-century Humanism. The first one, and my main interest here, is the traditional Humanism that came to predominately ground the neo-Humanist revolt in the Dostoevskyan idea of the freedom of the "being" of the human "sub-ject"; the second that also informs neo-Humanism promotes the idea of the freedom of "Being," that is the ground of both natural "being" and human "being." The first face of Humanism is found in Husserl's Vienna lecture of 1935, *Philosophy and the Crisis of European Humanity.* In the same year, the second face of Humanism is to be found in Heidegger's Freiburg lecture course *Introduction to Metaphysics* (1935) (Heidegger 2000: 154, 159, 173,

213). But it is in the famous *Letter on Humanism* (1947) that the import of Heidegger's anti-scientific declaration of 1935 and the turn to poetry is made quite clear: against the phenomenological Humanism of Husserl and hence the existentialism of Sartre, Heidegger pits his fundamental ontology of Being which he denominates as a "'humanism' in the extreme sense" (Heidegger 1993: 245, 245–55).

That Husserl presents traditional Humanism as a magnificent expression of the Dostoevskyan spirit can be seen in the close of his Vienna lecture.

> The crisis of European existence can end in only one of two ways: in the ruin of a Europe alienated from its rational sense of life, fallen into a barbarian hatred of spirit; or in the rebirth of Europe from the spirit of philosophy, through *a heroism of reason that will definitively overcome naturalism*. Let us "good Europeans" do battle with this *danger of dangers,* with the sort of courage that does not shrink even the endless battle....If we do ... the phoenix of *a new inner life of the spirit* will arise as the underpinning of a great and distant human future, for the spirit alone is immortal.
>
> (Husserl 1970 [1935]: 192, emphasis provided)

In the *Phenomenology of Perception* (1962 [1945]), Merleau-Ponty, on the one hand, articulates the humanist objection to science that "Notes from Underground" has expressed, and, on the other, carries forward Husserl's theme of "overcoming naturalism," the "danger of dangers."

> Husserl's first directive to phenomenology ... to return to the "things themselves" is from the start the forswearing of science. *I am not the outcome or the meeting-point of numerous causal agencies which determine my bodily or psychological make-up.* I cannot conceive of myself as *nothing but a bit of the world*, a mere object of biological, psychological or sociological investigation. *I cannot shut myself up within the realm of science.*
>
> (Merleau-Ponty 1989 [1945]: viii, 434, emphasis provided)

In *Being and Nothingness* (Sartre 1965 [1952]: 137–46, 263–68) Sartre rounds out the Husserlian tradition of the Humanistic revolt against science in reference to the social sciences.

> All knowing is consciousness of knowing. Thus the resistance of the patient implies on the level of the censor an awareness of the thing repressed as such, a comprehension of the goal toward which the questions of the psychoanalyst are leading, and an act of synthetic connection by which it compares the *truth* of the repressed complex to the psychoanalytic hypothesis which aims at it. These various operations in their turn imply that the censor is conscious (of) itself. But what type of

self-consciousness can the censor have? It must be the consciousness of being conscious of the drive to be repressed, but *precisely in order not to be conscious of it*. What does this mean if not that the censor is in bad faith? ... Will anyone speak of the unconscious here?

(Sartre Ibid: 144,146)

Thus human reality does not exist first in order to act later; but for human reality, to be is to act, and to cease to act is to cease to be. [And so], if *human reality is action*, this *means* obviously that *its determination to action is itself action*. If we reject this principle, and *if we admit that human reality can be determined to action by a prior state* of the word or of itself, this amounts to putting a given at the beginning of the series. *Then these acts disappear as acts in order to give place to a series of movements. Thus the notion of behavior is itself destroyed as* with Janet and *with the Behaviorists. The existence of the act implies its autonomy.*

(Sartre Ibid: 264, emphasis provided)

Sartre's revolt is seen here in his celebrated dismissal of Psychoanalysis and Behaviorism for their joint commitment to science and Determinism against Humanism and Freedom: the concept of bad faith replaces the concept of the unconscious, and the concept of action replaces the concept of behavior as physical movement. To be sure, Sartre's conception of action presupposes a theory freedom:

As Sartre memorably put it, the nothingness that "lies coiled in the heart of being" –"like a worm" – is the source of human freedom. Without it, he suggests, determinism might be true of human thought and action: nothingness, intervening between every putative "cause" and "effect," makes it the case that the former cannot necessitate the latter.

(Richmond 2005: 4)

In view of the fact that Husserl, Sartre, and Merleau-Ponty were committed to and thus perpetuated the Humanist defiance of science and its determinism, their important position on the question of human freedom must now be considered. Since Heidegger's preference for poetry as a general artistic process of intuition in defiance of the "mathematical formalism" of modern science is what he shares with the three above, he is included in this consideration (Heidegger 2000: 294). I will show that he is nonetheless to be set quite apart from them on the issue of human freedom, for, to Heidegger, it is an *ontological* and not a *phenomenological* issue. Hence, the relevant question to my thesis of recovery with regard to the latter is this: why is there a problem in the fact that the phenomenological theory of freedom is nothing more than an affirmation of Humanist belief? What I will now uncover is that the conceptual substance of this theory, *against Merleau-Ponty himself*, can be plausibly read to be more than the affirmation of freedom. Which is to say, that there is a prospect of recovery that is implicated, but not implicit, in Merleau-Ponty's discussion of freedom. In fact, because of that very implication, we will see that Giddens could well have been inspired, perhaps only in part, to articulate his "Call" as a direct result of the connotations of that conceptual substance.

Freedom: affirmation by default

Concerning the problem of structure and agency with reference to the alternatives of rescuing agency or recovering agency, the position of Husserl, Sartre, and Merleau-Ponty on the nature of human freedom is certainly consistent with the tradition of rescue. But now we can explicate their conception of freedom to see its connection to the prospect of recovery. First of all, their position is true to the theme of Kant's theory of freedom: freedom as a "spontaneity" of mind and action is an experience that a community of individuals inwardly have of themselves as individuals. We've seen that Dilthey transformed Kant's noumenal version of "inward experience" into a phenomenological version of "lived experience." However, and here's the rub, there is a serious limitation of this Diltheyan idea of freedom that ramifies throughout the phenomenology of Husserl, Sartre, and Merleau-Ponty. But it is, I think, most clearly brought out in Merleau-Ponty's discussion of freedom in the last chapter of *Phenomenology of Perception* (1989: 434–56). Indeed, his discussion, in my judgment, is the culmination of the discussion of human freedom in the phenomenological tradition. As it makes very clear, in stemming directly from the two perplexities of the Kantian problem, the discussion is still carried on in the very terms of those perplexities. When Merleau-Ponty presents the idea that freedom is a "power," the perplexity of comprehension and the perplexity of unification are, in effect, being brought forward as implied issues. *What he winds up with is a concept of the "power" of freedom the efficacy of which can have no ground in the natural world of causation.* This special failure of "comprehension" demands that a unification of the "power" of freedom and the "power" of causation be somehow realized, on pain of utter and total irrelevance. In other words, the phenomenological tradition winds up with a theory of freedom as an affirmation because of a failure to provide a genuinely viable theory of freedom as a power. In short, in failing to take up Heidegger's problem of the unification of the two causalities it is an affirmation by default.

Phenomenology of freedom: if not an experience, what power?

Ironically, for Merleau-Ponty the reality of freedom is not, strictly speaking, phenomenological. Note from his earlier quote the assertion that "I cannot *conceive* of myself as nothing but a bit of the world." What is it, exactly, that he cannot conceive? Certainly, it is revealed in what came before the above assertion: "*I am not the outcome or the meeting-point of numerous causal*

agencies which determine my bodily or psychological make-up." Of course,
this means that Merleau-Ponty, himself, could not possibly have the phenomenological experience of being the outcome of a determinism. But still,
why isn't the issue strictly phenomenological? In other words, why isn't it a
matter of our "experience" of ourselves in our own human being rather than
our "conception" of ourselves with regard to our own human being? Merleau-Ponty is here showing himself to be a very good Kantian who has
learned a key lesson of the *Critique of Pure Reason* that "thoughts without
content are empty, intuitions without concepts are blind" – he understands
that, from the transcendental perspective of the possibility of an experience,
freedom can only be an experience exactly because "percepts without concepts are blind" (Kant 1998 [1781]: 193–94). And this is absolutely right. To
see this with the sharpest clarity, note in the quote below that Levi-Strauss is
going to tell us, not about what he *conceives or does not conceive,* but rather
about what he *perceives or does not perceive* in his "lived experience" with
regard to freedom and determinism. In other words, we are going to see here
the irony of an anti-humanist structural anthropologist who is speaking as if
he is an existential phenomenologist! This is certainly odd coming from the
mechanical determinist against whom Bourdieu revolted in his celebrated
Outline of a Theory of Practice (1977); and of course, we are therefore right
in being suspicious.

> [One should] remember that I have written that myths get thought in
> man unbeknownst to him. [Identically in my case]. ... I have the feeling
> that my books get written through me. ... [Thus] for me [this] describes a
> *lived experience, because it says exactly how I perceive my own relation
> to my work.* ... I never had, and still do not have, the perception of
> feeling my personal identity. *I appear as the place where something is
> going on, but there is no "I," no "me." Each of us is a kind of crossroads
> where things happen. The crossroad is purely passive; something happens
> there. There is no choice, it is just a matter of chance.* [*Of course*] I don't
> pretend at all that, because I think that way, I am entitled to conclude
> that mankind thinks that way ... [Nevertheless] ... the fact that I per-
> sonally have this idiosyncrasy perhaps entitles me to point to something
> which is valid, while the way in which my colleagues think ... are
> equally valid.
>
> (Levi-Strauss 1979: 3–4)

Merleau-Ponty and Levi-Strauss are in a flat-out contradiction of each other.
Given that each human being "is a kind of crossroads," for Merleau-Ponty,
his "lived experience" is such that there *is* a "self," thus there is an "I" and a
"me," and the crossroads of this is of a self that is *purely active;* for Levi-
Strauss, his "lived experience" is devoid of an "I" or a "me," thus *there is no
self,* only a *purely passive* "individual"! However, Levi-Strauss deserves to be
severely chastised here since he evidently has not properly learned the

Kantian lesson about the necessity of conception for perception: his "lived experience" of himself as a purely passive crossroads has been made possible because of his tacit acceptance of the Kantian principle that determinism is the rule of phenomenal experience. Clearly, speaking technically, he denies Dilthey's distinction between the "phenomenal" and the "phenomen-ological." In short, because Levi-Strauss therefore cannot conceive of him-self as anything but a bit of the phenomenal world, since that is the only world that exists, he has the appropriate perception and the correct "lived experience," in this case, namely, of being a patient and not an agent. And the metaphysical character of that tacit conception comes out in his cele-brated critique of Sartre's appropriation of the Kantian idea of the absolute spontaneity of human freedom that turns up in his work as the "absolute spontaneity of consciousness" (Sartre 1957: 98–99, 106).

> Sartre seems to have remembered only half of Marx's and Freud's com-bined lesson. [Given that man sees himself living meaningfully in every-day life] ... *this meaning is never the right one*: superstructures are *faulty acts* which have "made it" socially. Hence it is vain to go to historical consciousness for the truest meaning.
>
> (Levi-Strauss 1966: 253–54)

The upshot here is that Levi-Strauss reveals the classic strategy of reification and its reality/appearance schema: to steal agency away from persons (hence the appearance of freedom) and to then ascribe it to an unobservable struc-ture (hence the reality of determinism) – in this case his transformation of Freud's psychological unconscious into an anthropological version of a Marxian social unconscious, a cultural cognitive/linguistic structure (Rossi 1974: 7–30).

And it must now be pointed out that Levi-Strauss's variety of reification can also be traced back to the metatheoretical principle that informs the theoretical focus and aim of his structural anthropology. The focus is on *Being itself, and not Being in relation to oneself* (Levi-Strauss Ibid: 62); and, given that (a) Being is culture, (b) Culture is language, and (c) Language is "human reason, which has its reason ... of which man knows nothing," the aim is to understand that unconscious collective "Reason" behind the con-scious individual "reason" of human beings (Levi-Strauss Ibid: 252). But, it must be asked, where does Levi-Strauss get this metatheoretical principle that has underwritten his structural anthropology? Well, he gets it from the man who is in the background differentially informing the work of both Levi-Strauss and Merleau-Ponty, Heidegger.

Heidegger: Being or power?

The metatheory of Levi-Strauss's structural anthropology can, and I con-tend, would have to be, traced back to the strange, and yet, on second thought, not so strange, amalgam of the realism of the scientism of Marx and Freud, and Heidegger's fundamental ontological turn to Being without Dasein. After all, it is the received view that

> In 1947 Heidegger wrote his famous *Letter on Humanism*. ... This essay is more or less a direct reply to Sartre's 1945 essay "Existentialism is a Humanism," and as a result became highly influential in France. Heidegger's critique of Humanism as a metaphysical concept and his displacement of man [and subjectivity] in favor of Being played a significant role in the recent emergence of anti-humanism in recent French thought (in Foucault, Lacan, and Derrida, among others [certainly Levi-Strauss]). ... Being appears through humankind [as the] "Shepard of Being" and [in the fact that] "language is the house of Being."
>
> (Moran 2000: 216)

In order to properly confront the contradiction between the concepts of pure agency and pure patiency we have to critically engage Levi-Strauss's not so strange amalgam, for, it must be declared here that for Heidegger fundamental ontology is itself a realism. This will extricate us from Levi-Strauss's bogus challenge, and thus allow us to take seriously Merleau-Ponty's discussion of freedom as a power.

In what he himself called a "turning" (die Kehre), Heidegger turned away from science in realizing that there was no subject matter left for metaphysics after the triumph of what he called the positive sciences, and later he even turned away from traditional metaphysics in realizing that transcendental philosophy is a secular theology that ultimately depends on divine creation as the measure of objects and subjects (Moran 2000: 208). However, this freed him to fully devote himself to his vision and investigate what has always been its major theme – the nature of Being, being, and human being, and its major principle – the grounding of being and human being in Being as the essence of freedom. In my understanding of Heidegger's vision and its relevance to the Merleau-Ponty/Levi-Strauss contradiction, this is a matter of seeing that the ultimate Kantian problem of the unification of the two causalities is the issue that is at the center of Heidegger's theme and principle. And in view of this understanding, from the standpoint taken here in this book, I see no other position to plausibly take than the following: the legitimacy of the Heideggerian problem of unifying the two causalities of nature and freedom, and thus the only way of saving that problem from dissolving into mystification after Heidegger's apparent abandonment of the realist metaphysics of nature and powers to a realist metaphysics of Being and beings (things and persons), will be found in returning to science and its variety of metaphysical realism. And I say "apparent abandonment," precisely because in Heidegger's ontological language, *the issue of its content to one side*, is not incompatible with the scientific language of nature and powers. In *Introduction to Metaphysics* a key thesis is that

> Being at bottom means nothing other than the coming to presence of what is present at hand. It is not present at hand in as crude and tangible way as tables and chairs.
>
> (Heidegger 2000: 213)

Note the obvious anti-positivist reference to the claim that Being is not to be identified with beings, that is the crudeness of an empiricism that reduces the Being of tables and chairs to mere tangibility. Now, Heidegger explicates the anti-positivist point he is making as he goes on to say that

> Being ... [is] not a present-to-hand fact. Being is the fundamental happening, the only ground upon which historical Dasein is granted in the midst of beings that are opened up as a whole.
>
> (Heidegger Ibid: 204)

In other to words, to paraphrase Heidegger with his own words: "the unconcealment of beings and thus of Being in the work [of nature art and history]" is the process by which "that which comes to presence is pro-duced into unconcealment" (Heidegger Ibid: 205). Thus there is a determinateness to Being in its unconcealment. Now the crucial question is, how so? Heidegger's answer is that

> The determinateness of Being is not a matter of delimiting a mere meaning of a word. It is *the* power that today still sustains and dominates all our relations to beings as a whole, to becoming, to seeming, to thinking, to the ought.
>
> (Heidegger Ibid: 217)

Hence, in order to promote the pursuit of the solution to the Giddens problem as the solution to the Heideggerian problem of uniting the two Kantian causalities of nature and freedom, I will formulate the compatibility of Heideggerian fundamental ontology of Being and beings and the scientific ontology of nature and powers in the following theses:

- Being is the production (pro-duction) of being.
- Being is to being as Power is to force.
- Power is latent force; and force is manifest power.
- In summary: Being is the ground of being as the power "to be."

Now, that that compatibility, it certainly seems to me, is genuine, and is so because it is closer to science than it is to positivism, consider a letter that Einstein wrote to Schlick.

> In general your presentation fails to correspond to my conceptual style insofar as I find your whole orientation ... too positivistic ... I tell you

straight out: Physics is the attempt at the conceptual reconstruction of a model of the real world and its lawful structure. In short, I suffer under the unsharp separation of Reality of Experience and Reality of Being. You will be astonished about the "metaphysicist" Einstein. But every four- and two-legged animal is de facto in this sense a metaphysicist.

(in Manicas 2006: 18)

Heidegger and Einstein, in being one of those two kinds of animal, should have known each other; what another "turning" there might have been.

Heidegger to Merleau-Ponty: power is the key

Now we will see that *the compatibility of scientific realism and Heideggerian realsim is, in effect, at the heart of the matter in reference to Merleau-Ponty's discussion of the nature of human freedom.* And we can begin by asking this question – what possible connection could there be between Merleau-Ponty's conception of freedom as a "power" and Heidegger's conception of freedom as the gift of "Being … [as the] 'quiet power' of the favoring-enabling … of the possible?" And more to the point: if Being is the power of production and human agency is a power to begin, how could the ideas of the power of Being and the power of agency be substantively different, and still remain metaphysically viable and thus coherent? I therefore am going to declare that there is no difference, on pain of the mystification and hence irrelevance of both ideas. We can thus leave the Heidegger question behind. As for Merleau-Ponty, now from this point we can say the following: he has not only learned the Kantian lesson that I pointed out above that Levi-Strauss never did learn concerning the need of perception for conception; in learning so much more from Kant, Merleau-Ponty has gone beyond Levi-Strauss in his understanding of the legitimacy of a belief in human freedom in a deterministic world. He was therefore absolutely correct to declare, "I cannot *conceive* of myself as nothing but a bit of the world." There can be no question here, I am convinced, but that Merleau-Ponty has dismissed Dilthey's move to "hide" the conception of freedom behind the "lived experience" of freedom. In other words, on the question of freedom as a power, we have been taken back to Kant.

Phenomenology of freedom: metaphysical incoherency

There is no freedom without some power.

Merleau-Ponty (1989: 454)

As a most excellent Kantian who knows something about the discussion of the third antinomy, Merleau-Ponty states that, "we should not seek freedom in the act of will" (Merleau-Ponty Ibid: 436), but must instead conceive of freedom as *"the power to interrupt," "a power to begin,"* and, that a question must be asked of freedom conceived of as a "power," *"But what is this power?"* (Merleau-Ponty Ibid: 438). At the same time, however, that freedom is regarded as the "power of action," and hence as somehow "real" in view of the fact that human beings *do* "interrupt" and *do* "begin" (again), that very "power" of human agency is not compromised in any relationship to structures of causation in the form of the physical world, the mind and body, and of society.

> Again, it is clear that *no causal relationship is conceivable* between the subject and his *body, his world or his society.* ... We ought, therefore, to reject not only *the idea of causality [as external], but also that of motivation [as an internal causality].* The alleged motive does not burden my decision; on the contrary, my decision lends the motive its force.
> (Merleau-Ponty Ibid: 434, 435, 452–54, added emphasis)

With this in mind, now let us remind ourselves that in an earlier quotation Merleau-Ponty has declared the following: the rejection of science, human beings are not objects, and the thesis that unites them both, *"I am not the outcome or the meeting-point of numerous causal agencies which determine. ..."* It must be presumed here that when Merleau-Ponty ends these comments with the definitive proclamation, *"I cannot shut myself up within the realm of science,"* we may come to a definitive conclusion. The import of all this is that the standard belief that causality and agency are opposing metaphysical categories underwrites Merleau-Ponty's position on freedom (despite the fact that he never realized the self-contradiction involved in referring to "causal agencies"). And this bodes ill for his explication of that freedom. The consequence of this separation of causality from agency is unmistakable: *the "power" of freedom is "power-less" – action is thus devoid of any natural ground of genuine efficacy.* And this consequence, it must be mentioned, issues from the standpoint of the premiere theorist of embodiment! The one who carried forth the phenomenological tradition of embodiment initiated by Dilthey and which was also carried forward by Husserl. There is, therefore, a fatal limitation to what has been a Husserlian heroic affirmation of human freedom in phenomenology and existentialism. *If freedom is a power that is not grounded in causality, then what is the ontological basis for its declared reality?* Especially in view of the critical fact that, in the case of Merleau-Ponty, he does not justify the belief in freedom by an appeal to Dilthey's or to Husserl's notion of "lived experience," or Sartre's "absolute spontaneity of consciousness," or, for that matter, Heidegger's radical notion that "Causality is grounded in freedom" (in Wood Ibid: 75; Heidegger Ibid: 205–8), but rather to Kant's understanding that freedom is a matter of conception (though as only a belief, it cannot amount to a genuine concept – knowledge). Clearly, at the very least, it can be said that Merleau-Pontyan existential phenomenology has not taken us beyond the legacy of Kant's and Dilthey's solutions to the threat to freedom from the determinism of the phenomenal world. The metaphysical incoherency of his position on freedom – a power that is power-less, a power of action that is unconnected to the body of the personal agent – makes that impossible.

And that metaphysical incoherency remains: 15 years after Merleau-Ponty's death in 1961, Zygmunt Bauman's Humanist treatise, *Toward A Critical Sociology,* systematically confronts the sociological "science of unfreedom"; the only "solution" that he, in effect, offers to the problem of nature's "unfreedom" as a threat to the freedom of culture, is the Husserlian declaration that human subjectivity "is an *entity* characterized above all by its intentionality, *the only active element capable of generating meaning*" (Bauman 1976: 47–49, emphasis provided). Now, this resort to, on the one hand, the phenomenological tradition of merely affirming human freedom and, on the other, the same tradition's disposition to suggest only, and no more, that the freedom affirmed is a power (of generation), strongly encourages me to say that Bauman's attempt to, in effect, maintain the relevance of phenomenology/existentialism to the Science and Humanism debate with regard to Giddens's problem clearly does not succeed. This is further seen in the fact that, in discussing the problem, Bauman's use of the vocabulary of structure and *action* is at best a theoretical step short of Giddens's vocabulary of structure and *agency*: Bauman never gets to (for he cannot) the metaphysical issue of the concept of agency that the concept of action is parasitic on (Bauman 1976: 47–48, 43–68, 79–81). What we have then at the center of the phenomenological theory of freedom, still, is a metaphysical dead end.

Phenomenology of freedom: metaphysical dead end

This definitive dead end can be extended to the philosophers of phenomenology generally. This is, first of all, seen in Sartre's own deeply flawed critique of Kant's atemporal argument for freedom.

> The free project is fundamental, for it is my being ... the fundamental project which I am is a project concerning not my relations to this or that particular object in the world, but my total being-in-the-world; since the world itself is revealed only in the light of an end, this project posits for its end a certain type of relation to being which the for-itself wills to adopt. *This project is not instantaneous, for it cannot be "in" time. Neither is it non-temporal in order to give time to itself afterwards. That is why we reject Kant's "choice of intelligible character."* The structure of the choice necessarily implies that it be a choice in the world. ... There is [therefore] only phenomenal choice, provided that we understand that the phenomenon is here the absolute. *But in its very upsurge, the choice is temporalized since it causes a future to come to illuminate the present ... .*
>
> (Sartre 1965: 455–56, my emphasis)

How can we get around the fact of this quotation that Sartre's rejection of the "choice of intelligible character" is so muddled that it is just not helpful: the project of choice all at once is such that, it "cannot be 'in' time" (and so its atemporal?), yet it is "neither ... non-temporal" (and so it is temporal?), for it is "a choice in the world," which is "only phenomenal choice" (and so it is determined?), and as such, "the choice is temporalized since it causes the future ... " (Sartre Ibid). As a consequence of my overall analysis to this point, I can only judge Sartre's conviction that "A special phenomenological method will be necessary in order make this initial project [of the ontology of human being in its freedom] explicit" (Sartre Ibid: 455) to be just that and nothing more, a conviction whose evidence is its sheer assertiveness. But of what? After all, what the method has made explicit is that it has led him to respond to Kant's noumenal/atemporal argument with one that either is self-contradictory, or is simply muddled. If freedom is temporal and therefore is phenomenal choice, how is determinism avoided? For example, when Sartre presents the idea of freedom by saying that

> We may therefore formulate our thesis: transcendental consciousness is an impersonal spontaneity. It determines its existence at each instant, without our being able to conceive anything *before it.* Thus each instant our consciousness life reveals itself to be a creation *ex nihilo.* Not a new *arrangement,* but a new existence
>
> (Sartre 1957: 98–99)

it is understood that he means that freedom is an "absolute spontaneity of consciousness."

But then, to name it "phenomenological," is a terminological dodge. For, in terms of Kant's logic, if choice is temporalized, it may well cause the future, but that "inward experience" must be judged to be the case precisely because it is being caused to do so. Marx and Levi-Strauss, Freud and Hull, and all other determinists understood the point and responded appropriately. Their responses, different in theoretical character, to be sure, nevertheless shared the same theme: "being caused" is the reality behind the appearance of "causing the future." Is it any wonder that Levi-Strauss reacted to Sartre in the way that he (in)famously did? Surely, the master of structural anthropology was mocking the entire phenomenological tradition in his donning the role of a phenomenologist, and reflexively reporting that determinism experientially structures his lived experience of his human being. And so, the lived being of us all. Which means, to be sure, the lived being of his dear friend, Merleau-Ponty, whose picture still sits, I believe, on Levi-Strauss's desk.

But even more clearly, the dead end can also be noted in Merleau-Ponty's attempt to abandon his work in *Phenomenology of Perception.* In the post-humous *The Visible and the Invisible* (1968) he is taking up (or he can be so understood) the problem that seriously mars his discussion of freedom that I have indicated above. Consider that the question, "But what is this power?"

suggests the following: some kind of notion of "causation" is presumed by some kind of notion of the "power" of freedom in Merleau-Ponty's declaration in the quote discussed earlier that human agency is not compromised by any of the classic deterministic structure(s) of naturalistic social science. In this posthumous work, that some kind of notion of "causation" is being offered in Merleau-Ponty's conception of "flesh." I have found at least seven interrelated formulations of "flesh" (Varela 2003: 127). Using three of Merleau-Ponty's own words for this new term – efficacy, power, fecundity – the following simple formulation is offered that integrates them around the theme of human agency: human agency is an *efficacy* that is the *power* of *fecundity* (Varela Ibid). Thus, agency entails that it is internally connected to causality, and that is because causality and power are internally connected. Clearly, Merleau-Ponty has returned, at the very least, to the spirit of Aristotle's ontological conception of living forms as quadratic causal entities. Quite simply, *what we have in the idea of human agency as the power of fecundity is the mirror image of the realist idea of causality as the power of production.* And here, exactly at this ontological moment that promises the dissolution of the principle that causality and agency are metaphysical opposites, Merleau-Ponty goes over the edge. He renews in this very volume his original commitment to the Dilthey/Husserl/Heidegger tradition of renouncing science (Varela 1994: 177–79). Thus, to the very end, *Merleau-Ponty proposes a conception of freedom as a power that cannot be "real," since without a grounding in a suitable realist metaphysic of causation, that power is power-less.*

Merleau-Ponty and Sartre: convergence

Now it can be acknowledged that Merleau-Ponty and Sartre can be reasonably seen to actually converge in their views on human freedom. For, if, as Sartre says, "man is free [means] man *is* freedom," his old existential principle that "existence precedes essence" is essentially discredited, and thus must be rewritten as a new principle – "*the essence of human existence is freedom*" (Sartre 2007: 17–25). Furthermore, when he also asserts that, "for human reality, to be is to act, and to cease to act is to cease to be," hence to be consistent with the new principle of existentialism, one is constrained to say that that is because action *is* real (Sartre 1965: 264). Hence, what can now be called the Sartre/Merleau-Ponty thesis can only be salvaged under this condition: *the essence of freedom as a power of fecundity must be grounded in a realist metaphysics of the causal power of production.* And that of course is precisely what Giddens's "agent causality" is calling for. However, if it is not, so that it is not either transcendent freedom – free will, or transcendental freedom – noumenal self, once again, we certainly have another theory of human freedom whose upshot is mystification. My own judgment is that, Sartre to one side, Merleau-Ponty was in effect stranded, and completely at a loss, at the very boundary of Kant's theory of freedom – "the power to begin" or "the power to interrupt" – and Kant's metaphysical realism – "the causal realism of matter in motion."

Freedom and the phenomenological tradition: final remarks

The phenomenological tradition itself, then, has, ultimately, given us an affirmation of human freedom: as a Humanist *antidote, not an answer,* to science, it too has rescued agency from the deterministic structures of the phenomenal world. But what it has not done, and cannot do, is to realize what the logic of its own theory of freedom actually demands: *the recovery of human freedom as genuine agency from the phenomenal world.* Hence, if that prospect is to be possible, the requirement that must be met to realize it I have just identified in the final assessment of Merleau-Ponty's theory of freedom in terms of the idea of flesh: the crossing of that line separating Kantian Idealism, freedom, and Kantian realism, causality. The metaphysical resources of the scientific realism that underwrites Kant's theory of freedom can provide a way for us to solve Heidegger's problem of unification by overcoming the metaphysical opposition of causality and agency. In that event, the shared conviction of Dilthey, Heidegger, and Husserl that the *"feeling of life in nature … is mysterious and inaccessible to explanation, [and it] will vanish in the analytic operations of science"* will have been discarded, once, and for all.

But of course, since this dismissal does not happen under the auspices of traditional Humanism, it can only take place with a renewal of Humanism that comes with the taking up Giddens's Call.

In this regard, the fact that traditional Humanism is dying out by the end of the 1970s is surely presupposed in Charles Taylor's *Sources of the Self: The Making of Modern Identity* (1989), which appeared at the end of the following decade. For, in that huge effort he systematically fails to go beyond the existential/phenomenological tradition of affirming human agency (Taylor 1989: ix–x, 3–52). In writing a history in which the conception of human agency as inwardness, freedom, and individuality is elaborately articulated, he vindicates agency, particularly freedom, against naturalist arguments that reject the *ontological reality of agency* by merely restating the received view of Kant's theory of freedom (Taylor Ibid: 363–67, 1985a: 15–44, 1985b: 318–37).

Humanism to Postmodernism: a new perspective

During the three decades from the 1950s up to the 1980s, then, the entire philosophical complex of Kant and Dilthey entwined with phenomenology and existentialism, fueled and drove the 1960s neo-Humanist revolt in the social sciences (Tiryakian 1962; Berger and Luckmann 1966; Natanson 1973; Roche 1973; Wolff 1978: 449–556). However, between the hey-day of neo-Humanism and the 1980s, something quite important was happening to the traditional revolt of that Humanism (Hughes 1964; Toulmin 1990). The ontological debate with science on the determinism/freedom issue was fading out at the end of the 1970s just as Postmodernism as an intellectual challenge to philosophy and to the social sciences was in ascendance with the beginning of the 1980s (Smart 1993: 11–39; Bertens 1995: 111–37; Best and Kellner 1997: 3–37). In pointing out the end of traditional Humanism and the crystallization of Postmodernism, the historical connection I intentionally have in mind is "coincidence," for, in my judgment, the latter has nothing to do with the former with specific regard to the ontology of human agency. While the fade out entailed that the phenomenological and existential traditions were disappearing as relevant resources for the very idea of having a debate, the ascendance of Postmodernism entailed the quashing of the legitimacy of debate with the insistence that any such debate is one of incommensurable language games that are thus ruled by fate, force, and chance. With respect to Kant and his relation to the social sciences, especially, the resources were certainly dissolving. Indeed, Clifford Geertz and Peter Berger (and Kellner) reveal this fact of the "end" of Kant's importance in their work of the early 1980s (Berger and Kellner 1981: 91–121).

In the introduction to his essays on anthropology and philosophy, *Available Light* (2000), for example, Geertz comments that he set off on his anthropological career by abandoning Kant to then be inspired by the late Wittgenstein (Geertz 2000: xi–xiii). And that importance of Wittgenstein over Kant is quite evident in his anthropological theory of mind presented in the paper of 1982, "The Way We Think Now" (Geertz 1983: 147–66): Geertz marries a notion of mind as a matter of semantics and not a mechanics with the notion of "forms of life." However, as a parallel to the failure of phenomenology, mind as a semantical act of freedom intrinsic to forms of life begs the question of its metaphysical relationship to the causal determinism that instantiates mechanics, and thus must instantiate those very forms of life that "house" freedom; abandoning Kant for Wittgenstein cuts Geertz off from any possible discovery of that deep problem, and hence from any possible solution. In short, in 1982, since Giddens's Call is completely missed here, Geertz's paper cannot possibly be the "way we *should* think now." In *Sociology Reinterpreted* in 1981, Berger (and Kellner) resorts to Kant's two-world solution in finding a place for human freedom in sociological theory, to be sure (Berger and Kellner 1981: 91–121). To my knowledge this is the last time in the social sciences that Kant's solution is used for that purpose within the framework of traditional Humanism. Outside of that humanism and in search of a different conception of the "human," Foucault is the only other "social scientist" who returns to Kant to retrieve human freedom; but, he does so by simply ignoring the two-realm solution for an esthetic one. And, I am afraid, that detour to freedom by way of esthetics is a theoretical dead-end: the Heideggerian problem of unifying the two causalities in order to save the failure of the Sartre/Merleau-Ponty tradition to find a metaphysical ground for freedom as a power in phenomenal nature is simply not identified, not addressed, and, therefore, never solved.

Lingering Humanism: voices of disappearance

In my judgment, in Ernst Cassirer's *The Logic of the Humanities* (1961 [1942]), and 25 years later in Jurgen Habermas's *On the Logic of the Social Sciences* (1989 [1967]), we already have an indication that the Science and Humanism freedom and determinism debate is ready for its clear disappearance in the decade after Habermas's volume of 1967. As a faithful Kantian, Cassirer maintains the same nature and science/culture and social sciences separation that was central to neo-Kantianism and philosophical anthropology in his treatise in the philosophy of social science: phenomenal causation (nature and nature-concepts) is reserved for the natural sciences, and the creation of form (culture and culture-concepts) is reserved for the humanities (Cassirer 1961: 158, 159–81). The Kantian question of freedom in nature Cassirer takes as given, and it is left absolutely untouched, for it never surfaces at any point in the book. Now, I cannot see that Habermas's unusually thick description of "The Dualism of the Natural and Cultural Sciences" differs from Cassirer's treatment in any substantive way with regard to the Science and Humanism debate at issue (Habermas 1961: 1–42). The concluding chapter, "Sociology as Theory of the Present," is, I believe, conclusive on this point: the discussion of causality and motives, and of causality and unconscious motives, is left at the very threshold of the problem of freedom and determinism (178–86). In the second half of the next decade Giddens's transforms that discussion into the new discussion that I have referred to as Giddens's Call. But of course, this would reasonably intimate what is at issue here in my discussion to this point, the dead-end to the traditional Science and Humanism debate on human freedom in deterministic nature which Cassirer and Habermas exemplify in their two works of distinction. In short, it is disappearing.

Audrey Borenstein's *Redeeming the Sin: Social Science and Literature* (1978) gives us reason to believe that the disappearance is certainly very well in evidence with the close of the 1970s, and does so in the fact that she now expresses the traditional defiance of Humanism against science as merely a *rhetoric* (in the sense of a linguistic style, and not a theory of social action; see Herzfeld, discussed below). In other words, without metaphysical content, we are given only the form of protest. Her take on the issue is given solely in the title: determinism is the original sin of the social sciences, and the magic of naming it as such is offered as our best answer to the hope of redeeming that sin by simply proclaiming our freedom. To be sure, there have been a few social scientists who were still defending freedom in more or less the traditional way of Humanism throughout the 1970s and in the early 1980s, for example, Isidor Chein in *The Science of Behavior and the Image of Man* (1973), John Shotter in *Images of Man In Psychological Research* (1975), Alan Dawe in "Theories of Social Action" (1978: 362–417), and Peter L. Berger and Hansfried Kellner in *Sociology Reinterpreted* (1981: 91–121), as I've already mentioned. But then, soon after, there is an exemplary demonstration of that disappearance in a social scientist who is, for many of us, one of the two greatest anthropologists of the second half of the last century. Clifford Geertz is certainly one of them, and the other would have to be Marshall Sahlins.

Sahlins: "It's history"

In Sahlins' 1982 publication "Individual Experience and Cultural Order," the anthropological variety of the structure and agency problem is taken up and a solution to it is being explored. Thus, Sahlins is certainly reaching for human agency, but it is not in order to rescue it from determinism. Is it then a recovery? What is clear is that in this paper, freedom is being declared in the name of G. H. Mead, against determinism in the name of Kroeber and White. But, paradoxically, while Sahlins pits Mead's freedom against the "determinism" of Kroeber and White, at the same time, he is embracing the "determinism" of Emile Durkheim. The relevance of Sahlins' situation is that he is doing it outside of the Science and Humanism debate, altogether (Sahlins Ibid: 277–91). The reason for that is to be found, I believe, in this fact: in being asked by me to comment upon the relevance of the traditional Science and Humanism debate in Anthropology as of 2003, Sahlins' response was marvelously witty, and unsuspected by him, unmistakably revealing. "It's history," he said. Sahlins' paper in the context of this comment is of such importance to the overall problem of the recovery of human agency from the marriage of Kantian freedom and Kantian realism under pursuit, that I must interrupt the immediate discussion of the theme of the disappearance of the Science and Humanism debate, in order to examine it. It will be shown that he, however inadvertently, is at the center of the question of the rescue and recovery of human agency, and in particular, he is peculiarly entangled with the issue of Kantian freedom and its noumenal argument.

Now, in looking at Sahlins' paper in relation to the themes of recovery and disappearance, I want to suggest this question. Can there be an anthropological recovery of human agency after Humanism, where the only resource in this matter is Postmodernism? Does this then leave the anthropology of recovery, as Frank Tortorrello has brought to my attention, in the space of Michael Herzfeld's "militant middle ground between Positivism and Postmodernism" (Herzfeld 2001: viii)? In the allusion to that position, I will simply point to the fact that, while embracing the structure and agency problem in order to give an answer to it by ethnographically exemplifying Giddens's theory of structuration rather creatively, Herzfeld, himself, in passing, makes this remarkable statement: "it is important not to separate rhetoric [as a theory of social action] from the material world to which, as a causative agent, it belongs" (Herzfeld 1997: 142). In other words, in effect, presumably acknowledging, if only in spirit, Giddens's Call, Herzfeld then leaves it unanswered, or, he leaves it for others to answer? And so, would Herzfeld

(Herzfeld 1997: 113) thus endorse Ortner's (1984: 143) answer to the structure/agency question in this assertion of hers?

> ... it is our location "*on the ground*" that puts us in a position *to see* people not simply as *passive* reactors to and enactors of some "*system*," but as *active agents* and subjects in their own history.
>
> (Ortner Ibid, emphasis provided)

In which case, by implication, not intention, is it not the case that Ortner, in effect, is dismissing Giddens's Call as an irrelevant appeal to "philosophy"? And that would be so for this reason: an appeal to the traditional empiricism (positivist empiricism or empirical realism) of the social sciences apparently will do. Ethnography thus is that empirical ground that "puts us in a position to see" "deterministic structures" and to see "human agency." Is this true for Herzfeld? Is this "truth" true about anthropology, today; I think not, certainly not in the case of Henrietta Moore's argument, in effect, against the philosophical naiveté of Ortner's residual empirical realism, that is that, for Moore, seeing human agency is a matter of an ontological and not an epistemological judgment (Moore 1999: 17–19)? Well, in the case of Sahlins, that Ortnerian truth not his, to be sure. However, in not appealing to Positivism or to Postmodernism, what could be the "middle ground" that he is looking for in reaching for human agency in "Individual experience and Cultural Order?" To explore this properly, I am going to address Sahlins' paper from the standpoint of *Culture and Practical Reason*.

Sahlins: anthropology after Humanism?

Culture and Practical Reason (1976a) offers a theory of *Culture* in five propositions that takes its point of departure from the basic and initial proposition of *Practical Reason* that *custom is not fetishized utility*. Thus, starting from the negative proposition of that view of custom

1   Meaning is the specific property of the anthropological project.
2   Cultures are meaningful orders of persons and things.
3   Since these orders are systematic, they *cannot be free inventions of the mind.*
4   *But anthropology must consist in the discovery of the system.*

(Sahlins Ibid: x).

I propose that Sahlins' last two propositions can be combined into a statement, such that it requires a solution to this problem: *If culture is a system, then it cannot be a free invention of the mind*. Now, in view of the problem of cultural structure and human agency, the question that must be raised is this: is culture, nevertheless, an invention? If so, what is the freedom of it, and how is to be understood? But note this comment of Sahlins almost 16 years later.

Traditions are invented in the specific terms of the people that construct them.

(Sahlins 1998: 408)

Obviously, after 1976, and with the 1982 paper, Sahlins makes it evident that he was always for invention; *but as regards the only concern of this critical review, the need for an adequate metaphysical grounding of freedom, it remains problematic* (Sahlins 1998: 399–421, 2000 [1982]: 277–91). Although culture as a system is not deterministic in the sense of Kroeber and White, yet, Sahlins insists that, "It seems incorrect to deny that individual action is culturally determined, since this is all it can be" (Sahlins Ibid: 281). He then leads us to the root of the cultural source of individual action, to be found in "Durkheim's famous sociological epistemology," stating that "Nothing is socially known or communicated except as it is encompassed in the existing cultural order" (Sahlins Ibid: 281). Paradoxically, so it seems, Sahlins is claiming *both*, that, from the Durkheimian standpoint, culture must be "deterministic," and from the Kroeber/White standpoint but contrary to it, culture is not "deterministic." For the sake of coherency let us restate the paradox: while culture is not "deterministic" (Kroeber/White rejected) it is, nevertheless, "determinate"(Durkheim accepted). I have no doubt that Sahlins certainly knows very well and believes that this must be so in some sense that escapes the Giddensian criticism that Durkheimian social structure is the traditional paradigm example of sociological determinism. In other words, to put it in the most challenging way, *Durkheim is the father of the very determinism of Kroeber and White's anthropological variety.* And so, Sahlins finds himself in a predicament: he is reaching for a metaphysical space in order to legitimately locate freedom or agency in reference to human action in such a way that it is not compromised by the "determinateness" of the cultural dimension of action. However, that space can only be available if there is a different and substantive sense to the second case of "determinism," and there's the rub. To tell the difference between "deterministic" and "determinate," in this context, a suitable theory of causality and agency that unifies them is required. This feature of Sahlins' predicament brings us to the direct relevance of the Giddensian critique of sociological determinism in the name of the new vocabulary of structure and agency.

Giddens: three-part insight

I now contend that Giddens too wants to realize that difference between "determinism" and "determinate" that will promote the recovery of human agency. For, first of all, the critique presupposes that any appeal once more to the noumenal or to the phenomenological is of no importance at this point in time. And second of all, this understanding is the backdrop to Giddens's three-part insight between 1976 and 1979: in *The New Rules*, we have seen that he calls for a non-Humean notion of determinism in order to have a concept of "agent causality" that can ground the concept of human agency for a theory of the human knower; in *Central Problems*, the old Parsonian vocabulary of (social) system and (individual) voluntarism is dropped, and the new vocabulary of (social) structure and (individual) agency is introduced; and thus the two works together simply suggest that *the "Call" is the reason for the new "vocabulary."* Hence, between the *New Rules of Sociological Method* (1976) and *The Constitution of Society* (1984), *the import of this trajectory is the overall realization that the Humanist failure to rescue human agency is total and definitive.* The implication here of course is that neither Kant's theory of noumenal freedom nor Dilthey's phenomenological theory of freedom are relevant to answering the "call." The crucial import of the trajectory is the suggestion of a New Humanism: the problem of establishing freedom in the teeth of determinism requires that the traditional Humanist strategy of rescue is to be supplanted by the strategy of recovery. And for recovery to be possible, as a realist theory of science permits us to see this as being implied by Giddens's Call, a new scientific metaphysical ground is needed to reconcile causality and agency.

Although Sahlins, and most of social science, missed Giddens's three-part insight (see Joas 1993: 172–87) and thus its relevance to his anthropological desire to reconcile agency and structure, yet, to his credit, it must be pointed out that he makes no such appeals to the phenomenological in his attempt at reconciliation As we will soon see, however, he must be judged to be making an appeal, of some sort, to the noumenal in his objectivist conception of "culture as constituted." And of course he does make an appeal to G. H. Mead (with Schutz in a marriage with the shifters of discourse) by simply taking on his theory of the agentic self (there is an innocuous resort to Sartre's existential notion of individuality as the indicator of freedom, but it merely agrees with the more basic Meadian thesis of the agentic self). Understandably, in missing Giddens's insight and its relevance to the White versus Durkheim problem, he also passes over the apparently metaphysically free-floating presumption of Mead's conception of the freedom of the self (Sahlins Ibid: 282–85).

> For, to adopt Mead's vocabulary, if there is a "me" that incorporates the attitude of some group at some level of generality, there is *also an "I" that retains a potential freedom of reaction* to the "generalized other"
>
> (Sahlins Ibid: 285, my emphasis)

I believe that we can now say that Sahlins has a double need for a theory of causality and agency that will overcome their oppositional relationship. In the 1982 paper in question, Sahlins is unable to metaphysically ground his conception of "culture as constituted" as a "determinate" "system" so as to avoid the charge of its reification as a "deterministic" system; and, in merely accepting without argument G. H. Mead's thesis of the agency of the human self, he also is unable to metaphysically ground that concept of human agency so as to justify the belief in its status of freedom. Concerning the former difficulty, for example, Sahlins' reply to me on the paper that Harré and I published on the reified character of the very idea of social structure, because of its violation of causal powers theory, was that he, Sahlins, merely ascribes somewhat of a more objective character to his notion of cultural structure (Varela and Harré 1996: 313–25). His only response to my skeptical reaction to his lingering objectivism, expressed by my question as to why Plato never dies, was that, "there is something real about it" (Varela 2003). Sahlins and I can only agree that, yes indeed, "there is something real ..." involved here, but about what "it" is, there can be no agreement between us. Why? For example, Sahlins specifies the reality of culture in the following way.

> [It is] a dual mode of existence. It appears both in *human projects* and intersubjectively as a *structure or system.* Intentionally arranged by the subject, it is also conventionally constituted in the society ... [In other words] *structure is a state; but action unfolds as a temporal process* ... [so that] the two dimensions of culture are indeed *mutually irreducible,* [although] ... they are *dialectically impenetrable.*
> (Sahlins Ibid: 286–87, emphasis provided)

Thus we have here a sixth proposition for his theory: *culture is constituted as a determinate system of meaning, but culture is lived as the indeterminate projects of personal being.*

Sahlins from Kant: muddle or what?

Is Kant's theory of freedom rattling sub rosa around in Sahlins' theory of culture as a system of traditions? Here, in effect, is an answer.

> Fundamentally, they [cultural states of structure] are *atemporal,* being for the people conditions of their form of life as *constituted,* and considered *coeval* with it. It follows that if such traditions are authoritatively narrativized, or when they contingently rise to consciousness, they will be aetiologized, that is, as *charter myths.*
> (Sahlins 1998: 408, emphasis provided)

And now we have a refinement of the sixth proposition: *as a determinate system of meaning culture as constituted is an atemporal state of a structure, but as the indeterminate projects of personal being culture as lived is a temporal process of action.* In other words, what we have then is the following contention: Sahlins' argument for the dual existence of culture is rooted in Kant's argument for the spontaneity which is the agency of human freedom, and the ground of the cultural moment of moral autonomy. *The point of Sahlins' appropriation of Kant's arguments is that he has transformed them into the problem of Durkheimian objectivism.* It is therefore relevant to ask this question: what are the properties of that objective reality of culture that are picked out by Sahlins, and how are they connected to Kant's argument for human freedom as it functions as the mechanism of the invention of culture?

Sahlins lets the Kantian cat out of the bag, so to speak, when he tells us that,

> In practice, the individual is the Archimedean point of the cultural universe: for the coordinates of his standpoint, hence of his interests, all of culture is *transcendentally laid out*, and all meaning, which without him are merely virtual or possible, become actual, referential, and intentional.
>
> (Sahlins Ibid: 283, emphasis provided)

The transcendental giveness of culture as a structural state of a system of meanings is not "actual" but "virtual." This distinction supposedly reveals the reality of cultural structure. Though virtual, cultural structure is objective in virtue of its being *atemporal, irreducible,* and hence *coeval* with culture lived as a temporal process of action. Care must be taken: while cultural structure is declared to be transcendental, the arguments for objectivity are not reflexively presented as being Kantian, that is as either derived or transformed from Kant's theory of freedom. Nor is there any direct indication that the arguments of atemporality/irreduciblity and coevalness are derived from the Saussurean principle of the ahistorical character of linguistic structure, though contextually that is quite a plausible inference (Sahlins Ibid: 286). Over all, what is to be made of this? To address that question, keep in mind Kant's atemporal argument for freedom from the first critique.

Kant to Sahlins: use and abuse of an argument

In order to intelligibly understand the alignments of the Kantian argument for freedom and the Sahlinsian argument for cultural objectivism, consider the following parallel between Kant and Sahlins in this regard. Whereas in *Kant determinism is phenomenal and freedom is noumenal, in Sahlins human freedom is phenomenal and cultural determinateness is noumenal.* The tell-tale property of "atemporality," when used by the philosopher and the anthropologist, reveals something rather odd. In the one, *freedom is atemporal,* for the other *determinateness is atemporal;* for the one, *determinism is phenomenal,* for the other *freedom is phenomenal.* Sahlins, then, it seems to me, has certainly rendered Kant's argument simply incoherent in transforming it for his purposes: *invented determinate culture is noumenal, inventing culture freely is phenomenal.* It is one thing for Dilthey to renounce the atemporality argument and then boldly face up to, though not all that well, the problem of relocating freedom temporally but not phenomenally, by inventing the sacred space of the phenomenological; it is quite another for Sahlins to relocate the "determinism" of culture in the noumenal realm of atemporality, and then, dismissing the phenomenological, to leave individual lived culture in the phenomenal realm of time and space, while the freedom of the individual is simply added on by an innocent appeal to Meadian theory. Under the structures of the problem of abandoning the Old Humanist tradition of rescuing agency and adopting the New Humanist tradition of recovering agency from a realist understanding of Kantian freedom, Sahlins' fashioning a theory of cultural structure and individual agency from the noumenal argument of Kant's theory of freedom is certainly incoherent. But, I also think that it is the fatal abuse of the entire Kantian argument for freedom: in being dismantled for no coherent reason, and then incoherently reassembled for use in his conceptions of constituted/lived culture, neither the objectiveness of Durkheimian structure nor the reality of human freedom as a variety of "agent causality" has been established.

Summary remarks

Stepping back from this examination of Sahlins' work, my judgment is that he is wandering, lost, and ultimately unfruitful, in his search for a way to ground culture and agency in an appropriate region of metaphysical space that avoids reification and honors the causal question that envelops them both in relationship to each other. This is the crucial import of the fact that Sahlins has not understood Giddens's Call for a conception of an "agent causality," nor the suggestion that that Call stands for a New Humanism. What is clearly presumed by the New Humanism is that it demands that one turns to the philosophy of science for help. But of course, a turn to the philosophy of science in search of any discussions relevant to the problem of understanding causality and agency in a way that would help to distinguish the determinism of a White and that of a Durkheim, is absolutely absent in "Individual Experience and Cultural Order." Or anywhere else in Sahlins' entire corpus of work that concerns structure and agency, for that matter (Sahlins 1976a,b, 2000: 271–583). And this is definitively revealed in an observation of Sahlins' work in relation to the history of anthropology, apart from Kroeber and White. This has to do with the Science and Humanism debate that Sahlins himself has dismissed as "History." At the time that that witticism was uttered, I had no doubt that it would someday come back to haunt him. Now it has.

Bidney: stranded in between humanisms?

In the Humanist Manifesto, *Theoretical Anthropology* (1953), David Bidney declares a clear and firm position on culture and human freedom.

> Human freedom may be conceived as the human *power of action* ...
> [Hence] the issue is *not* whether man's will is free ... undetermined or
> causeless, but whether man as a whole is or is not to a limited extent the

active agent and efficient cause of cultural process. ... [In short] *culture is to be conceived as the ... invention of human freedom.*
(Bidney 1996 [1967, 1953]: 123, 124, 114)

In a nutshell, Bidney's thesis is that culture is certainly a human invention; but that is so by virtue of the fact that human freedom, not free will, is a variety of efficient causality (Bidney Ibid: 14). Is this the kind of solution Sahlins needs? Well for sure, he absolutely makes no reference to Bidney on this issue, and we may add, apart from Sahlins, and in all fairness to him, that there is very good reason for that. Bidney's thesis comes off as didactic and stilted, at the very least. But worst of all, in view of the characteristic misunderstanding that science is positivistic that has plagued the history of the social sciences, the mixing of the categories of freedom and efficient causality, *especially at that time*, comes off as jarringly muddled and just plain weird. After all, as I have indicated, the perfectly simple way to state the problem of deterministic structures and human agency is precisely in terms of the conflict between efficient (agent-less) causality and freedom (a-causal agency). And so, of course, from that standpoint, Bidney's thesis is what Sahlins needs in the resort to Mead, *but only with Giddens's Call understood and answered*. Hence, Bidney's Kantian notion that freedom is an efficient causal power of action, and thus is the basis for the thesis that human culture is an invention, is a notion that was not properly understood, then, or now, by social scientists restricted, as Sahlins is, to the confines of the traditional Science and Humanism debate, which he has dismissed, and the Postmodern aftermath, which he so rightly challenges. The reason I think is now eminently clear: Bidney was stranded between the Old Humanism that, in already being metaphysically bankrupt by the early 1950s with regard to the issue of the ontology of human agency, was thus on its way out and eventually so by the 1980s, and a New Humanism that as yet had not emerged, and had not taken center stage in the philosophy of science. Indeed, the latter may only be happening in the early part of the twenty-first century. And clearly, that is exactly why Sahlins never could have thought of revisiting Bidney's *Theoretical Anthropology*. But note: the relevance of Bidney's notion of the efficient causality of freedom to Sahlins' search for a solution to the structure/agency problem is, of course, the very fact that it is Kantian. And Kant again comes up in reference to Sahlins' search when one remembers how Sahlins gets freedom into his theory of culture – his resort to Mead. I would venture the guess that Sahlins has never imagined to this very day that there is any connection between Mead and Kant concerning Mead's conception of the agentic self. Now, as a matter of historical fact, there is a surprising dimension here with regard to Mead's notion of the self whose freedom is in fact internally related to Kant's theory of freedom. That dimension takes us to the very center of the recovery thesis in relation to Sahlins' metaphysical difficulties.

Mead and Whewell: the Kant connection

It is absolutely important to know (as Harré has informed me) that Whewell
brought the idea of causal powers from Kant in Germany to England, and
Mead was reading Whewell on this general theme, and, he had also been
reading Kant's two critiques at the very least (Harré 1986; Joas 1985). This
reading subsequently figured in the publication of his first major theoretical
paper in 1900, "Suggestions Toward a Theory of the Philosophical Disciplines." Here, he is focusing on the agentic status of the human being, and
indeed conceives of the self as active in being a problem-centered actor situated in an environment that has a social character (Mead 1900: 6–24, 19).
Now, it is quite important to consider that in this first effort of Mead's
reaching for a concept of the self as an agent, there is implied, however
sketchily, an association with Kant's conception of causal powers. In a footnote, Mead makes a reference to Whewell's observation that, in the scientific
thinker's systematic connecting of facts together, it is done not simply as a
result of "*logical induction,*" nor from the "*suggestions of the situation,*" but,
"*from an element of novelty*" (Mead 1964 [1900]: 19; Varela 1993: Chapter
7). Here we have then the link between Kantian freedom and causal powers,
Whewell's mediation, and Mead's conception of the active self. *Now note,
carefully, that Kantian spontaneity of "consciousness" turns up as Whewellian
"novelty," which then becomes the Meadian "active self."* This "novelty" of
the self's solutions to situational problems indicates that the property of
being "active" is the property of autonomy; in turn, that autonomy is
internally connected with the idea of a power of action grounded in causation.
And lo and behold, Mead's active self winds up in Sahlins' 1982 paper, and
does so absolutely innocent of all of these pregnant and most important
connections. The point here is that Kant's notion of human agency was
explicitly formulated in the two critiques as the efficient causality of freedom.
Thus, with this in mind, I will finally declare that the answer to the question
of Bidney's relevance to Sahlins' metaphysical needs then must be, now, an
absolute yes. *To be sure, once more, his updated restatement of Kantian
autonomy as efficient causal power can only be effectively relevant when
human agency is recovered as an answer to Giddens's Call.*

Humanism: Old to New

While in Sahlins' 1982 paper the Science and Humanism framework is
deliberately excluded, by the mid-1990s there is one last work of the twentieth century in which, although that framework remains intact, yet the disappearance of the debate concerning the ontology of human agency now
seems to be complete with the closing of the twentieth century. Kenneth
Bock's defense of human agency in *Human Nature Mythology* (1994) is my
cardinal evidence. In his introduction Bock ends the discussion with this call
that centers his entire book.

> In the *Essay on Man,* Ernst Cassirer called for a renewal of the unified image of humans that once prevailed in the Western world. Amidst the growing signs that we are losing our nerve in the face of an increasingly complex social life, *we need a restoration of faith in human dignity*
>
> (Bock 1994: 10, my emphasis)

The defense is being cast in the exclusive terms of a moral or ethical prescription, that is it is a plea to affirm human agency. Bock therefore presents it as matter of *mythology* and thus not *metaphysics*, that is *faith* and not a proto-theoretical *conception*. This is sharply exposed in the discussion of the social sciences where Giddens's stance on agency and causation is actually noted!

> John Calvin at least allowed people the power and the freedom to decide to do evil. ... The point is made by Anthony Giddens when he calls for recognition of the *causal* significance of human intentions, reasons, and motives in any explanation of social activity. ... When Giddens turns, then, to acknowledge and deal with the fact of society as a collectivity, it is with due caution to avoid losing sight of "the necessary centrality of the active subject." Structure exists, and ... we should ... activate structure itself, to view it as a process of "structuration" in which primacy is reserved for acting persons. *How successful this effort to reconcile human freedom and the aims of sociological analysis might be will depend on different readings, but Giddens has surely proceeded with unusual sensitivity about the predicament in which social science has placed humankind.*
>
> (Bock Ibid: 97, emphasis provided)

Despite my deep respect for Bock's elegant and impassioned plea for a renewal of faith for the affirmation of human freedom, he, as the saying, almost, goes, is only preaching to the departed. He simply has not recognized that Cassirer's call for the renewal of the unified image of human being in fact has resurfaced in something quite beyond Cassirer's understanding, that is Giddens's Call. After all, in Cassirer's discussion of the concepts of "substance" in traditional premodern philosophy and "function" in modern mathematics and science in his classic, by the very name of those two concepts, there is absolutely not even a hint of the conception of causal power (Cassirer 1953). Indeed Bock has glided over Giddens's Call, insight, and the implied demand that a return to the philosophy of science must take place in order to conceptually realize that "agent causality" is the real ground of human agency. Otherwise, how is that faith in and affirmation of human freedom to be seriously realized?

And so it is absolutely no surprise that, at the beginning of the second millennium, Todorov's reconstruction of the legacy of Humanism for the future presents the theme of affirming freedom against determinism as if the Science and Humanism debate *never existed.*

> Against the proponents of scientism, the humanists maintain ... the possibility of freedom: the human being is not the plaything of forces from which he cannot hope to escape
>
> (Todorov 2002: 33)

Nowhere in Todorov's book in which he presents a chapter entitled "The declaration of autonomy," is the ontology of the freedom/determinism issue revisited, re-examined, evaluated, and a response of any traditional kind offered (Todorov Ibid: 47–79). Or a new one provided, or even its need suggested. Consider now for a moment the fact that the classic Humanist defiance of Science and its determinism is again being rehearsed in 2002 in this manner: clearly, for Todorov, Giddens's call for a new understanding of determinism, causality, and agency in order to ground human freedom in the phenomenal world of science *has never been heard of.* And this is not conjecture on my part.

> Rather than a science or a dogma, humanist thought proposes a practical choice: a wager. Men are free, it says; they are capable of the best and the worst. Better to wager that they are capable of acting willfully, loving purely, and treating one another as equals than the contrary. Man can surpass himself; this is what makes him human. "You must wager. ... " Not to wager is to make the opposite wager; and in this case there is nothing to gain.
>
> (Todorov Ibid: 236)

From the "sin" of determinism and the redeeming of our freedom by the magic of naming our freedom, to "The Declaration of Autonomy" through the taking up of a "wager" in its favor against the necessity of its opposite, is once again to indulge in magic. *What we are presented with here from Borenstein to Todorov is the death, not, I contend, of Humanism, but of the Old Humanism of the twentieth century in philosophy and the social sciences.* It is, to repeat, my declaration that Giddens's Call for a new metaphysical approach to the Science and Humanism debate on the ontology of freedom constitutes the rebirth of Humanism. And while it certainly is not Heidegger's fundamental ontology that constitutes that rebirth, since that ontology is divorced from science, nevertheless, it is a Humanism in the extreme. And, that extreme is the "Real Humanism" that Louis Althusser could not have reached; and in this regard, I contend, that the critiques of Anthony Giddens and Susan James of the Althusserian project carry just that point by implication: when Althusser announces his central thesis, "Ideology interpellates individuals as subjects," and thus its corollary, "There are no subjects except by and for their subjection," it is clear that the theory of "Ideological State Apparatuses" is a return to a sociological determinism which, ultimately, gives us a Marxist (and especially a Durkheimian) cultural/normative version of the structure and agency problem;

in other words, we have an exemplar of reification: the ideological constitution of the subject *is* the structural determination of the subject and the appropriation of its agency (Althusser 1995: 100–40, 128, 136, 129–36, 1996: 242–47; Giddens 1986: 217–18; James 1990: 151–56) For, the "Real Humanism" comes to us with the rebirth of a Humanism that is constituted by this fact: with the realism of scientific practice from Newton to Faraday to modern physics that makes Science for Humanism finally possible, the recovery of human agency is a prospect that is thus realizable. In Ernest Gellner's "The Scientific Status of the Social Sciences," one clearly sees that this promise is entirely lost in another merely ritual appeal to the traditional deterministic argument against the traditional Humanist defiance of science in the name of freedom (Gellner 1986: 124–25).

Perhaps it now will not be too far fetched to suggest the following: the idea of Giddens's Call more than simply resonates with Corliss Lamont's 1949 proposal of a new theory of "Contingency, Determinism, and Freedom" (Lamont 1990: 155–69). It fulfills it.

> Every free choice is equivalent to a *free cause*. In short, *you* – a thinking, initiating, choosing agent – can be and frequently are the free cause of your own actions. ... [Hence], If my position on freedom of choice is correct, we must discard as untrue all systems of religion and philosophy that are fundamentally deterministic and fatalistic.
>
> (Lamont Ibid: 169)

The only correction here is this: Lamont's position on freedom is originally Kant's.

2 Theoretical framework

Postmodernism and after

Science for Humanism: the new encounter

Although it certainly is the case that the traditional Science/Humanism debate has taken the thematic form of Science against Humanism, the historical reason for that fact must now be fully identified. Between the second half of the eighteenth century and the early part of the nineteenth century, science is being conflated with the positivist view of science (Manicas 1987: 7–36; Keat 1971: 3–17). This conflation then becomes institutionalized into the very fabric of the tradition of the Science and Humanism encounter (see its persistence in an eminent serious critic of traditional Science and Humanism, Lemert 1997: 131–46, especially 131–36). Thus, the traditional debate concerning the problem of freedom and determinism has not in fact been between Science and Humanism, but between Positivism and Humanism; and that is why we can now say that the theme of antagonism and defiance is an expression of *Positivism against Humanism* in the history of the social sciences. In light of this clarification, I can now say that Sahlins' reply, "It's History," to the question as to the contemporary relevance of the "Science and Humanism" debate is right, in one sense; but that is because it is wrong in another. In view of the fact that it is wrong to presume that Humanism has been in a debate with science as it is, that is a realist practice, it thus can be said, and rightfully, that the debate that has been going on, which has been the debate with Positivism, is now "History." However, as I think is clear at this point, that difference makes all the difference. Particularly with respect to the problem of structure and agency, and the competing solutions of the rescuing of freedom from the natural world, the Old Humanist strategy, and the recovery of freedom from the natural world and from culture, the New Humanist strategy.

But now, for some of us in the social sciences who agree with Porpora that "realism is humanism," there is an important consequence (Porpora 2001: 264). That natural science is correctly understood to be a realist practice that is to underwrite the New Humanism and its strategy of return, changes the very terms of the "Science and Humanism" encounter. We now can regard the debate to be a *conversation*, not an *antagonism*. In this regard, such a conversation, especially on the matter of realism and methodology, has been going on since the 1980s, for instance, in the work of Andrew Tudor (1982), Andrew Sayer (1992 [1984]), and Ray Pawson (1989). Science for Humanism hence is to be the new and proper theme defining this encounter. *I thus locate the ontological problem of structure and agency at the interface of science and social science, and hence understand it to be a scientific, and therefore, a social scientific problem.* This means that I am making a distinction between two kinds of freedom: the freedom of agency and the freedom of liberty, respectively. The distinction will be further discussed at the end of the chapter.

Postmodern knowledge: fatal irrelevance

My understanding of Postmodern knowledge is in firm agreement with Christopher Norris's characterization of it as a strong negative turn against the enlightenment project, that is the paradigm of rational inquiry in its commitment to the values of truth and reason, realism, and objectivity (Norris 2000: 84, 101, 153; see also Rosenau 1992: 3–24). The theological theorist uniquely challenging the social sciences today, John Milbank, has recently captured Norris's perception, exactly, when he declares that Post-modern knowledge is the "realization that discourses of truth are so many incommensurable language games ... [and therefore] ineluctably impose upon us the conclusion that the ultimate overarching game is the play of force, fate, and chance" (Milbank 1993: 278–79). And the import of the Norris and Milbank assessment for the social sciences, and thus for my endeavor here, has been given by Pauline Marie Rosenau in her *Post-Modernism and the Social Sciences* (1992).

> [Post-modernism] haunts social science today; [it] rejects epistemological assumptions, refutes methodological conventions, resists knowledge claims, obscures all versions of truth, and dismisses policy recommendations.
>
> (Rosenau 1992: 3)

The Norris and Milbank assessment is true enough in both a historical and a general sense, but such a characterization, in pertaining to modern philosophy and the social sciences in their embracing of the Enlightenment Project, even in the case of Rosenau, is simply too broad a critique. Thus, I will need a more specific and sharply focused investigation of the relationship of the two Postmodernisms to the social sciences. I have already defined that focus, and will restate it here in order to get started.

How exactly is the Postmodern (or indifferently, Post-modern: see Rosenau Ibid: 18–19) theory of the subject and of scientific knowledge irrelevant to the proposal that the recovery, and not the rescue, of human agency is the solution to the problem of structure and agency? And even more to the point: can Postmodernism possibly help us understand the central nut to crack at the heart of the problem of recovering agency, namely, that of overcoming the metaphysical opposition of causality and agency? And, that the way to do that is to trace this opposition back to the metaphysically conflicting theories of Kant and Dilthey, with respect to the relationship of freedom to its location in the noumenal realm and to its location in the phenomenological region? Thus, the ultimate understanding that is required here is this: how can causality and agency be reconciled so that we realize a concept of "agent causality." To arrive at this understanding is to answer, today, Heidegger's question of yesterday. As I now will show in some systematic detail, the heart of the matter in my essential charge of the fatal irrelevance of Postmodern thought was captured by Daniel Bell's insight that "the postmodern split between signifiers and referents precludes unambiguous definitions" (cited in Antonio 1998: 24). As a matter of fact, I contend that the split renders it impossible to arrive at any definitions at all concerning fundamental theoretical/metaphysical conceptions, for instance, such as agency, structure, and embodiment.

Postmodernism of knowledge: Derrida, Foucault, Baudrillard

> Eliminate the subject, and, as with the author, the tools central to modern inquiry such as causality and agency vanish.
>
> Pauline Marie Rosenau

Giddens's discussion of "Structuralism and the Theory of the Subject" in *Central Problems of Social Theory* (1979) certainly promotes the argument that, in moving beyond structuralism, yet, ironically, Postmodern knowledge continues the anti-humanist strategy of structuralism: to decenter the subject through reification and its denial of human freedom. Specifically in the case of Giddens, he has only shown this to be the unfortunate consequence of Derrida's pursuit of linguistic formalism (Derrida, see Giddens 1979: 28–38; Moran 2000: 435–74). But beyond Derrida, this consequence is also found by Dreyfus and Rabinow in Foucault's theory of causally empowered discourse (Foucault, see Dreyfus and Rabinow 1983: and Freundlieb 1994: 52–80), and is the implication of the studies of Bogard, Bauman, and Smart of Baudrillard's theory of the disappearance of reality (Baudrillard, see Smart 1992: 109–40; Bauman 1992: 149–55). I can now express this denial of freedom in Giddens's own terms: both the subject as *agent* from the *New Rules*, and the subject as *knower* from *Central Problems,* are lost. And that loss is irretrievable. In this section I will discuss only Derrida and Baudrillard, for I cannot agree with the latter that we should *Forget Foucault* (Baudrillard 2007), certainly not with regard to his later work. For Foucault reaches the point of transcending the error of agentifying "Discourse" and correctly ascribing agency where it belongs, to persons in their relationships to each other. Thus, I would have to advise that we forget Baudrillard and remember

Foucault. However, Foucault's return to Kant In "What is Enlightenment" does no more than reinstate Kantian freedom, and note that he does this in terms of Baudelaire's version of the consciousness of modernity.

> Modernity is often characterized in terms of consciousness of the discontinuity of time: a break with tradition, a feeling of novelty, a vertigo in the face of the passing moment. And this is ... what Baudelaire seems to be saying when he defines modernity as the "the ephemeral, the fleeting, the contingent." But, for him, *being modern* does not lie in recognizing and accepting this perpetual movement; on the contrary, it lies in adopting a certain *attitude* with respect to this movement; and this ... *consists in recapturing something eternal that is not beyond the present instant, nor behind it, but within it.* Modernity is not a phenomenon of sensitivity to the fleeting present; *it is the will to "heroize" the present.*
>
> (Foucault 1994: 310)

This reinstatement of the free act of the Kantian subject "within the present instant" rather than "beyond" or "behind" it, is a verbal dodge; the phenomenological thesis that freedom as a power that is power-less and thus must be grounded in the natural world of causal powers of agency, is not even identified, let alone addressed. For this reason, Foucault's return to Kant is one that, in this book, is not relevant. It will, however, be given the examination it deserves in another work.

Derrida: language and reification

Derrida's spectacular idea of language or signification as the process of the "structuring of structure" is a vigorous critique of Saussure's dualism of the signifier and the signified (Giddens Ibid: 30–31). The price, however, that has been paid in this regard is that that concept is *a radical retreat to the signifier at the expense of the signified* (Giddens Ibid: 30). As "be-ing" in time, in the specification that signification is the endless spontaneous production of pure signifiers, we have, it seems to me, an unfortunate implication with regard to the problem of structure and agency. Signification is being presented as a linguistic variety of reification: agency is taken away from *persons in their use of language* and it is given to *the activity itself of that language in use.* This has been wonderfully captured by Peter Mullen's "poetic" mockery of Derrida's standpoint (found in Lehman 1991).

> D'ya wanna know the creed'a
> of Jacques Derrida?
> Dere ain't no no reada,
> Dere ain't no wrider
> Eider.

But how does the alleged reification in Derrida's theory actually work? My contention is that it has to do with, first of all, Derrida's most powerful expression of his general campaign to banish the metaphysics of presence and its logocentric bias, that is the myth that there is a rationally knowable reality of mind contained in language and ideas carried in words behind the appearance of world, history, people, actions, and language. Specifically, Derrida aims to banish Saussure's residual mentalism that is tucked away in the dualism of the "signifier" and the "signified." That mentalism has to do with the fact that in Saussure's concept of the "sign" he is

> treating the signified as a determinate "idea" or a "meaning" fixed by the conjunction of word and thought. He thus left open the possibility that the signified could exist as the "pure concept" ... independent of the signifier. ...
>
> (Giddens Ibid: 30)

Derrida's expression is found in the very difficult notion of "archi-writing." The notion is defined by the four key ideas of "differance," "trace," "spacing," and the "principle" that space and time are so unified that to "differ is to defer." Thus, signification is the spontaneous temporal production of meanings that are nothing but the formal chaining or formal play of differences; a "meaning" then would be a trace, that is a moment of difference in that chain. Giddens has, I think, chosen the right Derridian quote to get at this.

> This chaining process ... is constituted from the trace which it carries in itself of other elements of the chain or system ... There are only differences from differences and traces from traces ... *Differance* is thus a structure and a movement which can only be grasped in relation to the opposition of presence/absence. *Differance* is the systematic play of differences, traces of differences, of the *spacing whereby elements are connected to one-another.*
>
> (in Giddens Ibid: 31, from Derrida 1972: 48)

Meaning or differance then is not a reference to the sheer physical fact of writing – marks on a page. In its reference to the *spacing* that differance logically presupposes, "it is *not*, has no existence, no 'being present'" (Giddens Ibid: 30, 31). The "presence" of any allusion to "Being" or "being" in its various traditional philosophical forms, for example, of the mental idealism and the physical positivism of the Cartesian Dualism of mind and body, respectively, has here been banished in the formalism of Derrida's doctrine that "meaning is created only by the play of differences in the process of signification [or syntagmatics]" (Giddens Ibid: 30). Here is the subtle point of the slogan that "to differ is to defer": differences only refer to other differences, and thus only defer, or rather, postpone the realization of the expectation of a "being present" that, forever, never is and never will be "present." *This is certainly an articulation of an anti-Cartesian overkill, and in that it captures something of what is the "spectacular" element in Derrida's theory of language. But it is also the Achilles heel of Derrida's theory, as I will show.*

As a closer lead into the problem that Derrida's theory of signification is an instance of reification, consider Giddens's explication of the way the theory specifies that language works. And let us do so especially in relation to the Wittgenstein/Strawson/Harré thesis that in the practice of a language persons are the only agents of that language.

> The thesis that writing is more fundamental than speaking. ... depends upon the proposal that writing expresses *differance, the spacing that alone makes the utterance possible. Differance is that which cannot be said, since it precedes and lends form to the act of speaking or to the inscription of marks on paper.*
>
> (Giddens Ibid: 35)

Now, we can simply restate the critical portion of the quote, the italics, into two theses and their joint implication (Giddens Ibid: 35).

- Writing is a chain of difference(s): it is the *spacing* which alone is the *source* of speaking.
- Spacing *gives form* to the act of speaking: hence it is that which *cannot be said.*
- Implication: *Spacing is agency.*

These two theses and their implication allow me to offer a formulation of Derrida's linguistic reification, in two parts. First, *the principle of the reification is this: the formalism of language produces the semantic meanings of speaking and writing. Second, the fact of reification is this: the act of speaking is not the actor, the speaker; the act of speaking is speaking itself.* We have here in the Postmodern dress of Derrida's theory of writing, on the one hand, the general continuation of the structuralist dogma that "language speaks the subject," and on the other, the specific continuation of Saussure's premise that language users are the passive prisoners of language (Giddens Ibid: 14). This assertion is the compelling implication that can be recognized in Giddens's point that, for Derrida, signification is not *langue,* exactly, but rather, it is

> *langue* interpreted as structuration; [however] it *does not reconnect*, as Wittgenstein's analysis reconnects, *what cannot be said with what has to be done. Derrida's Differance acknowledges only the spacing of the signifier.* Language is a "situated product" only in the juxtaposition of the marks and traces of marks. For Wittgenstein, on the other hand, language is a situated product involved in the temporal, material, and social spacing of language-games or so I want to interpret Wittgenstein here.
>
> (Giddens Ibid: 35)

The metaphysical import of Mullen's mockery then, I now contend, is deadly accurate. The mistake of Derrida's theory of language is that it lacks an explicit and adequate metaphysical conception of agency and the person. And retrospectively, from the standpoint of this book, that lack has to do intimately with the lack of any understanding of the relevance of a metaphysics of scientific realism and the concepts of causality and agency that would enable us to recover human agency from the ever present danger of the reification of human structures, in this case, in the specific form of Derrida's "the structuring of structure." *After all, hasn't Derrida missed the realist inference of "power" in the implied thesis that "spacing is agency?"* I think he has, and for a simple reason: without argument, it is theoretically incoherent to imply that "spacing" is a mechanism (not mechanicalism) of causal production. And from the standpoint of the philosophy of science, while "spacing" is thus a vacuous attempt at explanation, in *Dispositions* (1998) Mumford has elegantly demonstrated in a new analysis that the concept of "powers" is certainly not. With this suggestion in mind, I will close this discussion with a quote containing certain of Giddens's comments on Derrida in reference to Saussure, which, I believe, are relevant to this issue of Derrida's metaphysical lack. It should be noted that the point of the comments is not what we already so clearly understand about the inadequacy of Derrida's theory its formalism. It has to do, instead, with Giddens's reference to Derrida's theory in relation to the philosophies of idealism and positivism.

> Derrida's work can thus be seen as giving new impetus to Saussure's formalism at the same time as it disavows the connection of that formalism with *langue* and synchrony: substance, or *the "concrete," is repudiated both on the plane of the sign (rejection of the "transcendental signified"), and on that of the referent (an objectively given world that can be "captured" by the concept). For each of these, which may be said to approximate respectively to idealism and positivism,* Derrida substitutes the productivity of chains of signification.
>
> (Giddens Ibid: 30–31, emphasis provided)

Derrida is renouncing idealism in the form of the transcendental signified and positivism in reference to the "empiricism" of knowledge, and doing so in the name of a metaphysics, to be sure, but of what ontological kind? Is it not the case that more, much more, than idealism and positivism has been dismissed here? Scientific realism, in effect, either has been set to one side or has been set aside in favor of privileging linguistic formalism. Thus, at the very least, the preference for the latter indicates that the metaphysical status of realism has been brought into the question: if language is the formal house of human being and we are its prisoners, what is real about the reality of the world, the social, and all the rest – persons as language users? As for "all the rest," with regard to Derrida's presumption that "space" as the "structuring of structure" is the agency of spontaneous production, this can be construed as the impoverished descendent of Dilthey's notion of human will as the "efficacy of power." This is suggested by the above point that "power" not "spacing" is the indicator of agency. And only a causal powers reading can legitimate such a tacit reference to such a kind of "agent caus-ality." Any disposition to linguistic formalism at the expense of scientific realism further deepens the truth that the Derridian ambition is misguided. The translation of "transcendental freedom" into the "transcendental sig-nifier," and the replacement of the latter by the spontaneity of linguistic production, is simply not a metaphysical advance over Kant's theory of the spontaneity of freedom. It cannot promote a theory of human agency that honors the integrity of human being in the ontology of its freedom.

Baudrillard: the end of reality, the social, and all the rest

In the work of Baudrillard, I cannot see how there could be a convincing argument against the conclusion that structure and agency have been dis-solved and lost in the hyper-reality of Postmodernity. Let us begin to exam-ine this thesis with this assertion of Baudrillard's.

> Abstraction today is no longer that of a map ... the mirror or the con-cept. Simulation is no longer that of territory, a referential being or substance. It is the generation by models of a real without origin or reality: a hyperreal. The territory no longer precedes the map, nor sur-vives it. Hence it is the map that precedes the territory – precession of simulacra – it is the map that engenders the territory.
>
> (in Poster 1988: 167)

Clearly he reduces the possibility of knowledge to the fashioning of "maps" for which there never is any possible reference to "territory," since the map is its own territory. Now consider Baudrillard's answer to the question "Who are you?" "What I am I don't know. I am the simulacrum of myself" (Poole 2007: 26). Wonderfully playful, and even delightfully amusing, perhaps; but keep in mind the fact that Baudrillard kindly confessed in 2002 that he essentially has a mystical reading of historical events (Poole Ibid). Thus we have in the above references, taken together, the expression of Baudrillard's *new revolution of value*, the definitive thesis of the death of the real: *simula-tion is the circulation of signs with never a reference to the real.*

> If the social is both destroyed by what produces it (the media, informa-tion) and reabsorbed by what it produces (the masses), it follows that its definition is empty, and that this term which serves as universal alibi for every discourse, no longer analyses anything. Not only is it superfluous and useless ... It conceals that it is only abstraction and residue, or even simply an effect of the social, a simulation and an illusion.
>
> (Baudrillard 1983: 66)

William Bogard has correctly understood the import of the revolution of value revealed in the above quote: modern sociology has no theoretical way of understanding the modern disappearance of the social, which actually, according to Baudrillard, never in fact ever existed (Bogard 1990: 8; Antonio 1998: 35–36). Thus, in the terms of this book, the categorical inadequacy of such a radical perspectivist standpoint is the upshot of the thesis of the end of reality, the social, and all the rest: not only is it the case that structure is not real, but it is also the case that neither is agency (Antonio Ibid). And so, ultimately, why should we take Baudrillard, "the Walt Disney of contemporary metaphysics" (Kellner 1989: 179), seriously? After all, to Bogard, Baudrillard has, himself, insisted, *sotto voce*, that Bogard should keep secret Baudrillard's private conviction that his thought on these matters should not be taken seriously (Bogard Ibid: 1). Yes, perhaps it is so that wit, humor, and a charming playfulness constitute the main business of his "theoretical" pronouncements (Lemert 1995: 79–81). Nevertheless, there is a radical implication of the simulation thesis that must be considered here that has to do with the principle of realism, and not simply the reality principle. Some commentators on Baudrillard's conception of hyper-reality seem to collapse the former into the latter, and, in so far as that is the case, that is unhelpful (Antonio Ibid: 41). For, what gets lost in the collapse, is the cardinal importance of the scientific realist model of nature as an array of causal powers; in which case not only is it true, as Lemert has insightfully remarked, that, "Disneyland probably is not emancipation," but, the deeper truth that emancipation is impossible because agency, both physical and human, can be neither rescued nor recovered (Lemert Ibid: 81).

Now, the radical implication of the theory of simulation is this: from the thesis of the end of reality there is lurking the idea that all theoretical explanation is a deception; at the heart of which we find what Harré would call a "thrilling" claim: *reflexivity is the reality behind the appearance of referentiality in all forms of knowing*. Now the reason that this idea and claim must be considered is that it is the message of the Postmodern Philosophy of Science of Nelson Goodman, Richard Rorty, Bruno Latour, and Ian Hacking (Harré 1998: 53–77). And *that* must therefore be taken quite seriously. Their work can be identified as varieties of a radical anti-realism the principles of which have been theoretically brought together with admirable clarity and conviction by Steve Woolgar.

Postmodern Philosophy of Science: impossibility of sociology of scientific knowledge

> Some conceptual boundaries have an importance for given societies which arises from the very nature of their situation, and cannot be abrogated. There is no shadow of doubt in my mind that, *in our society*, the concept of the "scientific" is of that kind. We need it, and it cannot but be an important and authoritative notion.
>
> Ernest Gellner (1986)

In Steve Woolgar's *Science: The Very Idea* (1993) a post-Kuhnian revolutionary manifesto is presented that usurps the role of the philosophy of science, and yet the very function of that role is slyly tucked away in the Social Study of Science (SSS), generally, and particularly in its extremist wing which is committed to historical and cultural relativism, the Sociology of Scientific Knowledge (SSK) (Woolgar 1993: 11–14). The function I especially have in mind is that of taking up a stance in reference to ontology and the question of which kind of realism is to be taken seriously. The pertinent examples would be, the realism of natural science practice – the reality of an external world and most importantly the reality of unobservables (particulars and causation, that is powers and dispositions, and liabilities), the empirical realism of positivist science – where the reality of unobservables is sacrificed to that of perception, sensation, experience and thus observation, and an extension of empirical realism that reduces scientific realism to social convention (culture) and/or language (talk and text). My take on this is that the SSK message of the post-Kuhnian revolution stems primarily from the stance of empirical realism that underwrites a conventionalist/linguistic twist, with a hell of a vengeance. Its message is that *human agency* is the reality at the center of scientific theoretical explanation and not *nature*, and thus that "nature" is a social construction. From this perspective, Gellner's point that the very idea of science is an idea that "We need ... and ... cannot but be an important and authoritative notion," is completely and absolutely rejected. *In so far as SSK defines its identity in terms of that message, SSK self-destructs: it is an impossible theory of scientific knowledge.* My standpoint will be seen to be consonant with Harré's critical evaluation of SSK. It leads him to declare that its view of science is at the very best, a "superior gossip"; from which comment I take him to imply (though he has never actually said it) by the final results of his devastating critique that the "superior gossip" of the SSK view is ultimately "superior rubbish" (Harré 1998: 359, 359–61).

In *The Truth of Science: Physical Theories and Reality*, Roger G. Newton, professor emeritus of physics at Indiana University, has made this very observation the center of his passing but compelling critique of the SSK deconstruction of the natural sciences. It seems to me that Newton's orientation to the problem of SSK is to offer his variation on the fact that Alan Sokal did not write his famous parody of Postmodern social science "to defend science against the supposed barbarian hordes of sociology" (Sokal 2000: 127). Hence, on the one hand, Newton devotes almost his entire book to a spelling out of the meaning and import of the title of it, and on the other, only almost two chapters are given over to the "the barbarian hordes" (Newton 1997: 1–22, 23–44). Given the historical fact that the unique adoption of scientific method in the seventeenth century in Western culture is a convention (that is its adoption was not inevitable), Newton discusses the understanding that certain aspects of scientific thinking (theories, laws, logic and mathematics) have elements of convention. With regard to the last one,

Newton levels a severe critical eye on the taking up of an extremist view of that truism. He makes the claim that there cannot be any rational justification for the sociological reductionism of the SSK conventionalist thesis of scientific practice (Newton Ibid: 11–22). And does so by relying on Poincaré's own instructive caveat of the conventionalist view in science itself.

> Some people have been struck by this character of free convention recognizable in certain fundamental principles of the sciences. They have wished to generalize beyond measure, and, at the same time, they have forgotten that *liberty is not license.* Thus they have reached what is called nominalism, and *have asked themselves if the savant is not the dupe of his own definitions, and if the world he thinks he discovers is not simply created by his own caprice.* Under these conditions science would be certain, but deprived of significance. *If this were so, science would be powerless. Now everyday we see it work under our very eyes. That could not be if it taught us nothing of reality.*
>
> (in Newton Ibid: 13, my emphasis)

This leads Newton into an analysis of SSK as an outgrowth of a nominalist/conventionalist standpoint that concludes with the judgment that that standpoint just cannot be taken seriously. For, these sociologists wind up with,

> … a perverse and grotesque interpretation of science, denying to rational cogitation and logical reasoning, based on empirical evidence, their proper, crucial role. This is the principle reason why most scientists indignantly reject these critiques.
>
> (Newton Ibid: 44)

The following year, Rom Harré too came to the same conclusion in his singularly focused and sustained complimentary critique of SSK in "Recovering the Experiment" (1998: 353–77). His offensive strategy is to rub the noses, as he would say, of the "barbarian horde" *in the systematic way the material practice of experimentation is the utilization of apparatus and instrumentation to directly implement the realist metaphysic of science, the modeling of nature's causal activity.* It is a perfect application of Harré's principle that

> Scientific rational practices are predominately material practices (using equipment and instruments for searching and finding) with some "thinking," and a severe stricture on deductivism.
>
> (in Varela 1995: 283)

With Harré's strategy in mind, I want to selectively move into its main criticisms by working through the essential principles of Woolgar's manifesto.

Woolgar: constructionism as the reality behind the appearance of realism

Now, Woolgar's capsule statement of the SSK message can be seen when he boldly proclaims,

> Thus far, much of *the argument* has been devoted to advancing *an inversion of the objectivist [realist] commitment associated with* traditional conceptions of *science*: we have *proposed* that, *rather than pre-existing our efforts to discover them, the objects of the natural world are constituted in virtue of representation. Several other inversions have also been suggested*: social norms provide an evaluative resource for the characterization of behavior, rather than governing that behavior; *logic and reason are the consequence (often, the "rationalization") of action rather than its cause*; rules are resources for post hoc evaluation of practice, rather than the determinants of practice; *facts are the upshot of knowledge practices, rather than their antecedents; and so on.* Then in chapter (5) we examined how *scientific discourse functions to resist these inversions*. The *methodological horrors are resisted by systematically setting apart scientific objects from analytic practice and establishing a "moral order" which defines the rights and obligations of persons, objects and machines, and which sanctions the relationship between these entities.* Given its pervasive influence, *what hope is there of challenging, let alone overcoming, the hegemony of this discourse?*
>
> (Woolgar Ibid: 83, emphasis provided)

The *central thesis* of this message is that, *in scientific practice, the objects of the natural world are not discovered but are constituted by the theoretical activity of scientists.* Woolgar is convinced that the ethnographies of the scientific laboratory confirm this thesis in their persistent discovery that scientific work is systemically messy. The construal of this "fact" is quite serious, he is convinced, for it is an indictment of the traditional presentation of the scientific self as rational by scientists and philosophers of science.

> In short, "scientists" actions are highly indeterminate. *Decisions about the kind of instrumentation to use, the types of experiment to run, the sorts of interpretation which are appropriate, are all highly dependent upon local conditions, circumstances and opportunities.* When rules of procedure are invoked, they tend to be used in a highly variable and often contradictory fashion.
>
> (Woolgar Ibid: 86–87, emphasis provided)

The very next point that Woolgar comes to is indicated by the alleged finding of the startling indeterminancy of scientific action, and it is crucial: scientific work is predominantly not concerned with "a dispassionate search for truth" (Woolgar Ibid: 87). This means that, the aim of the day-to-day activities of the lab is to make things work: *the concern* of the majority of scientists *is instrumental and not epistemological* (Woolgar Ibid). This is believed to be direct evidence for the conclusion that the activity of *science is constructive* and *not descriptive*. In other words:

> Scientists have little time for a reflective evaluation of the epistemological status of their actions and interpretations. "Philosophizing" of this kind is most common among the elder statesmen of the field or among the disaffected and marginal members of the community. ... If you tell me that a certain alloy exhibits a glass transition temperature around the ambient temperature of the laboratory I might get excited, not because truth has been revealed, but because this piece of information enables me to set up a different kind of experiment, to apply for a research grant, or to once and for all defeat the claims of my competitors.
>
> (Woolgar Ibid)

And so the upshot is this:

> In virtue of this kind of ethnography, it is suggested, science can be understood as essentially similar to non-science in most respects. The *main conclusion* is that *science is an ordinary enterprise, neither to be feared nor accredited special (epistemological) status.*
>
> (Woolgar Ibid: 92)

How are we to understand the conclusion that science in its essence is simply like any another local cultural way of life in society – that is epistemological/ontological (metaphysical) practice in science is not a difference that could make any significant difference compared to the same practice in, let us say, religion? Well, to take the most pertinent example for this conclusion: in virtue of the fact that both God and nature can only be constructions, and therefore located within a historical and cultural relativistic perspective, supernaturalism and naturalism are on equal metaphysical footing. Of course, there is an implication here of no small moment: on the level of explanatory legitimacy, the significance of the scientific revolution has been understood to have been the ontological revolt against all varieties of supernaturalism and the consequent ontological victory of naturalism. As we will see in Chapter 9, in the history of physics the victory of a dynamic theory of matter over a materialist theory of matter crucially involved the freedom to fashion a conception of causal powers that was a natural power and not a spiritual power. The implication then is that this rather important feature of the scientific revolution has been undermined: explanatory legitimacy is nothing more than a matter of social opportunism in the service of conforming to cultural values, beliefs, and ideology. At the very least, from the standpoint of that implication, the thesis of causal powers has no possible purchase as a realist ontological proposal that physical and human particulars have the property of powers and liability. We will, in this regard, see that *this very implication is the Achilles heel of SSK.*

Woolgar: science as self-deception

Thus, there is an evident implication of great moment with regard to the ontological equivalence of all the explanatory practices of cultures: *the concept of nature cannot play any explanatory role in science.* Scientists then are apparently guilty of an endemic self-deception, which, one would gather, is to be accounted for by (or by some kind of variation of) the Marxian theory of a collective unconscious and the defense mechanism of false consciousness, or of the Freudian theory of the individual unconscious and the defense mechanism of repression. In other words, as presented by Woolgar, it would seem that SSK theory implicitly depends on the very explanatory tradition in social science that is the critical focus of this book: human beings are patients, since the structures hidden from consciousness are the real agents in the lives of the practitioners of all cultures. And yet, of course, there could be a straightforward account of scientific behavior that is something other than self-deception, and thus on the conscious level. For instance, this is seen in one of the examples often cited by SSS/SSK scholars as a paradigm of natural science studies. Here I am referring to Paul Forman's explanation of the acceptance of quantum mechanics by Weimar scientists: having lost their high social standing and therefore wanting to regain it, once they realized that the acceptance of non-deterministic quantum mechanics would likely raise their level of public esteem, this became the real reason for their adoption (Brown 2001: 115–18, 131). Of course, as Poincaré's caveat suggests, since the scientists in question would have denied that interpretation, then we are right back to the interpretation of the unconscious (collective or individual) and self-deception, or worse. However, ultimately, the question of which account is involved to one side, what cannot be avoided is the realization that the SSK thesis that nature can play no explanatory role in scientific practice presumes that agency is real, and, since nature is not the agent, then only persons can be.

Woolgar: agency in science not nature?

And this is exactly Woolgar's view in his position that the hegemony of scientific discourse is that of the ideology of representation and thus a rhetoric and not a genuine metaphysic of realism. And now it must be noted that,

> As has already been hinted, *the notion of agency is at the heart of the ideology of representation.* The key relationship to be negotiated is that between the objects of the world and their representation through signs, records, and so on. *Agents of representation* are those entities which

mediate between the world and its representation. *Their role is presumed to be the relatively passive one of enabling or facilitating representation. ... Agents are considered passive in the sense that they are not thought capable of affecting the character of the world. ...* The strength of the ideology of representation is the notion that ... any other agent could equally have produced the same results, facts, insights, and so on. This is the corollary of the view that the same facts were already there, enjoying a time-less pre-existence, merely awaiting the arrival of a transitory agent.

(Woolgar Ibid: 101–2, emphasis provided)

The presumption of a hidden agency that is evident in this alleged false practice of realist representation is fatally exposed, and along with it the full force of Woolgar's condemnation of scientific realism. There is a relation of reciprocity that centers representation and its relation to the subject:

The insinuation and articulation of agency detracts from the facticity (representations) claimed by the subjects ... at the same time, the deletion of agency enhances the facticity (representations) claimed by the author's own report. In terms of chapter 6, the strangeness, and hence constructed character of the activities of the subjects are highlighted while the attention to the activities of representer is played down, minimized and otherwise backgrounded. This difference between observer and subject/object is established and sustained throughout the course of texts which purport to be merely reporting upon the character of the other.

(Woolgar Ibid: 100)

To combat a scientific realism that entails the denial of the fact that scientists are the exclusive and secret agency of the construction of the idea that nature is the objective site of explanatory causal forces, a new kind of ethnography of science is the key. Its decisive target

is the practice of representation itself. *In order to come to terms with the way in which representation pervades science,* our approach should be reflexive since we need to explore ways of investigating our use of representation. At the same time the notion of ethnography suggests we treat as strange the practices of representation as we engage in them. Hence, our ethnography should be a reflexive ethnography rather than just an instrumental ethnography of science. ... [For] ... *the task is to see what can be done to reconstitute the moral order of representation, not only to explore alternatives to the current dominance of the rhetoric of realism, but also to dispute its right to define what counts as an alternative.*

(Woolgar Ibid: 92, 105–6, emphasis provided)

It is thus very clear that Woolgar is declaring that scientific realism is to be dismissed precisely because it is a mistake, and so it is the case that the strength of a scientific explanation is no more than its degree of resistance to deconstruction. The difference between science and social science lies not in method but in the extent of resources invested to build and establish resistance.

(Woolgar Ibid: 108)

Woolgar and Harré: recovering realism

Now, Woolgar's concept of the "technologies of representation" is the bridge that connects the post-Kuhnian anti-realist manifesto to Harré's realist conception of the experiment which, he declares, scientists have designed to complement their discursive devises (theories) that function to model the varieties of natural kinds of causal activities. That bridge pertains to what Woolgar refers to as the population of various inanimate agents that mediate between the world and its representations: such inscription devices as experimental apparatus, measuring instruments, chart recorders, oscilloscopes, and so on (Woolgar Ibid: 102–3). In this regard, Harré's critique of the post-Kuhnian manifesto rests exactly on exposing a deadly inconsistency at its very core. SSK rejects the metaphysic of scientific realism while tacitly embracing a metaphysic of empirical realism: only observable things and events are real – everyday objects, animals, people, and events such as scientific talk and conducting experiments. The critique is this: ultimately, SSK rejects scientific realism in favor of empirical realism (or actualism) not because scientific practice does not work (after all, theories actually explain, predict, and are practically effective – engineering) but rather because of its commitment to empirical realism. *Consequently, in treating the experiment as a form of discourse and so as a text, the materiality of the very work of experimentation, its material stuff and its embodied act of manipulation, is simply not taken seriously because it is never understood in its scientific context.* Harré makes exactly this very point.

> For example, a manipulation to decompose water into hydrogen and oxygen, and to reconstitute water from hydrogen and oxygen, seems to have been forgotten.
>
> (Harré op cit: 364)

And the key here, as it has been indicated in Harré's earlier quote, is that *the predominate work of science in reference to its basic strategy of modeling nature is that very work itself of the material practice of experimentation*. But now we must have a deeper understanding of this material work in its function "as an alternative form of representation" (Harré Ibid: 366). What Harré is after is a new distinction: it is not that between the *artificial and the natural* – here the experiment as artifact is detached from its connection to the world as natural – but that between the *domesticated and the wild* (Harré Ibid: 368).

What happens when a Stern–Gerlach apparatus is switched on; when a reagent is poured into a test tube; or a Bunsen burner is ignited under a retort, or a population of drosophila are left to breed in a suitable enclosure. We have certainly created models of certain aspects or portions of the World. But we have also done something else, since the apparatus is made of material stuff, and fruit flies are fruit flies. We have domesticated, and so brought partly under control, certain aspects of the wild. *Experiments are not just discursive representations of nature in a material medium. They are natural phenomena.*

[However,] in so far as models are treated as representations of reality they are in no better case against the post-modernist critic of science than propositions, but if they are taken as mini-worlds, they are part of nature, bench-top apparatus, that belongs within the same type-hierarchies as some wild/naturally occurring mechanisms. *Models, bench-top, not cognitive, are domesticated portions of the wild world. Just like cows are domesticated versions of the aurochs, primeval wild oxen.*

(Harré Ibid: 368, my emphasis)

Note Harré's specific clarification of the critical feature of nature's causal activity for the scientific act of modeling.

If the bits of apparatus in an instrumentarium are domesticated chunks of nature, then the general outline of Hacking's account of the [theoretical] stability of some parts of science [geometrical optics, Newtonian mechanics, the nineteenth-century parts of inorganic chemistry, and so on] is a consequence. *The phenomena are in the laboratory, but the powers to produce them, in these circumstances are the powers of nature, and they are very much present in the laboratory.*

(Harré Ibid: 371, my emphasis)

This brings out *the Achilles heel of the SSK manifesto*: *with the ruling out of nature as a reality*, and, since experimentation depends on the reality of nature for its function of modeling a portion of nature in its causal activity, ultimately, therefore, *there is the ruling out of nature's causal activity as a reality*. With the idea of the Achilles heel in mind, Harré's response to the unsophisticated trick of rejecting scientific realism because of a commitment to empirical realism is to reiterate Poincaré's claim, but in his own way.

Interesting though this view [of sociological reductionism] is, it does seem to ignore certain quite general features of scientific activity. Not least, it overlooks the fact that the scientific community continues to exist and to maintain its place, whatever that is, in relation to the rest of society. If in some way or another the scientific community did not continue to produce the "goods" in the form of workable, reliable, and usable knowledge, it would hardly have continued to prosper.

Furthermore, the achievement of a scientific reputation, good or bad, cannot be just a matter of the exercise of social power in a community. *The success or failure of experimental tests cannot be irrelevant to the acceptance or rejection of theories and hypotheses, even if we must admit that no empirical test could determine our attitude to theory.*

(Harré 1985: 191, my emphasis)

The theme of what has been spelled out here is the well-known objection to all forms of epistemological relativism – the commitment of the genetic fallacy.

It does not follow that because one has given a correct account of how some belief came to be held that we are not entitled to ask about its truth as well. ... The revelation of how that belief was caused has no bearing on its value as knowledge.

(Harré Ibid: 194)

Upon reflection, what the review of various lines of critique from Newton and Harré that we have just completed certainly shows us is that, together in their convergence, they constitute the collapse of the SSK manifesto in its commitment to delegitimize the authority of science's causal explanation of nature. But that is not all.

The Achilles heel of SSK: human agency presupposes natural agency

There is one more critical point to be made that finalizes the collapse in question. And it is this: *SSK cannot coherently justify its denial of the reality of nature, and especially, the causal character of the World's activity, and at the same time insist on the agency of human beings as the exclusive constructors of ideas, for example, such as God and nature.* After all, to do so carries the consequence that SSK is an impossible theory of scientific knowledge. *For human agency "to work" in its "work" as social "construction," human agency must be a real causal force.* In other words, Giddens's reference to "agent causality." And therefore, the reality of the "agent causality" of human agency must be grounded in the "agent causality" of the world's activity. In short, if human agency, hence the presupposition of natural agency. But if "nature" is denied its real causal status, what are we metaphysically left with as a justification for the SSK belief that human particulars, not natural particulars, are agents? Since it would be impossible, under the constraints of SSK, to accept the reality of the traditional Judeo-Christian God as the original real causal force of creation, in order to have an account of human agency, there can be no reliance on a supernatural particular(s) with which to justify human agency as free will. Therefore, that only human beings are real causal agents is ultimately metaphysically incoherent. But Bhaskar has conclusively shown that there certainly can be the restoration of metaphysical coherency with regard to the very idea of human agency. And that is found in this marvelous irony: the discovery of certain kinds of agency in the natural world is the direct and exclusive result of the human productive act of the design and execution of experimentation.

> Mechanisms endure even when not acting, and act in their normal way even when the consequents of the law-like statements they ground are, owing to the operation of intervening mechanisms or countervailing causes, unrealized. *It is the role of the experimental scientist to exclude such interventions, which are usual; and to trigger the mechanism so that it is active.*
> (Bhaskar 1979: 46, emphasis provided)

Since it is the case, then, that knowledge of natural agency requires the special exercise of human personal agency, it must also be the case that the SSK theory of knowledge self-destructs.

Scientific theories then can never be solely reflexive and so, never referential. The worst nightmare of the Durkheimian sociology of knowledge would thereby be fully realized in that event. For now we indeed would have, on the one hand, Durkheim's original thesis that society is religion and God a symbol that reveals society worshiping itself, and on the other, we would also have the derivative thesis that science is a secular religion and nature a symbol of science worshiping itself in talking only to itself. Science therefore cannot be guilty of the grand self-deception that reflexivity is the truth behind referentiality. After all, in HBO's production *Rome*, Brutus is presented as saying to Cassius, "You may name a cat a bird, yet, it will not fly." But of course – not only scientists are realists.

Postmodernism and the recovery of human agency

The foregoing discussion compels me to declare that it is impossible to conceive of a conversation between realist science and humanism in reference to any of its important problems of knowledge and the human subject under the auspices of the Postmodernism of knowledge and the Postmodern philosophy of science as it has been identified and discussed here. Even with respect to Rosenau's discussion of an affirmative Postmodernist call for "the return of the subject," it simply is not up to the mark (see Rosenau Ibid: 53–61): when she actually refers to Giddens's calling for a decentering of the subject but not its "evaporation," Giddens's Call is absolutely missed (Rosenau Ibid: 59); and there is never any reference to realist social science, particularly concerning the "the return of the subject." And this is absolutely critical here. For, while Rosenau certainly acknowledges that the skeptical Postmodernist substitution of "the post-modern individual" for the "modern subject" is inadequate, and thus approvingly brings in the affirmative Postmodernist "return of the subject" indicated above, the fact that she misses Giddens's Call in this move proves to be devastating to her position (Rosenau Ibid: 50–56). To see this, consider this statement of Rosenau.

The post-modern individual repudiates the responsibility imposed by humanism, that each modern subject carries on his/her shoulder. *S/he adopts a post-modern anti-causal point of view because s/he has no desire to assume responsibility or insist on his/her role as an agent. ... In the absence of cause and effect the post-modern individual cannot be held personally accountable because these things "just happen."*

(Rosenau Ibid: 55–56)

Now, the point is this: when Rosenau moves from noting a variety of social scientist's call for "the return of the subject," *in each case of which the "agency" of this returned subject is clearly referenced, particularly* to Giddens's "structuration analysis," the omission of the call for a conception of "agent causality" in order to fashion a theory of personal agency blatantly stands out (Rosenau Ibid: 57–59). In other words, *there can be no "return of the subject" without answering Giddens's Call.* This captures precisely the deadly accuracy of Porpora's insight into the failure of the Postmodern theory of the subject: "Postmodernism pretends to give us free-floating resistance and agency – but all somehow without ontological agents" (Porpora 2001: 264). Furthermore, we have to note that this very ontological failure parallels the phenomenological tradition in its affirmation of human agency without any possibility of finding its validating place among the other kinds of agency in the world of physical and biological particulars.

Hence, with respect to the realist/humanist problem of the human subject, I can conclusively declare that under the auspices of the Postmodernism of knowledge and the Postmodern philosophy of science no fruitful reformulations of this problem with the genuine promise of a possible solution under the auspices of such thought-ways could be forthcoming. Thus, the bottom line of this understanding is that the deep need for a suitable philosophy of realism for science has been salvaged from the debacle of these two forms of Postmodern knowledge. A salvage, nevertheless, that then frees us, thankfully, for the hard work of the renewal of the social sciences that may lead us to the provision of promising results in addressing its fundamental problems. This is precisely the reason why I believe that, in the matter of the problem of embodied discursive agency in a world of deterministic structures, science can be *for* humanism. To see this is to understand that realism of the relevant kind truly comes after the implosion of Postmodernism (Lopez and Potter 2001: 3–16).

After Postmodernism: position and theses of the new humanist project of the recovery of agency

Paradoxical as it may seem at first sight, determinism cannot be regarded as complete unless what may be called *freedom* or spontaneity of *every* concrete [material or cultural] object is taken into account.

Bunge (1979 [1959]: 181)

Science For Humanism: The Recovery of Human Agency is rooted in the contention that for modern philosophy and the social sciences the problem of deterministic structure and human agency originates in Kant's theory of freedom. (This particular view will be given a systematic formulation in Chapter 3.) With the 1960s, what has always been taken to be the Kantian truth of the rescue of human agency from the natural world defining the Science and Humanism debate on the two theses of structure and agency, has finally been articulated. Its full exposure is found in this excerpt from Ralf Dahrendorf's well known discussion of these matters in his essay *Homo Sociologicus* (1968: 19–106). The essay, as expected, is actually framed by the specific debate between Durkheimian naturalistic sociology and Kantian Humanistic sociology.

> According to [Alfred] Weber, whereas sociology after some decades ... has come considerably closer to a rational understanding of ... society, the autonomous human being and his freedom have been lost sight of in the process. ... Sociology has paid for the exactness of its propositions with the humanity of its intentions, and has become a thoroughly inhuman, amoral science. Alfred Weber and the many who share this view are mistaken in one important respect. It was no accident that in the course of time sociology lost sight of people as human beings; *rather, this development was inevitable from the moment that sociology emerged as a science. The two intentions with which sociology began are incompatible. As long as sociologists interpret their task in moral terms, they must renounce the analysis of social reality; as soon as they strive for scientific insight, they must forgo their moral concern with the individual and his liberty.* What makes the paradox of moral and alienated man so urgent is not that sociology has strayed from its proper task, but that it has become a *true science*.
>
> (Dahrendorf 1968 [1958]: 77, emphasis provided)

The "two incompatible intentions" of "true science" and "the autonomous human being" that are the conditions of the debate between Science and Humanism, are defined by the "paradox of moral and alienated man" in the terms of "conflict," "dilemma," and "problem." The incompatibility of the conflicting "intentions" entail the "dilemma" that with science, freedom must be lost, and with humanism, science must be lost. The "problem" is based on the dogmatic belief that underwrites the "dilemma." And it shows up with particular clarity in the peculiar way in which Dahrendorf resorts to Kant's theory of freedom in order to accomplish the traditional rescue. The peculiarity is this: the rescue is justified on nothing more than a *moral* complaint against the principle of determinism, and that is because the principle of determinism is simply beyond challenge. And this reveals that the substance of the "problem" is a "*stalemate*": *a deep categorical conviction that (1) the principle of determinism absolutely rules out freedom (causality and agency are mutually exclusive metaphysical opposites) and that (2) the principle of determinism does so because it represents the ontology of nature.* This is the essence of the received view of Kant's transcendental philosophy in the history of Western modern philosophy, and this view is inscribed in the history of the social sciences: the phenomenal constitution of the natural world as we know it from the categorical constitution of the human mind. In their second look at *The Interpretive Turn*, three decades after Dahrendorf's essay of 1958, Rabinow and Sullivan relegitimate the traditional conflict and stalemate between naturalistic and humanistic social science as a definitive paradigmatic conflict (Rabinow and Sullivan 1987: 1–32). And by the time of Charles Lemert's *Sociology After the Crisis* in 1995, the conflict and its stalemate are completely absent; and is so in an otherwise important discussion of the history of sociological theory and the crisis that is ultimately rooted in its systemic disposition to structure away human differences in order to declare strong structures in the service of its scientific ambitions (Lemert 1995: 114–30, 207). The strong implication here is that, it is no surprise that the Science against Humanism debate fades out with the 1980s, amounting to what has been taken to be the fact of the matter – the death of the Science and Humanism encounter. In other words, "Its History." As this chapter has tried to make clear, however, this of course is the exact point of the purpose of this book: upon the death of the Old Humanism a New Humanism is possible. The possibility hinges on a new metaphysical question concerning the solution to the problem of structure and agency. I now want to spell out the position that underwrites that question and the four theses that constitute it.

As a metaphysical question located at the interface of science and social science, human agency, as I have already indicated, must be seen as a theoretical problem that is, first of all scientific and, second of all, social scientific. I will introduce the substance of the distinction with the statement of the American poet Robert Lowell.

> Free will is sewn into everything we do. ... Yet the possible alternatives that life allows us are very few.

"Everything we do" presumes our "agency," and the "life" in which we are agents is a "structure" that offers us only certain possibilities and not others, and just this range of them and not others, in a given historical moment. Now, this informal statement of the problem of human agency can be restated formally.

> As a *scientific theoretical issue* the relation of the concepts of structure and agency is a problem of the freedom of agency in a natural world of deterministic structures. It concerns the relationship between determinism, causality, and the stratification of the variety of natural kinds of agency. As a *social scientific theoretical issue* the relation of the concepts of structure and agency is the problem of liberty in the social world. It

concerns, at a minimum, the relationship between the demands for the social integration of the individual and the provision of individual independence, and in some cases, emancipation, in ordered societies. And therefore it should particularly focus on the nature, significance, and distribution of authority, power, and the ideological appropriation of various forms of knowledge for hegemonic ambitions that threaten the ontological integrity of human being.

Thus, I have contended throughout this chapter that a fruitful understanding of the structure/agency problem that carries a legitimate prospect of its solution requires that we return *anew* to its well-known origin in *Kant's Theory of Freedom* (Allison 1995: 11–30). What is new has to do with the fact that as Kant went on from *The Critique of Pure Reason* to *The Critique of Practical Reason* he then refers to the determinism of objects in the phenomenal realm and the freedom of subjects in the noumenal realm with an explicit and persistent special emphasis. In the former case, we have the *"efficient causality of nature,"* and in the latter, we have the *"efficient causality of freedom"* (the initial details are in Chapter 3 and the full details in Chapter 10). The important point to note is that Kant is highlighting a naturalist thesis that physical objects and human subjects are both efficient causes. The importance of the point here, in my judgment, is that the noumenal character of human agency is set to one side (though it is not set aside), while Kant is deftly suggesting the natural character of human agency. In other words, *conceived of as a problem in the metaphysics of science, the solution to the problem of deterministic structure and human agency is the recovery of persons as causal agents in the natural world of other causal agents.* Hence I am asserting the position that Kantian Transcendental Idealism is grounded in a commitment to naturalism, and, that that commitment can be traced to the realism of his metaphysics of nature. And Kant's fundamental view is consistent with this assertion when, as we have carefully noted in Chapter 1, he declares that freedom is a transcendental and not a transcendent (spiritual: soul as free will) *"power of spontaneously* beginning a series of successive things or states." In other words, *the idea of freedom as "spontaneity" from his transcendental Idealism is grounded in the idea of freedom as "power" from his metaphysics of nature.*

And from Mario Bunge's quote above, it can certainly be seen that this view of Kantian freedom is fully in keeping with the twentieth century declaration that "determinism cannot be regarded as complete unless what may be called *freedom* or spontaneity of *every* concrete [material or cultural] object is taken into account."

Now, in light of this position, my argument can be stated in the following four theses.

- The stalemate of the structure/agency problem is traceable to the seemingly intractable problem of reconciling the phenomenal/noumenal divide: *it is this difficulty that must be overcome for the recovery of human agency to be possible.*

- The solution is found in the idea that the phenomenal/noumenal divide is to be rejected: *thus it will be shown that physical objects and human subjects are both efficient causes, but of course of different natural kinds.*

- The first move in the above demonstration is the idea that efficient causes are causal agents, thus physical entities must have the properties of causal powers [and liabilities]: this is to be shown in the triumph of the dynamical theory of matter (immaterial forces or powers) over the materialist theory of matter (material stuff) in physics between the seventeenth and mid-nineteenth centuries. From Newton to Faraday, causal powers theory of classical physics becomes the field theory of modern physics. *The recovery of natural agency in the physical world is now taken to be the basis for the recovery of human agency in the cultural world.*

- The recovery of human agency involves three stages. (a) Kant's noumenal theory that freedom is an atemporal act must be wrong since it violates a major stipulation of the dynamical theory of matter that moving bodies must be continuous in space and time. (b) Kant himself actually offers a counter-noumenal theory of freedom that does not violate the stipulation in (a), in suggesting that freedom is the property of a primary autonomy. (c) Hebb offers the neurological evidence for the primary autonomy of the human cortical brain: that evidence permits us to draw a definitive line separating instinctive behavior and intelligence, especially human. *Human freedom or agency as a primary autonomy is thus the basis for regarding human embodied activity as genuine action; and therefore human beings are to be regarded as genuinely agentic persons.* The action of an embodied object and the action of an embodied subject are, equally, actions of causal agents, that is efficient causal entities or powerful particulars. The organization of the material bases for the structure of these two forms of efficient causes, however, are of course different: physical in the one case and neurological in the other (Mayr 1985: 43–83, 1997: 1–78).

The solution that I have articulated here to the problem of structure and agency can now be restated in a new formulation of the Thomas theorem. That enriched reformulation is to be called the Thomas–Harré theorem: *people defining situations as real so that they are real in their consequences, is a possibility by virtue of the fact that human beings are real powerful particulars in a world of other beings that are also real powerful particulars* (see Thomas's actual reference to powers in his theorem, Thomas 1972: 41). In the achievement of this solution from the scientific realism of the dynamic theory of matter in conjunction with the resources of the *Critique of Practical Reason*, Giddens's Call for a conception of "agent causality" with which to ground a theory of human agency, I believe, will have been answered. That Call and its answer points to the intimate connection between Kant and Giddens that centers this entire discussion.

> Much can be learned from what Kant had to say on the subject of *agent causality in the human context. Any* adequate account of the concept of a person as a rational being in general, requires both the concept of a transcendental source of unity of an individual's consciousness, the transcendental unity of apperception, and must invoke the concept of a transcendental ego which *has the power to perform unconditioned acts and make unconditioned choices.* ... The same transcendental ego, [thus], is the source of both the unity of consciousness and of unconditioned actions.
>
> (Harré 2006: 5, emphasis provided)

3 Kant and the stalemate of the social sciences
Prelude and transformation

Prelude to a stalemate: Hobbes and Rousseau

The scientific revolution of Galileo and Newton provided the metaphysic of naturalism and its principle of determinism, within which the Science and Humanism debate concerning the modern problem of structure and agency is going to be framed, conducted, and, especially, is going to be understood. That debate is anticipated with the appearance of Hobbes's materialist and mechanistic social theory and the challenge to it from the Cambridge Platonist's spiritualist theory of human freedom in the seventeenth century (Mintz 1996: 80–133). The emerging debate seamlessly continues with the advent of Newtonian mechanistic physical theory and Rousseau's reaction to it with his free-will theory in the eighteenth century. Let the proto-scientist Hobbes and the proto-Humanist Rousseau representatively speak to this point.

[For Hobbes, Mind is] ... nothing but motion in some internal substance of the head.

(Mintz 1996: 110)

[The upshot of which is that, like] a wooden top that is lashed by the boys, and runs about sometimes to one wall, sometimes to another [doing this or that] ... *if it were sensible of its own motion would think it proceeded from its own will, unless it felt what lashed it. And is a man any wiser* ... because he thinks [he does this or that] without other cause than his own will and *seeth not what are the lashings that cause his will?*

(Mintz Ibid: 112, emphasis provided)

[For Rousseau] *The motive power of all action is the will of a free creature; we can go no further.* It is not the word freedom that is meaningless, but the word necessity. To suppose some action which is not the effect of an active motive power is indeed to suppose effects without causes, to reason in a vicious circle. *Either there is no original impulse, or every original impulse has no antecedent cause and there is no will properly so-called without freedom. Man* is free to act, therefore, and as such he *is animated by an immaterial substance.*

(Rousseau 1996: 243, emphasis provided)

[Furthermore] *No material creature is in itself active, and I am active ...* I have a Body which is acted upon by other bodies, and it acts in turn upon them; *there is no doubt about this reciprocal action; but my will is independent of my senses. ... When I yield to temptation I surrender myself to the action of objects.* When I blame myself for this weakness I listen to my own will alone. ... The feeling of freedom is never effaced in me but when I myself do wrong, and when I at length prevent the *voice of the social* from protesting against the *authority of my body.*

(Rousseau Ibid: 242–43, emphasis provided)

In taking up the question of the ontological status of human action in the natural world of Galileo and Newton, Hobbes and Rousseau (continuing the Cambridge Platonist tradition) are presenting a discourse that presumes the traditional Judeo-Greco-Christian question of freedom and determinism discussed in Chapter 1. However, since that question is now to be conducted under the auspices of Cartesian Dualism, it will be of central importance for the discussion that follows to remind ourselves of what is taken to be axiomatic concerning this Cartesian beginning of modern philosophy.

[For Descartes] "the special prerogative of the *soul* is to *originate* action. (Singer 1959: 277)". Since it was not part of the material world, it did not obey natural laws, but was free. Lacking this free will, lower animals were capable only of automatic actions. To him they were *machines*, like impressive hydromechanical *automata* at the Austrian palace of Hellbrunn. Although Descartes did not originate the concept of *reflex*, he focused attention on it and gave it wide currency.

(Holt 1989: 144–45, emphasis provided)

Cartesianism presumes Rousseau's special doctrine of free will conceived of as an immaterial autonomy, and the theory of the Newtonian laws where its mechanical action is conceived of as material automaticity. This doctrine of free will with regard to defining the freedom of the human *mind* will be intimately associated with and therefore quite naturally indicated by the idea of *reflection*; at the same time, as the human *body* is now being defined as a machine, its mechanical character will be indexed by the idea of *reflex*. Coeval with the term reflex during this time, the idea of *instinct* too is emerging into special explanatory prominence (Varela 2003: 103–5). Indeed, the two concepts are being understood to capture the exact sense of determinism as mechanical action that has thus the precise character of automaticity; and with that sense in tow they come to be used interchangeably (Varela Ibid: 105–10). Moving toward the advent of the nineteenth century, then, we have an ontological battleground framed by Cartesianism, within which, from the perspective of the Hobbesian and Rousseauan traditions, the fundamental Western question of freedom and determinism is transformed into a modern problem that is to be played out in the emergent and developing histories of modern philosophy and the social sciences.

What is of great relevance in this context and must be brought out here is that Rousseau, in fact, takes special pains to make clear that the mentalist side of Cartesianism certainly implies that free will is a transcendent theory of freedom by virtue of the fact that it is a religious conception ("the special prerogative of the soul is to originate action"). It therefore presupposes the theology of supernaturalism against which the metaphysics of naturalism is being pitted with the emerging and developing scientific revolution. Hobbes, on his part, has presented what is to become a naturalist schema that is a response to a transcendent theory of freedom: mind or will as a material object that is a motion in the head, is caused by the actions of other material objects inside and outside of the head (Ryan 1974: 3–19). For, since this modern problem of freedom can now be located originally in nature, the principle of determinism becomes the source of a fundamental metaphysical tension in modern thought on the question of freedom. That tension is found, as Hobbes has shown, in the radical fact that the principle of determinism is being taken as ruling the material world, of which the physical and the human are thus to be understood as but two complementary material parts. And clearly, it is to this metaphysical tension that Dahrendorf's inadvertent articulation of the absolute stalemate of the structure–agency debate can be directly traced.

Metaphysical tension: the initial agenda

From within the metaphysic of naturalism and with regard to the future of the problem of freedom and determinism in philosophy and the social sciences, it is clear that the search for solutions has an initial agenda. If, now, human freedom can only be understood within the paradigm of science and its metaphysic of naturalism, what conceptions of freedom are to be possible alternatives to the tradition of transcendent freedom? A deep metaphysical question is therefore emerging here: since the very idea that human freedom has been conceived of as a "power" (of the will) that is free precisely because it resides in a realm transcendent to nature, *how is that power now to be understood when human beings are taken to reside, instead, and originally, in the natural world?* Thus, what is to be the fate of transcendence in modern theories of freedom? And, reciprocally, what is to be the fate of modern theories of freedom without transcendence? Ultimately, is a metaphysical conception of power for explanatory science possible without transcendence?

In the above quote of Rousseau, while keeping in mind the expected declaration that free will is a religious conception, we should also keep in mind the unusual declaration that human freedom must itself be "causal," since, after all, Rousseau claims that human action is the effect of an "active motive power." This sharpens the issue: can the power of human will retain its "causal" status of *freedom* when it is to be relocated in the *natural* world of "causal" *determinism*? In other words, *pace* Rousseau, how can the "active motive power" of the will cause an action without, *pace* Hobbes, the "*lashings that cause [that] will*"? The issue, however, can be sharpened even further: given the Newtonian context within which he is theorizing, is Rousseau asserting the *causal* status of free will *in spite of, or because of,* his religious conception? If it is the former, then the Hobbesian choice seems to wins out: the "will" that causes the action is itself caused. If it is the latter, then, on what grounds can Rousseau's choice possibly win: the "will" as "cause" is a spiritual form of causation? The supernaturalist metaphysic and its principle of spiritual causation *("and [only] I am active")* is challenged and replaced by the naturalist metaphysic that claims the reality of natural causation, alone ("I am active [but only because I am caused]"). More to the point, and of cardinal interest here, *natural causation is strictly construed according to the Newtonian laws of motion, specifically in this case, the law of inertia.* And it is of paramount importance to be precise here on the issue of the construal of this law.

Metaphysical tension and inertia: proper and improper construal

It is from the understanding of the very fact of the proper and improper construal of that law that the logic of the metaphysical tension can be precisely spelled out. This will definitively reveal the connection between Dahrendorf's conception of the stalemate at issue and its origin in the *improper* construal of the law of inertia. Let us therefore consider the following mid-twentieth-century representative statement of this law so that it may concretely inform the discussion to follow; and let us do so up against Kant's own contrary statement of inertia. Here we have the standard view corrected by one of the architects of Newton realist metaphysics.

> Hence, no sooner was the conception of *inert bodies passively following the dictates of blind forces* seen to be applicable [by Newton] to the motion of mass-points, than it was *immediately generalized into a world-philosophy.*
>
> (Singer 1959: 294 [referenced in Holt Ibid] the second emphasis is added)

> matter is the movable insofar as it is something having a movable force [power].
>
> (Kant 1985b: 95)

I am going to call what became the standard and absolutely exclusive interpretation of inertia ("a generalized world philosophy") *outside of physics,* in modern philosophy and the social sciences, the *"ultimate thesis."* The thesis emerges in the agreement between Hobbes's telling closing line, "seeth not what are the lashings that cause his will," and Rousseau's assertion that, "No material creature is in itself active." The substance of the thesis is this: the *inertia* of material particulars in motion entails that material particulars are *inert*. In short, Hobbes and Rousseau agree to the principle that *material particulars are patients not agents*. All these considerations with respect to Hobbes and Rousseau and with respect to, especially, the ultimate thesis, constitute the critical import of the metaphysical tension that is fundamental to modern thought. *That import, I now maintain, remains in tact straight through the demise of the Old Humanism, continuing with the ascendance of Postmodernism, into a world not quite After Positivism – a Steinmetzian non-positivistic period in which "a revised positivism is alive and well in many of the social sciences, and is persistently being challenged by alternative epistemologies"* (Steinmetz 2005: 1–56). The sterile continuation of a "revised positivism" that is, thus, still a caricature of science, is testimony to and the guarantee of the persistence of the ultimate thesis as an unproblematic belief in the social sciences (Steinmetz Ibid).

It is exactly with this metaphysical import in mind that we must remind ourselves here of something that is quite important concerning the naturalist metaphysic and the social theory of Hobbes which it frames. While the naturalist metaphysic gives us an example of the absolute sovereignty of the determinism of *nature* over material objects, yet, at the same time, Hobbes's theory, despite its naturalist frame, gives us the special example of an absolute sovereignty of the determinism of *society* over human subjects; and for Hobbes "society" means of course the determinism of the *civil ruler* over, presumably, "willing," that is "consenting" human subjects. It is very well known that this is a serious crack in the theory: despite Hobbes's earlier quote on determinism against freedom, and hence against himself, Hobbes implicitly shows that the determinism that is to rule in both the physical and the human worlds seems *not* to be the same (Hobbes 1957: Introduction by Oakeshott). Cassirer, by virtue of his standpoint as a Kantian, captured this difference accordingly in his essay on social contract theory in *Myth of the State* (1975 [1946]).

> The contract of rulership which is the legal basis of all civil power has, therefore, its limits. *There is … no act of submission by which man can give up the state of a free agent and enslave himself.* For by such an act of renunciation *he would give up* that very character which constitutes *his nature and essence*: *he would lose his humanity.*
>
> (Cassirer 1975 [1946]: 175, emphasis provided)

Nonhuman material objects are nothing but material objects, to be sure, and hence must of necessity suffer the sovereignty of the determinism of their material nature (Hobbes's wooden top). However, while human beings are certainly material objects, nevertheless, in virtue of the fact that they are members of society they are still subjects (Hobbesian wooden tops who seeth, or believeth, what?). The critical reason for that is that they enter a contract and thereby submit to the sovereignty of the determinism of their society. To be quite sure, as Alan Ryan has shown us so lucidly in his "The Nature of Human Nature in Hobbes and Rousseau," that sovereignty is supposed to be a formidable determinism (Ryan 1974: 1–10).

> Leviathan is more than a mere contractual arrangement. It is, as Hobbes says, a real and perfect unity of them all. *We become literally one body – though an artificial one, none the less a real one.* ... Since the Leviathan is, although a body, a body whose *sinews are conventions*, its *parts the citizens*, must have as little choice about keeping these conventions as have things in the natural world about obeying the laws governing them.
> (Ryan Ibid: 12, emphasis provided)

Nevertheless, despite Hobbes's attempt to insure that the citizens of Leviathan become that Leviathan by coercion and socialization in his recourse to the sociobiological imperatives of fear of death, selfishness, survival, and social order through contract, the theory has never been fully convincing. The force of the argument is the force of rhetoric, and not the force of a demonstration. But on Hobbes's very own terms human beings are subjects and not completely objects: convention, contract, and choice, are still presumed and their accepted reality a resistant feature of the theory itself. And perhaps most revealing of all, is Hobbes himself, the theorist: the sociobiological determinism – an impersonal force – of Leviathanian theory reveals *his determination* – a personal force – to see to it that in theory human subjects *will* submit to the civil ruler of society. It is Hobbes's formidable will to believe that is the driving force of his rhetoric. And it is *that* which gives the theory the illusion of being a demonstrative truth. That illusion masks the deep question the theory does not confront. The "will" of the theorist, the will of the sovereign, and the will of each citizen, displays a "force," the nature of which is actually the root question of the ultimate thesis. How is it to be accepted that the will of human material subjects must be an instance of a "law" that is itself, apart from those subjects, taken to reference the agency of "force," "causation," and "energy." Thus, Cassirer's crucial Kantian insight that submission cannot be the renunciation of human agency could not but have been taken seriously in the modern world of philosophy and the social sciences. It was and is the bone of contention in the Science and Humanism debate on structure and agency. We certainly have here the seed of what will become the problem of reification – the agentification of structures and their laws, the logic of which entails the theft of human agency. Clearly, Hobbes's theory itself is an exemplary expression of the modern metaphysical tension that informs and drives what will become the modern problem of structure and agency.

Kantian transformation: stalemate and the structure and agency problem

With Cassirer's insight in mind, I want to insist that it is not enough to claim that the Hobbesian and Rousseauan traditions together constitute a schema for what will become the paradigm of the debate between Science and Humanism concerning the problem of structure and agency. This claim, thus, must be spelled out in the following proposals. The first and central proposal is that it is primarily through the authority of Kant's theory of freedom that the Hobbes/Rousseau schema and its traditional problem of freedom and determinism will be transformed into the Science and Humanism debate on the new problem of deterministic structures and embodied human agency. In reference to deterministic structures, the second proposal is that, as we will see, Kant highlights the determinism of both the physical world and the instinctivism of human biology as his deep metaphysical concern. Kant's highlighting of the structures of the physical and the biological is the occasion to point to the way in which the determinism of the physical and that of the biological are intimately connected. This leads to my third proposal: the ultimate thesis binds the determinism of the physical world to the determinism of the biological world; the mechanistic principle that material objects are patients has its parallel in the reflex/instinctivist principle that organismic objects too are patients and not agents. My fourth proposal then is that, with the concept of instinct in the background, the concept of reflex action becomes the primary conceptual unit of behavioral analysis in biology and the social sciences in their inter relationships; and that this is especially true for psychology in the schools of behaviorism and psychoanalysis. As a matter of historical fact, as it will be made clear, the fifth proposal is that *the concept of reflex instantiates the ultimate thesis*. And since, six, at the very least, sociology and anthropology must presuppose a psychological theory of some kind in its sociocultural theorization, the ultimate thesis and the reflex concept are together a built-in presupposition. Usually, in view of the historical fact that reflex comes to be conflated with instinct (and its late modern cognate, the parasitic idea of "hard wiring"), the latter will smuggle the former into the thought-ways of these two social sciences. Now, the seventh proposal is that the ultimate thesis is crucial to understanding that the stalemate of the Hobbes and Rousseau debate concerning the problem of freedom and determinism, *before* Kant, is transformed into the stalemate of the Science and Humanism debate concerning the problem of structure and agency, *after* Kant. What is critical to realize here is that the stalemate is being driven by the ultimate thesis, the result of which is that the *patiency of Hobbesian citizens is prescribed as a natural theory and the agency of Rousseauan citizens is therefore prescribed as an extra-natural theory*. Now, and this becomes the center piece of the interlocking set of the above proposals, although Kant's theory of freedom is unquestionably the mechanism by which the Hobbes/Rousseau debate becomes the Science and Humanism debate, it is the fate of the question of how to understand Kantian freedom in this regard that turns out to be pivotal in all this. That the predominant outcome of attempts to understand Kant all come down to the failure to see that transcendental freedom is not transcendent freedom in noumenal dress, seals the future, so to speak, of the course of the Science and Humanism encounter in the history of philosophy and the social sciences. In other words, *the failed understanding of Kant's theory of freedom prescribes that the old stalemate of the former debate on freedom and determinism is to continue as the new stalemate of the latter debate on structure and agency.* And thus, as I have earlier indicated, here precisely we have further insight into the roots of Dahrendorf's version of the stalemate of the structure–agency problem that is to serially mark the intellectual landscape of the history of the social sciences to date.

In order to facilitate the demonstration of the cogency of these proposals in my presentation of the select details of the history of the social sciences in the chapters to follow, the above discussion can be given in a succinct summary form.

Metaphysical tension and the ultimate thesis: summary statement

> Man the machine – man the impersonal engine. Whatsoever a man is, is due to his *make*, and to the influences brought to bear upon it by heredities, his habitat, his associations. He is moved, directed, COMMANDED, by exterior influences, solely. He *originates* nothing, not even a thought.
>
> Mark Twain *What is Man?* (1905)

The theme of the metaphysical tension that centers the Science and Humanism debate on the structure–agency problem is this: the Kantian theory of freedom and its contemporary representation in Giddens's Call, together, are internally connected to the stalemate of the social sciences on the debate at issue. The mistake that Kant's theory of freedom is free will theory cast in the language of transcendental philosophy, determines that the Humanist answer to the determinism of science is to return to Kant in order to rescue human freedom from the natural world; the rescue takes the form of either reinstating Kant's noumenal freedom for Humanist social science, or declaring a phenomenological freedom for Humanist social science. In either case the return and rescue are a dead end to the debate. This state of affairs on the Science and Humanism debate at issue constitutes a stalemate that signals the end of the (Old) Humanist tradition on the problem of structure and agency. Giddens's Call for a realist theory of human agency is the contemporary representative of Kant's *unrealized* realist theory of freedom. The mistaken view that both Giddens and Kant stand for a Postmodern form of free-will theory perpetuates the stalemate, promotes not only the death of Humanism, but insures the impossibility of a New Humanism; and this leads to the essential delegitimation of the problem of structure and agency in the social sciences. Finally, in the next sentence we have the essence of the Dahrendorfian conception of the stalemate: the theme of the *metaphysical tension* revolves around the *ultimate thesis* and its reciprocal concepts of *inertia and freedom*, and is defined by *five kinds of interrelated misunderstanding*:

(1) Determinism as Inertia: patiency is natural and agency is extra-natural.
(2) Kant and Rousseau: transcendental freedom is transcendent freedom in disguise.
(3) Human freedom is thus necessarily an extra-natural theory of free will: any alternatives are merely variations – two paradigm examples are the traditions of Kantian transcendentalism and Diltheyan phenomenology.
(4) Kant and Giddens: agency theory is transcendental, and hence, a transcendent theory in disguise; both are anti-scientific theories.
(5) Inertia and reflex: inertia as inertness is represented by the reciprocal concepts of reflex and instinct.

The history of the structure–agency problem: a series of footnotes to Kant

As suggested in the summary, there are two ways in which the history of the structure and agency problem in the social sciences – the Sociological Tradition and Modern Sociology – has been a *series of footnotes to Kant. One* way is where it is *presumed* in theorization, and thus the treatment of Kant's theory of freedom is *muddled* (Simmel), is *distorted* (Durkheim), is puzzling (Weber), or, where it is *reinstated* in theorization either in its *transcendent* form, and therefore the treatment of Kantian freedom is irrelevant (Stark, Benton), or in its *transcendental* form, in which case the treatment of Kant's theory of freedom is either a questionable substantive or an empty ritual of return (Parsons, Dahrendorf, Berger, Foucault); and *the other way,* is where the freedom of Kantian theory is *reconsidered,* but its transcendentalism is dropped in favor of relocating its ground in the *phenomenological* region of the human world of *lived experience* (Husserl), *lived existence* (Sartre), or *lived flesh* (Merleau-Ponty). From this point on in this chapter and in Chapter 4, and then in Chapters 5–8, I present the historical truth of the stalemate of the social sciences concerning the structure and agency problem. And I do so accordingly: I will be focusing on the last representatives of *The Sociological Tradition* exemplified by Simmel, Durkheim, and Weber, and then on the initial representatives of Modern Sociology exemplified by Parsons, Dahrendorf, and Berger.

This of course continues the obvious and correct focus on sociology, primarily, and anthropology in passing mention; but I will be also paying strict attention to psychology and psychoanalysis (in Chapter 4). The reason for the latter is found in my proposal that the ultimate thesis is the basis for the stalemate of the social sciences with regard to solving the problem of structure and agency. My outright contention is that Hull, Skinner, and Freud are profound and systematically explicit exponents of the Science against Humanism dogma of the ultimate thesis; hence their strategy of looking for some kind of psychological causal structure that is the reality behind the appearance of human consciousness and action. It will be a supreme historical lesson to actually discover in each particular case the unique way in which the ultimate thesis drives their scientific theorizing. Now, in seeing how vividly clear and boldly direct is the connection between the ultimate thesis, theoretical work, and resultant stalemate in behaviorism and psychoanalysis, we have an added bonus. It is that of having been prepared to appreciate that very same connection, but not in so clear and direct a way, in the work of the three giants of *The Sociological Tradition* to be examined. In the case of the three prominent sociologists of Modern Sociology, it is only in Parsons's theory of the social system and individual voluntarism that the ultimate thesis and stalemate connection comes through adequately; as for Dahrendorf and Berger only the Kantian part of the ultimate thesis – agency as extra-natural – shines through. Even here, however, the absence of the first part, nature as patiency, can quite comfortably be assumed to simply have been taken for granted. I think this can be easily recognized in the fact of my using Dahrendorf's theory of homo sociologicus as the paradigm statement of the stalemate of the structure–agency problem in the social sciences. In the view that determinism is the ontology of nature and therefore freedom is ruled out, we have a perfect translation of the ultimate thesis into the principle of determinism.

Now, overall, this presentation of the internally connected series of footnotes to Kant in the social sciences will strongly bring out this major point: *a thorough understanding of the truth of the ultimate thesis/stalemate connection at issue,* in reference to the several returns to Kant in order to take up his theory of freedom as presumption, as reinstatement, or as reconsideration under the old auspices of the tradition of rescue, *will give us a thorough reason for taking seriously the thesis of the return to Kantian freedom under the new auspices of the recovery of human agency.* And there is another and complementary major point: I am engaging in the project of fundamentally rewriting the history of the Science and Humanism debate on the structure and agency question. Thus, I intend to set the record straight on this issue; and consequently the *historical record* is of paramount importance, even though it is certainly secondary to the primary *theoretical record* of the themes of rescue and recovery.

In order to set the stage for the above analysis to follow, Werner Stark's Humanist Manifesto in *The Fundamental Forms of Social Thought* (1963) and Ted Benton's in *Philosophical Foundations of the Three Sociologies* (1977), along with a brief look at Martin Albrow (1990) on Weber's relation to Kant, will give us exactly what we need in that regard. For, in these two works we have two major statements of the neo-Humanist revolt in its intimate connection to Kant that crystallized with the 1960s. In reference to the background to the 1960s revolt and the Kant connection, certainly we should remind ourselves of the earlier mention (Chapter 1) of David Bidney's *Theoretical Anthropology* (1996 [1953]). This was, as I have shown, a Humanist Manifesto for anthropology that comprehensively made it definitively clear that its philosophical point of departure informing its theory of culture and freedom was the German Idealist tradition in which Kant was of pioneering importance. And that importance could not be significantly recognized until it was placed in the context of Giddens's Call. And, in between Werner Stark's 1963 work and Ted Benton's in 1977, we will see in Chapter 8 that Peter Berger and Thomas Luckmann's renowned *The Social Construction of Reality* in 1966 implicitly assumed Kant's theory of freedom as the ground of their idea of "social construction." This will come to the fore in my discussion of Berger's actual but not quite satisfactory reinstatement of Kant's noumenal theory of freedom in (with Hansfried Kellner) *Sociology Reinterpreted* (1981).

Stark's Humanist Manifesto

In his classic study of *The Fundamental Forms of Social Thought* (1963), namely, society as an organism, a machine, and as culture, Werner Stark's final and definitive conclusion is that culture theory is in principle superior to the other two theories. The cardinal feature of cultural theory is that it is "an act of liberation – liberation from erstwhile bondage to the natural sciences" (Stark Ibid: 218). The theoretical point of the liberation is the realization that,

> Society ... is neither a creation of the laws of mechanics nor a reflection of the laws of biology: it is *man's own, sprung from his will, sustained by his will, perfectible through his will.* ... *[This] third philosophy* (*the "idealism of freedom"*) ... however, is dualistic. It allows that the laws of nature are imperative, but it also insists that they leave room for an area of indeterminacy. It is as if we had a country with concentric circles: an outer belt under the sway of *mechanical* forces, an intermediate ring under the sway of *vital* forces, and an inner core where *cultural* forces reign supreme.
>
> (Stark Ibid: 218–19, emphasis provided)

Cultural theory, then, is itself based on a theory of freedom that Stark believes is a special variety of idealist philosophy, notably, subjective idealism. That its theory of freedom is constituted by "a principle of life, spirit, and will," is because its principle authors, for instance, Aquinas, Kant, and Vico, reveal that there is a "religious side to this system ... a personalistic theism" (Stark Ibid: 8). As a catholic sociologist, Stark makes it quite clear that, for him, the triumph of Humanism over Science at the beginning of the neo-Humanist revolution is necessarily a fusion of the sacred and the secular.

Kant and Vico are expressive of that fusion, since for them, according to Stark, the theory of freedom is a theory of freedom as spirit and its manifestation in the effort of will that, nevertheless, is located in but in principle not reduced to a natural world of physical determinism and biological laws. The implication is unavoidable: *Kantian transcendental freedom is transcendent freedom, and that is the heart of the idea of freedom for Humanism in the social sciences* (see also, Dawe 1978: 362–417).

Benton's philosophical foundations

Almost 15 years later, Ted Benton's work is a replica of that standard view of Kantian freedom, in near-perfect form. The two lengthy quotes to follow show this quite clearly: in the first, we have a general characterization of the Science and Humanism debate, the second zeros in on its Kantian grounding.

> Historically speaking, the debate ... as to the status of the social sciences ... has centered around the mutual opposition of "positivist" and "humanist" philosophies. Characteristically, positivism has claimed the territory of human social relations and their history as a proper object of scientific study. ... Those I have referred to as "humanists" have argued against this, [on the grounds] that the utterly distinctive character of the object of social, historical or cultural understanding (*the "free will" of the human subject*, "intentionality" "meaning," or whatever) renders the method of the natural sciences quite inappropriate.
>
> (Benton 1977: 81, emphasis provided)

> This, then, is Kant's way of posing the central problem of combining the mechanistic conception of a causally ordered, "deterministic" nature with belief in the *free will*, and hence moral responsibility of human agents. Kant's "solution" to the problem is to argue that the human subject participates in both the noumenal and phenomenal world. As part of the phenomenal world the human individual is an object of possible experience (through external sense in the case of other selves, through introspection in the case of oneself), and also part of the causal order of nature. To this phenomenal aspect of ourselves belong our desires and impulses. But as part of the noumenal world, the self is thus *outside* the scope of the synthetic a priori categories and principles of natural science, including the category of *cause*. There is, then, conceptual room for the "noumenal" subject, possessed of free (i.e. not causally determined) will, capable of subjecting itself to universal moral duties.
>
> (Benton Ibid: 103)

From the discussion surrounding the above quotes, after pointing out that the Humanist approaches of all varieties, such as the Hegelian, neo-Kantian, phenomenological, existentialist, ethnomethodological, Wittgensteinian, and even certain Marxists, seem to argue for their status as heterogeneous philosophical sources, Benton (Ibid: 101) rightly dismisses that argument. Instead, he avers, albeit in general terms, that they all stem from the philosophy of Immanuel Kant, at the center of which is the doctrine of free will (Benton Ibid). As a Marxist, Benton's presentation is not exactly Stark's: the ontology of Kant's theory of freedom is not explicitly confronted and laid out, and in such a way that its idealism is subordinated to a personal theism. Thus, Benton appears to leave it open whether the noumenal world that is "outside" of the phenomenal world of causation is transcendental or transcendent; or rather, he is implying that the two terms, after all, are simply interchangeable. However, if we consider, briefly, the case of Martin Albrow's discussion of the philosophical foundations of Max Weber's interpretative sociology, there is no such state of ambiguity with regard to this matter of the metaphysical status of the Kantian theory of knowledge.

Albrow's Weber: Kant as Rousseau in disguise

Opening up the last decade of the twentieth century with his study of Weberian sociology, Albrow (1990: 31–42) contends that its prime interest in rationality in its various forms in relationship to the multiplicity of historical reality, is informed by the central idea of the radical individualism of the human being as the bearer of reason. Albrow contextualizes that interest and idea with this claim.

> We are now nearer to appreciating the force of that paradox that individuals for Kant are *in the world but not of it*. The individual is at the core *not even human*, for its ultimate quality is unity, the fount of reason. In this way *the individual is close to the divine, to the other-worldly, rather than this world.* ... The complementarity of Kant's ideas of the world and the individual should now be apparent. They belong on either side of a dichotomous system of ideas. The "world" is associated with chaos, the senses, the variable, the material; the "individual" is associated with mind, reason, unity, the eternal. ... It is impossible to appreciate the direction of Kant's argument unless one bears in mind *the Christian belief in two worlds, the material and terrestrial, on the one hand, and the spiritual and the heavenly, on the other. Kant's individual drew its meaning from the latter and lived in the former.* ... Now closely associated with this doctrine was a nexus of ideas about freedom, the will, causality, duty and personality. *Weber's idea of the individual is pervaded by these ideas.* ... *[and the deep question at the center of them all] How does one combine the idea that everything is caused with the belief that the human will is free?*
> (Albrow Ibid: 37, 39, emphasis provided)

As exemplary representatives of the social science tradition, particularly as it was understood during the three-decade period (1950s, 1960s, 1970s) of the neo-Humanist revolt, Stark, Benton, and Albrow evince one of the cardinal mistakes of the social sciences. Kantian theory is conflated with free-will theory. Kant is Rousseau in disguise: the very idea of freedom is cast as a secular form of the traditional religious doctrine of freedom, wherein its ontological status is extra-natural. Hence, it will be the case, that any change in vocabulary, for instance, from free will to noumenal freedom, noumenal freedom to vitalism, vitalism to voluntarism, and from voluntarism to agency, will be regarded as purely terminological. In short, ultimately, from this standpoint, despite the change in vocabulary from theorist to theorist, there has been no change in metaphysics. Thus, a theory of freedom must, in the nature of this metaphysical case, be judged to be non-scientific, if not anti-scientific. We have seen earlier in this chapter that Rousseau's theory was certainly the paradigm example of freedom as free-will at the beginning of the modern period. But, now, we must begin to systematically ask this question. Can this actually be said of Kant, particularly from his own words on the matter? Of the two chapters devoted to Kant, the second will continue the systematic examination of his theory of freedom which I will now take up. Hence, here, in order to meet the needs of this chapter, my consideration of his theory of freedom will therefore be brief and restricted to the *Metaphysical Foundations of Natural Science* (1786), particularly in reference to the metaphysical work at the end of his life, the *Opus Postumum* (1796–1803).

Kant on his own theory of freedom: transcendental, not transcendence?

Regarding the *Opus Postumum*, which he was still working on a year before his death in 1804, it is certainly relevant to reveal that Kant himself thought that this was "his most important work" (Kant 1995: xvii). The importance, for him, resided in the fact that it completed his system of philosophy, and that that system was explicitly informed by a realist metaphysic. To actually appreciate that Kant was articulating Newtonian theoretical science, I am going to also provide Newton's own statement of its realist metaphysic.

> The moving *forces* of matter are *powers*, either purely dynamic or mechanical. *The latter are based on the former.*
> (Kant 1995: 58, emphasis provided)

> All bodies are movable and endowed with certain powers (which we call the inertia) of preserving in their motion.
> (Newton in Cohen and Westfall 1995: 117)

From the unmistakable realist standpoint that understands nature to be constituted by powers manifested as forces, we now consider Kant's comment on freedom in relation to nature, so constituted. This is only one of a number of statements in the *Opus*.

There is in man an active, *supersensible* principle which, *independently* of nature and the causality of the world, determines nature's appearances, and is called freedom.

(Kant Ibid: 242)

We have here, in what in fact he calls a "Theorem," Kant's selective restatement of his doctrine of human freedom and agency in its standard form. On the one hand, "supersensible," for instance, refers, deliberately, to the noumenal realm, and thus, deliberately, not the "supernatural" realm, and on the other, "independently of nature," surely, from Kant's naturalist standpoint, does not mean here "outside" of nature, that is "other-worldly." It means, rather, "outside" of our sense-dependent experience of the world. In other words, *this is a statement of a realist metaphysics against the metaphysics of positivism.* That Kant is certainly struggling here, there can be no doubt, yet, I think that this is to be expected. But from other statements in the *Opus*, what can be taken to be a somewhat problematic grounding in powers and thus forces, is certainly cleared up, though just as certainly, imperfectly.

> *Freedom of the will* [willkur] is a fact which cannot be attributed to the object as a natural being; but, yet it is *a principle of causality in the world,* and appears to contain effect without cause in its very concept. That which commands as a person (categorical imperative), hence as God, hence as if a person.
>
> (Kant 1995: 230, emphasis provided)

Despite the fact that Kant does use the phrase "freedom of the will," we must quickly note, once more, that he directly asserts it to be "a principle of causality in the world." But not only that, in the last sentence, the grounding of freedom is first to be done in the terms of the categorical imperative, *and then* God. My above point, exactly. And now consider, in this last regard, this statement of Kant's on the location of freedom in metaphysical space. Indeed, it may be the last statement of its kind on such matters that the great man ever made; it is found in what is called the VII fascicle, sheet X, page 2, and although the approximate date for it is given as between April and December 1800, this may not coincide exactly with the actual date of composition. Having worked as late as 1803 on one other fascicle, he apparently left off such work, and died February 2 1804.

> The concept God is the idea which man, as a moral being, forms of the highest moral being in relation according to principles of right, insofar as he, according to the categorical imperative, regards all duties as commands of this being. Concept of *freedom. Moral-practical reason is one of the moving forces of nature and all sense-objects.*
>
> (Kant Ibid: 199)

In the quote before this one, the declaration that freedom is "a principle of causality *in* the world" now can be compared to this assertion that freedom "is one of the moving forces *of* nature." Does not Kant tell us something here in speaking of freedom as a causal force "in" nature, and then that it is "of" nature? After all, although we can say of Rousseau that he regarded free-will as a causal force "in" nature, what we cannot say is that he meant by that, "of" nature. In Kant's case that is, at the very least, what we must say he did mean. But there is one other comment that Kant makes in this last work on the philosophy of science that deepens the plausibility of our view here on this issue of *freedom being "in" nature because it is "of" nature.*

> One can, in fact, also draw on the concept of *organic* (as opposed to *inorganic*) nature, in the consideration of the moving forces of nature, without, [thereby], transgressing the limits, determined a priori, of the transition to physics, or mixing into it what belongs to the material part of physics.
>
> (Kant Ibid)

The thesis that dynamical powers constitute mechanical forces binds together the *Critiques* and informs the theory of transcendental freedom unifying them, can now to be enriched.

The latter is realized, as the quote above intimates, with a thesis proposing a connection between physical and biological generativity. That Kant is graduating toward this new thesis in the *Opus* is suggested by the fact that he carries forward a theoretical analysis found in the short version of the first critique, the *Prolegomena to any Future Metaphysics* (Kant 1985b), into the *Metaphysical Foundations*. In the *Prolegomena*, what is emphasized is that physical objects – "matter" – and human subjects are both active due to their respective internal principles, but yet, nevertheless, they are radically different, since only subjects are active and free; in *Metaphysical Foundations* the idea of the radical distinction between "matter" and "freedom" from the *Prolegomena* is restated as the equally radical distinction between "matter" and "life" (Kant 1985b: 96, 105–6). This last distinction presupposes the basic principle of mechanics that underwrites the law of inertia, namely, "matter is the movable insofar as it is something having a movable force [power]" (Kant 1985b: 95). Here, too, "matter" and "life" are material particulars active by virtue of their internal principles of "movable [power]." Furthermore, matter is an expansive force that, in filling space, "must be termed *original*, because it cannot be derived from any other property of matter" (Kant 1985b: 44–45, emphasis provided). Thus the "force" that is "movable" as a "power," is "original," in that it refers to the expansiveness of matter filling space. And now Kant presents the basis for the radical distinction separating "life" from "matter": the "expansiveness" of life, speaking in this case figuratively, is a movable force and thus power, of self-determination;

the latter specifically is composed of the internal principle of desire, an internal activity of thought, and two aspects of desire – pleasure and pain, appetite and will (Kant 1985b: 105). *Presumably, "life" is a term now used to stand for the components of freedom.* It can be seen that, insofar as Kant also means by "life" the freedom of subjects *and* the actions of non-human subjects, that is animals, he is at the very edge of spilling over into a vitalist conception of "life." But, evidently, if that is so, I want to emphasize that he is attempting to insinuate the dimensions of freedom into the very structural dynamics of matter. Hence, any accusation that Kant is a vitalist must be carefully qualified by the dynamical theory of matter that centers his entire work. Notice this carefully: in Rousseau's conception of the will as an "active motive power," that "power" is "transcendent" to matter, while Kant's will as the freedom of a dynamically embodied (movable power/force) subject is a "power" immanent in nature.

As we move further into Kant in the *Opus*, where the above quote opens his discussion, we note the following theoretical theme that essentially exhausts what he has to say on the issue of the inorganic/organic connection.

> Organism is the form of a body regarded as machine, i.e. as an instrument of motion for a certain purpose. The internal relationship of the parts of a body, whose purpose is a certain form of movement, is its mechanism. All the laws of motion of matter are mechanical; but only if the internal relationship of the parts is represented as formed for a *purpose* of a certain form of motion, is a mechanism attributed to the body.
> (Kant 1985b: 61)

Of course by today's standards and knowledge, while Kant was giving us some very rudimentary ideas concerning the inorganic and organic, nevertheless, the realist framework informing this offering is quite sophisticated. The deep insight is the realist treatment of matter and animals in terms of powers of generativity, and this insight is far reaching in its theoretical originality. Today, at the frontiers of biological evolutionary theory, some biologists are attempting to examine, perhaps for the first time, the notion of causality that is implicated in the conception of "natural selection," and doing so from the point of view of the "organism" as the site of a "selective" process that is "natural" to the activity of its environmental encounters.

For example, Brian Goodwin in *How the Leopard Changed its Spots* (1994) and Richard C. Lewontin in "Genes, Environment, and Organisms" (1995) are only *beginning* to entertain the radical idea that organisms must be reconceptualized in terms of powers of generativity; actually in the former, and by implication in the latter. In this specific regard, I maintain that Kant's realist treatment of matter and animals was revolutionary. And not only for his time.

Kantian freedom: an initial formulation

From the above last statements in the *Opus*, and in his own words, we can put together this formulation that represents the most persistent and promising features of Kant's theory of freedom: *there is in human beings a unique active principle of causality, which, being called freedom, is one of the original moving powers of nature in the world.* In this last metaphysical work where we are given Kant's last word on freedom as a unique active principle of causality, we certainly have confirming consistency with his initial statements in this quote I have already referred to from the first critique (Chapter 1):

> It is possible to admit present things,
> substances, which have the power of
> acting out of freedom.
>
> Kant (A 450, B 478).

Note, "activeness" as the very idea of "power" is the telling link – *freedom as transcendental is a power of spontaneity that is a property of things or substances.*

However, as a reminder of how difficult it is to nail a definitive distinction between Kant's transcendental theory of freedom and the transcendence theory of freedom, from Kant himself, and how equally difficult it will be to completely justify any such distinction by showing that the causality of nature and the causality of freedom can be reconciled in reference to the realist theory of causal powers that is found in Kant's *Metaphysical Foundations of Natural Science*, consider one final quote from the *Opus:* "It is utterly impossible to unite the principle of causal relations in the world with freedom; for that would be an effect without a cause" (Kant 1995: 223).

Of course, a century and a quarter after this statement of Kant's on the issue of the unification of the two causalities, I have already pointed out that Heidegger implicitly presumed that it could be addressed positively. He presumed so in transforming the statement into a *problem* of unifying these two original moving powers that were, at one and the same time, of nature and of culture. And as a consequence of the realist appreciation that Heidegger's solution to the problem in terms of a metaphysics of Being is far less promising than a solution in terms of a metaphysics of Powers, Kant's statement can now be understood to have been a last judgment, surely, but certainly not a final one. Perhaps that is our task.

Transcendental rather than transcendence: a new look

From the above discussion, we are in an even stronger position to assert that the scientific realist theory of matter Kant was pioneering in *Metaphysical Foundations* was the ground to the figure of the theory of freedom that underwrites the three *Critiques*. I now want to propose something new in reference to this last point. It is important to initially recognize that it must have been very difficult for Kant to have been definitively clear in forging the distinction between divine causal power and human causal power, because, I propose, *in order to do so presupposes that Kant had in effect taken up the primary problem of making a distinction between divine powers and the powers of matter, and then proceeded to address it in his metaphysical theory of matter.* Simply put, he was not doing that. Now, clearly, this shows us that Kant was absolutely not involved in the metaphysical problem of distinguishing the powers of matter from the powers of divinity. However, it is central to my proposal that the latter is relevant to the problem of the conflation of Kant's transcendental theory of freedom with Rousseau's transcendence theory of freedom. I want to carefully explore just how the difficulty of making the latter distinction is rendered more complicated by the difficulty of making the more basic distinction between divine and material causal powers in matter. The clarification of that distinction and its importance for understanding Kant's theory of freedom is what I mean by a new look.

The problem of transcendental versus transcendent freedom for Kant is not simply the traditional one that has to do with the rejection of supernaturalism in the name of naturalism at the center of the scientific revolution. Thus, the direct implication of the revolution is that, since Kantian freedom is allegedly a transcendence theory, the theory is damned because any talk of the "powers" of spontaneity is talk of "spiritual powers," and so, ultimately, of "divine powers." For, there is the other tradition involved here, that of the revolt of positivism against immaterialist metaphysical theory in science in the name of a materialist metaphysical theory for science. Hence, any such reference to "powers," whether they are divine and thus spiritual, but especially if the reference is to "powers" that are taken to be natural, there is the positivist authorization to regard all such concepts for natural science as fictions, and hence they are outlawed. Remember, as a cardinal historical example, how Dilthey took it for granted that any reference, for instance, to substance and powers in science is evidence of a resort to the "phantoms of metaphysics." In the particular history of this problem, these two traditions have been effectively collapsed into the one predominate tradition, ultimately, of logical positivism (Mach) or logical empiricism (Carnap 1995: 196–207, 247–56). Thus, the problem here then is one between *realism and positivism*: the world seen in terms of matter as powers and forces, and the world seen in terms of matter as events and laws, respectively (Mumford 1998: 216–38).

My proposal, then, has to do with a problem that is subtly different. First, we have this given: scientific realism and the theory that matter is composed of immaterial powers and their manifestation as the material forces of particulars in their interacting movements; second, we have the new problem as to whether or not these immaterial powers are natural or spiritual, or, perhaps both? Cambridge Platonism seriously raised this very novel and intriguing problem from *within* the metaphysical context of the conflicting dynamic and materialist theories of matter in physics in the seventeenth century.

Cambridge Platonism: More's reading of Boyle

Cambridge Platonist Henry More examined Boyle's experimental work that seemed to encouraged a powers reading of the nature of matter, and in direct response to that reading, declared that, exactly because causal powers are immaterial, they thus must be spiritual. Hence, he is forcing upon science the subtle task of having to demonstrate that, in being *immaterial*, the "powers" of natural particulars that ground such particulars in the *materiality* of the work they perform as "forces," are ultimately not "spiritual powers." It is this issue that constitutes the intimate inter-relationship between the *realism of religion and the realism of science*. Now, we must be exceptionally clear here: in the former issue of the tradition of positivism, science, and freedom, the confrontation is between the ontology's of supernaturalism and trans-cendence and of naturalism and imminence. Thus, we have the stark contrast separating free-will as a divine/spiritual power from determinism as the physical regularity of material events. This view of the scientific revolution that simply highlights the opposing metaphysics of *supernaturalist powers* and *naturalist events*, and leaves it at that, tends to seriously lose sight of the above significant fact that religion and science are realist metaphysical brothers under their intellectual skin. After all, in Western thought, God and Nature are objectivist/realist categories, par excellence, so that they are not taken to be metaphysical fancy, theoretical fictions, or, social constructions. (After all, try to convince Job, and thus Western civilization, that the power of God and the forces of nature are not external realities.) And, as a result, there is the further tendency to miss the fact that the old realism of religion is being updated by Henry More in the sly manner indicated above, that, in effect, is insinuating itself into the very constitution of the new realism of science. Hence, from More's perspective, *divinity is, technically, implicated in the theoretical ontology of modern science.*

The import of this situation, I suggest, is that the task of clearly separating transcendental freedom from transcendent freedom has now been particu-larly complicated. For, with More's thesis, it becomes very difficult to see how the power of noumenal freedom is not the power of free will, when divine power (the other-worldly realm of supernaturalism) and natural power (the this-worldly realm of naturalism) are now conceived to be internally connected.

This special difficulty of the intertwining problems of the conflation of transcendental and transcendence theories of freedom *and* the separation of divine from natural power, I want to relate to the fact that, in my judgment, Kant, himself, was never able to see all this that clearly at the time. However, while I do believe that Kant *intuitively* was convinced that divine and natural powers were separate realities, it is quite clear that he never was able to *articulate* the meaning of all that. Now, the point to make at this juncture is that the problem of the conflation of transcendent and transcendental theories of freedom that mar the history of the social sciences, is deepened by the fact that social science cannot even conceive that the separation of divine and natural power is a problem to solve; and is one that is to be taken seriously. And of course, this is exactly true in virtue of the fact that the positivist/empirical realist tradition that still dominates social science makes it just about impossible for the social sciences to understand that science is a realist practice of causal powers explanation. It remains to seen then, what general impact on the philosophy of science thinking in the social sciences, today, will Peter T. Manicas' *A Realist Philosophy of Social Science* have.

Therefore, the above consideration should help us to see why a Martin Albrow can simply state, as a matter of fact, that, under the direct influence of Kant, Max Weber had to face up to the central question, *"How does one combine the idea that everything is caused* [phenomenal realm] *with the belief that the human will is free* [noumenal realm].*"* Albrow, in 1990, remember, has made it very clear that, for him, the "power" of human will is not natural: Kant's individual lives in "the material and terrestrial" world [phenomenal], but he draws his meaning from "the spiritual and the heavenly" world [noumenal?]. So of course, then, we find that at the start of the *twenty-first century*, as we shall soon see below, the Loyal and Barnes critical dismissal of the Parsons/Giddens theories of voluntarism and agency, respectively, and thus Kantian freedom by implication, can innocently repeat the same deeply suspect "fact" about Kant's theory of freedom.

Giddens and the stalemate of modern social science: neglect and dismissal

The New Humanist discourse for handling the structure–agency problem that Giddens promotes revolves around the direct confrontation of the problem of freedom and determinism. The latter, I have argued, is necessarily informed and hence defined by the ultimate thesis and its attendant misunderstandings. With this in mind, we can now recall that, for Giddens, the reason for the New Humanism is that Durkheimian sociological determinism is carried forward in Parsons's work, so that, consequently, the "voluntarism" of the actor easily disappears in what becomes Parsons's alleged deterministic social–psychological system (Giddens 1993 [1976]: 100–6, 1984: xxxvii; see also Dawe 1978: 400–8). In other words, Giddens is implying that the 1937 theory of "the structure *of* social action" is, with the 1950s, transmuted into the theory of "structure *and* action." And thus, as I have been insisting, Giddens proceeded to shift away from the vocabulary of structure and voluntarism to that of structure and agency in order to inaugurate a fresh start on the problem of determinism and freedom in sociological theorizing. But Giddens's Call tends to be neglected, and even dismissed, in modern social science.

For example, with regard to that transmutation, the premier apologist of the Parsonian enterprise, Jeffrey C. Alexander, not only dismisses the standard critique, but he completely omits an examination of Giddens's use of it for a proposal of a New Humanism (Alexander 1978: 177–98, 1982, 1983). Clearly, Alexander implies that Parsons's system and voluntarism standpoint is not a problem that requires a New Humanism and a relevant vocabulary shift (Parsons will be fully discussed in Chapter 8). This is also the implication of one other prominent Parsonian apologist, Bryan S. Turner. In *Classical Sociology* (1999) he recently laid out a comprehensive presentation of the several traditions of critique in his defense of Parsonian theory, and as impressive as it is, nevertheless, Giddens's Call is absolutely absent (Turner 1999: 175–78, 178–82). This state of affairs, however, is not restricted to these two eminent social scientists. This specific absence of Giddens's Call is also found in the comprehensive and systematic discussions of the current status of sociology by Donald N. Levine, *Visions of The Sociological Tradition* (1995), and by Chris Shilling and Phillip A. Mellor, *The Sociological Ambition* (2001).

Turner and Homans: Giddens's neglect

The critique of Jonathan Turner and George Homans leveled at Parsonian theory, too, has taken our attention away from Giddens's Call. And it should be remembered that both Turner and Homans are critics here of Parsons, especially from the standpoint of a metaphysical defense of positivistic sociology. In other words, their critique is taking place in reference to the neo-Humanist revolt as I have located it in the context of Kant and the ultimate thesis. *It is, therefore, important to insist, that it is the determinism of the Parsonian system/voluntarism theory that is the critical point, rather than, for example, the Turner/Homans complaint that the theory of action "was a theory of action with darn little action"* (Turner 1988: 3). For, strictly speaking, since by "action" Homans meant Skinnerian "behavior" and not Taylorian "action," the issue of determinism is again relevant; but then, it is never confronted, and so the problem of human activity being assimilated to patiency ("behavior") and not agency ("action") slips by, again seriously unnoticed (Taylor 1964).

Actually, as it is very well understood, the slippage is deeper than that: there is the standard implication in positivistic social science that the problem is considered to be an irrelevant issue because it is deemed a philosophical preoccupation rather than a scientific one. Thus, Turner's preference for "inter-action" against Parsons's "action," although not unimportant, is a distraction, since it covers over the fact that he still misses the entire meaning of Giddens's Call. The point is that that Call is a *scientific* issue, precisely because, as rightfully fundamentally *philosophical*, it goes to the *metaphysical center of scientific theory, the ontology of kinds of causal power-entities and processes.* As one who believes in *The Promise of Positivism* (1990)

Turner seems to have particularly missed the realist insight into the ontological nature of scientific theory (Turner 1990: 156, 158). Leaving Turner for a closer look at the example of positivism's promise in a deeper examination of Homans's standpoint, let Max Planck's 1909 assessment of Mackian positivism for the practice of physics frame the discussion to follow.

> When the great masters of exact investigation of nature gave their ideas to science, when Nicholas Copernicus removed the earth from the center of the universe, when Johannes Kepler formulated the laws named after him, when Isaac Newton discovered gravitation ... the series could be long continued-surely, economical points of view were the very last thing to steel these men in their struggle against traditional opinions and dominating authorities. No, it was their unshakeable belief-whether resting on artistic or religious basis-in the reality of their world picture. In view of these certainly uncontestable facts, one cannot reject the surmise that, if *the Mack principle of economy* were really to be put at the center of the theory of knowledge, *the trains of thought of such leading spirits would be disturbed, the flight of their imagination crippled, and consequently the progress of science perhaps fatefully hindered.*
>
> (quoted in Frank 1957: 63, emphasis provided)

Giddens confronted: Homans

That George Homans too has missed the realist nature of theory is certainly the case, even though his situation is significantly different. This is because he *has* examined Giddens's proposal of structuration theory, but, despite the fact that he has found it quite interesting, yet, his claim is that he must conclude that it is scientifically wanting. Although it is absolutely expected from one who believed that "Bringing Men Back In" with the aid of Skinnerian behaviorism and the Hempel D–N model of explanation, is the answer to the problem of the sociological reification of structure, and an answer to the problem of science in sociology, the result, nevertheless, is tellingly odd (Homans 1964: 809–18). Homans should speak for himself.

> But the acute reader of Giddens will note that he provides no explanation how and why the actions of people create or maintain structures, nor how and why structures in turn maintain or change the actions of people by affecting the contingencies of behavior. To do so, Giddens would have had to bring in behaviorism, under that name or another, and he does not even begin to do so. To that extent, his theory is a good description but an inadequate explanation. ... [In this regard, generally] the reasons for rejecting or ignoring behaviorism are often emotionally, but never intellectually, compelling.
>
> (Homans 1986: xiii–xxx, xxv)

From the realist standpoint that Giddens's Call presumes, the oddness of this commentary must be made very clear. To put it in Giddens's terms: for Homans, in effect, to actually believe that Skinnerian "behavior" is the theoretical conception that will satisfy the need for a theory of personal agency, is astoundingly incoherent. That Homans is handing over agency to the presumed laws of operant instrumental conditioning, and thence assigning patiency to human beings is, of course, the ultimate thesis incarnate in the principle of determinism; and of course it is the very kind of determinism that Giddens is renouncing. He favors a new principle that allows us to properly assign agency to persons and recognize as improper the assignment of agency to such fictions as, for instance, "laws" of behavior. After all, the content of a scientific law, as Manicas has beautifully demonstrated in his proposal for a realist theory of social science (e.g. psychology and sociology), must reference some relevant type of agent causality (Manicas 1987: 266–93; 2006: 7–41). And, further, Homans's incoherency is deeper than I have indicated, for it points to a fatal self-contradiction at the metaphysical center of Skinnerian behaviorism.

Skinner and Homans: metaphysic of behaviorism

We have a serious contradiction in the Skinner/Homans metaphysic of behaviorism with regard to the concepts of "behavior" (patiency) and "action" (agency). The standard understanding that this metaphysic prescribes the concept of "behavior" and hence proscribes the concept of "action" is, actually, at the very least, confused, at worse, simply wrong. Skinner's concept of behavior is of course the concept of operant behavior, that is he shifted away from elicited to emitted behavior; but in that shift, under the watchful eye of scientific realism, it must be said that he "walked backwards" into the Taylorian fact that animals are agents, after all (Taylor 1964: 268–73). And of course, precisely because of Skinner's positivist (Mach/ Carnap) commitments he was never able to recognize what indeed he had discovered. Having first realized that, practically speaking, outside of Pavlovian conditioned reflexes, a psychologist can never empirically find a "stimulus" for every "response," he came to understand that, even apart from that, animals *naturally* "behave" all the time without having to be "stimulated" (a fuller discussion with references will be given in Chapter 4). But that's the point of the fact that animals "operate" their activity: to "behave" independently of stimulation is the sign of agency. In other words, *emitted behavior is action!* Thus, here is the fatal contradiction referred to above: how can *laws be the agents and the person the patient, when they are laws of the agency of persons in action?* The Skinnerian behaviorism embraced by Homans has given him the appearance of a concept of "behavior," where in reality he has been given a rudimentary concept of "action." From the standpoint of a realist metaphysics of science, a given concept of "action" must be a species of "agent causality," and thus fits better Giddens's Call for a realist sociology than it does Homans's Call for a positivist sociology. The upshot is that the treatment of so-called "laws" of reinforcement as the agents determining the activity of human beings, while human beings are the effects of law-driven activity, can only be another instance of reification in the social sciences. And of course, we therefore have the following:

(1) the agent/patient schema that informs Homanian behaviorism is the logic of reification;
(2) that logic is the direct expression of the agent/patient schema that informs the ultimate thesis: inertia entails that the agency of the laws governing material particulars means the patiency of material particulars.

Thus, with regard to Turner and Homans, from their commitment to positivistic social science, Homans' discussion of Giddens makes it clear that Turner's neglect of Giddens's Call can be to taken to mean that it and the problem of structure and agency are to be dismissed. As a direct consequence, the serious examination of the traditional issue of determinism and its justification of treating human patiency as the reality behind the appearance of human agency that their work entails, is never confronted. And in view of his tracking the uncanny persistence of positivism to date, especially with regard to the magical trick of marrying positivism and realism, Steinmetz today would add that there is little hope of any such confrontation in the future. And this of course means that the whole problem of structure and agency and its history that takes us back to Kant, the ultimate thesis, and the attendant misunderstandings, too, will not be discovered and thence be confronted. Yet, all this will not go away.

Giddens and the Parsons/Kant connection

The apologies and critiques of Parsons reviewed earlier have, together, neglected an important constituent feature of his theoretical enterprise. Because of that neglect, the apologies and the critiques bring us right back to the Science and Humanism debate: that feature is the Parsons/Kant connection. And what this fact also suggests is that, in effect, since Giddens's Call presumes the recovery of a viable form of Parsonian voluntarism, we have here as well a specific indication of a Giddens/Kant connection that must be explored. With this in mind, note the thesis of the eminent Parsons scholar Richard Munch that

> Parsons's sociology cannot be understood apart from a consideration of Kant's critical project. [Indeed] we have to read *The Structure of Social Action* as the sociological equivalent of Kant's moral philosophy.
>
> (Munch 1981: 713)

Thus Giddens is connected to Kant indirectly through Parsons. Furthermore, by virtue of the thesis that *The Structure of Social Action* is the

Critique of Practical Reason in disguise, Munch encourages the following assertion: the *voluntarism* of the *actor* is the sociological equivalent of the *noumenalism* of the transcendental ego (Varela 2004: 4–5, to be discussed in greater detail in Chapter 8). As the transcendental ego in sociological dress, it is no accident that Parsonian voluntarism in *The Structure of Social Action* is, to begin with, going to be identified with free-will terminology. It is important to now recognize that the critique of voluntarism as a variant of free-will theory will be conducted with an implied reference to nineteenth-century vitalism. The latter, as I will explore below, is the form that updates free will theory and brings it to us through nineteenth-century biology, and into the twentieth through Freud's biopsychological theorizing. And so, this is not unique to Parsons, for, specifically, we will see that Freud's concepts of energy and the ego have been rejected as vitalist categories within psychoanalysis itself, for example, at the hands of Robert R. Holt's brave critique in *Freud Reappraised* (1989: 114–40, 141–68). Giddens's rejection of Parsons's action theory is thus a rejection of voluntarism as a free-will/vitalist answer to the determinism/mechanism problem inherited from nineteenth-century biological debates. Giddens thus has crucially missed the Kantian side of Parsons' action theory, in which Parsons is reaching for a voluntarism that I will show is connected, on the one hand, to Kant's efficient causality of freedom, and on the other, to Giddens's own theory of personal agency.

Vitalism and the structure–agency connection

The above recovery of the connection of the structure and agency problem to the problem of vitalism in biology and psychology demands an enrichment of the four discourses of freedom and determinism of Rousseau, Kant, Dilthey, and Giddens. In short, this means the inclusion of the discourse of *mechanism and vitalism*. Essentially, as I have just proposed, vitalism is free-will theory updated and given new life, so to speak, in its being relocated in an anti-mechanistic philosophy of modern biology. Rousseau's idea of the "causal power" of the will of freedom that is other than the causal forces of Newton's phenomenal matter in motion, resurfaces through Kant's co-mingling of freedom and life, in the guise of the principle of the vital force of life. While the rise of behaviorism and the concept of "behavior" as patiency is justified in a positivist empiricism that rules out all causes as powers and forces in the name of Newton's first law, we will explore below the fact that we have the emergence of psychoanalysis as it too is trapped in a metaphysical tension of, on the one hand, a mechanistic biological theory of the mind as the brain centered on the first law, found in the *Project for a Scientific Psychology* (1954), and, on the other, a vitalistic psychological theory of the unconscious mind appearing with *The Interpretation of Dreams* (Holt 1989 Ibid). From my perspective here, it is clear that the Science and Humanism debate over human agency has reared its troublesome metaphysical head from within the depths of Freud's metapsychology. The identification, then, of the metaphysical problems of mechanism and vitalism that underwrite behaviorism and psychoanalysis, firmly locates them in the Science and Humanism debate concerning structure and agency as we have taken it thus far. And in view of the fact that the ultimate thesis underwrites behaviorism and psychoanalysis, it will be shown that behaviorism and psychoanalysis are both implicated as obstacles to the discovery of the interconnections between Giddens and Kant on the matter of recovering a realist theory of human agency.

Freud and the Kant/Giddens connection

Thus, we have to remember, right here, Freud's intimate connection to both Kant and Giddens. On the one hand, Freud has claimed that the psychoanalytic theory of the structural unconscious was a Kantian psychology in the precise sense that he believed he gave Kant's theory of mind what it needed; and on the other, Giddens has grafted on to his theory of the person in structuration the idea of an unconscious that complements the concepts of reflexive and practical consciousness (in Rapaport 1959; in Giddens 1984: 41–60). To see this point now, and for the ensuing discussion, concerning the intimate connection between behaviorism/psychoanalysis and Giddens/Kant, we have to examine just how the concepts of mechanism and vitalism are understood in the traditional debate.

Giddens and vitalism: clarification

In Holt's detailed examination of Freudian theory and the mechanism/vitalism debate that was the center of Freud's medical student days, consider this moment in that discussion.

> Regarded from the empiricist standpoint, the *mechanist* and *vitalistic* systems [of theoretical biology] show a fundamental affinity. ... Common to both systems, in the first place, is the view of causality in the sense of an *executive causality*, while in the empirical sciences of the present day the causal connection is usually conceived in the sense of a *consecutive causality*. Both systems seek for an explanation of the organic event by reducing it to a *"principle" or "category" which is "at work" in it, which "causes" it.*
>
> (Mainx 1955: 628, quoted in Holt 1989: 162, emphasis provided)

Note the obvious and expected resort to the classic Humean/positivist rejection of "causal powers," that is "executive causality," in terms of the science/positivist conflation, and hence its endorsement of "event regularity," that is "consecutive causality." The resort to the metaphysics of vitalism in the nineteenth-century biological debates between mechanists and vitalists argued for an ontological dualism that pitted the latter against the former; a

non physical "energy" that is other than matter, and that defined the principle of life, that is the principle of vital impulsion (Holt Ibid: 155–56). Giddens's rejection of free will is, by implication, also a rejection of the vitalist
version of free will, the latter as a mysterious impulsion that is other than
matter and other than brain. But, obviously, the rejection is not the standard
one that is expressed by Mainx's explication. After all, "executive causality"
is Giddens's "agent causality." Yet, to be sure, the reference to "executive"
will be restricted to being a reference to only a certain species of agentive
causal particulars – especially human beings. Over all, Giddens's dismissal of
free will in its classic or vitalist version, then, only pertains to the implication
of a special case of reification in Mainx's emphasis on a "principle" "at
work" "in" organic particulars that act as "causes" of them. In the inno-
cence of a positivist authority that was only possible in 1955, and by virtue
of the positivist dogma that power ascription is in principle reification,
Mainx engages in a blanket renunciation of any hint of a "power" of causality. The importance of the example of Giddens and Mainx concerning the
obstacles to understanding the New Humanism, can be brought out further
in an examination of the Loyal and Barnes critique of Parsons and Giddens.
"'Agency' as a Red Herring in Social Theory" is a critique aimed at the
alleged importance of the problem of structure and agency (2000: 507–24).
The Parsons/Giddens connection is center stage, with Kant backstage, as their
theories of voluntarism, agency, and freedom, respectively, are dismissed as
variants of free-will theory.

The Loyal/Barnes dismissal: mistaken identity

Loyal/Barnes take Parsons and Giddens to be the prime exemplars of their
thesis that *agency is a scientifically useless concept*. Note their reason, and a
reason that tends to identify Giddens not only with Parsons, but, by implication, with Kant.

> If we say that an action was chosen and "could have been otherwise,"
> what does that signify? The immediate thought is that an *absence of
> causation* is indicated, the existence of *an act of will uncoupled from a
> causal nexus, perhaps even the intervention of a nonmaterial agency into
> the ongoing sequence of a material world*. But none of this has any
> empirical significance.
>
> (Loyal and Barnes 2000: 521)

Loyal and Barnes are straightforwardly contending that the very idea of
human freedom as agency is the idea of free will in disguise. If Kant
authored the original and seminal formulation of the problem of deterministic structures and human agency for philosophy and the social sciences,
then there is an implication in the above quote that is unmistakable. Kant's
theory of freedom is a theory of "an act of will" (transcendental ego) which,

as the "intervention of a nonmaterial agency in the material world (noumenal status)," is "uncoupled (transcendent) from a causal nexus (phenomenal world)." If this is the case with Kant, then, the implication is that, Giddens, in replacing the vocabulary of system/voluntarism with that of structure–agency, is deceived if he believes that, in effect, he has eliminated the final traces of the terminology of free-will theory; and by implication, that he has gotten free of the Kantian tradition and any of its derivatives – German Idealism, vitalism, and phenomenology. Now, the authors must have presumed that the concept of agency as free will in disguise is scientifically useless for one and only one metaphysical reason: as a transcendent or a transcendental concept, it is rooted in the metaphysics of supernaturalism. In other words, the will, first of all, is a power, and second, a derivative of divine power, spirit. Indeed, from the traditional social science standpoint of the conflation of science and positivism, their notion of causation, in being Humean/empiricist/positivist, prescribes that the very idea of agency is outlawed. In the nineteenth century, this dogma of Positivism has been assimilated to the first two Comtean laws of mental evolution, in which agency is believed to appear as either personalized sacred formulations – religious ideas like spirits/gods/souls – or impersonalized secular formulations – philosophical/metaphysical ideas like vital impulsions/forces/powers. In time, the two categories are collapsed into one category, with various name tags, e.g. "spooky," "ghostly," "ethereal." And therefore, by the time Loyal and Barnes come on the scene deep in the twentieth century, any such talk of "agency"/"agent causality," has long since been believed to be a reference to something that is, not so much extra-natural any longer in the traditional religious sense, but as something extra-rational, in the sense of being abnormal and even paranormal; and therefore strange as in esoteric, or even theosophical. Indeed, to speak negatively, the connotation is borderline psychotic, or to speak positively, the connotation is rhetorical fancy, literary license, or an altered consciousness of an idiosyncratic individualism and/or of a cultic groupism. In other words, the very idea of "agency as a power" has been, root and branch, radically delegitimized. Thus, it is no wonder that Loyal and Barnes have completely missed Giddens's Call for "agent causality." For, in demanding that the theory of agency emerge from a new and suitable metaphysics of causation, and to do so from within the authority of science, the entire preceding history of the gradual de-legitimation at issue that began from the initial mistake about agent causality, renders such a demand simply impotent. *But then it must be the case that their critique is, of necessity, irrelevant to the theory of structuration.* It is with reference to Giddens's proposal of a new theory of agency, when seen in this specific recent case of its being critically attacked, that we have a new compelling demonstration of the extraordinary significance of his Call. It is certainly to be appreciated that Loyal and Barnes have implied the identification of Kant and Giddens on the issue of structure and agency, through Parsons, however unintentionally; yet, at the same time, it must also be appreciated that, in the suggestion of a Kant connection, we certainly understand that it was a telling mistake for them to have declared the Parsons/Giddens theory of agency against structure a failure, on the grounds that human agency is the notion of free will.

I can only conclude from this investigation of the Loyal/Barnes thesis, that we have fresh evidence of the fact that, once again, the ultimate thesis that inertia means inertness, and hence human agency is just another name for the anti-scientific notion of free will, has spawned another renunciation in the name of science of a theory of freedom offered in the name of Humanism. Clearly, as long as both Scientists and old Humanists (Giddens excepted) labor under the delusion that science is a positivist practice, the debate over structure and agency will be the stalemate that Dahrendorf's announcement has doomed it to be.

Indeed, even in the case of "The Uncanny Persistence of Positivism" into the second millennium, for instance, in the oxymoronic form of what Steinmetz calls "positivist realism," or "depth-realist positivism," the delusion of conflation still persists. For, in this bizarre form,

> What they retained was an updated version of the constant conjunctions model, now renamed (by Hempel) the deductive-nomological model. According to this D-N model, events are explained by being subsumed under a general law that can take both deductive and "inductive-statistical" forms.
>
> (Steinmetz Ibid: 33)

Well, in this light, it would certainly seem like Loyal and Barnes are out of step with those uncanny persistent positivist social scientists who have chosen to marry Humean positivism and Harréan realism. In other words: natural world activity is composed of both acausal events *and* causal actions, and these are assimilated to Hempel's D-N model in which scientific laws are the agents that "determine" patient particulars which are the events in process. In view of Planck's setting the record straight on the value of a positivist physics, that is the marriage in question, it cannot be true that the "integration of theoretical and unobservable constructs into a covering law framework" in the case of the new positivist realists can be taken seriously. Thus, with regard to these Steinmetzian new positivists, it is not possible that there has been on their part any genuine knowledge and therefore one jot of an understanding of the victory of the dynamic theory of matter over the materialist theory. In view then of this position, I am even firmer in my conviction above, that in the Loyal/Barnes critique we do have another near-perfect representative example of the persistence of the tacit acceptance of the ultimate thesis in the social sciences in their persistent positivism. To be sure, in Homans's case, I have shown that that tacit acceptance is much clearer. However, in the discussion to follow this chapter of Hull and particularly Skinner and Freud, that acceptance, as I have already suggested, turns out to be most explicit in the last two cases, its impact direct, and its influence systematic in their scientific thinking.

The neglect of Giddens: transitional remarks

Though it is true, that even when social scientists like Loyal/Barnes and Homans engage Giddens on his proposal of structuration, the Call that grounds it is simply completely not understood, there still are other obstacles to understanding the Call. Giddens, too, surprisingly, can be seen to be his own obstacle here (see another example of missing the Call, Joas 1993: 172–87). With regard to a particular critical problem with Giddens's own defense of his theory of structuration, which I will address next, he makes it easy for social scientists to miss the point that that theory is grounded in his Call, and that a radically different return to Kant is required in order to solve the structure–agency problem. With regard to our major interest in the Giddens/Kant connection, it will be instructive to now meet this difficulty head on. For, while Giddens has surely met the difficulty at issue, strangely, the encounter, though honest and straightforward, is actually ineffective.

Giddens and agency: critical problems

Giddens has not *explicitly* connected his theory of human agency as "agent causality" to Kant's theory of freedom. And although he does connect the theory to his argument against the reification of social structures, in view of the fact that the argument is formulated as a theory of structuration, nevertheless, there is an important difficulty to be brought out in this regard. In *New Rules*, observe Giddens himself making the connection between reification and structuration.

> The dissolution of reification is evidently tied to the possibility of the (*cognitive*) realization by actors that structures are their own products; and to the (practical) recovery of their control over them.
> (Giddens 1993 [1976]: 132, emphasis provided)

Giddens is tracing the solution to the problem of the reification of human structures primarily to a "cognitive" realization that those structures are human productions (and thence to the resultant practical control over them). The difficulty of this argument is as follows: how is this idea nothing more than Giddens's own rewording of the traditional Kantian view that the physical world is the product of nature's laws and the cultural world is the product of human laws? In Cassirer's Kantian-inspired words, that very idea is simply the Humanist belief that the *nature and essence of our humanity is freedom*. Certainly to his immense credit, in transforming this Humanist doctrine into the idea of agency as a species of "agent causality," Giddens has taken us up to but not into a new philosophical horizon. However, so far as I know, he has clearly not *explicitly* and *systematically* understood that he should be looking to the varieties of realism in the philosophy of science in order to finally formulate his theory of human agency as "agent causality" in the terms of Harréan causal powers theory (Giddens 1993[1976]: 91–92, 1984: 345–46). Since Giddens's has not yet discovered this, I suggest that this means that (1) Giddens's theory of human agency as agent causality will remain a dogma, never to be realized; the upshot of which is that the dogma becomes a dead end in the social sciences, and (2) as a direct consequence, it permanently leaves him (and everybody else so involved) without any *principled* and hence *definitive argument* against the reification of human structures (Giddens and Pierson 1998: 75–93, especially 78–79). For, the mere "cognitive" realization that human agency produces human structures does not, in and of itself, provide us with a way to understand some very odd events in the philosophy of social science since the second half of the last century.

We have already seen the import of the Merleau-Ponty/Levi-Strauss predicament: the "cognitive" realization of freedom in the phenomenological experience of one major thinker on the issue in question, is contradicted by the "cognitive" realization of determinism in the phenomenological experience of another major thinker on the same issue, and that this reveals that "cognitive" realization is of little metaphysical value in fruitfully addressing the problem of freedom and determinism. But now, there is also the other intriguing event that pertains to contemporary Freudian and Durkheimian theory in reference to the structure and agency problem: the resurrection of Freudian and Durkheimian causal realism.

How are we to understand that both the Edelson/Gardner resurrection of Freudian causal realism in support of the traditional deterministic conception of psychological structure (Edelson 1988: 359–60; Gardner 1991: 136–69) and the Bhaskar/Archer resurrection of Durkheimian causal realism in support of an anti-deterministic conception of social structure, must both be judged to be a failure? Harré and I, together and separately, have decisively demonstrated that the two attempts at resurrection have been guilty of an improper assignment of causal powers to human structures; and although it is true that the debate continues (see Elder-Vass 2007: 25–44, 463–77; Porpora 1993: 212–29), Paul Lewis and Peter T. Manicas have recently taken up the question, and have concurred with us (Varela 1995b: 363–85, 2001: 63–74, 2002: 105–11, 2007: 201–10; Varela and Harré 1996: 313–25; Harré 1984: 3–14, 2001: 22–28; Lewis 2000: 249–68; Manicas: 67–74, 75–76). In this regard, consider that Manicas's examination of the issue with respect to Bhaskar, Archer, Porpora has led him to fashion a revealing argument that goes to the heart of the decisive demonstration of the failure in question (note, in effect, the same unavoidable conclusion in Margaret Gilbert's discussion of holism, despite her defense of it (1992: 288–314)).

Of course, if social structure is reified – made independently real – it could be causal, but not only is this ontologically dubious, it is not a move available to the position defended by Porpora. A similar argument has been made by Margaret Archer (1995) who argues, following Bhaskar, that structure and culture are both emergent properties and as such that "the realist is committed to maintaining that 'the causal power of social forms is mediated through social agency'" (1995: 195).

The question to ask is this: *why postulate the existence of structure or culture as causally relevant if, to be causally effective, these must be mediated by social actors?*

(Manicas 2006: 72, 67–74, 75–76, emphasis provided)

Manicas's argument has expressed the key point of our demonstration. Since the logic of causal powers theory requires the conclusion that only social persons are powerful particulars, that the parties on both sides of the quarrel absolutely agree that structures can only be effective in terms of the agency of persons, *the agreement is the reason for the conclusion* (Manicas 2006: 75–102).

Now, to return to Giddens's "cognitive realization" argument, it is clear that, in addressing both the problems of structure and agency and reification, it is no longer good enough merely to point to the fact of the realization that human beings are agents, and hence are free to produce structures of various sorts. After all, the traditional Science and Humanism debate has always been based on the conflicting interpretations that, for science, human nature is deterministic, and for Humanism, human nature is free. The Merleau-Ponty/Levi-Strauss predicament, then, is merely an instance of that traditional theme. The upshot is a shock of recognition, that is that an instance like the Merleau-Ponty/Levi-Strauss predicament is actually a throw-back to the *pre-Giddensian* days when the Parsonsian vocabulary of system and voluntarism was the only metaphysical "game in town." Giddens's point about "cognitive realization," it must now be said, *is itself* pre-Giddensian, and hence is further evidence that he truly has nothing much more than a *belief* that human agency is a species of agent causality. And so, it is no wonder that he has to be dogmatic about his Call, for, he certainly does not have a *conception* of "agent causality." It is thus to be concluded, that the dissolution of reification is only connected *to*, but clearly not demonstrated *by*, the thesis that human agency produces human structures. Now it can be appreciated how the failure to see the point of this conclusion prevents Giddens from meeting a serious challenge to his contention that structuration theory is indeed a definitive argument in the defeat of the reification of human structures.

Giddens and Pierson: unmet challenge

Christopher Pierson's presentation of a challenge to structuration theory dramatically highlights Giddens's inability to mobilize an effective argument against the reification of human structures. (Giddens and Pierson 1998: 75–93). Just under 20 years after *Central Problems in Social Theory* (1979) and just shy of 15 years after *The Constitution of Society* (1984) Pierson, as a devil's advocate, can ask Giddens the following question.

> What would you say to an unreconstructed structuralist who insisted that the agency of which you speak doesn't really exist and that where an agent appears to be making a choice, in fact there is something else behind her or him, which is driving her or him to choose in a particular way? Such a structuralist might say that you have the appearance of actions because you have the appearance of choices, but in some sense there is always something behind pulling the strings, a ventriloquist putting words in the mouth of a puppet.
>
> (Giddens and Pierson 1998: 78–79)

To which Giddens gives this reply.

> Well, your structuralist would have to tell me *what* this something is. Assuming they aren't unconscious emotions, which structuralists aren't talking about in this context, what could these forces possibly be?
>
> (Giddens and Pierson Ibid, emphasis provided)

Neither the devil's advocate nor Giddens, it should be noted, do anything more in the ensuing discussion than to repeat themselves, predictably (Giddens and Pierson Ibid: 79–88); each awaits on the other to give some definitive account that will end the matter; hopefully for Giddens, that it will lead to an acceptance of the answer of structuration theory, because it is supposed to end the structuralist question (Giddens and Pierson Ibid). The acceptance, unfortunately, never happens in their discussion. *But, more to the point, why does it appear, as it does in this case, that such a question will forever be asked?* I would like to suggest that that is because *the same kind of answer will be given.* Giddens, in effect, presumes, I think, what he does not mean to, namely, *that* such "structures" as, for instance, unconscious forces of whatever kind, *could* be, at least, genuine powerful particulars, so that, as a consequence, the only question to ask is the specific one that he does ask, namely, *what* "kind" could *that* be; so, there is the presumption that there is no distinction of any importance between "that" and "what" in such scientific matters. Speaking from the standpoint of Harréan realism, however, Giddens seems not to understand that the issue of unconscious, psychological, social, or cultural explanatory structures is, in realist terms, the issue of proposing that they are genuine – real causal powers – and plausible – unobservable causal powers. Thus, one can, as in physics, successfully propose *that* an unobservable causal structure does exist, or not, *before* its "whatness" can be worked out in some detail. In short, "that" and "what" in such cases constitute a significant distinction, and hence are separate but related questions, and have their own answers; furthermore, since "that" should not be conflated with "what," raising the former as a question does not automatically license raising the latter as a question; the former must be settled first. For example, even Rudolf Carnap had to acknowledge, against his logical positivism no doubt, exactly that very idea when, in discussing unobservables in physics, he commented that "Today, little is known about [the] structure [of electrons]; tomorrow a great deal may be known" (Carnap 1966: 256).

In other words, "that" electrons exist is not in question (not since it has been settled) though what is in question is "what" their structure consists of, particularly, in some systematic detail. In the case of proposing that human structures are causal agents, the point is, Harré and I have shown that there are good reasons to think that they cannot even be a "that," to begin with; hence, the question of their "whatness" can or should never arise. Giddens, therefore, could have shown Pierson that the kind of question he asked in the name of an "unreconstructed structuralist," is just no longer viable. And so, Giddens could have answered the "unreconstructed structuralist" decisively, from the standpoint of Harré's complementary theories of causal powers and plausibility with their provision of *principled* and hence *definitive arguments* against the reification of human structures.

4 Kant and the stalemate of the psychological sciences

Behavior and energy

Introduction: Hamlet, the ultimate thesis, and modern psychology

With the advent of the nineteenth century, the Western world is going to view Hamlet as the exemplification of the fate of theories of freedom in an intellectual world in which naturalism is dominating, and, where the ultimate thesis has established the meaning of determinism in science, and hence for the social sciences already on the rise. Thus, for example, in 1803, Schlegel singles out what, at the end of the nineteenth century, 1899, Freud winds up riveting the attention of virtually the entire twentieth century on in the west. What is singled out of course, to use Schlegel's phrase, is the "dreadful enigma" of Hamlet's fateful delay in fulfilling the ghost's duty for him to avenge the murder of the former king, his father, by the current king, his uncle (Freud 1998 [1900]: 298–99). The issue of "delay" interpretively grows to assume the sure sign that the "I" in Descartes's "I think" is in radical doubt.

> The destiny of humanity is there exhibited as a gigantic Sphinx, which threatens to precipitate us into the abyss of skepticism all who are unable to solve her dreadful enigmas.
>
> (Hoy 1963: 156)

Thus, the suggested deeper point transcends the play, as Schlegel seems to be reaching for a grasp of the nature of our humanity that is rendered highly problematic in its supposed essence as a Kantian freedom. It is not so much that Cassirer's declaration that living humanity cannot give up its essence of freedom that is at issue here, but rather, that living Hamlet's failure to convince us on the detailed ground of experience that we are free, is unnerving us. Is there in fact a "freedom" that we can do with what we will? We thus are empirically bewildered, and in time find ourselves theoretically and so ontologically adrift. This is adumbrated by the phrase, the "abyss of skepticism." Indeed, Schlegel's observation is actually an after shock, since it seems to have been already fully absorbed in the previous century's serious encounter of the play.

In 1756 Thomas Hanmer charges that Hamlet's delay is, from the stand-point of human nature, an absurdity – an incomprehensibility for which there is no excuse (Hoy Ibid: 145–46). In 1765 Samuel Johnson, in effect, answers that earlier charge when he declares that,

> *Hamlet is, through the whole play, rather an instrument than an agent.* After he has, by stratagem of the play, convicted the king, he makes no attempt to punish him, and his death is at last effected by an incident which *Hamlet has no part in producing.*
>
> (Hoy Ibid: 147, emphasis provided)

The answer in this statement seems to suggest an explanation, whether or not it may also be an excuse: throughout the play, what Hamlet intends (e.g. to kill Claudius in his chamber), he does not do (he cannot kill him while he is praying); and what he does (the sword is sheathed), he does not intend (yet, still, the intent to kill remains). Kant's Copernican Revolution is dangerously challenged: the authority of the subject in matters of knowledge, and hence in life in matters of responsibility, is being dangerously threatened. The twentieth century begins with the transformation of Johnson's interpretive suggestion that Hamlet is a patient not an agent, into a spectacular instance of Freud's scientific canonization of the theory of unconscious determinism. Ernest Jones understood and expressed it perfectly in *Hamlet and Oedipus* (1949): "Hamlet's advocates say he cannot do his duty, his detractors say he will not, whereas the *truth is that he cannot will*" (Jones 1949 [1911]: 59, emphasis provided).

From the Hobbesian principle that human beings "seeth not what are the lashings that cause his will" to the Freudian refinement of that principle with the pronouncement that human will "cannot will," we have the emergence of an "effective conception" of the unconscious that has been all but enshrined as our fate, and virtually established as a law (Whyte 1960). Now, I have argued that the tradition of Science against Humanism is a tradition in which determinism is defined in terms of inertia as inertness, against a freedom that is defined in terms of the conflation of transcendental and transcendent freedom. The paradigm case of Hamlet perfectly illustrates that very point: the delay is being interpreted as a sure sign that the prince is a patient, hence the instrument of the forces of Denmark and his family that engulf him. The growing predominance of this principle of interpretation can be persuasively revealed with the help of two telling nineteenth-century examples in philosophy.

The nineteenth century and the ultimate thesis: philosophy and psychology

As an exemplar of the romantic movement, Schiller proclaims the Hobbesian dogma that, if man is only a material creature of the natural world, it is then that he avows man to be nothing more than a "Mere turnspit, acted upon by external forces" (Berlin 1992 [1959]: 220–22). And, as certainly more than expected, the romantics are of course supported by premier nineteenth-century positivists in this regard. John Stuart Mill, in a confession on the matter at mid-century, reveals his anxiety as he feels himself to be under the fate of nature's ultimate thesis.

> I felt as if I was scientifically proved to be the helpless slave of ante-cedent [external] circumstances; as if my character and that of all others have been formed for us by *agencies beyond our control, and was wholly outside of our own power.*
>
> (quoted in Baumer 1977: 321, emphasis provided)

Actually, we have to respectfully restate John Stuart here, and instead, risk the pain of saying the obvious: the "power" of the (extra-natural) "will" that Mill alludes to is itself "outside" of the (natural) agencies that are themselves "inside" the world in their manifestation of the first law of movement.

By the twentieth century and with the arrival of behaviorism and psycho-analysis, modern psychology decisively follows suit in profoundly embracing the traditional belief in the ultimate thesis in the very constitution of its fundamental scientific thinking. The import of the arrival of these com-plementary psychological deterministic theories was expressed perfectly in two witticisms about modern psychology. The context of these witticisms is an epigrammatic saying concerning its early history: *"psychology has a long past – as philosophy (theology and metaphysics) – and a short history" – as science (positivism and realism)*. In giving up philosophy for science the first witticism is expressed in the comment that

> In the nineteenth century psychology lost its soul, in the twentieth, it was about to lose its mind.

In breaking with philosophy and in becoming a science, the standard story is captured here: the "soul" is lost, and with it, human freedom in its only availability, that is in the terms of free-will theory and its secular variations, Kantian freedom and so on. The second part of the comment picks up on the possibility of the loss of the human mind to the scientific ambitions of modern psychology in this lovely joke; one that only a Cartesian could especially relish.

> Two psychologists, A and B, meet at the corner of whatever: A says to B – "You certainly feel fine, now, *you* tell *me*, how do I feel?"

Can there be any doubt but that the two anti-philosophical psychologists are exactly who they seem to be? I now want to specifically encounter behaviorism and psychoanalysis, in that order, concerning which the treatment here will be brief and directly to the point. We can orient ourselves for the examination with this simple observation: since the forces of determinism are external, so must knowledge of their activity take the form of the external observer. In behaviorism, laws of reinforcement determine the variety of behaviors that correspond to the variety of ordinary human actions; in psychoanalysis (classical and ego-psychology), the laws of the structural unconscious of superego, ego, and id, generate conscience, consciousness, and desire, respectively, in the individual, in conjunction with the precipitating events of the environment (see Varela 2003: 96–103). For the examination to follow I want to foreshadow what is to be revealed concerning the absolute centrality of the ultimate thesis in behaviorist and classical psychoanalytic thinking. I do this with another declaration of Mark Twain's from his *What is Man* essay of 1905. In the earlier quote he gave a general outline of the implication of the law of inertia – as the ultimate thesis: "Man the machine" is determined by "exterior influences. ... [while he] originates nothing, not even thought." In this second pronouncement he moves from the machinery of mind to its biological substrate, the brain. Note, that on the eve of both of these naturalistic psychologies a literary writer has fully anticipated the positivistic metaphysic that defines both theories and propels them to reify laws and the unconscious.

> A man's brain is so constructed that *it can originate nothing whatsoever.* It can only use material obtained from the *outside.* It is merely a machine; and it works automatically, not by will power. *It has no command over itself, its owner has no command over it.*
>
> (Mark Twain 1905)

Hull: the reflex arc and inertia

In the 1936 American Psychological Association presidential address of Clark L. Hull, "Mind, Mechanism, and Adaptive Behavior," one finds a heroic proposal for the realization of the dream of determinism. What is proposed is Hull's once renowned, but long since extinct, hypothetico-deductive "theoretical system in miniature," of postulates, operational definitions, and theorems. There is a critical feature of such a scientific system, Hull insists, that distinguishes it from an equally rigorous system of the formal kind that can be found in philosophy, for example, Spinoza's Ethic (Hull 1937: 6). In the former it is the case that

> From these postulates there should be deduced by the most rigorous logic possible under the circumstances, a series of interlocking theorems covering the major concrete phenomena of the field in question, [specifically those] concrete manifestations of the higher forms of human behavior.
>
> (Hull Ibid: 5, 9)

A truly momentous accomplishment of Hull's miniature system is to be seen in theorem IV, since,

> This theorem is noteworthy because it represents the classical case of a form of *spontaneity* widely assumed, as far back as the Middle Ages, to be inconceivable without presupposing consciousness.
>
> (Hull Ibid: 12, emphasis provided)

Thus, for instance, Kant's freedom as the spontaneity of the mind and action is lost in being translated into an instrumentally conditioned mechanism of adaptive behavior (Hull 1936: 1–32). That "mechanism" had been constructed by combining the Pavlovian and Thorndikean s-r learning theories, giving us the essential theoretical model of "a human machine interacting by reflexes with its environment" (Hull Ibid: 11,15–28). In a nutshell, freedom as the spontaneity of consciousness is thus explained away in terms of the notion of differential reinforcement. At a given moment when, apparently "all of a sudden," response A instead of response B is experienced in the consciousness of an animal or human animal, that phenomenology of spontaneity is thus accounted for in terms of the critical difference in the reinforcement history of responses A over B in a given stimulus situation. Being ignorant of the laws of one's reinforcement history, Hull wanted us to believe, accounts for the illusion of spontaneity – "all of a sudden" – in the appearance of response A rather than response B. It is important here to emphasize the fact indicated above that Hull, in part, derives the "determinism" of his system directly from the systems of Pavlov and Thorndike. But he also derives it from the classic logicist mistake of conflating logical deduction with causal production (Harré 1971: Chapter 1). With regard to the former source of "determinism," note Hull's concluding comment to his discussion of that connection between Pavlov and Thorndike in reference to theorem I postulate 2: "The *automatic,* stimulus-response approach thus examined is characteristic of the remainder of the system" (Hull 1933 Ibid: 11, emphasis provided).

Automaticity is the indicator of determinism, and the referent to its mechanism, of course, is what John Dewey called the reflex arc concept in psychology (Dewey 1896). *In the fact that the automaticity of the s-r reflex machine replaces the autonomy of the mind of a person, we therefore have the "instantaneity" of the reflex, that is an immediate/direct reaction, substituting for the "spontaneity" of the mind.*

Let's now look at Hull's own view of the classic problem of freedom and determinism in its historical dimension that frames his presidential address. The context of the display of his view is, to be sure, Darwinian evolutionary theory and the accepted conviction that human beings are "evolution's crowning achievement." Hull then takes it from there and asserts that

> It is equally clear that man's preeminence lies in his capacity for adaptive behavior. Because of the seemingly unique and remarkable nature of

adaptive behavior, it has been customary to attribute it to the action of a *special agent or substance* called "mind." Thus "mind" as a hypothetical entity directing and controlling adaptive behavior attains biological status possessing survival value and, consequently, a "place in nature." But what is this mysterious thing called mind? By what principles does it operate? ... Are they those of the ordinary *physical world* or are they of the nature of *spiritual essences* – of an entirely different order, the *nonphysical*.

(Hull Ibid: 1, emphasis provided)

Hull of course aims to show, as we have already specified, that the system of postulates covers several of the key characteristics of human complex adaptive behavior that traditionally have led to the standard thesis of free-will conceived of as a spiritual mental entity; but that in his miniature system such behavior can now be accounted for in terms of the physical, but never the psychic (Hull 1936: 28). Hull simply gives the expected reason for the presumed necessity of this state of affairs.

In the miniature theoretical system, no mention of *consciousness* or *experience* was made for the simple reason that no theorem has been found as yet whose deduction would be facilitated in any way by including such a postulate.

(Hull Ibid: 30)

But we know from hindsight that much more than that is entailed by a magnificent scientific ambition that was rivaled at the time only by that of Sigmund Freud (McClelland 1964: 1–15).

If this deduction were accomplished we should have an unbroken logical chain extending from the primitive electron all the way up to complex purposive behavior. Further developments may conceivably extend the system to include the highest rational and moral behavior. Such is the natural goal of science ... a complete scientific monism. ... [that promises] an electro-chemical parallel to the conditioned reflex.

(Hull Ibid: 29)

From the above discussion of Hullian behaviorism it is evidently clear that it is a near-perfect example of the fact that in its commitment to determinism, the science of behavior and reflexes is against the Humanist study of freedom as consciousness and experience. For, Hull has offered the explanation that consciousness and experience are characteristics that stem only from, on the one hand, the idea of "primitive animism," and on the other, from "the preservative influences of medieval theology" (Hull Ibid: 2, 31). In so far as determinism is instantiated in the s-r principle of the automaticity of reflex chains of behavior, not only is there no room for a "special agent" of spirit/

mind, there is no room for the very idea of agency at all. In short, as Hull has stated above, the postulate of mind cannot, by way of deduction, lead us to a theorem that shows such an entity in the reflex behavior, innate and learned, of the human animal. Thus, in that declaration what is revealed is that the spirit and the letter of the law of logical positivism or logical empiricism drive the machinery of the Hullian miniature system (Mackenzie 1977: 144–51).

But now, what of Hull's relationship to the ultimate thesis. Well, certainly the upshot of the major part of the thesis is followed in Hullian psychology; since animals and humans engage technically in "behavior" and not "action," they are patients not agents. And just as certainly, the theory of freedom is an extra-natural theory, that is a spiritualist theory having its source in primitive animism, and its persistence due to medieval theology and its idea of God/man/freedom as substance (Hull Ibid: 6). Hence, the free-will theories announced by Cambridge Platonists, presumed by Cartesian Dualism, promulgated by Rousseau, and allegedly transmuted into Kantian transcendental Idealism, and all the rest, are simply not worth mentioning by Hull. They, no doubt, must be dismissed as proposals that were mere repetition-compulsive variations of a delusional belief in powers, perpetuated by a genuflection before the sophisticated version of such belief of Augustine, and its religious rationalization in the metaphysics of Aquinas. However, while all of the above appears to be straightforwardly true, yet, there is no explicit direct connection, at least in the work we are dealing with, to the law of inertia. And so, the suggested line from inertia to the reflex arc is not openly in direct evidence in Hull's work. However, in virtue of the fact that the concept of reflex grounds Hullian theory, one would have to think that the law of inertia is taken for granted. Hence, can we not garner some good evidence that Hull does actually presume such a line? And that, in time, he would have brought it forth? Or simply acknowledge it, if pointed out to him? Consider: if he indeed was in pursuit, and he was, of a systematic deductive connection that would derive behavior as a reflex machine originally from a parallel on the electron-chemical level of material activity, Newton's laws are of course directly implicated (Hull Ibid: 29). But, such speculation aside, although I assert here its near-perfect persuasiveness, in the operant behaviorism of B. F. Skinner, the thesis that there is a line from inertia to reflex is confirmed; the connection is explicit, even systematic, and it thus is tied to the same kind of rejection of freedom as agency, on the one hand, and the acceptance of environmental determinism, on the other, that Hull, in his own formalist fashion, embraced.

Skinner: inertia to the behavior/environment machine

Skinner's work makes it eminently clear that the ultimate thesis is explicitly influential in two ways. First, humanity is a paradox of the principle of inertia: the person is a patient, but, his/her behavior is emitted. Second, there is a line from the determinism of inertia (things are the instruments of external forces) to the machine system of environment and behavior (mechanical determinism). This reveals the principle that mediates the connection between inertia and machine, namely, the general idea of reflex behavior as the model of mechanical determinism. And I expressly want it to be understood here that I am convinced that B. F. Skinner was every bit mechanical determinist (in the sense indicated above) as the two classic paradigm examples in psychology – Clark L. Hull and Sigmund Freud. If the statement by Skinner that I am now going to quote has ever been recanted, by him, I have not been able to find it in any of his works. In what is to follow, it will be seen that, in the crucial sense of being deterministic, the distinction between reflex and emitted behavior is *cancelled*. In a nutshell, Skinner has actually declared that, just as the reflex reaction of *"coughing in church"* cannot be a matter of responsibility, so is it the same for the operant behavior of *"whispering in church"* (Skinner 1953: 115–16)! Here is his analytic justification.

> The distinction between voluntary and involuntary behavior is a matter of the kind of control. It corresponds to the distinction between eliciting and discriminative stimuli. The eliciting stimulus *appears* to be more coercive. Its causal connection with behavior is relatively simple and easily *observed*. ... The discriminative stimulus, on the other hand, shares its control with other variables, so that the *inevitability of its effect cannot be easily demonstrated*. But when all relevant variables have been taken into account, it is not difficult to *guarantee the result – to force the discriminative operant as inexorably as the eliciting stimulus forces its response*. [If so], we may say that *voluntary behavior is operant and involuntary behavior reflex*.
>
> (Skinner Ibid: 112, emphasis provided)

We appear to be free and responsible, but in reality, we are determined by the automaticity of simple/static and complex/dynamic reflex arc systems. In this regard, E. G. Boring, in effect, introduces us to the basis for seeing the role of the ultimate thesis in Skinner's radical behaviorism. It is found in the key proposition of his 1931 Harvard dissertation.

> Skinner. ... defended the proposition that the psychologist should regard the *reflex as a correlation between stimulus and response*. He *ignored* the possibility of intervening physiological links, which, for the psychologist, ... are a dummy physiology doing duty for truth when the facts are missing. Skinner ... [developed] a stimulus-response psychology that is not in any sense a physiological stimulus-response psychology. ... Such functional relations as $R = f(S)$ are established by observing the covariation of a stimulus S and a response R and lack the *physical continuity* between terms which most *scientists prefer*. Skinner's functions are

> *Humean correlations* of discrete variables, not causal continuities, and Skinner has sometimes been said ... to deal with the empty organism.
>
> (Boring 1950: 650, emphasis provided)

Skinner is here preparing himself for a psychology that is radically divorced from the realism of scientific practice. The Humean interpretation of the functional equation takes Skinner, by way of the ultimate thesis, straight to the idea of human activity as behavior and not action. But we can certainly go one step further beyond Boring's insightful Machian portrait of Skinnerian theory. The general omission of the "causal continuities" that "scientists prefer" entails not only the specific omission of the "physical." Much more importantly, there is the omission of the "person." John Dewey's renowned classic paper, "The Reflex Arc Concept in Psychology"(1896), can help us further in regard to this serious second omission.

Skinner and Dewey: reflex arc to organic circuit

Dewey certainly understood that the general idea of the reflex was the direct occasion for a mechanistic psychology. Evidently, 17 years before Watson's paper in 1913, "Psychology as a Behaviorist Views It," and 3 or 4 years before psychoanalysis began with Freud's dream book (Freud 1998), he anticipated the germinal idea that both behaviorism and psychoanalysis shared. In the quote that follows, Dewey is actually critiquing the reflex arc concept from the opposite point of view of what he called the "organic circuit." A cardinal thesis of his paper is that, on the one hand, a mechanistic psychology is an *artifact* of the imposition of the reflex arc concept on intelligent human activity, and on the other, that activity is best understood instead in terms of an organic circuit concept. With this in mind, consider Dewey's remarks.

> The result is that the reflex arc idea leaves us with a *disjointed psychology*, whether viewed from the standpoint of development of the individual or race, or from that of the analysis of the mature consciousness. *As to the former*, in its failure to see that *the arc* of which it talks is virtually a *circuit*, a *continual reconstitution*, it *breaks continuity and leaves us nothing but a series of jerks, the origin of each jerk to be sought outside the process of experience itself, in either an external pressure of "environment,"* or else in an *unaccountable spontaneous variation from within the "soul" of the "organism."* As to the latter, *failing to see the unity of activity*, no matter how much it may prate of unity, *it still leaves us with* sensation or peripheral *stimulus*; idea, or *central process* ...; and motor *response*, or act, as *three disconnected existences, having somehow adjusted to each other, whether through the intervention of an extra-experimental soul, or by mechanical push and pull.*
>
> (Dewey Ibid: 139, emphasis provided)

Dewey is here highlighting the pragmatist insight that intelligence in action displays a unity of activity; that the "activity" involves a "continual reconstitution" of terms such as "stimulus" and "response" as part of the vocabulary of language in use by an individual; that intelligence in action with its individual use of language is located in an ongoing problem-centered situation. And of supreme importance, Dewey's concept of the "organic circuit" in fact presupposes the Kantian subject of the phenomenal, not the noumenal, world. But this time, nevertheless, as an active Darwinian subject whose problem-centered "activity" is more or less a "unifying" (organized) activity. But Dewey's concept also foreshadows Giddens's personal agent of structuration. In other words, *Dewey's active subject is the "person" that is strictly implied*, but not so *mysteriously denied, by Skinner's concept of emitted behavior.* Clearly, behaviorism and pragmatism radically depart from each other on the issue of the status of the subject. Behaviorists insist that the scientific study of human beings demands the dismissal of the subject, since agency is not a legitimate conception; the pragmatists, to the contrary, imply that a science of human beings demands the inclusion of the subject in any such study, and thereby are implying that agency is indeed very much a legitimate conception. Now, of course, Skinner would never have accepted Dewey's paper on exactly that issue of the subject. But, more important, is that his rejection is rooted in the crucial paradox of his theory of behavior. That paradox demands that we ask this question: how can the person be a patient while his/her behavior is emitted? Isn't Skinner fatally inconsistent here? We are, I do think, closing in on "bad news" for the theory of operant behavior.

In my earlier discussion of Homans's adoption of the Skinnerian standpoint of subjectless behavior, I declared that Skinner in fact is self-contradictory on exactly this very question. *For, as a matter of fact, the concept of "behavior" is a concept of "action," in disguise.* In other words, human beings are agents and not patients; and so behaviorism is metaphysically or ontologically absurd, and hence an impossible science. They simply can't get their metaphysics straight, and so they constantly talk out of both sides of their metaphysical mouths. As we will now see in his own words, and what Boring had actually missed, that Skinner denies that human beings are *agents of production* (the import of Boring's observation), and then categorically declares that there are external *productive causes that make them behave* (Boring's failed observation). But of course Skinner would do just that: it is exactly what the ultimate thesis prescribes. This was revealed earlier in the Homans case: scientific laws are the agents and human beings the patients. This is the perfect time for Skinner to speak for himself, step by step.

The problem of emitted behavior: identification and assignation of agency

Let's start with a standard Skinnerian declaration in *Beyond Freedom and Dignity* (1971).

> As a science of behavior adopts the strategy of physics and biology, *the autonomous agent to which behavior has traditionally been attributed is replaced by the environment* – the environment in which the species evolved and in which the behavior of the individual is *shaped and maintained.*
>
> (Skinner 1971: 175, emphasis provided)

In order to discover that Skinner actually derives this rejection of agency from the same source from which he derives the acceptance of patiency, the ultimate thesis, one must return to the 1953 text *Science and Behavior.* In this text it will be seen that it is *not*, exactly, the idea of "the autonomous agent" that is the real enemy in Skinner's world. After all, as implied above, he certainly does accept the idea of an "autonomous agent" – as external productive causes – when he announces in *Beyond Freedom and Dignity* that "the environment takes over the function and role of autonomous man" (Skinner op cit: 176). In other words, *the environment is an autonomous but impersonal agency.* I know of no place in Skinner's discussion of these matters where he is ever aware of the conceptual necessity to distinguish "agency *of* the individual" from "agency *in* the individual." I am convinced that the absolute rule for Skinner is the systematic conflation of the former with the latter.

> [Thus] *the free inner man* ... is only a prescientific substitute for the kinds of causes which are discovered in the course of a scientific analysis. *All these alternative causes lie outside the individual. The biological* substratum itself is determined by prior events in the *genetic* process. Other important events are found in th*e nonsocial* environment and in the *culture* of the individual. *These are the things which make the individual behave as he does.*
>
> (Skinner 1953: 447, emphasis provided)

Since "the free inner man" is the problem that Skinner always focuses on, the real enemy, of course, is Cartesian Dualism. However, in Skinner's indiscriminate over-reaction, the idea of the "person" is discarded along with mind. In using the phrase "of course" to emphasize the fact that Cartesianism is the root of the problem, I do not mean only the received view of recent discussions of Skinner in his relationship to philosophy. For, as excellent as some of them truly are, in those discussions one only finds the traditional emphasis on the legendary problem of mentalism – dualism, and the mind's internality (interiority, not inwardness) and privacy (Hocutt, 1996: 81–95; Kitchener 1996: 108–25; Garrett 1996: 141–48). But here, in this structure/agency context, the significance of the Cartesian mind in its internality and privacy is that these features are a code for the transcendence of the mind in its freedom. Thus, we have mentalism's internal connection to the Descartes/Rousseau doctrine of free will. Therefore, it seems to me, the famous "I think therefore I am" principle can be seen slightly differently: the "I think" is a problem of such fundamental importance, precisely because the freedom of the "I" *to* think, is the deep reason why thinking demonstrates the certainty of our existence. Human existence is the certainty of the freedom of the human "I" to be its mindful self. Kant must have picked up on this and transformed it into the transcendental ego. It cannot, then, be a surprise that in Skinner's radical behaviorism there is precisely this focus on the internal connection between mind and freedom. In keeping with my point above, Skinner's behaviorism is radical in that it steals autonomy from the individual or person and gives it to the environment, and does so under the excuse that human freedom is scientifically illegitimate because of its Cartesianism. Now this is clearly revealed, I think, in Skinner's shift from elicited to emitted behavior, for, the latter once again brings back the problem of freedom and determinism. The reason is straightforward: *if an R (response) can occur independent of S (stimulus) and on its own (autonomy), then how is emitted behavior not agency, and thus not freedom?* So, the mind's internality and privacy really is a problem for the science that Skinner demands. And that is because its presupposed traditional theory of free will could be used, contrary to Skinner's wishes, to equate freedom and emitted behavior, and thus escape what Skinner believes are science's twin aims of predictability and hence practical control. But absolutely, Skinner can not allow *that* to happen. In his 1974 book *About Behaviorism* he's making sure it doesn't: "A *person is not an originating agent*: *he is a locus,* a point at which many genetic and environmental conditions come together in *a joint effect*" (Skinner 1974: 168).

Thus, it is no wonder that Skinner reveals over and over again the close tie between the Cartesian Dualist issue of the agency of the "I" to "think" and the radical behaviorist issue of the agency of the environment to be the cause of that "think" without the "I" whose agency has been magically stolen. The last paper that Skinner published in the 1990 November issue of the *American Psychologist*, "Can Psychology be a science of Mind," was finished the evening before he died, 3 months earlier. When he states that "There is no place in a scientific analysis of behavior for a mind or self," there is no question that he means the "mind" or "self" in its freedom that is the alleged discovery of introspection (Skinner 1990: 1209). For, he opens his paper with this ever so typical pronouncement.

> Many *psychologists*, like the philosophers before them, *have looked inside themselves* for explanations of their behavior. They have *felt feelings and observed mental processes through introspection*. Introspection has never been very satisfactory, however. … [besides it] is no longer used very much.
>
> (Skinner Ibid: 1206, emphasis provided)

Granted, that introspection is an inherently and fatally flawed "method" – "looking into yourself" can only be an act of imagination and not an act of imaging (Harré 1970: Chapter 1). This book rests on the understanding that the issue of causation as agency and the question of the agency of the human subject cannot be settled and answered, respectively, on the basis of the legitimacy or illegitimacy of introspection as a method. The latter is a matter of epistemology, the former, that of ontology. And both are twin aspects of the metaphysics of science. Thus, the empirical realism of Machian positivism is the wrong metaphysics with which to address the problem of causation and agency. "Agent causality" is a conceptual and not an empirical matter that has to do with the world of matter, life forms, and not exclusively with the world of culture and the individual. In other words, as I have declared in Chapter 2, freedom as the problem of agency is a scientific, and therefore, a social scientific problem. Besides, in the realist practice of science, that issue has been settled, and it has nothing to do with Carnap's insistence that it is a mere preference and a practical decision (Carnap 1995: 255–56), or with the insistence of Barnes, Bloor, and Henry that it is the trick of using a realist mode of speech (Barnes *et al.* 1995: 205).

From the preceding considerations we can provide the following framework for a critical analysis of radical behaviorism. The theme is that the ultimate thesis explicitly directs Skinner's systematic presentations of his operant conditioning theory of behavior. Three assertions of radical behaviorism are thus entailed: the causes of human activity

(1) are external to the individual: *outside* agency as natural;
(2) are never internal to the individual: *inner* agency is extra-natural – free will;
(3) are constitutive of operant conditioning: behavior is emitted not elicited, yet the environment is the only agency determining (a) what behavior is emitted and (b) what kind of behavior it will become in terms of a developing reinforcement history.

In Skinner's last paper of 1990 he reveals, I believe, the deep theme of freedom and emitted behavior that unites these three features of radical behaviorism: "Operant conditioning must solve the 'problem of the *first* instance': how and why do responses occur *before* they have been reinforced" (Skinner Ibid: 1206, emphasis provided).

Yes, indeed it certainly does. Just as Hull could not escape the problem of dissolving the spontaneity of the autonomous Kantian subject in the instantaneity of the automatic reflex machine, so Skinner too cannot escape the autonomy of the Kantian subject by replacing it with the autonomy of behavior that is miraculously emitted without (the honest acknowledgment of) the subject. Skinner's final solution to this problem, without the slightest awareness of its connection to the structure/agency problem in the social sciences, seems to resort to one of the classic forms of reification, cultural determinism.

> Modeling, telling, and teaching are *functions of the social environments called cultures.* Different cultures emerge from different contingencies of

variation and selection and differ in the extent to which they help their members solve their problems. In other words, *cultures evolve, in a third kind of variation and selection.* (Cultures that shape and maintain operant behavior area exclusively human. ...)

(Skinner Ibid: 1207, emphasis provided)

Surely, we have here in Skinner's last effort an eerie resonance with the Hobbesian machine, Leviathan. He is the engineer who gives Hobbes exactly what he needs, a technology that transforms, through the mechanism of operant conditioning, operants who happen to be people into the Leviathan of Culture. Let Alan Ryan speak to this suggestion: "Who, after reading Noam Chomsky's devastating attack on B. F. Skinner's view of language, would not agree that Hobbes's difficulties are alive and unsolved and living in Harvard" (Ryan 1974: 9).

Our task is to examine and especially challenge the cardinal thesis of operant conditioning that behavior is emitted. This is a special problem, and it goes like this: Skinner in effect is arguing that, since agency is external to the individual and never internal, emitted behavior is not agency but patiency. What is special then about the problem of emitted behavior is the paradox of how behavior can be emitted but not agentic. What is omitted here in Skinnerian theory is the possibility that emitted behavior *is* agentic, first of all because that is the fact of the matter that Skinner empirically uncovered, and then mistakenly conceptualized what he had found according to the ultimate thesis; second, because the individual displays behavior that is emitted and not elicited, while that certainly does mean that it rules out the idea of "agency *in* the individual," it does not necessarily rule out the idea of the "agency *of* the individual." In virtue of the fact that Skinner is a Machian positivist, the ultimate thesis that is presumed in that standpoint dictates that he thus can only identify agency with the Cartesian extra-natural theory of the "the free inner man." This, I think, can be seen in the following comments in the chapter on "Freedom" in his classic *Beyond Freedom and Dignity.* Skinner here examines Leibnitz's assertion that "Liberty consists in the *power to do* what one wants to do," along with a similar one of Voltaire's, in which the word "can" instead of "power" is used in defining freedom or liberty (Skinner 1971: 34, emphasis provided). In indicating that these were found by Bertrand de Jouvenel, Skinner then exclaims, that

Jouvenel relegates these comments to a footnote, saying that the power to want is a matter of "interior liberty" (the freedom of the inner man!) which falls outside of the "gambit of freedom."

(Skinner Ibid)

From my discussion of the helpful distinction between two kinds of freedom, agency and liberty, the "power to want" is most certainly within the "gambit of freedom." Obviously, Skinner chose Jouvenel rather than Kant, or Bunge, or Harré. I dare say that he was seeking reinforcement rather than under-standing. But that is exactly what is to be expected from the great man – science for him is only about predictability and control, not understanding (Garrett 1996: 142–43). Although it certainly does not save him, it never-theless may be of help in understanding Skinner and his relation to science to suggest the obvious. Perhaps he does conflate science with engineering, which is to serve a political ideology of social predictability and control.

Threading the entire network of ideas that make-up this special problem is perhaps a heretofore unnoticed dimension. This was already suggested before in the critique of Homans's use of Skinnerian theory. All of these inconsistencies, together, stem from the fact that, though Skinner's Machian behaviorism dictates that there are only "correlations of events" and no "causes of production," he constantly violates that rule. Consequently, one is tempted to say that Skinner routinely "talks the talk" and "walks the walk" of Machianism, as Kitchener has excellently argued, but often, at critical moments, a certain choice of vocabulary strongly reveals that he also implies scientific realism (Kitchener 1996: 113–15).

Emitted behavior: Skinner's original sin

We begin thus with Skinner's original sin: an attempt to solve the "problem of the first instance" by an implicit denial, not of autonomy, but of the autonomy of the person. *He is able to do this by conflating the person with the Cartesian mind.* Therefore his basic trick: dismissing mentalism brings with it the collateral dismissal of the person, but without confronting the latter as a separate issue. For, the question of the person is central to the problem of emitted behavior. How can there be behavior without the person as the source of the behavior, therefore, emitted behavior without agency, and hence the agency of the environment without the agency of the persons who constitute it? In other words, it is fatally inconsistent to deny the agency of the person while ascribing agency to the environment, of other persons, particularly, the Skinnerian psychologist. Skinner, again, but selectively, can speak to this question: "As a science of behavior adopts the strategy of physics ... , *the autonomous agent to which behavior has traditionally been attributed is replaced by the environment*" (Skinner 1971: 175, emphasis provided).

This statement is Skinner's version of Newton's first law and has been restated by me as the first two assertions of radical behaviorism. Both of them comprise what I have called the ultimate thesis: since causation is a natural state of affairs under the law of inertia, it is external to the individual and never internal; hence, freedom as agency can only be an extra-natural theory – free will and its historical variants. Cartesianism is the modern paradigm case. Hence, from this standpoint, *the ultimate thesis is the bald commitment of radical behaviorism.* Thus, this is the root of why Skinner can say that, "we assume that no behavior is free" (Skinner 1953: 111). With regard to the "the problem of the first instance" my thesis is as follows: (a)

The stalemate of the psychological sciences   117

emitted behavior is not "behavior" (patiency), but "action" (agency); (b) the concept of "behavior" is a prescription and not in fact a description; (c) this is why Skinner is forever fending the idea off, and defending not so much operant behavior, but defending *against* the sense of its agency. In short, *paradoxically, the hidden premise of emitted behavior is its agency.* Now let us see how Skinner actually works out the concept of emitted behavior.

Operant behavior: how emitted behavior is agency, or, how a rabbit is pulled out of a hat

The initial part of my evidence is the sheer fact that Skinner, at the very end, announces "the problem of the first instance": he knows that, in being emitted and not elicited, behavior is autonomous; thus he must prove this premise wrong. His commitment to the law of inertia and the positivist dogma that reality is what is observable, so that all else are "explanatory fictions," demands the denial of the premise. With this in mind, consider these two statements of Skinner's on self-control.

All reinforcements are self-administered, since a response may be regarded as "*producing*" its reinforcement. ... It is also more than simply *generating* circumstances under which a given type of behavior is characteristically reinforced. ...

(Skinner 1953: 237, emphasis provided)

Self-reinforcement of operant behavior presupposes that the individual has it in his *power* to obtain reinforcement. ...

(Skinner Ibid, emphasis provided)

The reference to such non-Humean causal words as "producing," "power," and "generating" is not atypical, for Skinner openly acknowledges that this is to be expected. Consider two examples.

In emphasizing the *controlling power of external variables,* we have left the organism itself in a peculiarly helpless position. ... It is true. ... the emphasis is still upon behavior, not upon the behaver.

(Skinner Ibid: 228, emphasis provided)

In characterizing a man's behavior in terms of frequency, we *assume certain standard conditions: he must be able to execute and repeat a given act,* and other behavior must not interfere appreciably.

(Skinner Ibid: 63, emphasis provided)

Note: Skinner's premise that behavior that is emitted is agency, is verified with the use of the word "power," that is the meaning of the phrase "able to execute." My observation of some earlier quotes identified the fact that

Skinner assigns autonomy to the environment, is confirmed by the specification of that assignment as referencing a "power of external variables." Now, it is so very clear here, that Skinner normatively resorts to the realist vocabulary of causal power/force. And, more to the point, the ultimate thesis and his positivism drive him to contradict that resort, and in so doing, he spills over into the reification of culture (Skinner Ibid: 228–29). Skinner is simply not in a position to realize that the hidden premise of the concept of emitted behavior and his occasional assertions that the human subject is "able to execute and repeat" reveal in broad daylight that he has indeed properly assigned powers to the appropriate human particulars – the behaver. This is exactly the case with respect to his articulation of the concept of emitted behavior.

> Operant conditioning may be described *without mentioning any stimulus* which acts before the response is made. In reinforcing the neck-stretching in the pigeon *it was necessary to wait for the stretching to occur*; we did *not* elicit it. When a baby puts his hand to his mouth, the movement may be reinforced ... , but *we cannot find any stimulus which elicits the movement* and which is present every time it occurs. Stimuli are always acting upon the organism, but their functional connection with *operant behavior is not like that in the reflex.* Operant behavior, in short, is emitted, rather than elicited.
>
> (Skinner Ibid: 107, emphasis provided)

> It is customary to refer to any movement of the organism as a "response." The word is borrowed from the field of reflex action and implies an act which, so to speak, answers a prior event – the stimulus. But we may make an event contingent upon behavior *without identifying, or being able to identify, a prior stimulus.* We did not alter the environment of the pigeon to *elicit* the upward movement of the head. *It is probably impossible to show that any single stimulus invariably precedes this movement.* Behavior of this sort may come under the control of stimuli, but the relation is not that of elicitation.
>
> (Skinner Ibid: 64, emphasis provided)

From the standpoint of the metaphysic of realism that is constitutive of scientific practice, I cannot see any way to invalidate the firm conclusion that the hidden premise of the concept of emitted or operant behavior is that such behavior is not a reflex; and that is certainly because such behavior is agentic. A species of Giddens's "agent causaliy," which in the human case, would be the display of personal agency – the agency *of* but not *in* the person. After all, the above quotes present the following assertions concerning emitted, but not reflex, behavior.

(1) Reinforcement: presupposes that one must wait for the animal to behave.
(2) Operant conditioning: presupposes that any stimulus acting before a response is unnecessary.

(3) Reason: as a rule, a stimulus before behavior that is present every time it is displayed, and which elicits the behavior in question, is impossible to find.

(4) Therefore: it must be concluded that emitted behavior is agency.

Skinner, then, is quite correct in accepting the standard condition that human beings "execute" an action by virtue of having the "power" that "enables" them to do so (Malcolm 1964: 141–62; Garrett 1996: 141–48). When, however, this is understood under the auspices of the realism of scientific practice, instead of the mistaken conflation of science with positivism, radical behaviorism is metaphysically exposed as a necessarily failed endeavor to promote a science of psychology at the expense of the Kantian free subject, or its contemporary representative, the Giddensian personal agent. In Richard Garrett's paper, "Skinner's Case For Radical Behaviorism," his argument against such a science and such an expense can certainly be reconsidered by the reference here to the Kant/Giddens human agent. And thus, the Kant/Giddens/Garrett view of human being gains definitive support by research he refers to on the Skinnerian enterprise.

In these experiments both linguistically incompetent (LI) children and linguistically competent (LC) children were exposed to the same contingencies of reinforcement. LI children responded in uniform ways to uniform contingencies of reinforcement *just as lower organisms do.* The behavior of LI children proved to be highly predictable and controllable; it was entirely a function of the external contingencies of reinforcement. LC children, in contrast, did not respond uniformly to uniform contingencies of reinforcement. Their behavior was not simply a function of external contingencies and so was not predictable or controllable. And this is precisely what we should expect of creatures that can think about goals, rules, and values, reason about them, and be motivated by them, i.e. it is exactly what we should expect of rational thinking creatures. For such creatures, exposed to the same external contingencies of reinforcement, may be expected to draw different conclusions about their situation, hold different values, consider different options, and arrive at different decisions. We conclude, therefore, that Skinner's radical behavioristic assumption (that adult human behavior is predictable and controllable) is unsound and needs to be rejected (Garrett 1996).

In light of Garrett's conclusion, the cardinal point of this entire discussion on Skinnerian behaviorism is that the ultimate basis of Garrett's rejection is the upshot of Skinner's original sin: to conduct empirical research from the standpoint of the ultimate thesis is to doom such a research enterprise from the very start. That Skinner could actually believe that there is no significant distinction between "coughing" and "whispering," and worse, that that must be true because emitted behavior is no less determined than elicited behavior, when it turns out that emitted behavior *is* agency, deserves the comment of one critic that "Behaviorism is such a perversion, that only a very brilliant fellow could have thought it up." But now, we are to enter an examination of the intimate connection between the ultimate thesis and another psychological theory of which it has been noted by a different critic, that the above witticism should begin with, "Behaviorism, *or Psychoanalysis.*"

Freud from Kant: the mechanism/vitalism problem

With the publication of the dream book at the turn of the twentieth century and in the tradition of Hobbesian conflict theory, Freud begins his journey toward the metapsychological reduction of the romantic freedom of the "will" to the deterministic materialism of the body. Spiritual power becomes physical energy. Down the road of this journey it will become evident that the crucial issue here will be the status of causality in this resort to the concept of energy. For, we now fully understand from the perspective of the Kantian metaphysics of nature, that *energy is the content of forceful particulars at work, and power is the potential force of which work is its manifestation.* The positivism of the day will completely deny all this. The theme of that reduction is what I have earlier called Freud's law (or the Hamlet principle) – *human beings cannot will.* By the mid-1920s, the instincts of the unconscious are developed into the final structural theory of id, ego, and superego. And as Norman O. Brown recognized in his declaration that psychoanalysis claims to "break through phenomena to the hidden 'noumenal' reality," the Kantianism of the structural theory is unmistakable (reference in Steinmetz Ibid: 50). Certainly, in Chapter 7, section F, of *The Interpretation of Dreams,* the "thing-in-itself" is implicit in Freud's initial and classic formulation of the conception of the unconscious – "the unconscious is the true psychical reality: in its innermost nature it is as much unknown to us as the external world, and it is just as imperfectly communicated to by the data of consciousness as is the external world by the reports of our sense-organs." Indeed, it is well known that Freud himself believed that he was giving Kant the very psychological theory of mind he needed. As we will now see, Kant returned the compliment.

It is right here at this juncture that we can explore the internal connection of Freud's structural theory of the unconscious to the conception of inertia that peeks out of a moment in Kerr's new discussion of the Freud–Jung relationship (Kerr 1993).

> It was commonly assumed that science decisively triumphed ... and that a complete materialistic account of the external world was nearly at hand. But how was man to conceptualize that other pole of experience – the self. *There seemed no place in the material world, with its endless antecedent causes for ... agency itself. The paradox was apparent to all. There was no agreed upon way of resolving it.*
>
> (Kerr 1993: 6, emphasis provided)

In his reference to "endless antecedent causes" Kerr has repeated the received view of the deterministic argument against freedom that is found in Kant's third antinomy. In this renowned antinomy, the determinism of the phenomenal world expresses Hobbes's principle that "the will that causes the action is itself caused." And in Hobbes's principle and Kant's third antinomy, the ultimate thesis unites them both. For the very idea of an "antecedent cause," the heart of Newton's first law, is the guarantee that particulars, physical and human, are patients, not agents.

While in Kerr's comment there is, at best, a fragment that merely indexes the relevance of the ultimate thesis, and with it as well the importance of the reflex arc, it is Robert R. Holt's ground-breaking work on the intellectual roots of Freud's theoretical thinking that makes all the difference in our understanding. His thorough examination of this above point reveals it all in the full light of day in "Beyond Vitalism and Mechanism: Freud's Concept of Psychic Energy" (1989: 141–70), and in "A Review of Some of Freud's Biological Assumptions and Their Influence on His Theories" (1989: 114–40). At the center of that examination is Holt's thesis that it is the science of psychoanalysis, its metapsychology, that causes such serious trouble for the Humanism of psychoanalysis, its clinical theory.

> The concept of *psychic energy* is central to Freud's metapsychology; in fact, it *was the principle means he called upon to help explain the events of clinical observation*. In its development during the past 40 years, the concept has steadily ramified into a conceptual thicket that baffles some, impresses many, and greatly complicates the task of anyone who tries to form a clear idea of what the basic theory of psychoanalysis is. Up to a point, one can get a good deal of clarification by tracing its place in the development of Freud's ideas, but the thoughts of no man are a closed system. *The search for historical understanding leads us* past Freud's immediate intellectual ancestors, past the bounds of psychology, and *into one of the major themes in the history of biology: the opposing views of vitalism and mechanism*
> (Holt 1989: 141–42, emphasis provided)

In the course of Holt's unusually thick analysis of the mechanism/vitalism problem of the metapsychology, what emerges is the realization that the traditional concept of energy, physical and psychical, is *dead*. And of great importance is the direct consequence of this event for Holt and his colleagues – they are left with the bare phenomenological fact "*[of] conscious experience that feels like energy?*" (Holt Ibid: 167). What Holt is coming to is that this phenomenological fact is a Call for a new concept of energy. But what is this "feel of energy," and especially, what is its relationship to "conscious experience." What I mean here is the problem of the determinism of the unconscious – the feel of energy – and the freedom of the individual – conscious experience. In Holt's discussion, this relationship and its problem is subsumed and obscured under the overall problem of mechanism and vitalism.

> Psychoanalysts are not much interested in such measurements [of energy in the nervous system] (no doubt properly so), for the kinds of motivational

phenomena they have in mind when they talk about energies have little to do with these microvolt quantities. They observe people who have violent importunate impulses; people who strive to attain their goals for long periods of time against tremendous odds and despite physical exhaustion; people who differ strikingly in the amount of pep, initiative, and zest they have, as against depression, lethargy, inertia, or fatigue. All these observations seem *to cry out for some kind of energy concept* – not just the energy that is released by the metabolism of food, *but some kind of directly experienced, psychological energy. So too, does the fact that thinking is hard work; if you try to make that into a quantitative statement, however, you end up with the assumption that thinking must use a great deal of psychic energy – quite the contrary of what Freud postulated.*

(Holt Ibid: 166–67, emphasis provided)

Having presented this paper in the early part of the second decade of the neo-Humanist revolt, it is natural to suppose that Holt is expressing the psychoanalytic version of the Science/Humanism structure/agency debate. And by the mid-1970s with the Klein/Schafer Humanistic revolt against the Scientific determinism of the unconscious, looking back at Holt, that is obviously quite correct (Klein 1975; Schaffer 1976). Although, to be sure, in his case, it is intricately imbedded in the thicket of his discussion of the mechanism/vitalism problem at the heart of psychoanalysis. In view of this, it is a virtual obligation then to assert my thesis concerning the issue that "conscious experience has the feeling of energy." For, the latter is certainly a restatement of the traditional issue concerning freedom, that is "conscious experience has the feeling of the effort of the will." Thus, my thesis: *Freud's roots in the mechanism/vitalism problem is the twentieth-century variety of Kant's noumenal/phenomenal problem.*

Indeed, Holt could just as well have said it for us in reference to his critical appreciation of Freud's failed *Project for a Scientific Psychology*. That failure to reduce psychical processes to the determinism of material particles in motion at the level of the nervous system is expressed in Freud's confession that "How *primary defense* ... is to be represented mechanically – this I confess, I am unable to say. ... [especially in view of the fact that] our consciousness furnishes only *qualities* whereas science recognizes only *quantities*" (Holt Ibid: 153). Holt's reaction to the confession reveals that the strict continuity between the nervous system of the *Project* and the *psychic apparatus* of the metapsychology is defined by the problem of mechanism and vitalism.

> Yet Freud ... thought that he had to [resort to] a deus ex machina, the Ego – not this time an ego as the total of cathected neurons, but in the *old philosophical sense contemporaneously described by William James (1890) as "the pure ego or self of selves," an ultimate prime mover and knower. Quite a voluntaristic and teleological concept for a man who also advocated exceptionless psychic determinism.*
>
> (Holt Ibid: 166, emphasis provided)

One has to correct Holt here: for a Kantian trying to contradict Kant's theory of freedom that is now understood to be grounded and hence justified in the metaphysical realism of modern science, it seems that Freud, the scientific realist that he actually was, therefore was bound to do just what he wound up doing. For, with regard to the realist metaphysics that must inform any understanding of the brain and the mind, the concept of the Kantian free subject *will* reassert itself. Now, what Holt fails to bring out right here concerning this reassertion is, in my judgment, *the* pivotal moment in Freudian metapsychology. The central *issue* is that Freud had to give up the *Project* in having to give *psychic* qualities a *major explanatory role* (Holt Ibid: 153). The critical *fact* here is that that role was taken over by an ego that self-consciously executes (Kantian noumenal freedom) the very primary defense that was suppose to be executed by the unconscious (Kantian phenomenal determinism of human instincitivism). Now, the absolutely critical *point* here is that, this means, that the very idea of an unconscious as the determinism that is supposed to explain that conscious experience of energy has been contradicted. The upshot of which, it seems to me, is that *psychoanalysis is right back where it started* – as a scientific revolt against the Humanist insistence that the feel of energy that constitutes conscious experience, after all is said and done, is the sign of an effort of will, that is freedom, and not a determinism that rules it out; and, that *that implication is coming from the side of science, not only from the side of Humanism.* In this case, there is the very important further implication: if the experience of energy is indeed the sign of freedom that has something to do with the concept of determinism itself, then the "power" of the will must be related to the power of determinate causation. In short, "agent causality" and the metaphysic of causal powers that grounds it. In that case, surely, then, Hobbes's law that "the will that causes the action is itself caused" and Freud's version of that law, namely, that "human beings cannot will," do not have it quite right, at all. This, of course, in raising the question of the origin of the Hobbes/Freud law, leads us to the ultimate thesis – the concepts of inertia and reflex. Hence, we must critically examine the problem of mechanism and vitalism that defines the continuity that binds Freud's concepts of brain and mind from the standpoint of its roots in the ultimate thesis. Thanks to Holt's superb analysis he lays out all of that for us. But unfortunately for him and psychoanalysis, Holt was not in a position to understand the fact that the failure of the *Project* was actually due to the fact that Kantian freedom had been illegitimately denied in the misguided conception of determinism that dominated Freud's day, and Holt's; and that that was exactly why Freud himself, against himself, reasserted the Kantian freedom of the ego. In other words, Freud simply did not understand Kantian philosophy, especially the theory of freedom; and he had no idea of Kant's scientific realism; let alone the internal relationship between his freedom and his realism. But of course, Freud was not alone.

As we now enter the examination indicated above, let us do so with this quote that Holt himself used with regard to the ultimate fate of the concepts of vitalism and mechanism as he moves toward the need for a new conception of energy. Since this quote is known to us from the earlier discussion of Giddens and vitalism (Chapter 3), thus I will only use part of it here. The context is Holt's conviction that the concepts of mechanism, as well as vitalism, must be shelved by psychoanalysis in the service of the above move.

> Common to both systems [of mechanism and vitalism], in the first place, is the view of causality in the sense of an executive causality [causal powers], while in the empirical sciences of the present day the causal connection is usually conceived only in the sense of a consecutive causality. Both systems seek for an explanation of the organic event by reducing it to a "principle" or "category" which is "at work" in it, which "causes" it.
>
> (Holt Ibid: 162, brackets inserted)

Keep the import of this quote in mind for the discussion to follow: in accepting Mainx's view that genuine causality is "consecutive causality" not "executive causality," Holt has thrown out the realist conception of "agent causality" as causal power. We will see the direct consequence of this state of affairs for Holt's Call for a new concept of energy. *In other words, which Call is the most promising, Holt's for a "directly experienced psychological energy" or Giddens's for a "directly experienced personal agency."*

Project and metapsychology: the inertia/reflex connection

The metapsychology that constitutes the psychoanalytic theory of personality and its principle of a deterministic unconscious is itself an articulation of the metaphysical message of The Solemn Oath. In a letter of 1842 to a friend, du-Bois-Raymond expressed the content of that Oath.

> Brucke and I pledged a solemn oath to put into effect this truth: "No other forces than the common physical-chemical ones are *active within the organism*. In those cases which cannot at the time be explained by these forces one has either to find the specific way ... of their action by means of the physical-mathematical method, or to *assume new forces equal in dignity* to the chemical-physical forces inherent in matter, *reducible to the force of attraction and repulsion*."
>
> ([Quoted by Bernfeld 1944: 348]; Holt 1989: 149)

Jointly authored by the brilliant students (Brucke, du-Bois-Raymond, Helmholtz, Ludwig) of Johannes Muller, "the most effective critic of mid-nineteenth-century mechanism," the purpose of the Oath was "to destroy, once and for all, vitalism, the fundamental belief of their admired master"

(Holt Ibid). So far this is the standard view of the Oath that surely informed and directed Freud's theoretical efforts to the end of his life. But I want to reorient the whole take on the importance of this anti-vitalistic program. My point of departure is Holt's critique of Freud's relationship to the program which he, Freud, directly learned about during the period 1874–78 from his professors Ernst Brucke and Theodor Meynert, and from his instructor Sigmund Exner, all at the University of Vienna medical school.

> By taking his teachers' statements about the nature of the nervous system not as empirical propositions subject to verification, but as unquestioned postulates, he put the whole theory further away from testability.
>
> (Holt 1965: 120)

The central unquestioned postulate at issue here is the concept of energy and its grounding principle of universal determinism (Holt Ibid: 94). The term "forces" of course entails both the concept and its grounding principle. While Holt separates these two I, instead, return to their head/tail relationship. To see the importance of this, we must return to the Oath and notice what is usually omitted in discussions of it concerning Freud. Given the usual emphasis on deterministic "forces" in reference to the twin reductionist sites of the nervous system and physics in biology, I want to explicitly pick out the usually unnoticed reference to "forces" that are not only *active within the organism*," but are "reducible to the force of *attraction* and *repulsion.*" Newton and Kant understood perfectly that the three laws of motion presume the realist metaphysical principle that the active causal forces of attraction and repulsion are active by virtue of being causal powers. We have already pointed out that both Mainx and therefore Holt treat the very idea of causal powers that are active within the organism as being explanatory fictions because they are an "executive causality." In short, in that treatment they are innocently honoring the idea of the ultimate thesis. And who in philosophy and the social sciences, until recently, would have disagreed with that thesis. Here, once more, is the classic mid-twentieth-century statement by Singer of the standard misunderstanding of the heart of the three laws of motion, the law of inertia.

> Hence, no sooner was the conception of *inert bodies passively following the dictates of blind forces* seen to be applicable [by Newton] to the motion of mass-points, than it was *immediately generalized into a world-philosophy.*
>
> (Singer 1959: 294, the second emphasis is added)

Now let's look at Richard Feynman's comment on the concept of force/energy. He is responding to first grade books in which the nature of science is presented in terms of the nature of both the central question that science asks and the central answer science gives. To the question, "what makes it [things] move," the answer is, "energy makes it move."

> Now energy is a very subtle concept. It is very, very difficult to get it right. What I mean by that is that it is not easy to understand energy well enough to use it right, so that you can deduce something correctly using the energy idea. It is beyond first grade. It would be equally well to say that *"God makes it move," or "spirit makes it move," or "movability makes it move"*. (In fact equally well to say "energy makes it stop"). Look at it this way: That's only the definition of energy. *It should be reversed.* We might say *something can move that has energy in it, but not "what makes it move is energy."* This is a subtle difference.
>
> (Feynman 2000: 178–79, emphasis provided)

Thus, the correct reading of inertia is that material particulars are agents and not patients, by virtue of the fact that "something can move that has energy in it." Technically, Harré encourages us to say that it is to be understood right here, that Feynman actually means by the phrase, "has energy *in it,*" not that there is "energy" *and* a "thing," but rather, that energy is *of* a thing (Harré in Varela 1995: 266–74). Note, in this regard, that "in it" and "outside it" both are versions of the mistaken idea, in effect, that there is "energy" *and* there is a "thing." Thus, Feynman is asserting that "energy" is not an external, or better, independent something that "makes" things move, as if things cannot move, even though they have their own energy. That, indeed, would be incoherent, for, if the energy of a thing indexes that such a thing is thereby an agent, that is why it can and does move. Hence, the "energy of" an entity (thing, animal, or person), is the complex of causal powers/forces and liabilities that constitute it as natural kind of agent causality. To separate "energy" and its internal connection to the idea of natural kinds of powerful particulars is conceptually dangerous. For, there will be the tendency to treat the energy concept exactly in the way that Feynman asserts it should never be treated. The history of the social sciences in their use of the energy concept is a testimony to that very danger of mistreatment. Holt is merely a paradigm example of that tradition, though in the context of this discussion of Freud, a special and very important example.

Now we will directly see that the upshot of Holt's otherwise magnificent critical examination of the fact that the "same set of biological propositions [of the *Oath*] were retained as fundamental assumptions in Freud's post-1900 theories, with only terminological changes," is a fatal paradox. The allusion to the above set of biological assumptions concerning the nervous system centers around the crucial notion of what Holt refers to as *"the passive reflex model"* (Holt Ibid: 96). Holt's theme is that that "model" is a major influence on Freudian theory that is continuous from the nervous system of the project to the psychic apparatus of the metapsychology. *In keeping with his Call for a new concept to handle the phenomenological fact of "directly experienced psychological energy," the reflex model must be rejected because the human subject is active and not passive.* Holt speaks precisely to this point when he reveals the views of both Brucke and Meynert on the reflex as a model of brain and mind. With regard to this reflex model, both a renowned natural scientist (Brucke or Meynert) and an equally renowned literary artist (Twain) are in perfect agreement.

> As a part of his rejection of the vitalism of his own teacher, Johannes Muller, Brucke introduced the idea that there was *no spontaneous central activity of the brain,* but explicitly declared that *the functioning of the entire brain followed the model of the reflex arc:* "voluntary movements ... too are originated by centripetal impulses; however, from them the conduction goes through parts of the cortex which serve consciousness, ideas, and will." The result was an implicit conception of the whole nervous system as a passive instrument which remained in a state of rest until stimulated, when it functioned so as to rid itself of the incoming exogenous energies.
>
> (Holt Ibid: 95)

Thus, the answer to the question, which Call is the most promising, Holt's for a "directly experienced psychological energy" or Giddens's for a "directly experienced personal agency," is unavoidable. Any serious attempt to reconcile Heidegger's two Kantian causalities now has no choice but to opt for personal agency. But that very choice contains the deep problem of recovery: Kant's realist idea of causality alone can transform "energy" into "agency."

Part II

Returning to Kant and the stalemate of sociology

5 Simmel

Sociation and the real a priori of power

Introduction: Simmel, Durkheim, Weber

With regard to the onset of the neo-Humanist revolt of the 1960s we have seen that both phenomenology and existentialism, *and now* the psychological sciences, were indeed self-destructing on the cardinal matter of the structure/agency problem. This of course was to show in two decades, as I have already averred, that the crisis of social science concerning the ontology of human being was surely on its way to dying out. In view of Chapters 3 and 4 we are strongly entitled to assert that the above self-destruction must, at bottom, be placed at the "doorstep" of the ultimate thesis and the conflation of science with positivism. Since the conflation cemented the legitimacy of the ultimate thesis we discovered the following consequences in philosophy and the psychological sciences: continental philosophy was doomed to insist that freedom is a power, but because of the metaphysical limitations imposed on phenomenology by the above-mentioned legitimacy, the power of that freedom was nevertheless going to be power-less by virtue of the fact that it is without recourse to a realist ontology of the natural world; while Hullian behaviorism was driven by the ultimate thesis to artificially substitute instantaneity for spontaneity, in being blinded by the same dogma that patiency is natural and agency therefore supernatural, Skinnerian behaviorism winds up with the basic premise of emitted behavior that it is actually contradicted by its own empirical observations to be the basic premise of agentive action; and finally in the case of classical psychoanalysis, even with Holt's stunning rejection of the "passive reflex/instinct model," it nevertheless was left stranded with the dead-end idea of "directly experienced psychological energy," and no means of ever giving it up for the more promising idea of a "directly experienced personal agency." Remember, and we can take this fact as fundamentally relevant to both behaviorism as well as psychoanalysis, Holt threw out Freud's having to reinstate the freedom of the Kantian ego. This meant, of necessity, that he would not be in a position to discover how to get from energy to agency. And, furthermore, consider this: as Holt had no idea that to move from energy to agency he needs causal powers theory, the premier psychoanalytic theorists of the next generation,

Gardner and Edelson, hit on causal powers theory, to be sure, but only to use it to reinstate the agency of the unconscious, all over again. The stalemate of the psychological sciences here must be judged beyond salvation.

Why would anyone say of psychology – both behaviorism and psychoanalysis – that "it is somewhere between fanciful and hopeless?" Perhaps the critical analysis presented in Chapter 4 and summarized above is one way to understand that.

On the eve of the 1960s, it is not surprising to discover that Dahrendorf expressed the predicament of being the victim of the ultimate thesis and of the conflation in an essay that had its roots in a crucial historical situation of German social science in the nineteenth century. That situation, thoroughly discussed in Chapter 4, was the fact that German social science was evincing a nationalist variety of the Science and Humanism debate, in which their natural science came forth with the formidable Solemn Oath with which to challenge the new structure/agency discourse of mechanism/vitalism. We have seen that the new discourse revealed the spectacular prominence of the ultimate thesis in its instantiation in the "passive reflex model," thus deeply explaining why there was that renowned rigid separation of the natural and the cultural "sciences." In other words, that thesis and model prescribed for Humanism as well as science its infamous fatal judgment: since the Kantian and Hegelian social and cultural realms were to be seen as extra-natural, hence as located in the world of "spirit," they were therefore to be condemned as being beyond any possibility of scientific analysis (Turner *et al.* 1995: 179). Now, while true for Hegel, that judgment was of course dead wrong for Kant: his sophisticated understanding of the causal realism of science contradicted the cardinal point of the Solemn Oath. Consider that the reminder here of the discussion of the "passive reflex model" in Chapter 4 definitively reveals the metaphysical thrust that is the subtext of Dahrendorf's "Homo Sociologicus." In short, the ultimate thesis is carried forward in that essay: Dahrendorf articulates the structure/agency problem around the idea that phenomenal determinism is the ontology of nature; and of course, since the ultimate thesis and its "passive reflex model" are mistaken, the categorical acceptance of phenomenal determinism is categorically mistaken. And we should note the significant fact that the "passive reflex model" would indeed be to taken to equally mean a "passive *instinct* model." I have shown elsewhere that it has been a commonplace mistake in Freud and the social sciences to conflate the concepts of "reflex" and "instinct" (Varela 2003: 106). It is now thus eminently clear that in the major discourses that express the metaphysical tension with regard to human being and the natural world – *free will and determinism* (the Hobbes/Rousseau and Romantic traditions), *noumenal ego and phenomenal world* (the Kantian tradition), *mechanism and vitalism* (nineteenth-century biology and the Freudian tradition), *social system and voluntarism* (the Parsonian tradition), and *structure and agency* (the Giddensian tradition) – the ultimate thesis and the conflation of reflex and instinct that articulates that thesis is a unifying metaphysical theme.

Historically speaking, the variety of discourses expressing the question of the metaphysical tension from the seventeenth century to the present allows us to notice a gap in the analysis of these discourses and the ultimate thesis up to this point. That gap pertains to the theoretical space in between the Freudian tradition of mechanism and vitalism and the Parsonian tradition of social system and voluntarism. In the sociologies of Georg Simmel, Emile Durkheim, and Max Weber, we have three new vocabularies filling that space which are also directly expressive of the structure/agency debate, and also of the ultimate thesis that constitutes it. They are, respectively, Simmel's *form* and *life*, Durkheim's the *social fact* and *social association*, and Weber's *system* and *persönlichkeit*. Kant's theory of freedom is at the heart of each thinker, therefore each theory, and thus of course each vocabulary. In their return to Kant the theory of noumenal freedom is treated quite differently: Simmel's is tragically muddled, Durkheim's is a fatal distortion, and Weber's is strangely puzzling. Thus, in so doing, the necessary upshot was that, together, they guaranteed that the stalemate of the debate in question would be continued under the authority of their enormous prestige. The important upshot of the discovery of the truly substantive and original returns of Simmel, Durkheim, and Weber for our later examination of Parsons, Bidney, Dahrendorf, Benton, and Berger in their relation to Kantian freedom, is that what we have here in the examples of Parsons, and especially, Dahrendorf and Berger, are *empty rituals of return*. While in the case of Bidney and Benton my discussion of their relation to Kant in this regard has already been sufficiently conducted for the purposes of this book, the examination to follow will be restricted to the remaining three sociologists. And, to repeat once more those purposes: along with the primacy of the recovery of agency, the intent here is to rewrite the history (though carefully selected) of the problem of the structure/agency debate, especially from the standpoint of the new perspective of Science for Humanism and, as a result, to see what can be learned about the failure of social scientists in the history of that debate to discover that the realism of science and the centrality of causal powers in scientific theory bears directly on the resolution of that debate. After all, to date, whether it is the American concern with the macro/micro link or the British concern with the structure/agency connection, it is still true for those two concerns, that getting the nature of causal powers right is *the* key to any possible solution to the problems of recovering agency and of resolving reification. In my judgment, that understanding has not as yet been explicitly and systematically manifest in the work of those in either the American nor the British concerns in question (to see this, revisit the British case in the recent discussions in the June 2007 issue of *Journal for the Theory of Social Behaviour* of Porpora, Varela, and King on the Archer/Elder-Vass defense of social realism in terms of Durkheim's emergence argument; and look at the proceedings record of the plenary session at the Critical Realism conference on Friday afternoon, August 17 in which all except King debated the defense in question). Setting the historical record straight, then, is of major importance here.

But I now want to give a further *general* sense of how Simmel, Durkheim, and Weber proceeded to guarantee the stalemate for the future. We will thus have a clear framework of the work to follow on the series of footnotes to Kant with regard to the question of structure and agency in the history of the social sciences.

Simmel, Durkheim, Weber: general introduction

Although the three giants of the late Sociological Tradition were engaged in the project of sociologizing Kantian philosophy of knowledge and mind, Durkheim's handling of the issue of deterministic social structures and individual human agency is the most prominent. It was not, as the traditional sociological view has it, *morality* that was front and center in his encounter with Kant, but *freedom*. To be more accurate, *morality was important to Durkheim exactly because freedom was the primary issue: for morality to be possible in society without the traditional god, freedom had to be made subordinate to the moral fact of society.* Society thus had to be god, and so the fate of freedom in Durkheimian sociology was sealed. His prominence thus consisted in the fact that he was the only one who directly confronted the problem of the noumenal metaphysic of Kantian freedom. In sharp contrast, while Simmel obliquely confronts the issue of the argument, Weber never confronts it at all, permitting himself to dismiss Kantian metaphysics through the safe distance of the received view informed as it was by the befuddlement of Pistorius. We will see that Durkheim's Sens lectures of 1883 and *Moral Education* of 1902–3 directly show his intimate struggle with Kantian freedom in no uncertain terms. As a matter of fact, because the latter can be reread in conjunction with the former, we now know that Durkheim was a traditional Kantian on the question of freedom in 1883, *and then* an anti-Kantian on that same question 1902–3. Indeed, it certainly can be asserted that, since the problem of determinism is the serious issue of Durkheimian social realism, that is exactly because, again, Kantian freedom remained an explicit issue in his theory of the social fact. And the import of that is the following: Durkheim had to somehow take the moral determinism out of the hands of the individuals in society, and give it to society. This would make the determinism of the social a fact for science to discover, and this would make freedom secondary to the primacy of the determinism of the social fact. Thus, although in the case of the social fact he was a determinist, he never quite renounced human freedom; after all, as the sociological Kantian that he was, freedom was a given. My point is that Durkheim was certainly not in a position to *deeply* understand the significant implications of the fact that his social realism was the metaphysical realism that science does indeed practice; thus, the point is that as a consequence of its rejection of positivism, it offers the concept of causal powers with which to properly understand the true standing of social realism with regard to the social fact and its reification as the theft of human freedom.

Had Durkheim been in a position to understand just that, this would therefore have put him on intimate terms with the possibility of recovering freedom from a sophisticated causal powers reading of the social fact that would
have shown him that social realism cannot mean reification. That particular
lack of sophisticated understanding of course cost his realism dearly: Durkheim
was never able to negotiate the belief in the relevance of the causal analysis
of social life with the idea of the causal efficacy of human freedom in the
practice of social life. The central reason is this: since, I am declaring, the
theory of the social fact was indeed the instantiation of the ultimate thesis, in
granting agency to the "social" the "individual" had to be, fundamentally, a
patient in the societal scheme of moral things. This is the metaphysical basis
for the above-mentioned subordination of freedom to the moral social fact.
This did not mean, certainly, that no degree of freedom was awarded the
"individual" for his or her good moral being, not at all, since that would
have been impossible for Durkheim; it did mean, however, that it had to be a
secondary feature of "individual" social being. In the chapter on Durkheim I
will spell this out in the following terms: *freedom is not rescued*, for Durkheim
was a naturalist and a scientific realist; yet, *freedom is clearly not recovered*,
in spite of his scientific realism. In actually forging his version of freedom
from his deep encounter with transcendental freedom, which he of course
rejected, he did so in resorting to Kant's own terms of "autonomy" and
"heteronomy." And this is why, in his return to Kant, Durkheim distorted
his theory of freedom: autonomy was lost in being subordinated and therefore assimilated to heteronomy. This metaphysical move is the machinery of
the metaphysical basis mentioned above. This allows us to appreciate the
problem of the Kantian theory of freedom for modern sociology, and most
assuredly, to realize that we have here one of the cardinal implications of
Giddens's Call. This of course is to say what has already been amply shown,
that the Call is a call for the solution to Heidegger's problem of reconciling
the two causalities of freedom and nature by transforming the noumenal
argument into the metaphysics of causal powers.

In Simmel's case, although Kantian freedom is an explicit concern, Arthur
Schopenhauer's answer to it, recent Simmelian scholarship informs us, has
particularly influenced the way it was handled. With the conception of
sociation that is the major theme of his seminal paper of 1908, *How is
Society Possible?*, Simmel's one attempt to negotiate the proper middle
ground between Durkheim's methodological holism and Weber's methodological individualism in forging a vision of society for a theory of sociology
reflects his vocabulary of "life" as against that of "form" (Simmel 1965: 337–56).
The deep point of that attempt is the domestication of Kant's theory of
freedom with the resource of Schopenhauer's metaphysics of the will – and
there's the rub. Any attempt to do so is certainly going to be muddled, and it
is – but what else could it be? How can Kantian freedom be adjusted to a
conception of will, and most particularly will as energy, that is grounded in a
deterministic metaphysics? We will discover that Simmel attempts to do so,

though certainly not systematically, and not, most fortunately, successfully, with a meandering allusion to something like a notion of causal powers. In his other attempt to negotiate the opposing terms of holism and individualism, he does so with his vocabulary of form. In that attempt, Simmel appeals to classical vitalism and something like the domestication of Hegel's social absolute with the idea of absolute life. We will see that, that bizarre fusion of vitalism and Hegelianism is another complete muddle.

Now with Weber, while Kant's theory of freedom is not intentionally explicit, yet, it is actually confronted in the forging of his interpretative sociology. Thus, Weber finds himself up against the Kantian problem of freedom in working out his position on human freedom in relation to causality and natural laws. The outcome of Weber's labors is truly surprising: he comes out with a view of human freedom that is actually struggling to realize an understanding of agency in relation to a causal powers reading of determinism; and he is doing all this as if it has nothing to do with Kant! That's the heart of what is puzzling about Weber's encounter with Kant and the structure/agency problem.

Kantian freedom and Schopenhauer's metaphysical determinism: Simmel's impossible marriage

In the conclusion to Rudolph H. Weingartner's renowned study of Simmel's work, *Experience and Culture* (1960), we have a tantalizing hint of the influence of Schopenhauer on Simmel with special regard to the usefulness of Kantian freedom for sociological theory.

> Moreover, while Simmel's emphasis on the *impulsive character of life* as process owes its inspiration to the Darwinian theory of evolution, when it is elaborated it comes more to resemble the development of Hegel's Idea. Nor does Simmel's emphasis on the impulsive character of life take him outside German idealism. His study of psychology leads him to see the significance of *impulse as the energy of life*. But when this idea is given a place in his philosophy, it comes to owe more to *Schopenhauer's conception of* will than to the work of psychologists. The *being* is that of Kant, the *becoming* that of Hegel, and the *impulse* that of Schopenhauer.
>
> (Weingartner 1960: 186, emphasis added)

We can use Weingartner's memorable closing line to formulate Simmel's problem with Kant's theory of freedom in this manner: *in accepting the idea that Kantian freedom constitutes the being of the human subject, Simmel's decision to construe the ground of the being of that freedom to be Schopenhauer's will as energy, unfortunately sets up a theoretical self-contradiction.* Under the auspices of the nineteenth-century revolt of mechanism against vitalism, and especially its most important realization in the social sciences, Freudian psychoanalysis, we have seen that, in the reduction of *will to energy,* the freedom of the former is contradicted by the determinism of the latter. In Simmel's study of *Schopenhauer and Nietzsche* (1991 [1907]) examine these comments on the former's metaphysics of the will with my idea of Simmel's problem in mind.

> For Schopenhauer the *will is like a fuel that energizes the most different kinds of machines.* Will lives only in singular acts, but *the causes producing singular acts do not explain what makes them acts of will.* Schopenhauer's whole approach seems to express a very deep and general, though dark, feeling – the same feeling that confers infinity to us and allows us to experience our ego as something infinite, despite the fact that life reveals itself only in finite and singular contents. ... *The reservoir of energy that facilitates the moments of the soul's life and the contents of that life are superior to any culmination in a single act of will: the creative totality of the soul is not exhausted in such an act* ... Thus *we experience ourselves* always as more than we are, *as something transcending given reality* and its continuous repetition of form through changing content. There crystallizes in consciousness the judgment that as finite we are more than finite, that *in every motion that is singular ... something infinite in itself gives voice to itself just by failing to give voice.* It is an aspect of this directive mood that Schopenhauer finds *a general act of will in every act of will that is singular on account of its separate content.* ... *Will is infinity within us,* because we sense that every finite act leaves part of the equation unsolved.
>
> (Simmel 1991: 25–26, emphasis provided)

> We must keep the above in mind lest Schopenhauer's metaphysic become a myth, a fantastic anthropomorphism. He has encouraged such mystification by claiming without qualification: *"The will is the thing-in-itself."*
>
> (Simmel Ibid: 24, emphasis provided)

We can extract from this magnificent reading of Schopenhauer Simmel's version of Schopenhauer's central proposition for his, Simmel's, purposes: *the particular will of the subject is the embodied causal energy that is grounded in the general will.* Note the difference between Schopenhauer and Simmel that is displayed in the proposition. The former, general will (the fuel of nature's various machines) is the reality behind the appearance of particular will; the latter, the free will of the subject is embodied in causal energy (the fuel of nature's human machine). The crucial fact revealed here is that Simmel's predominate response to the theory of noumenal freedom is that of treating the causal character of *freedom* in terms of *energy* rather than *agency.* I say predominate response, and thus not his only response, because Simmel, as we will see, does indeed marginally refer to human freedom in terms of some kind of an *idea* of causal power; what he does not do, of course, is to regard human freedom according to the *theory* of causal powers, for no such theory had yet been articulated in the philosophy of science. Hence, Simmel's response (predominate and marginal) to Kant's noumenal theory of freedom does not, I think, indicate that he understood it to be a *problem*, but rather that it was understood instead to be *troublesome* (this will all be spelled out later). My exemplary example of understanding the noumenal theory as a *problem* is Heidegger's impressive thesis: extra-temporality is the key issue of noumenal freedom and the unification of the two causalities is the problem. Now, from the fact that Simmel has taken Schopenhauer's theory of the will seriously in response to Kant's troublesome theory of freedom, and therefore was led to view freedom as energy and not agency, the lesson learned from Holt's similar treatment in his discussion of Freud is absolutely relevant. I have no other alternative then but to dismiss Simmel's granting the concept of the will a philosophical legitimacy. My reason is that the legitimacy is given, while, at the same time, admitting that Schopenhauer's will is of no possible relevance to scientific explanation, and, by implication, that that has no bearing whatsoever on the intelligibility and hence the possible relevance of such a conception to social science theory (not just sociological theory) (Simmel Ibid: 42).

With regard to this criticism, examine Simmel's above statement that Schopenhauer's thesis is that there is "a general act of will in every act of will that is singular," in relationship to Simmel's other statement that Schopenhauer means by this that "Will lives only in singular acts, but the causes producing singular acts do not explain what makes them acts of will." This is a paradox that admits of no possible resolution in logic or theory; thus, in a nutshell, it reveals why, today, for us, Schopenhauer's concept of will can have no possible relevance to scientific realist explanation generally, and thus, specifically, can have no possible relevance to the problem of the recovery of agency from a realist understanding of the deterministic structures of the natural and human worlds. Furthermore, when, in this context, Simmel can say, in discussing Schopenhauer, "Thus, the demotion of the rational character of life in favor of its character as *being or power* is based on the will," he makes matters absolutely worse (Simmel Ibid: 30, emphasis provided). For, again, from the standpoint of scientific realism, there can be no theoretical purchase granted to Schopenhauer's claim that the will references a "being of power" that has nothing to do with causal power, and yet is supposed to explain "what makes them [human acts] acts of will." Now, the upshot of this critique of Schopenhauer is not good news for Simmel's intention to use Schopenhauer's concept of will to somehow promote the acceptance of human freedom for sociology. With such a proposition as the one given above for this purpose, namely, that the particular will of the subject is the embodied causal energy that is grounded in the general will, Simmel is in a hopeless theoretical situation. The very idea is simply hopeless.

With the reason for my dismissal in mind, look now at the relationship between Schopenhauer's metaphysics of the will and Heidegger's metaphysics of being for a moment, in order to further appreciate this point: the two answers to Kant's theory of freedom that we have here are strikingly similar. In this regard, consider that Schopenhauer's answer fails for the same reason that Heidegger's fails: while for both the concept of the will and the concept of being are deliberately divorced from science, yet, they are believed to be relevant and significant answers to Kant's theory of freedom. Given my above critique, from the standpoint of the recovery of agency, not only must I insist that the problem of Kant's theory is best understood as the problem of unifying the causality of freedom and the causality of nature, but I also have to insist that Schopenhauer's will as his answer to the problem of Kantian freedom is best understood in the same way. However, if it is reasonable to conclude, as I have earlier, that a (causal) powers reading of the problem of unifying the two causalities is more fruitful than a reading from the perspective of Heidegger's concept of being, I will then argue that a similar powers reading is also superior to a reading of that problem than from the standpoint of Schopenhauer's concept of the will. And now that we find Simmel revealing the idea that Schopenhauer's will is a being of power, my argument is of course even stronger. My reason is this: the failed conception of will as a power can only be redeemed by the realist version of power as causal. And indeed we know quite well from Schopenhauer's "Critique of the Kantian Philosophy" in conjunction with the "Prize Essay On the Freedom of the Will," that the powers treatment of causation suggested there is not the realist version of power as causal (discussed further in this chapter).

In this regard, Giddens, for example, would never have been able to Call for a concept of "agent causality" if it had to be derived from Schopenhauer's powers reading of causation: agency would have again been lost to a reinstatement of the very strict version of mechanistic determinism that Giddens intends to get away from. That, to me, is the definitive blow to the philosophical integrity of Schopenhauer's theory of the will. Now this is directly relevant to Simmel's use of Schopenhauer's concept of will to yield the above proposition that the particular will of all subjects is embodied causal energy that is grounded in the general will. For, what can be the fate of Simmel's domestication of Kant's theory of freedom via the marriage of Schopenhauer's will and nineteenth-century vitalism for the sociology he is forging? "How is Society Possible" with regard to such a marriage? Precisely put, on the one hand, Simmel embraces the idea that Kantian freedom is somehow the embodiment of causal energy, and, on the other, Simmel seemingly embraces the idea that freedom is grounded in Schopenhauer's will that is a "being of power" that is not causal. *How is freedom efficacious in the world of human acts of will if its "agent causality" does not explain that efficaciousness, but then the agentless and hence acausal general will that grounds it is supposed to explain it?* How can this impossible theory of freedom account for Simmel's conviction that he has indeed shown how society is possible by the domestication of Kantian freedom for a sociological theory of society? For Simmel, his theory is that what makes society possible, is sociation; his strategy is to locate freedom in the constitution of sociation.

And the theme of the possibility is the unity of Simmel's three sociological a priori's: individuals together are a social force by virtue of the fact that the self-determination of each of them becomes the mutual determination of each other as well. How is *that* possible?

How is sociation possible?

As we enter Simmel's "How is Society Possible," in which Kantian, Hegelian, and Schopenhauerian influences are variously indicated, it is important to keep in mind two facts: Simmel's *Schopenhauer and Nietzsche* came out in 1907; and in 1904 his book on Kant appeared on the scene. The dominate import of these facts is that, given Hegelian social philosophy, Kant's transcendental philosophy of freedom is especially Simmel's ground which orients him to the figures of Schopenhauer and Nietzsche. And it is specifically that triadic set of philosophical perspectives that systematically informs this little masterpiece in the philosophy of social science.

> The processes of consciousness which formulate sociation [Simmel's contribution] ... presuppose something fundamental which finds expression in practice although we are not aware of it in its abstractness. The presupposition is that individuality finds its place in *the structure of generality*, and furthermore, that in spite of the unpredictable character of individuality, *this structure is laid out, as it were, for individuality and its functions* [Hegelian influence]. The nexus by which each social element (each individual) is interwoven with the life and activities of every other, and by which *the external framework of society is produced*, is a *causal* one (phenomenal realm). But it is transformed into a *teleological* nexus as soon as it is considered from the perspective of the elements that carry and produce it – individuals [noumenal realm]. For they *feel* themselves to be *egos* whose behavior grows out of *autonomous, self-determined* personalities [Kant's ego as autonomous enriched by Schopenhauer's will as feeling?]. The objective totality yields to the individuals that confront it from without, as it were; it offers a place to their subjectively determined life-processes, which thereby, in their very individuality, become necessary links in the life of the whole. It is this dual nexus which supplies the individual consciousness with a fundamental [a priori synthetic] category and thus transforms it into a social element [sociation]. ... The sociological inquiry is directed toward abstracting from the complex phenomenon called social life that which is *purely society*, that is, sociation. It eliminates from the purity of this concept everything which does not constitute *society as a unique and autonomous form of existence* [Hegelian influence], although it can be realized only historically in society [Simmel's contribution: sociation under the a priori category of time].
>
> (Simmel 1965: 355–56, 351, emphasis provided)

Setting Hegel's and Schopenhauer's influences aside, for the moment, it is shown here in this quote that the standard Kantian dualistic schema of the phenomenal realm – causal nexus – and the noumenal realm – teleological nexus – frames the 1908 paper. Let us first consult another paper in *The Sociology of Georg Simmel* to get from Simmel the cardinal premise that informs the theoretical utilization of Kantian freedom.

> Freedom is not *solipsistic existence but sociological action*. It is not a condition limited to the *single individual* but *a relationship*, even though it is a relationship from the standpoint of the individual.
>
> (Simmel 1964: 121, emphasis provided)

We can now see in this following comment how Simmel treats his construal of Kantian will in relation to Schopenhauer's will in his theory of sociation.

> A society is, therefore, a structure which consists of beings who stand *inside and outside* of it, at the *same time*. This fact. ... [points to] the *feeling* of being *independent and separate* from all these [societal] *entanglements and relationships*, a feeling that is designated by the *logically uncertain concept "freedom."*
>
> (Simmel 1965 [1908]: 347–48, emphasis provided)

Kant's theory of freedom is being domesticated by its conversion into a structural feature of social interaction. Now, it seems to me, that Simmel's strategy of converting the transcendental idea of freedom into a sociological a priori certainly permits the following interpretation. Simmel never really understood that the key specifications of Kant's theory of freedom that *one* and the *same* subject participates *simultaneously* in the noumenal *and* phenomenal realms, and that participating in the noumenal realm of extra-temporality, or atemporality, is therefore a participation in freedom, was a *discovery of a problem, rather than the presentation of a solution.* To be sure, since, with few exceptions, the entire history of the structure and agency problem is a testimony to the fact of that failed understanding, Simmel is not alone in this. It is instructive in this regard to think about Schopenhauer's ultimate conclusion that from Kant's noumenal theory of freedom *"arises a delusion of the individual's unconditioned freedom* (discussed later more fully)." In this case of Schopenhauer on Kant's two specifications ("unconditioned freedom"), we have an example of the complete failure to understand that they amount to the discovery of a problem, and not, as he is declaring, the discovery of psychological pathology ("arises a delusion"). I am encouraged to think that Schopenhauer's standpoint is the deep reason why Simmel never understood the genuine theoretical status of Kant's theory of freedom. The reason being that the acceptance of Schopenhauer's theory that the non-rationality of the general will (blind forces of nature) is the reality behind the appearance of the rationality of human particular will, seems to have encouraged Simmel to argue in *Schopenhauer and Nietzsche* that, for instance, philosophical positions were ultimately not rational choices, but issuances of temperament (discussed later). Now, while it is reasonable to believe that Simmel, in proposing that freedom is located in the act of "standing outside of societal structure," is thus indexing Kant's noumenal realm and its twin specifications, it is, thus far, certainly arguable. However, in *Schopenhauer and Nietzsche*, we catch Simmel in fact actually repeating Kant's conception of noumenal freedom by way of an example of his own (Simmel 1991: 36). As he begins a critical examination of Schopenhauer's thesis of the metaphysical unity of all things by virtue of their grounding in the general will, he is exploring Kant's concept of the transcendental ego in relation to Schopenhauer's concept of the transcendent will.

> Our soul has a *mysterious potency*, readily observed, to combine into one unified idea a plurality of elements that come to mind, one after the other. The process of conceiving the sentence, "Life is pain," depends *neither on space nor time nor any of the applications of a principle of causality*, but is rather *a process of the soul* by which different elements are brought into a form containing *no before and no after*.
>
> But even *if the constituent elements are transformed, the result is not merely an absolute and transcendental unity*: a strangely composed multiplicity remains as an irreducible residue. The incomparable construct of the human sentence combines multiplicity and unity in such a *miraculous way* that the multiplicity of its elements survives the *termination of the space-time configuration*; and *the unity, which is palpably alive, is independent of all opposition and all relativity*, the latter condition which *Schopenhauer finds only in the realm of the transcendent*.
>
> (Simmel 1991: 36)

First, Simmel is restating Kant's noumenal argument for freedom: as a gestalt unit, the "sentence," "Life is pain," is a conception that is "an absolute and transcendental unity" that "depends *neither on space nor time nor any of the applications of a principle of causality.*" Second, he is enriching Kant's original argument with Schopenhauer's metaphysical contribution: the "sentence" is also "[a] unity, which is palpably *alive*, [and] is *independent* of all opposition and all relativity (emphasis provided)." In bending over backwards to make a place for transcendence in relation to the transcendental act of freedom, the long standing problem that I have been discussing throughout this book of conflating "transcendental" with "transcendence" concerning Kant's theory of freedom, is never raised by Simmel. The critical point of the category, "transcendental," was to provide the safe haven of imaginative space for such dimensions of the human subject in order to avoid what would otherwise be taken as evidence of a transcendent other-worldly realm. Therefore, in the case of Schopenhauer's use of the term "transcendence," if the religious other-worldly ontology is not the reference, then what other ontology is left? The reality of the general will manifested in the appearance of particular wills is certainly not the world of science. In which case, it seems clear to me, we have lurking here in the background to all this the traditional issue of the mistaken conflation of science with positivism. Since the general will is a secular metaphysic that declares the reality of "being" or "power" against the metaphysic of empirical realism, Schopenhauer had no available metaphysical space other than that provided by the traditional category of "transcendence" to so locate it. This move of Schopenhauer's, though quite understandable but yet regrettable, in view of a proper understanding of the realist metaphysics of science, is no longer required. Both Schopenhauer and Heidegger simply lacked that proper understanding.

I must now examine what appears to be Simmel's own contribution to Kant's theory of freedom that is referred to as *metaphysical individualism*, or *absolute individualism* (Weinstein and Weinstein 1991: xlv–xlix, then Simmel 1991: 38–39). This contribution is the context that surrounds the above quote just discussed.

> *Metaphysical individuality*, however, is totally different from and even opposed in its essence to *phenomenal individuality*. In contrast to the world of experience, in which each unit [individual] is an expression of its complementary relation with other essences, metaphysical individuality, which is beyond empirical imagination, must be conceived of in terms of absolute units. The life and life-forms of each unit express its inner-most essence, and the elements of each unit are internally related to the whole. Whereas in the world of experience everything is or is such as it is only because of the other units, *in absolute individuality there is an ultimate element of being that is, perhaps, comparable to the feeling of freedom and being-for-itself of a single soul. Absolute individuality is under no external or relational necessity.* ... its essence is not based on other things but only its innermost and radically independent facticity.
>
> (Simmel Ibid: 38, emphasis provided)

How has Simmel given us something other than a restatement of Kant's noumenal theory of freedom? What is the metaphysical status of "the ultimate element of being?" What is the substantive difference between the "feeling of freedom and being-for-itself of a single soul" and the noumenal feature of extra-temporality or atemporality as the condition of freedom of a single mind? First of all and foremost, noumenal freedom is now considered to be a "mysterious potency." Pistorius singled out as the issue of his absolute befuddlement the "mysterious" simultaneous participation in Kant's two realms; the deeper befuddlement was and is the "mysterious" participation in the other-worldly realm that is the point of the traditional charge that the individual's freedom is free will in disguise. What is not confronted by Simmel in any clear and systematic way is the metaphysical status of the "potency" of freedom that is now highlighted as something "mysterious," better, even "miraculous." Hence, from Simmel's quote at issue I can now conclude what I only asserted earlier in the discussion, that Simmel was not in the position to understand that the conception of noumenal freedom is the discovery of a problem. In other words, it is not "problematic," that is a problem in the traditional sense that Kant's transcendentalism is a new word for transcendence; and that makes the theory suspect. Remember, Simmel is historically located between the phenomenological tradition of Dilthey and then Husserl, and the yet to come ontological tradition of Heidegger. Thus, he has only phenomenology as the alternative site to locate freedom; while Heidegger's problem of the two causalities and his solution to it with the idea of Being has not yet arrived, of course. But, since he accepts as a mystery that the "potency" of Kantian freedom is "a feeling of freedom" that is "beyond empirical imagination" in being an "innermost essence," neither Dilthey's nor Husserl's phenomenology of lived experience is suitable. And his only objection, not quite a criticism, is in the form of a qualification: leaving Kant's theory of freedom as a "mysterious potency" that is only transcendental and not transcendent *untouched*, he adds Schopenhauer's theory of a deterministic will whose generality is a unity that is transcendent and so more than transcendental. In other words, the mystery of the potency is set aside in fact, and the potency itself is translated into impulse or energy. Furthermore, despite this acceptance of Kantian freedom along with that translation, Simmel has not, I do think, precisely hit on the idea of trans-forming Pistorius's complaint into the *problem* of unifying the two causal-ities. For, as I have already declared, Simmel is committed to an impossible theory of freedom: the absurd paradox of marrying the transcendental will of Kantian theory and the transcendent will of Schopenhauerian theory. That is obviously in stark contrast to Heidegger's two causalities: the latter permits the possibility of unification, the former rules it out. This would suggest that a Heideggerian conception of a problem could not have been grasped by Simmel, on his own, as an independent insight. But, even supposing, for the sake of argument, that it was, the conception would have been rejected in light of that marriage. This leaves open the suggestion that, since Simmel does see mysterious *freedom* in terms of causal *energy*, rather than causal *agency*, some sense of a solution to some kind of a problem was intuitively picked up on. But what that "problem" could be, is forever unclear with Simmel on this matter. *He has a solution – energy – in search, or in need, of a problem.*

In view of this above possibility of an intuitive sense of a solution without any sense of its problem concerning the idea of freedom as causal energy, it should not be *entirely* astonishing to note that, in the above quote presenting freedom as a sociological a priori, there is a faint *glimmer of trouble* hinted at in the characterization of Kantian freedom as a "logically *uncertain* con-cept." Weingartner's identification of the influences of Kant – being – and Schopenhauer – will – seems to imply that Simmel settled for

Schopenhauer's conception of the will as energy as his way of coming to metaphysical grips with Kant's troublesome theory of freedom. However, I do not think that's quite right. Thus, to the contrary, my argument, instead, gives us a significantly different view. The reason for that has been already declared: Schopenhauer's determinism is the heart of Simmel's problem of locating freedom at the site of sociation. The determinism of Schopenhauer's theory of will, then, now, must be seen directly for ourselves, for, Simmel is never exactly and systematically clear about Schopenhauer's determinism in his discussion of his philosophy, and particularly in its relation to his. And I, as yet, have not found that issue of determinism discussed by Weingartner, the Weinsteins, or by Levine, either.

On this issue of determinism, Schopenhauer's renowned "Criticism of the Kantian Philosophy" is without doubt the perfect place to go for our critical purposes.

It is also from this immediate knowledge of one's own will that in human consciousness the concept of *freedom* arises; for certainly the *will as world-creating, as the thing-in-itself, is free* from the principle of sufficient freedom, and thus from all necessity, and hence is completely independent, free, *and indeed almighty. Yet actually this holds good only of the will in itself, not of its phenomena, not of the individuals, who, just through the will itself, are unalterably determined as to its phenomena in time.* But in the ordinary consciousness not clarified by philosophy, *the will is at once confused with its phenomenon, and what belongs only to the will is attributed to the phenomenon. In this way arises the delusion of the individual's unconditioned freedom.* Precisely on this account, Spinoza rightly says that even the projected stone would believe, if it had consciousness, that it was flying of its own free will. For the in-it-self even of the stone is certainly the one and only free will; but, as in all its phenomena, so here also where it appears as stone, it is already fully determined. ... By *failing* to recognize and overlooking this immediate origin of the concept of freedom in every human consciousness, *Kant now places the origin of that concept in a very subtle speculation. Thus* through this speculation, *the unconditioned*, to which our reason must always tend, *leads to the hypostasizing of the concept of freedom*, and the practical concept of freedom is supposed to be based first of all on this transcendent Idea of freedom. ... [Hence] *the transcendental freedom of the will ... is by no means the unconditioned causality of a cause ... because a cause must be essentially phenomenon, not something toto genere different lying beyond every phenomenon. ... Therefore* in spite of all transcendental freedom (i.e. independence of the will-in-itself of the laws of the connexion of its phenomenon), *no person has the capacity of himself to begin a series of actions*, a thing which, on the contrary, was asserted by the thesis. *Therefore, freedom also has no causality, for only the will is free, and it lies outside nature or the phenomenon. The*

> *phenomenon is only the objectification of the will, and does not stand to it*
> *as a relation of causality.*
> (Schopenhauer 1969 [1819]: 503–4, 506–7, emphasis provided)

Schopenhauer is absolutely clear on the matter of Kant's theory of freedom: it is a categorical failure in three specific ways.

- There is only the phenomenal realm: without the *unconditioned causality of a cause* there can be no problem of unifying the two causalities.
- The noumenal theory of the unconditioned causality of a cause is a thoroughly misleading piece of *subtle speculation:* the theory is *the hypostasizing of the concept of freedom.*
- From the hypostasizing of the concept of freedom there *arises the delusion of the individual's unconditioned freedom: the will as world-creating, as the thing-in-itself, is free. … Not … the individuals, who, just through the will itself, are unalterably determined as to its phenomena in time.*

If Weingartner is correct, so that sociational freedom as the transformation of Kantian will into the embodied causal energy of Schopenhauer's will *is* Simmel's theory, then, it *is* an impossible one. The upshot is final: his attempt to save freedom from the threat of determinism has failed.

And, yet, isn't there something odd, and hence telling, about the actual fact that, nevertheless, Simmel does *not* seem to write as if his theory of freedom is impossible? After all, obviously, he never says that "the *feeling* of being *independent and separate*" is a "logically [*impossible*] concept [of] freedom." For, given what he does say, its complementary meaning is that the feeling of freedom is certainly "logically possible, but nevertheless, there is something about it that is still logically uncertain." And, ontologically speaking, must it not be the case that the uncertainty is simply the fact that freedom is a "mysterious potency"? Perhaps, but it is necessary to be precise in a way that is relevant to the purpose here of recovering human agency: *since the potency of freedom is a mystery, yet as a power, what is the mystery of the power that grounds that potency?* Remember, in bringing out the idea that Schopenhauer's "being" is a "power," in an earlier quote we've seen that Simmel does not do so under the canopy of the determinism of the general will.

> The reservoir of *energy that facilitates the moments of the soul's life* and the contents of that life are superior to any culmination in a single act of will: *the creative totality of the soul is not exhausted in such an act.*

Hence, *ontologically,* what is the connection between, freedom as a *power,* and, freedom as *energy*? The implication of the above quote is evident: "*the creative totality of the soul*" is the energy of Kantian spontaneity. In short, *power is the energy of agency.* In sharp contrast to this, Freud's deterministic view of Kant led him to reduce agency to energy and thus, in effect, to suggest the reductionist idea that *power is the agency of energy.* The critical difference is this: the Kant/Simmel position emphasizes *agency not energy,* and hence the agency of powerful particulars, the Kant/Freud position emphasizes *energy not agency,* and thus particulars as the vehicle of power whose energy referent lies at level lower than the person. Now this is an implication, but it has not been clear in Simmelian scholarship that Simmel is actually thinking that way. Indeed, to my knowledge, this question, and certainly this answer, are not to be found anywhere in the scholarship of Weingartner, the Weinsteins, nor in that of Levine. The answer to one side, I have not seen in any of their discussions of Simmel concerning the problem of freedom and sociation, or freedom and methodological/absolute individuality, the linking up of the two properties of *power and energy.* And certainly never apart from the context of Schopenhauer's metaphysics of the will. I want now to examine the specification of the theme of domesticating mysterious potency *and* the will in sociation, apart from the determinism, in terms of the connection between energy and power.

Sociation: potency of the will and energy and power

To get started on the above examination, I want to pick up on the phrase, "the feeling of embodied energy," that I have used in my discussion of Simmel and Schopenhauer on the problem of domesticating freedom. In this regard, Simmel himself approvingly uses the phrase, "this feeling of existence," in order to capture Schopenhauer's key principle that "we feel in every singular act of our soul an energy which bears this act but also surpasses it"; and further, that the "feeling of existence" as energy is also referred to by Simmel as a "moving force" (Simmel Ibid: 27, 28). Thus, in view of the fact that my line, "the feeling of embodied energy," and Simmel's, "the feeling of existence [as a] moving force," are substantially identical, here we have one piece of evidence that, for Simmel, *the feeling of the moving force of existential energy is the feeling of agency.* How then does Simmel's exploration of the idea of human freedom avoid Freud's destiny that was realized in the work of Holt? In this comment from the 1908 paper at issue, in effect, Simmel speaks to such a question.

> *Things in nature are further apart than individuals are.* In the *spatial* world, each element occupies a place it *cannot share* with any other. Here, there is *nothing analogous to human unity,* which is grounded in understanding, love, or common work. On the other hand, *spatial elements fuse in the observer's consciousness into a unity that is not attained by the assemblage of individuals.* For here, the objects of the synthesis are *independent beings, psychic centers, personal units.* They therefore *resist* the absolute fusion (in the observer's mind) to which, by contrast, the "self-lessness" of inanimate things must yield. [This is why] society, by

contrast, is the objective unit *which needs no outside observer* ... This image of general society [hence] ... can be grasped only through an analysis of the *creativity and experience* of the component individuals [as sociation].

(Simmel 1964: 339)

Keeping in mind the fact that, four years before "How is Society Possible" the Kant book was published, anyone who knows Kant's metaphysics of nature that is presented in the two works that I have already discussed in earlier chapters, can instantly recognize the more than possible influence of Kant's realist theory of matter (attraction and repulsion as the basis for the individuation and assemblage of things) throughout this above quote. The point here, of course, is to indicate that there can be no serious doubt that Simmel was determined not to lose Kantian will in Schopenhauer's will, while intending to take both very seriously in the theory of sociation. And so, certainly, any such doubt cannot be relevant when *Simmel's central interest in saving individuality from its dissolution in the holistic tendencies of social forms can certainly be acknowledged as his version of the problem of structure and agency* (Weinstein and Weinstein Ibid in Simmel: xlix–lii). Furthermore, note that what Simmel was calling for in the use of Hegel was a brand of "sociological inquiry" that

eliminates from the purity of this concept everything which does not constitute society as a unique and autonomous form of existence [Hegelian influence], although it can be realized only historically in society.

(Simmel Ibid: 355–56, 351, emphasis provided)

To be quite sure, this looks dangerously like a Simmelian version of the Durkheimian social fact, but, it would, I think, be quite wrong to actually think that. For, in his concept of society as a unique and autonomous form of existence Simmel is reaching for a higher level of human freedom called "The Turning." This is Simmel's turn away from biology to culture. Weingartner presents this concept quite well.

The *propelling impulses* still come from *life* which is their *only* source. But the *direction* is changed, they are sublimated. "In general we see in order to live; the artist lives in order to see" and "goes on to create art." "At first men know in order to live; but then there are men who live in order to know." And their lives are at the service of science. Similarly in the moral sphere ... And so it happens with all the different forms. With the turning toward free action, the process of differentiation of subject and object is in principle completed. The individual sees himself as a subject, surrounded by realms of formed contents [e.g. art, science, religion] which have in the full sense become the objects of his activity. His

actions are not merely directed toward these objects, but they are per-
formed for the sake of these objects.

(Weingartner 1960: 55, emphasis provided)

As Simmel is trying to preserve human freedom in his Hegelian version of
the social fact, not Durkheim's, it is more than reasonable to expect to find
that he was as well doing so for Kantian freedom in reference to Schopenhauer's fatally flawed vitalism. The critical line in the above quote that
justifies this expectation is the first one: freedom as *"propelling impulses still
come from life which is their only source."* Elsewhere Weingartner rounds out
Simmel's notion of freedom that is directly relevant here.

In the free. ... the *impulses* to action, the *causal energy* which propels us
to do anything whatever and toward whatever end have their sources in
the process of life.

(Weingartner Ibid: 51, emphasis provided)

That Weingartner chose as the proper contrast to the word "compelling,"
not the word "impelling" but instead, the word, "propelling" is absolutely
revealing. Note that "causal energy" then must be subordinated to the idea
of its causal character as that "which propels us to do." Though quite
enough for that time, Weingartner, however, does nothing else to inform us
of the deeper import of that choice and its implication of subordinating
causal energy to causal propulsion, for any further understanding of Simmel's theoretical ambitions. In other words, the ambition of getting at a
robust theory of sociation: the social interaction of *Kantian actors* who, as
individuals, are both *inside and outside* of the social life they *own*, and
that is because they originally *produce* it. If, in Simmel's thinking, there is an
important connection between energy and power that is in the direction of
realizing that the feeling of the moving force of existential energy is the
feeling of agency, the idea that life is the source of impulses that, technically
speaking, are "propulsive" and not "impulsive" is a promising insight to
pursue. The implication that the *metaphysical point of energy is the power of
agency, not the power of energy, that is that energy is the agent*, certainly
looks more like a fact of the matter than an implication. After all, the
reading of causal energy as causal propulsion makes that point clear. In
other words, Weingartner got it right, but not right enough. Although the
above discussion shows that Weingartner had the necessary ideas in his
hands, yet he never makes absolutely clear the point just made above: *the
metaphysical point of power is agency not energy.* Not to make that clear, in
that case, risks the Freudian consequence that agency winds up being
contradicted by the determinism of energy. After all, Freud's example *was*
the sign of the times; vitalism was doomed, it was only a matter of time.
Writing in *1985* on "How Biology Differs from the Physical Sciences," Ernst
Mayr commented that, "Among biologists vitalism has been dead for some

forty or fifty years" (Mayr 1985: 46). Simmel died in 1918, that time was short.

On the real a priori: energy or agency?

To pursue this promise, let me begin with an important insight of the Weinsteins. It has to do with getting hold of the point, according to them, of the *overall character* of Simmel's development from the early period (1890s–1900) where he focused on the prospect of a *positive moral science*, to the *skeptical Humanism* of his middle period (1900–1910), and then to the final period centered as it was in a *classical philosophy of life* (1910–1918) (Weinstein and Weinstein 1991: xvii).

> The unity of Simmel's thought proceeds not from a single vision [as Weingartner maintains] but from a project, his quest to *reground form in a real a priori*. That search ended in a tragic vitalism based on intuition.
>
> (Weinstein and Weinstein Ibid: xvi, emphasis provided)

Since the only source of the *"propelling impulses"* of human freedom come from life, Simmel is consequently looking for an understanding of that kind of a priori that will provide the grounding that will do justice to the special reality of the *"propelling* character of impulse." And, the reality of "propulsion" and not the reality of "impulsion," is to be more accurately conceived of as *agency, not impulse as energy.* The key to doing so is this idea: to find a real a priori that will give us the grounding site for freedom, and, therein the basis for blocking off the reification of form, yet, without eliminating form. We should notice, right now, the intimate connection of Simmel's key idea with Giddens's idea of structuration: to get hold of real causation for a conception of human agency in order to block the reification of structure without losing structure. Now think about *this* assertion of Simmel's that the a priori "is an objective *power*, an operative *reality* within us" (Weingartner 1960: 58). If we amend this marvelous declaration by modifying the ending to read, " within *and* between us," clearly, a major breakthrough has taken place. One that takes Simmel toward realizing his key idea of finding the "real a priori" he was in search of. For, note carefully, the "objective power" of the a priori, in my amendment, locates that power at the site of the very structure of sociation! That the implication that "power is the agency of energy" (and not Freud's the "energy of agency") is not only looking good as the fact of the matter, it *is* the fact of the matter, I now take to be a fait accompli. It is at this juncture that it is necessary to pause for a moment to point out the following observation concerning Simmel's key idea and its connection to sociation in reference to Deena and Michael Weinstein's dynamic portrait of his life's work.

The Weinsteins and Varela: conflict of interpretations

From the Weinsteins' portrait, given the above suggestion of locating power at the site of sociation, we uncover an important conflict of two interpretations, mine and theirs. It is in regard to the challenge of reading *Simmel's theory of sociation and freedom in relationship to his attempt to transcend the dualism of form and life* that plagued him during the middle and late periods of his work. To help us in this, I now want to once more present the idea of a parallel of Simmel and Giddens: Giddens too is trying to understand how *a theory of structuration and freedom can transcend the dualism of structure and agency.* Indeed, stepping back and looking at Simmel's dualism in the context of the history of the structure/agency problem, it makes perfect sense to now say that that dualism of *form and life* is Simmel's terminological contribution to the development of that problem at the time. In other words, *from Simmel, through Weber and Parsons, to Giddens, sociation has graduated into structuration, and freedom has been refined to the problem of agency as we have it in Giddens' Call.* In the following discussion I want to argue that Simmel's aim can be better realized if we assimilate his theoretical situation to that of Giddens's in the manner I have just illustrated. And the critical reason that I think does the trick, is the connection between Simmel's search for the real a priori and his allusion to powers. We will discover that Simmel was meandering toward the very idea of *causal* powers, and just about hits it on the head; and clearly without explicitly knowing where he was going, or knowing what indeed he had walked in on. In the case of Giddens, several decades later, he Calls, in effect, for Simmel's search to be fully conscious and systematically directed by the relevant auspices of the philosophy of science rather than the philosophy of vitalism.

Holism/individualism or structure/agency? Alternative interpretations

The Weinsteins do not recognize the breakthrough that I have associated with Simmel's work, nor its intimate relationship to Giddens's Call, and that is because they understandably restrict themselves to laying out in rich detail the trajectory of Simmel's three periods and *their* reading of its import. But now, with the breakthrough and its suggested relationship to Giddens in mind, we are properly prepared for the Weinsteins to speak for themselves.

> In the major production of his late period, *Lebensansschauung,* Simmel returns to the duality posed by nineteenth-century philosophy of life. But now he has his own idea of what he calls *"absolute life,"* which had a *"unified character"* and is metaphysically *prior* to personal existence, to the *individual.* From this vantage point Simmel is able to accomplish what he could not do in *Schopenhauer and Nietzsche,* that is, to synthesize the opposing positions. Simmel argues that "Schopenhauer's [general] will to life and Nietzsche's [individual] will to power doubtless lie in

the direction of concrete fulfillment of his own idea of life ... " Thus, Simmel makes the distinction between *holism and individualism* – a distinction he had held to be irreconcilable in his middle period – relative to a *commanding unity*: "what. ... constitutes life, is the absolute unity of both. ... " Simmel attempts to achieve a genuine synthesis through a notion of absolute life ... [which] is able to comprehend and unify the opposites of *flux and fixed, continuity and individuality,* because it is defined as a *self-transcendent process,* in the two senses that it perpetually *generates* more of itself (it is "more life") and *objectifies itself into crystallized forms or individuals* (it is "more than life"). Life, then, is a broken unity, but *somehow still a unit.*

> (Weinstein and Weinstein in Simmel Ibid: xlix–l,
> emphasis also provided)

The Weinstein's unequivocally judge this resolution of the form/life dualism into the elements of "holism and individualism," both of which are originally rooted in an "absolute life" that generates "forms [and] individuals," to merely be a "speculative possibility" (Weinstein and Weinstein Ibid: l). And one whose only possibility is speculation that is a sterile redundancy.

> His purely speculative unity, though psychologically well grounded in the inward grasp of individual lived experience, is an absurd absolute, for it continually precipitates meanings and destroys them without even the remediation of an evolutionary development. Yet, to transform the self-transcendence of personal existence into a symbol of being itself is not merely dogmatic, it is ethically gratuitous. It gives us nothing more than ourselves, though on a grand scale.
>
> (Weinstein and Weinstein in Simmel Ibid: li)

But more, much more than that turns out to be the upshot of their assessment. In their final criticism they interestingly end with Simmel's relationship to Schopenhauer. What is particularly interesting about this has to do with my point that Simmel's relationship to Schopenhauer concerns the protection of Kantian freedom from the threat of the latter's theory of general will. In the following quote we should pay strict attention to Weinsteins' failure to explicitly highlight what Freud well understood with the id-centered conception of the unconscious, the exceptionless determinism of the general will. And I say this for a most special reason: Simmel does indeed make it very clear that as a philosopher of classical vitalism that kind of determinism is to be renounced. In his celebrated essay, "The Conflict in Modern Culture," he insists that the very idea of a "closed system" is an anathema. Simmel continues, thus:

> This is a view against which life ... must defend itself. The philosophy that exalts and glorifies life insists firmly on two things. On the one hand it rejects *mechanics* as a universal principle. ... On the other hand it

rejects the claim of *ideas* [as laws] to a metaphysical *independence and primacy* [reification]. Life does not wish to be *dominated* by what is *below it*; indeed, it does not wish to dominated at all, not even by ideas which claim for themselves a *rank above it*.

> (Simmel 1968 [1914], emphasis provided)

Keeping Simmel's central concern with the problem of mechanical systems that deterministically close off the freedom of sociation in mind, the import of the final Weinstein critique is open to a richer understanding of Simmel's final period than that offered in their critique.

> Simmel's synthesis does not give equal weight to the respective parties [holism/individualism]. It is difficult to discern *any significant difference* between *absolute life* and Schopenhauer's *metaphysical will*, both of which *objectify* themselves into individuals but also ceaselessly move beyond them.
>
> (Weinstein and Weinstein in Simmel Ibid: li, emphasis provided)

A richer understanding is possible here as I have indicated, for the Weinsteins restrict their concluding remarks to an appreciation of Simmel's relationship to the historical moment of philosophy astride the end of the nineteenth and the beginning of the twentieth centuries. After and beyond their long, informative, and truly absorbing introduction to *Schopenhauer and Nietzsche*, they publish their own book on Simmel. *Postmodern(ized) Simmel* (1993), which, I am afraid, speaks for itself. Sociology, its history as a social science, and the fundamental problems concerning Science and Humanism, especially the one examined in this study, are left behind. But, truth be told, in their otherwise excellent introduction, Kant and Schopenhauer and the problem of freedom/individualism and determinism/holism are in fact never discussed from the point of view of the traditional history of social science that certainly deals with the serious issue of the possibility of naturalism. It's as if all that never existed. Thus, particularly because of this last point and my analysis of Simmel's work here, I am setting to one side their examination of Simmel's glide into his own brand of post-Schopenhauerian pessimism and its comparison with related developments in culture critique and the modern crisis, in order to pay attention to the appraisal of Simmel in relation to the above allusion to the historical moment of philosophy at the time. The relevant question in that regard has to do with their tantalizing criticism in the above quote that no significant difference can be discerned between *absolute life and the general will*. The bone of contention is that both ideas are an appeal to a metaphysic – life vs. will – that *mysteriously* "comprehend[s] and unifies the opposites, [representatively: holism and individualism], because they are a *self-transcendent process*" (Weinstein and Weinstein Ibid: l, emphasis provided).

> Simmel here *closes down* the discourse on *philosophy of life*, occupying a position between the optimistic *holism* of Bergson's creative evolutionism and the optimistic *individualism* of James's pluralistic universe. Bergsonian life is present in his vision, but without an upward dynamic. The Jamesian individual is there, but without the compensation of the will to believe. As one of the three great closures of vitalism, Simmel's is the closest to the *psychological facts of person existence*. Its tragic vision, which grew out of Simmel's quest for a real *a priori*, not only reflects his own life-struggle, but is far more pertinent to the cultural and person life of the twentieth century than are those of his more optimistic counterparts. Simmel's strain of thought was continued in the succeeding generation as a reflection on the personal life in existentialism. His own turn to metaphysics produced one of the last great monuments of that art, a monument to deconstruction, a life that deconstructs philosophy and a philosophy that deconstructs life.
>
> (Weinstein and Weinstein in Simmel 1991: li–lii)

It is quite true that Simmel "*closes down* the discourse on *philosophy of life*" with regard to the problem of a "*self-transcendent process*" that mysteriously resolves the holism/individualism dualism. However, it is one thing to make that claim for Simmel, on the one hand, in his own time and in terms of his theoretical predicament, *as they have articulated it*, and on the other, to do all that as if the structure/agency problem *doesn't exist*, or, that it has *nothing to do with Simmel's predicament*. But it certainly does: if Simmel is on a "quest for a real *a priori*" that will be a grounding site for freedom in sociation, and, thus will be the basis for blocking off the reification of form, yet, without eliminating form, surely the intimate connection between this quest and that of Giddens's in reference to his quest for a conception of real causation that will recover human agency, control for the reification of structure, without losing structure, must now be taken analytically seriously. Thus, it must be asserted that Simmel's dualism of form/holism and life/individualism is indeed his terminological contribution to the development of the Science and Humanism debate on the structure/agency problem. Once again, from Simmel to Giddens, sociation and structuration turn out to be metaphysical cognates of each other, and freedom as casual energy is best understood in terms causal powers as the ground for human agency. As I have just established, *the shift from energy to powers, and then to agency, is certainly verified with Simmel's assertion that what is real about the a priori he is in quest of is that it is an objective power within us*. Now let us track Simmel as he meanders toward the idea of causal powers without quite realizing that he has walked in on exactly what, metaphysically, his quest is, ultimately, all about. The last link in the chain is implicit in his walk-about: *that the point of the energy of agency is not energy but agency, hence, that agency is grounded in powers, not that agency is grounded in the fuel of machines, can only be the case if those powers are causal*. The history of the problem of structure and agency has made that clear in the exemplars of Schopenhauer and Heidegger, and now Simmel. This amounts to the resurrection of Simmel's theory of sociation that was originally constituted of the impossible marriage of Kantian freedom and Schopenhauer's determinism. After all, now, freedom is efficacious in the world, since the "agent causality" of human acts of will does explain that efficaciousness.

Energy to agency: causal powers and the ontological gap

Simmel neither understood that his theory of freedom in sociation was impossible, nor therefore did he forge his theory in the realization of a causal powers theory of freedom. However, what he did do was more or less come in upon the different necessary component ideas for such a realization, but without the required systematic understanding of the import of what he was actually accomplishing. In this sense, precisely, the failure of his theory of freedom in sociation, nevertheless, left us with the important fragments that together hold the promise of the recovery of agency. We can now proceed to finally see this in two ways: first, to show that he indeed finds himself walking around the idea of causal powers, especially with reference to the idea of the "energy of agency"; second, then to show that his inability to understand what he had accomplished turns out to be the result of an ontological gap between two eighteenth-century views of the nature of human being. On the one hand, we have the view that "nature" is conceived under the auspices of natural law, and on the other, that "nature" is conceived under the auspices of ethical (moral) law. Now, the problem is that in the former case, "generality" loses freedom to determinism, while in the latter, "generality" realizes freedom in determinism. The implication here is that, *the failure to see the relevance of the gap to the theory of sociation, is the reason why Simmel's theory is a stalemate.* And, that reason has to do with the fact that, on closer examination, natural law is an expression of the ultimate thesis. Hence the gap: human agency cannot come from a world of patiency.

To set up for Simmel's movement among fragments of ideas that together were pointing to causal powers, let's systematically reconstruct his theory of freedom in sociation. This can be done in terms of a cardinal premise and three sociological a prioris.

Cardinal premise
  Freedom is not *solipsistic existence but sociological action*. It is not a condition limited to the *single individual* but *a relationship,* even though it is a relationship from the standpoint of the individual.
                                        (Simmel 1964: 121, emphasis provided)

Sociological a priori 1
  In practice, this fundamental process. ... within an existing society operates as the a priori condition of additional interactions that arise

among individuals. Every member of a group ... sees every other member not just empirically, but on the basis of an a prioric principle which the group imposes on every one of its participants. Among officers, church members, employees, scholars, or members of a family, every member regards the other with the unquestioned assumption that his is a member of "my group. ..." By virtue of [some common basis of life] people look at one another as if through a veil. This veil does not simply hide the peculiarity of the person; it gives it new form. *Its purely individual, real nature and its group nature fuse into a new autonomous phenomenon. We see the other not simply as an individual but as a colleague or comrade or fellow party member – in short, as a cohabitant of the same specific world. ... Evidently, this is true also of the relations of members who belong to different groups. The civilian who meets an officer cannot free himself from his knowledge of the fact that this individual is an officer....* In all these cases, reality is veiled by social generalization, which, in a highly differentiated society, makes discovering it altogether impossible. Man ... both distorts and supplements [the picture of the other], since generalization is always both less and more than individuality is. The distortions derive from all these a priori, operative categories: from the individual's type as man, from the idea of his perfection, and from the general society to which he belongs. Beyond all these, there is, as a heuristic principle of knowledge, the idea of his real, unconditionally individual nature. It seems as if only the apprehension of this nature could furnish the basis for an entirely correct relation to him. But the very alterations and new formations which preclude this ideal knowledge of him are, actually, *the conditions which make possible the sort of relations we call social.* The phenomenon recalls *Kant's* conception of the categories; they form immediate data into new objects, but they alone make the given world into a knowable world.

(Simmel 1965: 344–45, emphasis provided)

Sociological a priori 2

A society is, therefore, a structure which consists of beings who stand *inside and outside* of it, at the *same time.* This fact. ... [points to] the *feeling* of being *independent and separate* from all these [societal] *entanglements and relationships,* a feeling that is designated by the ... *concept* [of] *"freedom."*

(Simmel1965 [1908]: 347–48, emphasis provided)

Sociological a priori 3

Kant's axiom that connection, since it is the exclusive product of the subject, cannot inhere in things themselves, does not apply here. *Societal unification needs no factors outside of its own component elements,* the *individuals. Each of them exercises the function which the psychic energy of the observer exercises in regard to external nature: the consciousness of*

> *constituting with the others a unity is actually all there is to this unity.*
> *This does not mean, of course, that each member of a society is conscious*
> *of* such an abstract notion of unity. It means that he is absorbed in
> innumerable, specific relations and in the feeling and knowledge of
> *determining others and of being determined by them. ... Again ...*
> *society ...* is the objective unit that *needs no outside observer.*
>
> (Simmel 1965: 338, emphasis provided)

The domestication of Kant's theory of freedom proceeds according to the
cardinal premise that freedom is a social relationship, and thence, into the
three interlocking a prioris that structure social interaction. The *first a priori*
refers to that structure as being centered on the idea that, *as individuals*
interact with each other indirectly through the medium of roles, they constitute
a social force. The "outside" dimension of relational freedom, the second,
pertains to the real a priori of objective power, the propulsive character of
impulse or psychic energy; the third a priori as the "inside" dimension of
freedom, is located at the site of life: the mutual determination between sub-
jects that gives rise to both forms and individuals. In short, sociation (or
structuration?) is the reciprocal exercise of the personal agency of interacting
subjects. My central focus will be the "outside" dimension of relational
freedom; the strategy is to systematically identify the ways in which Simmel,
in effect, is enhancing what I am going to call his major *neo-Kantian thesis*:
the real a priori of human freedom is an objective power of agency. The main
source of such knowledge will come from the work that I have been mining
throughout this discussion – Weingartner's superb study of Simmel's philosophy of human being, freedom, and the social. I also want to situate my
presentation of Simmel's indicators of causal powers in the framework of
Aristotle's philosophy of biology. The reason is based on Ernst Mayr's
declaration concerning the scientific relevance of Aristotle to modern biology.

> What is generally lumped under the term *vitalism* includes a hetero-
> geneous mixture of theories of various degrees of validity. Delbruck
> (1986) demonstrated that for *Aristotle vitalism was actually the postulate*
> *of a genetic program, as we would now call it,* and when one carefully
> reads what Johannes Muller wrote about the *Lebenskraft* postulated by
> him, it is again a perfect description of the genetic program.
>
> (Mayr 1985: 46, emphasis provided)

The importance of Mayr's information is that Aristotle's vitalism, in being a
postulate of a genetic program, is an excellent reminder that he is the father
of scientific realism and thus causal powers theory. The relevance of this is
that Simmel's enhancement of his neo-Kantian thesis is best understood
under the auspices of Aristotelian realist biology. There is, perhaps, another
reason. Kant's venture into biology, we have earlier indicated, was itself
related to his scientific realism and the causal powers reading of human

agency. Although Weingartner makes no mention of any of this, nevertheless, the Aristotle/Kant connection is important for the understanding of the topic of Simmel's enhancement of his neo-Kantian thesis. It cannot be an accident that Simmel's work on the problem of finding a place for freedom in a theory of social life is connected, on the one hand to the thesis that freedom is an objective power of agency, and on the other, to the two major causal power theorists in Western philosophy of science. This, then, encourages my realist reading of Simmel's work, even though he himself could not have taken up that standpoint at the time; and in his philosophical efforts, Weingartner and the Weinsteins show that clearly by referring to Simmel's classical vitalist standpoint that particularly distinguishes his last period. My only caveat here is that, I would not underestimate the excellence of Simmel's intuitive sense of a problem: Kantian freedom is deemed conceptually troublesome, causal powers "talk" crops up in his work, relevantly, while not only is Kant, certainly, foremost on his mind, but Aristotle, very likely, is in the background, very much alive for him.

With respect to the encouragement to read freedom in sociation from a realist standpoint, we now can point out that there are three other clear moments where Simmel reveals his causal powers "talk' explicitly in reference to freedom. In an essay of the first period published in 1896, we have one of those moments, and, in one of the three most important of his philosophical works, *Lebensanschuung* (1918), of his last period, we have the other two moments. Together with the reference to the real a priori, there are four all told (Weinstein and Weinstein in Simmel 1991: xxvii).

The essay of 1896 is an "Outline of a Theory of the Will" whose main topic is a theory of volition by way of a critical dismissal of that part of the theory of instinctual drives that stresses drives as causally producing action (Weingartner 1960: 19–20). The general interest in this problem of instinct and will, Weingartner claims, is to promote Simmel's fundamental focus on human life as it is "lived," and hence to emphasize its temporality (Weingartner Ibid: 15–17, 19). No mention is made of any interest remotely connected to science and nature and the problem of causality and freedom. Nevertheless, Weingartner's own text leads one to believe that the realist vocabulary he uses to discuss its content, *is* a mirror of the actual content that Simmel employs himself; and that, surely, resonates with an interest in science and the problem of causality and freedom. The actual relevance of the theory of volition here is not the quality of temporality, that is the Bergson-like non-mechanical flow of action; instead, it is the relationship between instinctive action and volitional action.

> His essay ... begins with a critique of a widely accepted theory of instinctual *drives*. ... *as forces existing prior to and productive of particular actions.* ... Simmel does not give up speaking of instinctual drives altogether, but proposes a fairly *drastic* reinterpretation. A drive is "the conscious aspect or sequence of an action already beginning." *The act itself is the*

consequence of *"innervation-occurrences that reside at a deeper level*; [*it*] *begins with starts that are themselves visible*, although they can already arouse psychic reflexes." [*Drive*] *is the psychic effect* of an already ongoing activity. It is a "state of feeling," *the psychological manifestation of the beginning of an activity*. ... [Correspondingly], volition is the psychic reflection of the first part of a process which begins with the triggering of nerve ends and issues in the accomplishment of the *intended* deed.

(Weingartner Ibid: 19, 20, emphasis provided)

With regard to the specific issue of denying the causality of instinctive drives, Weingartner shows in this above quote that Simmel comes up with an insightful, though sketchy, alternative account that favors human agency, that is the individual as the source of the causal production of action (*the act itself is the consequence of "innervation-occurrences that reside at a deeper level"*). This assertion is fully justified as an implication of the denial that agency should be assigned to instincts, rather than to the human individuals whose acts themselves are consequences (grounded in?) of neural events residing at a deeper level. Note, parenthetically, that, like Dewey, actually at the same time that he was distinguishing between the reflex arc and the organic circuit in 1896, Simmel's anti-mechanical standpoint leads him too to emphasize the continuity of neural events from innervation to intention to enervation. The implication of the idea of causal powers (not the theory) is to be found not merely in Weingartner's vocabulary mirroring Simmel's, but also, arguably, in Simmel's own text language: neural events *"at a deeper level" and other neural events "not themselves visible."* The last two references from *Lebensanschauung* are, in my judgment, at the very least, impressive, in their allusion to a realist sense of causation.

Freedom is nothing negative, not the absence of coercion, but the completely new category to which man's development rises, as soon as he has left the level of teleology, which is tied to his inner physis [satisfying needs of the individual apart from other individuals] and its mere continuation in the area of action.

(Weingartner Ibid: 51)

The context of this quote is Weingartner's discussion of "The Turning" and its central idea, that of cultivation. Thus, [cultural] freedom [under its key ideal of cultivation] is something positive: "the completely new category" that is beyond biological needs/drives – the social life of culture. In other words: freedom in sociation on the level of forms of knowledge – art, science, religion. Note then Weingartner's commentary explicating this new category that is freedom.

As regards freedom, it is irrelevant to ask whether or not an action is determined by *antecedent conditions; its efficient cause is quite beside the point.* ... In the free, just as in the teleological stage of life, the *impulses to action*, the *causal energy which propels* us to do anything whatever and toward whatever end have their sources in the process of life. *Only* the direction of the action [biology or culture] changes as one moves from one stage to the next.

(Weingartner Ibid, emphasis provided)

The new category of freedom is an efficient cause that does not require antecedent efficient causes, for example, instinctual drives, for their actions: generally independent of external causation, human freedom is autonomous. Simmel, in effect, has contradicted himself here: *this* is the *potency* of Kantian freedom that is now no longer *mysterious.* Simmel was not in a position to discover that, with the new category of freedom in hand, which I have reformulated, and from his own statements, half of the "back," so to speak, of the ultimate thesis has been "broken." Kantian freedom now located in sociation is not in any way an extra-natural thesis; either in the traditional terms of free-will theory, or any of its variants on the theme of mysteriousness – from Dilthey to Husserl, and, now, to Simmel. Of course, the very much tougher realization would have to ask this kind of a question. If freedom in sociation is an efficient cause whose autonomy certifies its agency, the fact that not all efficient causes are autonomous, for example, physical particulars, would, nevertheless, imply that, in being efficient causes, physical particulars too are agents. Indeed, Simmel, at the very least, certainly came across that idea from Kant, and, so, all he would have had to have done in this context is to remember it. But of course, that he did not do so precisely follows from the fact that Simmel simply happened to have hit upon, without recognizing, the idea that the new category of freedom is Kant's conception of the efficient causality of freedom.

Now, we can raise this question of Simmel's discussion of this new and unmysterious potency of an efficient causal productive energy. Is his reference to the fact the neural events of freedom are at a "*at a deeper level*," and other neural events that may be involved are also "*not themselves visible*," implying the idea of "powers"? What is, actually, "objective" about the "power" of the real a priori? Is it the "power" that grounds the energy of efficient causality? We turn to that part of Simmel's discussion under examination where the last moment of what I have called "causal powers talk" is identified. Weingartner continues discussing "The Turning" and Simmel's idea of cultivation, now wanting to pick out its distinction from enculturation. The difference is that between being a member of the culture who lives the culture only as a practical instrument of survival, as against being one who lives the culture as a symbolic opportunity of realizing its ideal forms of knowledge and meaning. To highlight the social fact of cultivation, the analogy to gardening nature (the career of a fruit tree) as against using nature (the manufacture of a mast for a schooner from a tree) is offered by way of clarification. Concerning the future state of a process of cultivation, it must be,

... latent in the *natural structural relations or motive powers* of the subject.... The pear tree itself seems to us cultivated, because a gardener, after all, develops only those possibilities which rest in the organic predisposition of its natural form, bringing it to the most perfect unfolding of its own nature.

(Weingartner Ibid: 73)

Yes, the new category of human freedom is efficient causal energy: it is the manifestation of force that is grounded in latent powers, which, themselves, are internally connected to the structural relations of the natural kind of agentive entity that it is. Simmel only implies this, since, of course, he never actually says it; yet, I dare say, he would certainly assent to anyone who would put all these separate pieces of his work together in the manner that I have. It would have saved him from the end that the Weinsteins have shown he did in fact wind up with. And that is the temperamental conviction that sociation is ultimately a totally mysterious *self-transcending process* of *absolute life* that miraculously saves human freedom and avoids reification. In this regard, we can turn to one more fact concerning Simmel's search for a way to articulate the objectivity of the real a priori of power that, I think, demonstrates why he could not have put it in the way that I have above.

Objective power of agency and natural law: the ontological gap

This "one more fact" is an allusion to what I have earlier called his thesis of the ontological gap. When that gap is located in "An Example of Philosophical Sociology," where he is discussing "Individual and Society in Eighteenth- and Nineteenth-Century Views of Life," it is presented as that between the "general man of natural law" and "general man of moral law." In that discussion, I want to especially bring out the key fact that Simmel, *unknowingly*, is actually presenting the gap in relationship to the ultimate thesis. The essay opens with a statement that presumes the fundamental principle of his Philosophical Sociology – sociation, with a scholarly acknowledgment of its antithesis – the social fact (Simmel 1964: 58–59). In the course of this essay, the Kantian constitution of the principle of sociation is tellingly revealed when Simmel asserts that

Our value lies in our good will – a certain quality of the *ultimate springs of our action that must be left undefined.* It lies behind all appearance of our actions which, along with the effects they may have, are its mere consequences. They sometimes express it correctly, sometimes distort it – since they are mere "phenomena," they have but an accidental relationship to the fundamental value, good will itself.

(Simmel Ibid: 62–63, emphasis provided)

The "ultimate springs of our action" we can of course take to be a reference to the real a priori, the objectivity of which is the reality of an agentive power. It is the objectivity of this real power that is at stake in the thesis of the ontological gap.

The thesis that this gap accounts for Simmel's being unable to understand the above reference to his new category of human freedom, is to be found in his discussion of systematic connection between, on the one hand, *scientific laws and individuality*, and on the other, *Kantian freedom and individuality* (Simmel Ibid: 67–69). The theme of the relationship between the first two components is that *natural law destroys individuality*; the theme of the relationship between the second two components is that *human (moral/ethical) law realizes individuality* (Simmel Ibid: 67–68). The issue of the destruction or the realization of individuality is the issue of freedom – the possibility of personhood and its agency. That there is a deep problem here between the two themes concerning this possibility is captured exactly when Simmel asserts that

> Any phenomenon, be it *an individual or a nebula* in the Milky Way, *is merely one of its instances.* In spite of the utter unrepeatability of its form, *the individual is a mere crosspoint and a resolvable pattern of fundamentally general laws.....*[Thus], concrete man is reduced to general man: he is the essence of each individual person, just as the universal laws of matter in general are embodied in any fragment of matter, however specifically it be formed.
>
> (Simmel Ibid: 67, emphasis provided)

What is revealed here strongly suggests why the two themes contradict each other? In the case of natural law *freedom loses out to determinism, in the case of moral law freedom finds itself in moral determinism.* Note the two italicized sentence fragments:

- since persons and objects *are* instances of laws;
- person-instances *are* crosspoints reduced to laws.

The implication of the two statements is that the concept of general laws itself is a restatement of the ultimate thesis. How could it not be? Since the elimination of particulars follows from the fact that they instantiate laws, then it must be the case that particulars are, in the case of human beings in relation to social being, predicates not subjects precisely because they are produced by the laws and not producers apart from the laws. *In other words, we have the ultimate thesis: laws stand for the agents of external causal forces in reference to patient entities upon which they act.*

Simmel, thus, never saw that this fact must mean that law and individuality cannot give rise to freedom and individuality. The crucial issue concerning the gap then is the radically different conceptions that underwrite the idea of "nature" in reference to natural law and individuality in the one case, and the idea of "nature" in reference to moral law and individuality in the second case. As I have just stated above, the "nature" of human being in the former (general man: natural law) is such that the individual is produced by laws of natural forces (phenomenal world); the "nature" of human being in the latter (general man: human law) is such that he/she is the producer of the laws of human forces (noumenal world). Simmel has simply restated, *and thereby implicitly accepted*, the subtle conflation of the "nature" of things via their natural laws and the "nature' of human beings via moral laws. For example, in this discussion Simmel accepts the eighteenth-century equation of what he refers to as "natural-law man" and "general-human man" (Simmel Ibid: 68). Thus, starting from that equation and the idea that they constitute an essence in each empirical man that is free of all sociocultural historicity, note Simmel's following comment:

> Thus, the crucial point of this conception of individuality ... is this: if man is freed from all that he is not purely himself ... there emerges as the proper substance of his being, man-as-such or humanity. This humanity [which] lives in all individuals. ... is their constant, fundamental nature. ... Freedom is the expression without restrictions or residues and in all domains of existence, of this essence of man ... of this unconditioned self, which alone reigns over man's existence. [In short,] only the free, self-contained individual is left. ... This generality of human nature. ... at the same time, makes freedom possible as an ethical concept. ... It is in the philosophy of Kant that this conception of individuality attains its highest intellectual sublimation. ... Thus the ego, not the accidental, psychological, individual ego, but the fundamental, creative, unchangeable ego [is] the vehicle and producer of objectivity. ... For Kant, [then], the identity of the egos [of all men]. ... is the notion [in which] he discovers the root of freedom.
>
> (Simmel Ibid: 68–69)

When Simmel can go on to the categorical imperative and declare that it is the most profound expression of the eighteenth-century conception of individuality, the ontological gap between the two ideas of "nature" at issue is sharply revealed.

> As long as we are mere parts of the mechanism of the world, including the social world, we have as little "value" as the passing cloud or withering stone. *Only when we cease being a mere product and crosspoint of external forces and become a being that develops out of his own ego, can we be responsible* ... Within the natural-social cosmos, "being-for-oneself" or "personality" do not exist. Only when we are rooted in *absolute freedom* do we gain both personality and the dignity of the moral.
>
> (Simmel Ibid: 72, emphasis provided)

What has been revealed here is this: in referring to the fact that natural law makes human beings "a mere product and crosspoint of *external forces*,"

Simmel had actually fallen victim to the ultimate thesis in his discussion of the theory of law and nature with respect to the problem of freedom and individual nature. He was therefore unable to recognize that the idea of "causal power" that he hit on in reference to his search for the real a priori could never to be connected to the theory of matter, because the latter was under the definition of the ultimate thesis that natural particulars are patients and agency must therefore be assigned to extra-natural particulars. Hence, Simmel's search for a way to articulate the objectivity of the real a priori of power was doomed: he would forever be unable to truly see that the new category of human freedom is indeed the energy of agency: a force grounded in latent powers, which, themselves, are internally connected to the structural relations of the natural kind of agentive entity that it is.

Final remarks: Simmel's return to Kant and sociation

The return to Kant in order to locate freedom in sociation thus has neither been the rescue nor the recovery of freedom, but rather the direct installment of Kantian self-determination as a sociological a priori, the grounding of which, however, hovers indecisively between an ambiguous allusion to scientific realism and a mystifying resort to vitalism in the spirit of Hegel. This, I think, is the character of Simmel's handling of Kantian freedom: inspired, serious, and tragically muddled. The tragedy of course is that the price he paid for his treatment of Kantian freedom is the failure to realize his neo-Kantian thesis that the real a priori of human freedom is an objective power of agency in sociation.

6 Durkheim

The social fact as a new third antinomy

Introduction: the "twins" theory problem

Even though *Simmel* did not fully realize his concept of sociation, I have argued that the three a prioris when understood in terms of causal powers theory constitute the answer to Giddens's Call. In this strict sense, sociation is the perfect standpoint from which to examine Durkheim's naturalistic theory of social life. While Simmel's return to Kant is certainly muddled, it was, one must say from my discussion in Chapter 5, certainly rich and, we've seen, potentially promising: of course, in spite of Simmel and not because of him. In the case of Durkheim, his return to Kant is never muddled, to be sure. After all, Durkheim's signature has always been that of a magnificent clarity, and his return is in keeping with that renowned marker of his work. Nevertheless, I now want to show in systematic detail that at the center of his social theory is the return to Kant in order to confront *the* question for his work, that of freedom in its relationship both to the possibility of naturalism in sociology and to the possibility of morality in modern social life. The directness of his confrontation of Kantian freedom and the intimate detail of his thinking it through has convinced me that it is certainly an impressive window into the making of the social fact. *But that very clarity reveals, in my judgment, his distortion of Kant's theory of freedom under the auspices of the ultimate thesis.* The price paid for the social fact was reification: it is intrinsic to the naturalistic project he forged, and in that machinery of making sociology a science the understanding of Kant's theory of freedom under the terms of his scientific realism was completely lost. Is this last judgment extravagant? It is, but only with respect to traditional Durkheimian scholarship. In what is to follow, I think not. We will see that one of the premier Durkheimian scholars, Edward A. Tiryakian, finally came to the conclusion that Saint Simone and Kant were the two major influences in Durkheim's sociological work; in the case of Kant, however, once again it is the traditional view that he upheld, that is that *morality* was the crucial category of influence. That of *freedom* is never mentioned (Tiryakian 1978: 237–86). In fact, I have yet to read a discussion of Durkheimian theory before or after the 1970s, in which, given Tiryakian's unique conclusion, the major Kantian category of importance for the theory of the social fact is freedom (Alpert 1961; Stark 1963: 236–43, 247–49; Nisbet 1974; Bierstedt 1966; LaCapra 1972; Lukes 1970; Pope 1976; Ceri 1993: 139–68; Joas 1993: 229–45; Lehmann 1993: 15–116; Levine 1995: 87–92, 152–80; Turner 1999: 87–110; Jones 1999; Schilling 2001: 40–56).

Durkheim: the Achilles heel of naturalistic sociology

Naturalistic sociology was the marriage of a moral philosopher and a social scientist, and, in its consummation, the offspring were the "*twin*" theories of the *social* fact *and* social *association*. The double question marks of course suggest that such a declaration, apparently, flies in the face of the received view that "for Durkheim, sociology's distinct reality was social reality, [and, in thus so being] understood as an emergent system of forces, was his premier argument for its *sui generis* metaphysical status" (Pope 1976: 203, 187–200). Of course, Durkheim meant just that when he declares that,

> The social fact *only* emerges when it has been transformed by association ...
> *Association* is – it too – an *active* factor which *produces* special effects.
> (Durkheim 1982 [1898: 252], emphasis provided)

But although on this account the two theories would certainly be identical twins, I am going to insist that they are, nevertheless, actually fraternal (thus the double question marks). Clearly, Durkheim's fundamental ontological *belief* is that the fact of the "social" *is* "association" – "the social fact *only* emerges when it has been transformed by [the "active factor" of] association." However, the problem of social realism for Durkheim has always been that he never provided the kind of account that would definitively argue against the paradox that although "the social fact" and "social association" are meant to be identical, and often are presented that way, yet, they are also persistently presented as separate theories (from now on this will be referred to as the "twin theories" problem). The upshot is that the separation means, on the one hand, that they are *identical* twins: one theory in two dimensions; and, on the other, that they are *fraternal* twins: two theories, kin related, but at odds. After he argued for Harry Alpert's thesis of identicality, this cardinal difficulty has led Werner Stark to also announce his reservation on that score.

> But it is at this point that we also see the *imbalance* in Durkheim's mind, the reason why he has been classed with the sociological realists, and why we have to regard him as, to some extent, *marginal rather than central to the cultural school* ... [This cultural school, or] third sociology ... [is] rooted in the *idealism* of freedom [Plato, Kant, Hegel] with a slight bias toward *objective idealism*, i.e. towards organicism.
> (Stark 1963: 240, 237, emphasis provided)

In his traditional and solid study of *Durkheim's Suicide* (1976), Whitney Pope, in effect, uniquely acknowledges the "twin theories" problem in bringing out from the latter the long-known implication of a group-mind.

> Durkheim's appeal to society as a *self-conscious entity* became more, rather than less, central to his general theory as it developed during his intellectual career (Pope 1975a). Thus, it certainly cannot be held that the *group-mind* doctrine was a *temporary aberration* later eliminated from his work.
>
> (Pope 1976: 194, emphasis provided)

With that particular emphasis, the distinction between the "social fact" and "social association" is brought out sharply into relief. But here it must be said that this feature of Durkheim's naturalistic sociology is persistent precisely because it is intrinsic to it; and, as such, it is certainly not an aberration. And so, as a necessary fixture of Durkheim's theory, my thesis is that it signifies the Achilles heel of Durkheim's theory of social life. *This, I argue, is what has to be understood about naturalistic sociology if it is going to be clear to us why Durkheim's position is a stalemate with regard to the problem of structure and agency.* And of course the latter problem too is intrinsic to Durkheim's position.

Naturalistic sociology and Durkheimian scholarship: positivism or realism?

Indeed, the naturalistic sociologies of Comte and Durkheim are singled out by Giddens as the *exemplars* of the problem of human agency in a human world of deterministic social structures (Giddens 1996: 65–77, 154–61). With regard to the issue of social reality, Pope's treatment of the issue is significantly contrary to Stark's.

> Durkheim's underlying objective, based on his conception of science and reality, was to legitimize sociology as a scientific discipline by proving that society is real. He believed that science is the study of reality. Every science studies its own distinctive realities; for Durkheim, sociology's distinct reality was social reality, understood as an emergent system of forces.
>
> (Pope 1976: 203)

For Pope, the connection to objective idealism vanishes, as if it never existed for Durkheim; the connection to scientific realism simply appears, though faintly, as if it has always been recognized that Durkheim is a scientific realist. Which of course can now be challenged to be simply not true. The problem of social realism has never, until the mid-to-late 1970s, indeed, could not have meant until then, the problem of Durkheim's *scientific realism*. And the latter, strictly understood in the context of the history of the philosophy of science and the fact of the dominance of positivism over realism. A simple consideration makes this quite clear: Giddens's *New Rules of Sociological Method* (1976) sets the stage for regarding social realism as a problem of Durkheim's scientific realism, and Bhaskar's (1979) *The Possibility of Naturalism* indeed is transforming that problem into the thesis of a critical realist solution.

More to the point, we will now see that Pope, unfortunately, does not take up the implication that Durkheim is a scientific realist seriously in his discussion of the problem of social reality. In the same year then that *The New Rules of Sociological Method* appears with Giddens's Call, we have a serious study of *Durkheim's Suicide*, with a rather oblique acknowledgment of its scientific realism, but, with no such Call in sight, and with no other implications either mentioned or pursued. In view of this uneventful allusion to Durkheim's philosophy of science we are led to ask what, therefore, do we actually have here in the way of a new understanding of Durkheimian theory? I say "uneventful" precisely because I do harbor a genuine doubt that, at the time, Pope actually understood that science *is* a realist practice, and thus *that's* why Durkheim's naturalistic sociology was informed by the realist standpoint of that practice. In other words, for Durkheim, it now must be said that objective idealism was dismissed for scientific realism, and *that* would have been the best reason for Pope to set aside objective idealism. Unfortunately, Pope presents the "scientific realism" of Durkheim's work as merely his belief, or his view of science, hence nothing more than a pet philosophical prejudice. Note Pope's comment on "Durkheim's perspective."

> *Today* one can *reject* Durkheim's perspective as *too restrictive*. The *debate* over emergence promises to continue. Whatever the ultimate *outcome* of this debate (if indeed, it is ever resolved and not dropped as unproductive), it *will probably have little impact upon sociology.* As Stinchcombe (1968: vi) has observed: "There is a good deal of *nonsense* talked in the social sciences about 'assumptions,' approaches, sui generis ... and the like. Mostly this nonsense does not interfere with the work of the discipline, but this is because exceptional men trust their *intuition* rather than their logical and *philosophical prejudices." The discipline of sociology is here to stay, regardless of ultimate evaluations of the validity of arguments for emergence like those proposed by Durkheim ... Similarly, there is no need to lend to sociology the mechanistic tone imparted to it when social reality is conceptualized* as a *power, current, force.* ... Since the language of force was integral to Durkheim's expression, removing it would alter his work; however, *nothing* of value would be lost. Hence, however basic to his thought, Durkheim's conceptualization of social reality as an emergent, irreducible system of forces may be rejected *without* diminishing appreciation of *Suicide*.
>
> (Pope Ibid: 203, emphasis provided)

For my purposes, the following consideration permits me to reabsorb *Durkheim's Suicide* back into the broader framework of his naturalistic sociology. To amplify what I have indicated above: since the mid-to-late 1970s, as I will later specify in select detail, it has been increasingly understood that the appreciation of Durkheim's naturalistic sociology is impossible without taking seriously the apparently "nonsensical philosophical prejudice" (to Stinchcombe and Pope) of conceiving of social reality as a system of causal *powers*. That Durkheim's "philosophical intuition" on that score was exactly right for the possibility of a naturalistic social science, of course, was ample testimony to his exceptionality at that time, and, as it so happens, it is particularly ample testimony of his exceptionality again, this time for the 1970s as well. And in view of our scientific realist standpoint of "today," we have to remind ourselves further, that, 1 year before, 2 years before, and 3 years after Pope's work at issue here, the very theme of the possibility of naturalism in social science was being explored by Keat and Urry, Harré and Secord, and, of course, by Bhaskar, precisely on the *only* philosophical prejudice concerning the nature of science that could make sense of *The Principles of Scientific Thinking* (Harré 1970). And this is especially the case in view of the nonsense of the traditional conflation of science with positivism that was of course still central to the social sciences in the 1970s. With this critique of Pope in mind, we should now point out that he has simply missed the connection between the issue of emergentism in Durkheim's problem of social realism *and* the issue of scientific realism in that same problem. And therefore, I contend, his taking leave of those issues in relation to scientific realism in Durkheimian naturalistic sociology now must be judged to have been based on an uninformed understanding of the realist status of the metaphysic of scientific practice. Let's look at this carefully.

The plausibility of the above assertion can be seen upon an examination of Pope's brief discussion of the connection between Durkheim's arguments of emergence and of superiority for the thesis of social reality.

> *Suicide* argues convincingly that the individual is transformed by his social existence. However, the explanation of this fact does *not* require an appeal to emergent social realities. Durkheim often noted that society is much more *powerful* than the individual, *but this statement simply shows that the many are much more influential than the one.* Nor does Durkheim's perspective adequately explain situations in which an individual is more powerful than the many (e.g. when a great charismatic leader is able to transform an entire society. ... Durkheim felt that the more vividly he demonstrated *the individual-social opposition,* and the more clearly he established *the relative power of the social,* the more convincing would be his argument for *society's reality.*)

(Pope Ibid: 196, emphasis provided)

This commentary and the other one above are at the center of Pope's discussion of "Durkheim's Case for Social Realism" (Pope Ibid: 187–204). Now, this commentary, I am suggesting, expresses the theme of getting rid of the nonsensical philosophical prejudice of emergence as an argument for the position that social reality is not the fallacy of social realism. Right here at this point I have to say that Pope, I believe, has picked up not the wrong end of the stick but the wrong stick. For Durkheim, *the relative power of the social* can only be an argument for *society's reality* if the reality of society *is* that of a casual power. This, exactly, was the deep reason for Durkheim's scientific ambition: the superiority of moral authority could only be truly superior to the egoism of radical individualism if its moral "necessity" also has the "force" of natural causal law. To think you can settle the issue of social realism, as Pope does, with the Nagelian-informed argument that emergence is a theoretical issue, and on that score, merely to point out that the proper part of science has been reductionist and not emergentist, though the latter is a case by case determination, is just no longer the critical point (Pope Ibid: 188–99). After all, today, and for some time now, to continue in that vein is a matter of not even being wrong.

Between the late 1950s and the late 1970s, Ernst Nagel's 1961 Carnapian conclusion that, in effect, a "powers" conception of causality is a matter of linguistic preference, was being overrun by the ascendance of the varieties of realism; the result of which was the deeper realist insight that scientific theory is ontologically driven, and, that ontology is about natural kinds of powerful particulars (Bunge 1979 [1959]: xv–xxii; Harré 1970, with Madden 1975; Wallace 1974; Nagel 1979 [1961]: 141–52, 277–335, 316–24). Therefore, to repeat, the ontological point of theory that is directly relevant to the problem of social realism is this: since reality is a matter of causal power, the critical conceptual question is whether society is a genuine or freakish and a plausible or implausible causal power. Then, from this it follows that *the crucial issue of "emergence" is the issue of the proper or improper ascription of causal power to the fact of the "social."* Now, in the case of Pope, the implication of this understanding is that one cannot throw out the philosophical intuition of "emergence" *and* at the same time retain the philosophical intuition of "scientific realism" for a naturalistic sociology, and seriously think one can understand that kind of sociology scientifically. And especially in its relationship to the problem of structure and agency. Of course, I am arguing that that ontological problem is the very one that defines Durkheim's theory of social life. And, by the way, his study of *Suicide* can now also be understood having as its principle meta-theoretical implication what amounts to Durkheim's solution to the structure/agency problem: social structure generates suicidogenic currents that determine the social types of suicides. Thus, the person's actual individual act of ending his or her life is apparently epiphenomenal. In other words, the implicit premise of the social fact is that structure determines agency. Hence, this premise surely signifies that *the question of human freedom is central to the formation of the theory of*

the social fact, and that the answer provided by the theory to that question
puts the status of human freedom into serious doubt.

With respect to the above discussion, we can return to my earlier question concerning Pope's departure from Stark's understanding of Durkheim. Note, again, the last three sentences of the Pope quotation in question.

> Similarly, there is no need to lend to sociology the mechanistic tone imparted to it when social reality is conceptualized as a *power, current, force.* ... Since the language of force was integral to Durkheim's expression, removing it would alter his work; however, *nothing* of value would be lost. Hence, however basic to his thought, Durkheim's conceptualization of social reality as an emergent, irreducible system of forces may be rejected *without* diminishing appreciation of *Suicide.*

As Pope is publishing his book with this comment, remember that both the structure and agency problem and the resurrection of Durkheim's social realism in the new terms of causal powers realism are coming into prominence. Thus, a new and deeper appreciation of Durkheim in relation to the possibility of naturalism is directly due to accepting the scientific realism of naturalistic sociology. *Indeed, it becomes the only way of understanding how a "mechanistic tone" can be rejected without rejecting Durkheim's scientific realism.* With these considerations in mind, then, I can say that, what we have, in effect, from Pope's departure from Stark is the implication of a dismissal of the structure and agency problem and its need for an answer to Giddens's Call. In short, instead of that Call, the consequence is that we have what I will call Pope's Dismissal. In so far as this is cogent, the deeper implication is that the conflation of positivism and science is still not going to be discovered for the falsehood that it is.

In my judgment, a clear point of the entire above discussion is that Kant is at the center of Durkheim's "twin theories" problem. After all, given my earlier demonstration of Kant's centrality to Giddens's Call, how could Kant not be at the heart of Durkheim's problems: Giddens's desire to preserve human agency on the grounds of a realist conception of "determinism" is of course directly inspired by the above-mentioned theoretical premise of naturalistic sociology that, in so far as the "social" is a fact, it is highly problematic that "freedom" is a fact. I now want to show this more deeply by presenting what I believe is the question that is driving the persistence of the "twin theories" problem.

Kant and the "twins theory" problem: the location of spontaneity

Durkheim ends his 1889 review of Ferdinand Tonnies's *Gemeinschaft und Gesellschaft* with a critical evaluation that is anticipating what will be, 4 years later, the theme of *The Division of Labor in Society.* Consider this statement in the overall critique.

But the point at which I will differ with him is in his theory of Gesell-schaft. … *It is essentially a mechanical aggregate; in it, all that remains of truly collective life results not from an internal spontaneity* but from the entirely external impulsion of the state. … Now, I believe that the life of great societies is every bit as *natural* as that of small aggregates.

(Durkheim 1982 [1889]: 121, emphasis provided)

For Durkheim, the task of forging a naturalistic sociology is the ontological one of identifying the *"spontaneity" of the human collective* that is to be at the same time a *causal explanation internal to the collective*. Furthermore, in providing that kind of explanation Durkheim, presumably, believes that the problem of freedom and determinism will be satisfactorily solved for the social sciences. My special point here is that Durkheim's ontological task is strictly a Kantian one: *the "twin theories" problem is rooted in his encounter with and critical response to Kant's theory that freedom is constituted by human spontaneity and reason*. The key issue here will be the conceptualization of that "spontaneity" as an explanatory force and its proper location in the relationship between the "social" and the "individual." It is *this* key issue, I believe, that will lead us to an understanding of how the theories of the "social fact" and of "social association" constitute the Achilles heel of Durkheimian sociology.

Simmel and Durkheim: the test case of "sociation"

I now will pursue the above formulation of the "twin theories" problem in relationship to Simmel's concept of "sociation." As the traditional mediator between Durkheim and Weber, Simmel brings together the "social" and "association" in his concept of "sociation." Now, Simmel's actual accomplishment, as I have already insisted, though quite excellent, was certainly short of the ideal. In other words, while Durkheim's conviction was that the social fact is sociation, the "twin theories" problem contradicts him, and, although Simmel's presentation of "sociation" went far beyond him, yet, we've deeply seen that Simmel didn't quite close the circle. But for the purposes of this examination of Durkheim's two theories, I am going to do just that for Simmel. Thus, as we have already seen, in conceiving sociation in terms of three Kantian-inspired sociological a prioris, *sociation is Simmel's principle of social force*: in social life individuals encounter each other indirectly through a *social role* (a priori no. 1: *social determination*); in that encounter each individual is both *inside and outside* the role (a priori no. 2: individual *self-determination*); so that social life is thus an *inter-action* of an individual with other individuals in terms of their roles (a priori no. 3: self/other *mutual self-other determination*). "Sociation," thus, is so constituted that it provides us with two cardinal givens: on the one hand, there is the inscribing of Kantian freedom in the conceptual structure of "sociation" (a priori no. 2: therefore necessarily presumed in no. 1 and no. 3) and, on the other, there is the grounding of Kantian freedom in the idea of causal powers (indicated in Simmel's later work). With these givens we can then say that, ideally considered, in Simmel's conception of "sociation" the relation of the "social" to "association" is a relation of identity. Moreover, if we then go one step further and regard this special conception of "sociation" as being actually located in the metaphysics of scientific realism, we have a happy consequence of some importance. The reification of either the "social" or the "individual" has been eliminated; agency thus has been recovered for *persons* now originally located in *action* interrelating with *other persons* in *action*. Using the two terms from Harry Alpert's classic study of Durkheim, we can assert that the theory of "sociation" is a "relational realism," not a "substantial realism," and therefore it fittingly applies to an understanding of the "twin theories" problem.

Having metaphysically framed Simmel's concept of "sociation" in this deserving manner permits me to then use this robust conception of "sociation" as a benchmark against which to "measure" Durkheim's "twin theories" as I proceed with a critical examination of them. Now, the central focus of my examination here is the traditional criticism that the ultimate failure of Durkheimian naturalistic sociology is its social realism, that is social "substantial realism" (from this point on, social realism is to mean "substantial realism"). In regard to what is substantialized, my contention is that *the "social" and "association" are taken to be separate, so that the "social" is then taken to be a deterministic force in relation to "association"; the "social" determinism of the "individual" is an instance of that primary case.* Given this contention, then, the traditional criticism is that to so regard the "social" as a "determinative force" in "association" is reification. Thus, with specific reference to the problem of Durkheim's social realism, it is my contention that the Achilles heel of naturalistic sociology has to do with the special relation between the theory of the social fact and the theory of social association: on the one hand, the relation entails the problem of the reification of the "social" in the "association" of "individuals," and, on the other, the relation entails the problem of freedom, that is the idea that "spontaneity" as an explanatory force is identified with the "social" and not the individual; freedom then is the problem of the proper location of "spontaneity" in the relationship between the "social" and the "individual." Reification and freedom are complementary problems: the former is the theft of the latter. What remains to be done is to clarify more sharply the exact nature of the special relation of the social fact to social association.

The twin theories: clarification

Since throughout all of Durkheim's works his two theories are presented as a matter of course, I certainly could begin this examination with a statement selected at random from any of the books, essays, and book reviews. Instead, I have deliberately chosen a statement from Durkheim's *Moral Education* (1961 [1901–2]) that expresses the two theories, to be sure, but does so in the context of a systematic reconstruction of Kant's theory of freedom. And we have Robert Alun Jones's *The Development of Durkheim's Social Realism* (1999) to thank for bringing to our attention the very important historical fact that Durkheim's reconstruction of Kant's theory of freedom in *Moral Education*, as a sociologist, actually followed upon an earlier reconstruction of Kantian theory, when he was a philosopher, in what is now called The Sens Lectures of 1883 (Jones 1999: 112). Later I will discuss the significant continuity and discontinuity between the two reconstructions in relation to the "twin theories" problem and Kantian freedom. But now, note carefully Durkheim's presentation of the two theories.

> We have viewed morality as essentially *idealistic*. What, indeed, is an ideal if not *a body of ideas that soar above the individual while vigorously stimulating* certain behavior? ... What we must above all cherish in society ... is not society in its physical aspects, but its spirit. And what is *this thing that people call societies soul or spirit* but a complex of ideas, of which the isolated individual would never have been able to conceive, which go beyond his mentality and which *come into being and sustain themselves only through the interaction of a plurality of associated individuals?* [But], while it is essentially an idealistic conception, this morality has its own *realism*. For the ideal with which we are dealing is not extraspatial or extratemporal. It clings to reality; it is part of it; it informs society – that concrete living entity which, so to speak, we see and touch and are involved in.
>
> (Durkheim Ibid: 123, emphasis provided)

The significance of the fact of the *social in association* is its determinism in relation to the individual ("a body of ideas that soar above the individual [in his relationship to other individuals] while vigorously stimulating certain behavior"). Furthermore, the quotations below will reveal the following: as Durkheim is making the transition from philosophy to sociology between 1883 and 1892, it can be clearly seen that, from his Latin thesis on Montesquieu (1892) to *The Rules of Sociological Method* (1895) to the "Debate on Explanation in History and Sociology" (1908), the idea of social force is asserted in terms of the realist anti-Humean idea of causation in the natural world.

> Montesquieu
>
> Are we, in other words, to understand that the state of society is the *efficient cause of the laws* or only their final cause? Montesquieu does not even suspect the possibility of the first of these meanings. He does not say that the laws of a democracy result necessarily from the limited number of its citizens as *heat results from fire*, but rather that they alone make possible the frugality and general equality which are in the nature of this kind of society.
>
> (Durkheim 1965: 41, emphasis provided)

The rules

When, then, the explanation of a social phenomenon is undertaken, we must seek separately *the efficient cause which produces it* and the function it fulfils.

(Durkheim 1964c [1938]: 95, emphasis provided)

Debate on explanation

Every causal relationship is unconscious, it must be divined after the event. ... If this is true for individual psychical facts, how much more so is it for *social events whose causes elude even more plainly the consciousness of the individual.*

(1982 [1908]: 212, emphasis provided)

The above three representative pronouncements of Durkheim's developing naturalism should do much more than encourage us to stop taking the determinism of the social fact to be the signature of his positivism. For, note what Durkheim himself is actually telling us: *the "social" is a "body of ideas," however, as an idealism, it is nevertheless grounded in a realism that therefore defines the "social" as an efficient causal force.* This compels us to consider this historical fact: during the defense of *The Division of Labor in Society* (1893) Durkheim made a declaration concerning the two theoretical premises of solidarity and charity in that work, and especially, he made a declaration concerning his standpoint as a social scientist in relation to the natural sciences.

I define charity as the attachment of a man to something other than himself. Solidarity and charity are related as *motion is to force. I am a scientist: I study motion.*

(Lukes 1972: 298)

At the metaphysical center of his work, then, we have here a fully self-conscious social scientist presenting his scientific ambition explicitly in the spirit of Newtonian science. Now, as I have already indicated, for the past some 25 or more years in the social sciences the following understanding has been graduating in clarity, focus, and conviction, concerning the Durkheimian project throughout its entire career. When you consider that the deterministic principle of Durkheim's naturalistic sociology is the idea of *efficient causation as a force of production*, and then you locate that principle in Durkheim's declaration of his Newtonian identity, you have much more than an *inviting suggestion* that naturalistic sociology is grounded in and informed by scientific realism. To appreciate that we have here, instead, a *definitive conclusion* on that score, certain additional scholarly developments than those discussed before regarding, now, an understanding of Durkheim's philosophy of science, must be briefly looked at.

Hirst on Durkheim: transitional understanding

The year before Giddens's Call, in *Durkheim, Bernard and Epistemology* (1975) Paul Hirst argued that Durkheim's naturalistic theory of the social fact is an impossible scientific project (Hirst Ibid: 1–15). His critical reasons for that state of affairs are a mixed blessing, however. Of the six major categories of the social fact Hirst singles out in his examination, the two most important ones he focuses on with respect to reification are "*structure*" and "*currents*" and their corresponding twin scientific values of *force* and *energy*, respectively (Hirst 1975: 96). In the following comment, the social "energy" – social sentiments – of the "suicidogenic current" is the focus of attention.

> *The "suicidogenic current,"* which explains the particular force of the social sentiments which establish each year a certain contingent of voluntary deaths, is no *idle metaphor*. It *is the particular form in which the notion of a society-subject's presence in "its" phenomena comes to the surface* in Durkheim's discourse. But *the "suicidogenic current," as the expression of an essence,* has no substance as an explanation, and it can never be specified as an explanatory mechanism. Its presence *behind the phenomena* is merely *referred to* and the space of its presence *is established by the way in which phenomena are organized.* For Durkheim, the rates of suicide are already "things" as expressions of the essence before the essence is brought into play. The essence, "social sentiments," justifies the "given" as the stage on which the essence plays its part as the *deus ex machina.*
>
> (Hirst Ibid: 103, emphasis provided)

The theme here is the explanatory idea of an analogy between "essence" – "phenomena" and "suicidogenic current" – "social phenomena" that is underwritten by the determinative relation between the "social" and "association." This theme of Hirst's is succinctly captured when he asserts what he believes to be the logic of that effort: "This combination of essentialism and empiricism, of the necessary given and its discovery through empirical knowledge, we will call *realism*" (Hirst Ibid: 6). The footnote for this statement on Durkheimian "realism," however, reveals that it is the Bachelardian view that nature is structured as a rational order constituted by invariant laws (Hirst Ibid: 179). But, consider carefully that, in an internal rearrangement of the above quotation that is to follow, clearly, we have an acknowledgment that "The 'suicidogenic current' ... is the particular form in which the notion of a society-subject's presence in 'its' phenomena comes to the surface ... [thus] the 'suicidogenic current' ... [as] the expression of an essence, 'the social sentiments' ... plays its part as the deus ex machina behind the phenomena ... ". What I am bringing out here is that Hirst is muddled in his understanding of the nature of Durkheim's actual realist practice, for, he has picked out the wrong theory of "realism" to refer to the right but unrecognized "realism" of Durkheim's scientific practice in his analysis of the problem of social realism. And furthermore, we thus have an interesting example of someone under the influence of a particular befuddlement with regard to realism and scientific practice, the result of which befuddlement winds up *dismissing Durkheim's naturalistic sociology by throwing out the baby of scientific realism with the bathwater of reification.* From the standpoint taken here, the point is that that move was as wrongheaded as Pope's similar move, and ultimately a dead end both for Hirst's study and for Pope's discussion of the problem of Durkheim's social realism in relation to the issue of his "scientific realism."

New look: a watershed in Durkheimian scholarship

I now want to follow out an idea that is implicit above, that we have been moving from an old to a new look at Durkheimian naturalistic sociology. In order to consider the latter, let's begin with the mention of the cardinal theme of Parsons's four-stage view of Durkheim's work: his early positivism must be pitted against an alleged later idealism, the result of which was that, in the process, Durkheim passed over voluntarism (Parsons 1949 [1937]: 304, 305, 441, 445; Pope 1973: 399–340; Joas 1993: 229). Now, that Parsons's view led us away from the opportunity of discovering the new look is evident in the critical apologetics of Jeffrey Alexander's career-long attempt to resurrect the Parsonian enterprise (Alexander 1983). First of all you have Alexander's abandonment of Parsons's view of Durkheim, and then, as Hans Joas has indicated, he proceeded to entrap Durkheim in the exclusive schema of utilitarianism and normativity (Joas Ibid: 230). However, with Joas's gentle dismissal, we are up against a failure to understand that Durkheim's central and profound commitment to a naturalistic sociology signified that the problems of that commitment had fundamentally to do with the question of the philosophy of science – the issues of social realism and the possibility of naturalism in relation to positivism and realism. Thus we have Joas's complete neglect of Durkheim's commitment to naturalistic sociology (Joas Ibid: 229–44). To be sure, it freed him to do two good things for us, on the one hand, to take leave of Parsons and Alexander, and on the other, to do that in order to pursue his own important insight that "Durkheim's work is best understood as a continuing attempt to answer the question of how a new morality can emerge" (Joas Ibid: 209–10; for a kindred view see Mestrovic 1988). But this question, at some point, surely, must be returned to its rightful place in the dynamic of Durkheim's scientific ambition. Certainly, therefore, and not only in this book of course, we must take leave of this line of development for the reasons so far articulated.

The theme of those reasons is of course that the recent trend in Durkheimian scholarship has been gradually uncovering the actual fact that the vision and point of Newtonian realist science does indeed underwrite his naturalistic sociology. Thus, we have from the mid-1970s and onwards into the 1990s the following scholarly achievements in this regard: in 1975 there is Russell Keat's declaration that Durkheim is part positivist and part realist, but only in so far as he is an essentialist (Keat and Urry 1975: 81, 80–87); the next year, in Whitney Pope's revisiting *Durkheim's Suicide*, the direct and unadorned statement that "Durkheim was a realist, not a nominalist," was centered in the uninspired acknowledgment that "Durkheim [conceptualized] ... social reality as an emergent, irreducible system of current [s] power[s] [or] forces" (Pope 1976: 187, 203); 9 years later, there is Christopher Bryant's counter-insistence that Durkheim is a "maximalist positivist," even though he rejected "the Humean notion of cause (Bryant 1985: 54–56)"; in other words, he is also a scientific realist; and the following year we have Stephen Turner's straightforward and casual statement in *The Search for a Methodology of Social Science* (1986) that Durkheimian social science is a practice of a Baconian realism committed to a "'substantialist' conception of social reality and a causal conception of the structure of social reality" (Turner 1986: 109–10). And finally, with Warren Schmaus's thesis in *Durkheim's Philosophy of Science and the Sociology of Knowledge* (1994) concerning the true character of Durkheim's naturalism, we have, I believe, a watershed in the history of Durkheimian scholarship.

> Durkheim consistently maintained a realist attitude toward unobservable entities ... and was never the positivist that some have taken him to be. ... *Throughout his career, Durkheim considered sociology to be the study of a type of unobservable, unconscious entity that he called collective representations. He conceived collective representations as real entities with causal powers that can be invoked to explain their effects, much as physicists explain natural phenomena through the postulation of theoretical entities.* Unlike physical entities, however, collective representations, as a kind of mental entity, have both semantic and causal properties.
>
> (Schmaus 1994: 37, emphasis provided)

Especially when this systematic and comprehensive demonstration of Durkheim's scientific realism is situated in the Bhaskar/Harré debate on the resurrection of Durkheimian social realism, Schmaus provides us with the definitive argument for the thesis that the problem of the "twin theories" and the issue of *social* realism must be located within the context of Durkheim's *scientific* realism. Hence, one of Finn Collins's passing assertions in *Social Reality* (1997) that the problem of social reality or the social fact has nothing to do with the scientific realism that informs the treatment of the social fact, simply jumps the gun, so to speak, and hence cannot, yet, be taken seriously (Collins 1997). After all, Finn has walked right passed the Bhaskar/Harré debate as if it doesn't exist, or, worse, as if there should not be such a debate. But, to repeat, of course it does, and is ongoing to date.

But, while I do think that Schmaus is quite right here – Durkheim "was never the positivist that some have taken him to be," nevertheless, in my judgment, he is not completely right. There is here a residual positivism that is intimately involved in the logic of the Achilles heel of naturalistic sociology. Stephen Turner has inadvertently revealed just that issue when he is spelling out Durkheim's utilization of the nineteenth-century vocabulary of thermodynamics and electricity, the cardinal terms of which are "current" and "impulses," based on Joule's principle of *energy* (Turner Ibid: 121).

> When Durkheim described individual actions ... he treated "impulses" as the more or less direct causes of action. Durkheim spoke of the effect of a collective current on the individual as an *"external impulse"* (1964: 101; 1986: 128; 1937: 101), and of what he called "prolongations of [collective] causes inside of individuals (1951: 287; 1930: 324) as a *"spark" of the collective current* (1951: 316; 1930: 357).
>
> (Turner Ibid: 157, emphasis provided)

What is the residual issue of positivism that is revealed here is what I have been calling the ultimate thesis: either as an "impulse" or a "spark," *the social energy of collective currents is the agents external to and thus acting upon human patients.* Clearly we have here the expression of the premise of social fact theory that structure determines agency: in so far as the social fact is an agent, the individual in the fact of social association is a patient. This is precisely Durkheim's problem of the reification of the social: "a body of ideas [the social fact] that soar above [association and] the individual while vigorously stimulating certain behavior?" This issue and its importance will be made definitively clear now as I work out the opening declaration of this chapter that there *are* the two theories of the "social" and "association," and that there is the crucial question of how their special relationship reveals an important fact about Durkheim's naturalistic sociology. *The "twin theories" problem is, first and last, the instantiation of the ultimate thesis; and that thesis intimately connects the "twin theories" with Kantian freedom and Durkheim's reaction to it.* Indeed, we will see that Durkheim, himself, makes these connections for us. To be sure, he does so inadvertently. Like everybody else had been doing, Newton's first law was automatically taken to mean that nature is a world of different natural kinds of patients, and thus the ontological status of agency must be extra-natural; hence, transcendence and transcendental are synonyms of each other. In regard to the latter, we will see in Durkheim's own words that he conflates the transcendental theory of freedom with Rousseau's transcendent theory of freedom. This conflation is one of the deep themes of his famous idea of the dualism of human nature.

Twin theories: further clarification

In the earlier quotation from *Moral Education*, the separation of the theory of the "social" and the theory of "association" is not as yet adequately established. To get that right, let us begin by examining these two expressions from the quotation in question: "morality ... is ... a body of ideas that soar above the individual while vigorously stimulating certain behavior," and, "this thing that people call society's soul or spirit ... comes into being and sustain themselves only through the interaction of a plurality of associated individuals." There is only a suggestion here of an inconsistency that is found in the fact that the first expression does *indicate* that the "social" is in but not of "association," and hence there is a separation between "social" and "association," while the second *implies* their identity. To make clear that Durkheim can and does mean the separation of the two theories I must resort to another statement of his in his paper "Sociology and Social Science" (1903). The statement that is an example of the separation, par excellence, comes from his critique of what will become Georg Simmel's concept of sociation. It is, I think, an example that is superior to the one Stark refers to in the quotation above where he highlights Durkheim's "unbalanced mind" (Stark Ibid: 242). The critique to follow is found not only in the text itself, but it spills over into a footnote, where, it seems, Durkheim is determined to bring home that distinction (one gets the impression that Durkheim was forever anticipating "hearing the penny drop," but was never quite convinced that he actually heard it).

Text

Yet by what right do we separate so drastically the "container" of society from its content? It is certainly absolutely true that not everything which occurs in society is social. But it is acknowledged that this does not hold good for everything not only *produced* in society *but by it*. ... But it so happens that *Simmel rebuts this conception. For him society is not an active, productive cause. It is merely the result of action and reaction between the parts, that is, between individuals.* In other words, it is the content which determines the nature of what contains it, it is the matter that produces the form. *But then how would it be possible to understand anything about the form if that matter which constitutes its entire reality were abstracted from it?*

(Durkheim 1982 [1903]: 191, emphasis also provided)

Footnote

In the author's thinking there is a *contradiction* which seems to us insoluble. According to him sociology must include all that is produced by society. This seems to imply a certain *efficacity* to it; for him it is only a *product*. In the end the social forms of which he speaks *have no reality in themselves, being only the pattern of underlying individual interactions, merely independent in appearance.*

(Durkheim Ibid: 208, emphasis provided)

Now we can show from the Simmel critique why one can believe that Durkheim is deliberately and definitively declaring that there is a separation of the "social fact" and "social association"; he is doing so in accordance with the schema of the reality of a *"productive cause"* in relation to the appearance of a *"produced effect."*

(1) Social fact: *"[the social] is an active, productive cause; it is [not] merely the result of action and reaction between the parts, that is ... the pattern of underlying individual interactions."*
(2) Social association: *"[association is the] action and reaction between the parts, [that is] it is only the [passive] pattern of underlying individual interactions*

Durkheimian theory of social life can now be seen as actually giving us two theories, each a set in which the "social" and "association" are related differently. In the case of what I will call the *"fraternal theory,"* we have the proposal that two factors are intimately connected but not identical: (1) *and* (2), and in the case of what I will call the *"twin theory,"* we have the contrary proposal that there is only one factor – (1) *is* (2). I now want to expose what I take to be the very nerve of Durkheim's Achilles heel: *the fraternal and the twin theories represent what I'm going to call Durkheim's version of Kant's third antinomy.* To set the stage for the specification of that antinomy I want to situate the two theories in the context of the thesis suggested above. The problem of Kantian freedom is of primary importance to Durkheimian theory, but while it is certainly the case that Durkheim's theory of freedom is a phoenix that rises out of the ashes of Kant's theory of freedom, its ascension is short lived.

Fraternal/twin theories: Kant and Durkheim's problem of freedom

Naturalistic sociology was indeed forged in Durkheim's lifelong dialogue with Kant's theory of the knowing subject, but more so with Kantian freedom. While it is very well known that the traditional view of the Durkheim/Kant relation has to do with the sociology of knowledge and Kant's categories of the mind, yet, even here that position is somewhat compromised by the fact that Marcel Mauss has claimed that it was Aristotle, and not so much Kant, who was the issue in the *Elementary Forms of the Religious Life* (Schmaus Ibid: 191). However that may be, and I am skeptical, I know of no one who centers Durkheim's fundamental theoretical problems in a dialogue with Kant's theory of freedom. For instance, not Robert Bellah, who gives us the ambiguous but yet inviting statement that, "In Kant he [Durkheim] found a compelling description of moral *obligation* which resonated deeply in his own personality" (Bellah 1973: x, emphasis provided). Note the obvious, what he does not say is that, Durkheim "found a compelling description of [*freedom*] which resonated deeply in his own personality." Remember in this regard, that for Kant there can be no separation of freedom and morality: the moral act *is* the act of freedom"; more importantly, the moral act is, nevertheless, absolutely parasitic on the theory of freedom. Thus, I suggest that *freedom, not moral obligation, must be the deeper connection between Durkheim and Kant on the question of working out a theory of the social fact.* After Bellah, in Edward Tiryakian's long essay "Emile Durkheim" (1978), for the first time in sociology and anthropology the position is taken that

> Saint-Simone and Kant hold a unique status in providing the key to the unity of sociology and philosophy in Durkheim's overall world view.
>
> (Tiryakian 1978: 213)

Indeed, Tiryakian goes further in this claim, asserting that

> He was not only thoroughly familiar with Kantian philosophy but also seems to have engaged in a life-long dialogue with Kant whenever he, Durkheim, reflected philosophically.
>
> (Tiryakian Ibid: 210)

On the question of the conception of the moral fact, Tiryakian goes on to repeat Bellah's point that Durkheim took from Kant the idea of its obligatory character, to which, Tiryakian notes, he added the character of desirability – "it is a good thing for the individual to perform" (Tiryakian Ibid). But, what is *never* mentioned by Tiryakian, not even a whisper, is Kant's theory of freedom; hence, there is no chance that we will get from Tiryakian the idea that Kant's theory was a major consideration in Durkheim's fashioning a theory of freedom for the naturalistic sociological theory of the social fact. Nevertheless, it can be shown that, in that dialogue with Kantian freedom, not only does Durkheim fashion a theory of freedom for the theory of the social fact, but, as I have proposed above, the theory can be understood as Durkheim's third antinomy. Let's now see how this works out.

Social fact theory: Durkheim's version of the third antinomy

I am approaching the idea of Durkheim's third antinomy in two ways. First, by returning to the earlier reference to Durkheim's task of properly locating spontaneity, we have the fact that he is taking his point of departure for his theory of social life from Kant's theory that the freedom of the individual is constituted by an inner spontaneity and the inner faculty of reason. The key issue, if you will recall, is Durkheim's identifying "inner spontaneity" as pertaining to the collective life of individuals as an explanatory force with regard to its proper location in the relationship between the "social and the association of individuals." Now we can declare that the "inner spontaneity" of collective life is an active principle and takes two forms: in the "*twin theory*," since the "social fact" is "social association," *"association" is the active factor of "social determination"*; in the *"fraternal theory"* the *"social"*

is the active factor determining "association." Thus, the "inner spontaneity"
of collective life is located at two different theoretical sites. In Durkheim's
theory of social life, then, the individual is both *active* – in "social association" – and *passive* – in "social association" in the relation to the "social."
This feature of Durkheim's theory shows that there is a fundamental contradiction built into the theory. *That contradiction between the "social" and
"association" with regard to the location of "inner spontaneity" (or agent
causality) is the precise meaning of Durkheim's third antinomy.* And second,
this clearly indicates what I have been asserting, namely, that in his dialogue
with Kant's theory of freedom, Durkheim is struggling with the problem of
freedom and determinism, *and*, in that struggle, I now add that he is fashioning a solution to the problem of freedom and determinism that is *a
paradox*. In spelling out that paradox, we are coming to Durkheim's confrontation with Kant's theory of freedom. I want to get to that confrontation
by working through Giddens's discussion of paradox in Durkheim's entire
corpus of work.

Giddens on Durkheim: paradox as liberty and as freedom

In the discussion of Durkheim's work, at one point Giddens claims that

> The *key* to Durkheim's whole life's work is to be found in his attempt to
> resolve the apparent *paradox* that *the liberty of the individual is only
> achieved through his dependence upon society.*
>
> (Giddens 1972: 45, emphasis provided)

Note, however, that in this comment, Giddens is not dealing with the
problem of deterministic social structure and the freedom of personal
agency, but rather with the historical fact of the change in the range of
liberty as one moves from traditional and thus mechanical society to modern
and hence organic society (Giddens Ibid: 27–29). When he does so, then
of course it is the problem of structure and agency, but, in that case, how are
we to understand such an idea of a paradox in Durkheimian theory of
freedom?

Let us return once more, but briefly, to Giddens's classic exemplar of the
structure/agency problem, the Comte/Durkheim tradition that defines the
orthodox consensus of mainstream social science (Giddens 1996: 65–77,
154–61). The second feature of the consensus, social causation, specifies the
import of the first, naturalism.

> That is to say, although as human agents we might seem to know a good
> deal about what we are doing and about why we act as we do, the social
> scientist is able to show that really we are moved by causes of which we
> are unaware.
>
> (Giddens Ibid: 65, 160–61)

Although Giddens has never explicitly formulated the idea of the Durkheimian paradox with regard to structure and agency, yet, that's certainly what it is, because, in effect, he *has* done so. Liberty and agency, in other words, are obviously the heads and tail of the paradox that centers naturalistic sociology. The only difference between Giddens and myself is a matter of priority of importance: agency is the primary issue of the paradox, in my judgment. Hence, we can explicitly formulate such an idea for him, and do so as a development of the second feature of the orthodox consensus. The telling idea here is that, according to the second feature, despite the fact that "human agents ... seem to know a good deal ... about why [they] act as [they] do, [they] really ... are moved by [unconscious] causes. ... " Now then, the paradox of freedom, not liberty, is going to especially come out of the Durkheim/Kant encounter: in forging the concept of moral individualism Durkheim is transforming what he implies is a Kantian theory of "ineffective autonomy" into a conception he in fact calls an "effective autonomy." That transformation is based on a principle of major importance for Durkheim, the fusion of freedom and determinism. Note that this of idea of fusion is expressed in the solution to the structure/agency problem mentioned earlier: that structure determines agency follows from the principle that freedom and determinism are fused. The fusion is actually asymmetrical: autonomy is placed in a strict subordination to heteronomy (the details of which will be given in the next section; Durkheim in Bellah 1973: 43–47, 1961: 111–19). As we know full well, although Durkheim has indeed talked about fusion many times, there are four main discussions where the principle is dealt with: Kantian philosophy, methodology, religion, and dualism (see also Durkheim in Bellah 1973 [1914]: 334–39). Let us start with The Rules.

> Psychical phenomena can only have social consequences when they are so closely linked to social phenomena that actions of both are necessarily intermingled. This is the case for certain sociopsychical phenomena. Thus, *the public official is a social force*, but he is at the same time an *individua*l. As a result he can turn his social energy in a direction *determined by his individual nature*, and thereby have an influence on the constitution of society. Such is the case with statesmen, and more generally men of genius. The latter, even when they do not fill a social function, draw from *the collective sentiments* of which they are the object an authority which is also a *social force*, and which they can put, in a certain measure, at the service of personal ideas. ... But it can be seen that such cases [of statesmen and geniuses] are due to *individual chance and consequently cannot affect the characteristics which constitute the social species, which alone is the object of science.* The limitation on the principle enunciated above [freedom: self-determination] is therefore *not* of great importance to the sociologist.
>
> (Durkheim 1982 [1895]: 145–46, emphasis provided)

Durkheim and Kant: paradox of freedom

Keep in mind the last sentence in the above quotation, for this is Durkheim the *scientist* speaking. But, during the Dreyfus Affair 3 years later in 1898, in "Individualism and the Intellectuals" we see Durkheim the *citizen* defending human freedom. With regard to the paradox of freedom, it is important to hear from this defense that Durkheim mounts what is of no surprise, the standpoints of Rousseau and Kant on freedom (Durkheim 1973: 45–48). To bring out a vital point about Durkheim's thinking in these matters, I want to juxtapose to the defense of freedom Snow's elegant comment on freedom that I have referred to in an earlier chapter.

Durkheim
It seems the moment has arrived to review in a brilliant move a polemic which was bogged down in repetitiveness. This is why, instead of resuming once again the discussion of facts, we have passed on, in a single bound, to the level of principles: it is the mental state of the "*intellectuals*," the basic ideas they profess, and no longer the details of their reasoning which are being attacked. If they obstinately *refuse "to bend their logic before the word of an army general,"* it is evidently *because the rights of the individual seem to them inalienable. It is there-fore* their individualism which has determined their schism ... This individualism *must be fought for tooth and nail.* ... And *a veritable cru-sade has begun against this public scourge, against "this great sickness of the present age."*

(Durkheim 1973 [1898]: 43, emphasis provided)

Snow
However much we may say and know that we are governed by forces outside our control and that the semblance of volition is only an illusion to us all, yet, that illusion, when it is challenged, is one of the things we fight for most bitterly.

(Snow 1983)

Durkheim's bitter defense of freedom against the politics of military authority strikingly illustrates Snow's theme. It reveals a deep "schism" in Durkheim's ontological soul that enriches the meaning of the paradox of his naturalistic sociology. And what is surely revealed here is that the relevance of the Science and Humanism debate concerning structure/agency is breaking through into the political affairs of everyday social life. Now, Durkheim seems to be trapped in a clash between two kinds of "great sickness of the present age": one of them is the denial of liberty and the other is the denial of freedom (agency). For, Durkheimian naturalistic sociology is caught up in the second: from the intellectual standpoint of *science*, freedom is of *minor* importance, and from the intellectual standpoint of *citizenship*, freedom is of *major* importance (Durkheim 1973 [1898]: 43–57, 43–44). However, in betraying something amiss in Durkheim's mind here, this second clash encourages us to suppose the following implication: the refusal of intellectuals like Durkheim to believe that their volition is an illusion before the determinism represented by the social fact of political (and/or military) power is rooted in a belief in the inalienable right to that volition. But in Durkheim, we now know that his fight against the very idea that volition is an illusion is a special case, for how could it be disconnected from his metaphysic of scientific realism? In fact, we can see such a *connection* at the end of Chapter 7 in *Moral Education* where the encounter with Kant and the problem of the autonomy of moral conscience seriously begins. In asserting that the rule of moral authority means that "our posture [of autonomy] is much more *passive* than *active*," then it is declared that the latter "must necessarily be a composite result of various forces derived from biological or social sources" (Durkheim 1961: 107, 108). Yet, Durkheim does not dismiss moral conscience in its vehement protest against this passivity, however, nor does he reject its insistent claims "for the person [of] even greater autonomy" (Durkheim Ibid: 108).

Note what he *does* do.

> Given the universality and persistence of this claim and increasing clarity with which it is affirmed, it is *impossible* to view it as a product of some kind of *delusion* of the public conscience. *It must certainly correspond to something real. It is itself a fact of the same order as those that would contradict it.*

> (Durkheim Ibid, emphasis provided)

With regard to Durkheim's thesis of passivity (social fact) *and* the antithesis of activity (social association), its confirmation in the quotation before the one above, and especially under the auspices of his scientific realism, what can one say concerning the import of Durkheim's remarkable statement in the above quotation? Let us make sure here of what we are talking about: it is the claim not only that human freedom is ontologically "real," but that it is "of the same order" of ontological reality as that of determinism. In other words, the fact of social determinism *and* the fact of the freedom of individuals in social association are of equal ontological importance. When this remarkable import of Durkheim's extraordinary statement is related to the contradiction between Durkheim as citizen and as philosopher of science and morality, we are led to an important conclusion. The determinism of social roles cannot be an argument against the freedom of individuals in social roles; and the reason for that is that political power is not a superior social power that reflects an ontology of a corresponding superior causal power. While there is no doubt that Durkheim certainly resisted that conclusion, his work implies it.

My commentary on Pope's observation of the weakness of the superiority argument for the social fact is directly relevant to the above conclusion. The emergence argument for the superiority of social reality needs the truth that the social is a causal power, and Harré and I have shown that that truth is not forthcoming. The ascription of causal power to the social in that sense begs the question as to the validity of the ascription; and the answer is that, in such an ascription, the social is a freakish and implausible powerful particular. Therefore, the critical question that has been crystallizing throughout the entire discussion has now arrived to be asked: *how in fact does Durkheim decide that the causal power of the collective is that of the "social"?* Remember, he did not have the relevant sophisticated critical tools – Harré's theory of causal powers and theory of plausibility – to discover a rigorous answer to such a question. Consequently, I propose that, for an answer to this question, one must look at his discussions of the social determinism of the individual in relation to the social fact as the instantiation of the ultimate thesis. And the upshot of this discussion in the last few pages that concerns the critical question and an answer to it, then, is that, Durkheim the citizen is contradicting Durkheim the scientist: political/military authority is not an instance of the general authority of the determinism of social roles that is supposed to be superior to the freedom of individuals in those roles. His writings on both Kant and freedom – The Sens Lectures – and Kant and the autonomy of moral conscience – *Moral Education* – are absolutely the only places to go in order to see Durkheim involved in discussions that directly bear on the answer to the critical question.

Confronting Kant: moral education

To set up for the first stage of Durkheim's confrontation, I am going to quote a long passage from *Moral Education* that closes Chapter 7. The passage is in two parts: first, a beginning reconstruction of the essence of Kant's theory of moral autonomy; second, the critique of the theory situated in a network of Durkheim's most important metaphysical ideas that ground and direct his naturalistic sociology. In Chapter 8, Durkheim continues the analysis in order to then work through what he implies is Kant's theory of "*ineffective* autonomy"; in his attempt to go beyond Kant, he is working to meet this standard guiding his theorizing of freedom – "What moral conscience demands is an *effective autonomy*" (Durkheim 1961: 114).

> Reconstruction
> Kant is certainly the moralist who has had the keenest sense of this double necessity [autonomy is an environmental product and a transcendent power]. ... [Kant] says "The autonomy of the will ... is the unique principle of all moral laws ...: all *heteronomy* in matters of the will ... is *opposed* ... to the *morality of the will*." Kant hopes to resolve this contradiction as follows: By *itself*, he says, the will is autonomous.

Were the will not subordinated to the influence of the senses, if it were so constituted as to conform only to the precepts of reason, it would move spontaneously toward duty through the impulse of its nature alone. For as purely rational being, the law then loses its obligatory quality, its coercive aspect. Autonomy would then be complete. But in fact, we are not beings of pure reason; we have sensibilities that have their own nature and that are refractory to the dictates of reason. While reason is geared to the general and the impersonal, our senses, on the contrary, have an affinity for the particular and the individual. *The law of reason is, then, a restraint upon our inclinations; we feel it as constraining upon the senses. But it constitutes an obligation, an imperative discipline only in connection with the senses. Pure reason*, on the contrary, depends only on itself: it *is autonomous. It itself makes the law that it imposes on the inferior aspects of our beings.* Thus, the contradiction is resolved in terms of the *dualism of our nature*: *autonomy is the product of the reasoned will, heteronomy the product of the senses.*

(Durkheim 1961 Ibid: 108–9, emphasis provided)

Critical evaluation

Obligation, in this case, would be some kind of *accidental* quality of the moral law. Of itself, the law would not necessarily be obligatory, but would be clothed with the authority *only* when it found itself in conflict with the *passions. Such an hypothesis is altogether arbitrary. Everything suggests, on the contrary, that the moral law is invested with an authority that imposes deference even upon reason. We do not only feel that it dominates our senses, but our whole nature, even our rational nature.* Kant has shown better than anyone that there is something *religious* in the sentiment that moral law inspires even in the loftiest reason. *But we can only have a religious feeling for some being – actual or ideal – that seems to us to be superior to the faculty that conceived it.* That is why obligation is an essential element of the moral precept; and we have suggested the reason for this. *Our whole nature has the need to be limited, contained, restricted – our reason as well as our senses.* For our *reason is not* a *transcendent* faculty; *it is implicated in society and consequently conforms to the laws of society. Everything in the world is limited, and all limitation presupposes forces which do the limiting.* In order to conceive a pure autonomy of the will, even in the terms that I have just put them, *Kant was obliged to admit that the will*, at least the will *insofar as it is purely rational, does not depend on the laws of nature.* He was obliged to create a *reality apart from the world*, on which the world exerts no influence, and *which*, reacting on itself, *remains independent of the action of external forces.* It does … seem. … [that] *this metaphysical conception, … can only mislead us in our thinking.*

(Durkheim 1961 Ibid: 109–110, emphasis provided)

We can now use the substance of the reconstruction and critique as we carefully examine the freedom that Durkheim allots to human beings as a scientist in the quotation on fusion, and this is to be done in reference to its insensitivity to the fact that Durkheim the citizen is contradicting Durkheim the scientist. As we do so, to begin with, one of several cardinal points that come out of the quotations immediately above should be brought out first. Durkheim does in fact conflate the *transcendental* theory of freedom with the *transcendent* theory of freedom. The significance of this observation for what is to follow is that Durkheim can no longer get away with concluding that Kantian freedom is an "ineffective autonomy," for that follows directly and exclusively from the mistake of conflation; hence, the theoretical adequacy of his complementary conclusion that his theory of freedom is, therefore, an "effective autonomy" is particularly open to serious question. Now, concerning Durkheim's allotment of freedom, he says, from the earlier quotation on fusion that "*he can* turn his social *energy* in a direction *determined by* his individual *nature.*"

If "his social energy [is] determined by his individual nature," then, that it is "*his*" "*energy*" is *incidental*, and that "*he can turn* his social energy" is *accidental: the individual is along for the ride*. With regard to Durkheim's scientific realism and his relation to Kant on the issue of freedom, what is he therefore presuming about the ontological status of the "can" of the "he?" It is, I think, this: that the "he" of the individual must be passive because the "can" is patiency, is because *agency* is ascribed to the "*nature*" of the individual, that "nature" is of two kinds, *biological* and *social*; hence, note that, on the one hand, the "energy" comes from the "biological" and, on the other, apart from the "individual" as "*he,*" it is ascribed to the "*social.*" It is here, from the 1898 paper that Durkheim now adds to the concept of the "individual" – egoistic individualism – the concept of the "human person" – moral individualism – in order to mediate the "social" determinism of the "individual" (Durkheim 1973: 47–48). But the "social," not the "person," is still the site of the agency of causal power – "personality is made up of supra-individual elements" (1964b: 339–40). This is brought out clearly in "The Dualism of Human Nature and its Social Conditions" (1914): that "the role of social being in our single selves" is that there is "something else in us besides ourselves [that] stimulates us to act" is because

> only the action of society arouses us to given our attention voluntarily. Attention presupposes effort: to be attentive we must suspend the spontaneous course of our representations and prevent our consciousness from pursuing the dispersive movement that is its natural course. We must do violence to certain of our strongest inclinations.
>
> (Durkheim Ibid: 339, 328–39)

Note Durkheim's slip of his theoretical tongue that reveals an anti-deterministic theme here: social agency is the occasion for personal agency.

Kant, however, is presuming something quite different concerning the ontological status of the "can" of the "he": the "*he*" of the individual is *active* because the "*can*" is *agency*; that is the "can" of the "he" is the agentic *nature of the individual*. In this way, Kant regarded the "nature" of the biological and the social as deterministic structures, opposed to and challenged by the "nature" of the agentic individual. Technically, therefore, the *Kantian individual is a "person" because he is an actor*; paradoxically the *Durkheimian individual is a person because he is a "reactor"* (the slip of his theoretical tongue to one side). The deep reason is this: the *Durkheimian person as reactor is the fate of human freedom when social fact theory is the instantiation of the ultimate thesis; the Kantian person as actor is the fate of human freedom when transcendental philosophy is the instantiation of a realist reading of Newton's first law.*

We still have to more accurately nail the paradox that the individual is a person because the person is a reactor. And this must be done in relationship to the scientific realism that grounds his naturalistic sociology. Now, we are going to discover that what is involved in this paradox is that, while the Durkheimian person is a *reactor*, despite the fact that, of course, he is not an *actor*, nevertheless, the Durkheimian person is *active*. And, if active, then certainly some kind of freedom or autonomy is being suggested. That suggestion must certainly be a reference to the minor freedom that comes from the psychosocial fusion of individual and social role. For Durkheim then, individual/role fusion means that the reactive person is passive *and* active. In short, what I am calling, an "active witness." In *Moral Education* we see that, in regarding this paradoxical freedom as an "effective autonomy," it is so

> ... not only for some unspecified ideal being [Kantian theory], but for such beings as we ourselves are [Durkheimian theory].
> (Durkheim Ibid: 114, emphasis provided)

He is in no doubt that this "is the only kind of autonomy to which we have any claim" (Durkheim Ibid: 118). But now I will offer the counter-claim that Durkheim's theory of autonomy is seriously problematic precisely because it is more accurately referred to as a "*compulsive* autonomy," and that is precisely why the individual is an "active witness." A major piece of evidence for this claim is found in Paolo Ceri's "Durkheim on Social Action" (1993), where he gives a more accurate insight into Durkheim's paradoxical freedom.

> In Durkheimian empirical analysis [of various kinds of action, e.g. suicide] the subject's *will* is not only not excluded, but it is recognized and postulated. But for Durkheim the topic of "will" concerns *the awareness of the consequences of action*, but *not* the matter of *causation*. *The element of will is denied any sense of self-causation so that it is not*

> *possible to recognize any role of autonomous causality in subjective*
> *intentionality.*
>
> (Ceri 1993: 152, emphasis provided)

Durkheim's person is *"active"* in being "[aware] of the consequences of action" stemming from both an embededness in the deterministic chains of the phenomenal world of nature, and an embededness in the deterministic chains of culture; *at the same time*, Durkheim's person is *passive* since there can be no awareness of the matter "of self-causation ... [that is an] autonomous causality in subjective intentionality." Note the following discovery: in the twin and fraternal theories, the premise that the individual is both active and passive, respectively, turns up as the premise of "compulsive autonomy." Based on the fact that the twin/fraternal theories prescribe the theory of "compulsive autonomy," how does Durkheim manage the view that he has of the relationship between Kant's theory of freedom and his? As the pre-Durkheimian Kantian subject, the individual as a person is an "ineffective autonomy"; but as the Kantian subject is transformed into the Durkheimian subject, the individual as a person is now an "effective autonomy." How does Durkheim get to the secondary premise that the person is "active" from the primary premise that the person is "passive"? Or rather, how can Durkheim be right that the "person" is a patient because the "social" is the agent, the "person" is "active" even though there is no "autonomous causality" that grounds that "active" property, and with all this, in being a scientific realist, the ground of the agency of the "social" is a causal power, that is an "autonomous causality"? In short, there is no ontological grounding for being "active." This is exactly the reason why, I contend, Durkheim's slip of the tongue – social agency is the occasion for personal agency – is a slip, and not an explicit proposal. In other words, *Durkheim's fraternal theory reduces sociation to the first a priori (Simmel), and thus he doesn't know how to expand it to the third a priori of mutual self-other determination; and that is because he fails to confirm the second a priori, the self-determination of the person in social roles.* In other words, his questionable understanding of Kantian self-determination is the key here. For Durkheim to think that Kantian autonomy is ineffective because the noumenal is his version of transcendence, *is not even wrong*; he could not have understood that the noumenal solution is the fate of human freedom because Kant did not see that, as a variety of efficient causality, it is an instance of his correct reading of Newton's first law. Hence, Durkheim's journey from Kant's "ineffective autonomy" to his "effective autonomy" was, in fact, a dead end: since "autonomy" is compelled by social forces and impelled by biological forces Durkheim's conception was actually a conception of "deceptive autonomy." Therefore, with regard to the social fact and concerning the location of causal power at the site of the latter, we must ask why is there an asymmetry in the relationship between the "social" and the "individual" in "association"? But of course we know why: as an instantiation of the ultimate thesis, the social fact thus prescribes the idea of "compulsive autonomy." It's back to Kant, then, for the source of Durkheim's difficulties here reside in his misunderstanding of Kantian freedom and his ignorance of its ground in Newtonian realism. In doing so, it will be important to remember that, in his discussion on Kant and freedom in Chapter 7, we discovered that Durkheim believes that autonomy *"must certainly correspond to something real."* To which we must add, that, as some kind of human fact, its "reality" must be connected to the very idea of causal power. Kant *and* Durkheim, after all, are joined at the hip: Newtonian realism is their shared metaphysic. We've always known that Newton got inertia right, and, thanks to Jones, we now know that Durkheim did not.

> Durkheim thus advanced four "special proofs" of the spirituality of the soul, the first three demonstrate a contradiction between the nature of mind and that of matter. ... [The third declares that] mind is endowed with *activity* and *spontaneity*, while matter is *inert.*
>
> (Jones Ibid: 146)

The Sens Lectures: confronting or becoming Kant?

Jones reports that the discussion of the Kantian doctrine of noumenal freedom and of phenomenal determinism in The Sens Lectures leads Durkheim to a firm position on the matter. Since Durkheim is clearly convinced that the noumenal/phenomenal divide is an ontological divide separating otherworldly and this-worldly realms:

> Durkheim rejected Kant's argument on the ground that the doctrine conserves, not *real* freedom, but only *possible* freedom. The actions of our lives, being purely phenomenal, would be determined, while the will, *imprisoned* in the noumenal world, would be unable to exert its influence on phenomena. The freedom Kant offers us is thus only virtual, sterile, metaphysical.
>
> (Jones 1999: 131–32, emphasis provided)

The judgment that, since the will is "imprisoned" in an other-worldly realm, Kant's theory of freedom is sterile is thus a cardinal contribution of The Sens Lectures. And of course we can certainly say that this judgment has promoted a major theme of the lectures on *Moral Education* concerning Kantian autonomy. In the latter work, Durkheim is realizing that if Kantian freedom is virtually "possible" but actually sterile, this means of course that it is an impossible theory of freedom: he thus concludes that Kant has left us with an "ineffective autonomy" (Jones Ibid: 112–19). However, as I have already remarked more than once, the judgment of sterility/ineffectiveness is seriously flawed because transcendental freedom is a "this-worldly affair, and

Kant did not know how to reconcile his Newtonian realism with phenomenological determinism. It can, thus, be no real surprise to discover that Durkheim's understanding of Kantian transcendental freedom is seriously wanting not only in *Moral Education*, but also in The Sens Lectures. Of course, this is because he was presenting the *received view* of Kantian philosophy, and doing so in his customary excellence of command (Jones Ibid: 139–132). If anything, Durkheim's reconstruction of the Kantian theory of freedom suffers from that very excellence: it is virtually a perfect, literal, representation. Either he never read the treatise on the *Metaphysical Foundations of Natural Science* or, if he did, it never influenced his understanding of Kant's transcendental philosophy. The former is certainly not an outrageous suggestion, after all, since one of the greatest Kantian scholars of the second half of the twentieth century, I have been told by one who was his student, has never read that very book.

This then, brings us to the uniqueness of Durkheim's representation of the received view, which involves two attempts to salvage the idea of human freedom in the face of his agreement "with the determinists that so long as we think of things solely under the form of causality, there is no *contingency*, and thus no freedom" (Jones Ibid: 132, emphasis provided). He is dealing with two kinds of determinists, the psychological (Lebnitz and Mill) and the scientific (Jones Ibid: 130–32). The former maintain that our intelligence, character, habits, etc. provide determining causes in the form of motives; even where there seems to be a choice among competing motives the struggle itself is determined by causes of some kind (Jones Ibid: 130–31); the latter claim that freedom is impossible in an external world of natural laws. Against this general view that "Everything, in short, passes mechanically in our wills," Durkheim mounts two kinds of argument for freedom (Jones Ibid: 131). With regard to the *psychological* mechanists, it is declared that

> Freedom ... does not lie between the *decision* and the *execution of the action*. But freedom does reside ... between the *conception of the end* of the action and the *choice of the strongest motive*. Indeed, it is this *capacity* for reflection and deliberation that distinguishes us from the lower animals.
> (Jones Ibid, emphasis provided)

And with regard to the *physical* mechanists it is also declared that

> If the *relation between* phenomena is determined, the *direction* in which the series of phenomena is tending is not. For the direction of the series is decided according to the principle of *finality*, and *the necessity called for by this principle is far less rigorous* than that of *causality* – that is the same end can be achieved through quite different means. *The ends assigned* to innumerable series of phenomena *can* be fulfilled in a variety of ways, and this *is where freedom can be introduced into the external world.*
> (Jones Ibid: 132, emphasis provided)

Durkheim supposes, one has to believe, that this admirable two-pronged defense of freedom gives us a fruitful answer to the sterility of Kant's conception of autonomy. For Durkheim as against Kant, self-determination, then, involves the complementary acts of reflection and deliberation: a capacity to conceive of ends for "innumerable series of phenomena," to assign ends to such series which "*can* be fulfilled in a variety of ways," and to engage in a "*choice of the strongest motive*" corresponding to one of the ends so assigned. We should note carefully the critical components of Durkheimian freedom that identifies the essence of autonomy: capacity, conceptualization, ends, choice – all unified by the ability to attain an independence of external and internal stimulation. Now consider, as Jones reports, that one of Durkheim's three Kantian-derived moral laws, the third, is the command to treat human beings as persons not as things (Jones Ibid: 137). The first essential conception of personhood is freedom, "to be the *cause* of one's own actions. ... [enabling one to] remove himself from external constraints, and to draw all action from himself ... [and to] place [himself] in movement" (Jones Ibid). With respect to this consideration, it is an understatement of the first order for Jones to announce to his readers that

> Durkheim's social realism was in some ways a sociological redescription of Kant. The treatment of ethics in the Sens Lectures is almost equally Kantian, but in an entirely different – and entirely unsociological – way.
>
> (Jones Ibid: 135)

Not quite that different. In reference to the above conception of freedom and autonomy that is presented as *Durkheim's*, minus the category of the *noumenal*, there is no significant difference between Kant and Durkheim. Indeed, *Durkheim is Kant in these Sens Lectures* on the specific issue of freedom. After all, which components of self-determination would Kant take issue with? How could he possibly object to the principle of independence unifying the components? Ultimately, independence is the whole point of autonomy: it is the agentic dimension of autonomy that Kant referred to as pure spontaneity. Clearly, Durkheim has simply restated, as his own, Kant's conception of freedom as autonomy, and the conception of autonomy as the freedom of moral action. With respect to the metaphysical grounding of self-determination, the truly critical issue, then, is the scientific realism they share in common. Thus, what is the realist ontological ground for "capacity" and therefore the "can" – its linguistic correlate – of the subject as a cause of his own effects, such as conceptualization, forming ends, choosing actions and their motives and ends, while, like a gyroscope, sustaining a dynamically continuous independence? In other words, Durkheim's term "capacity" is the idea of "causal powers," but of course he has, as yet, no such conception in mind.

When he becomes a sociologist inspired by the realism of science, we've seen exactly what happens to causal powers in his specific conception of psychosocial fusion. Remember, as *agency* is ascribed to the *biological* and *social* "nature" of the individual, reciprocally, the "he" of the individual is *passive* because *patiency* is ascribed to the "can" of the "he"; for Kant, since the "can" of the "he" is the agentic *nature of the individual*, the "*he*" of the individual is *active* because *agency* is ascribed to its roots in "*can.*" The Kant of the last sentence is of course Durkheim of The Sens Lectures. It is the perfect expression of the *sine qua non* of Kantian personhood and Durkheim's third moral law: "to be the *cause* of one's own actions." In other words, Durkheim follows Kant in ascribing to the person an autonomy grounded in an "autonomous causality." In dropping only the noumenal as the site of autonomy, and retaining the primary essence of Kantian personhood, at this time Durkheim therefore is hovering over empty metaphysical, that is onto-logical, space. How are Kant's "noumenal realm" and Durkheim's "empty metaphysical space not of equal significance or insignificance? But we now must ask this question: how does it happen, that, as we move to the recon-struction of Kant in *Moral Education*, the essence of Kantian personhood, that is "autonomous causality," is there renounced? And as Ceri has allowed us to point out, Durkheimian freedom is thus a paradox: the person is pas-sive and at the same time active.

Returning to Kant? Stalemate or promise?

To understand that Durkheim's "twin theories" problem and its paradox of freedom is an instantiation of the ultimate thesis, is to understand that Durkheim had returned to Kant neither to rescue nor to recover human agency. Instead, as we have seen in the very meaning of the paradox of freedom, he returned in order to reconcile agency to structure, autonomy to heteronomy. *It is in the logic of that very reconciliation that we have Durkheim's distortion of Kant's theory of freedom.* Note here the radical difference in the idea of recovery. In Kantian/Durkheimian terms, Giddens's Call is a call to dismantle heteronomy, Humean determinism, and to refashion determinism so that heteronomy is reconciled to autonomy. This of course is the point of calling for a conception of "agent causality" to ground a conception of per-sonal agency. I have insisted that this can only be done under the auspices of an appropriate philosophy of scientific realism. Thus, Durkheim's return, on the contrary, culminates in a stalemate with regard to the structure/agency problem, and quite clearly, since social fact theory instantiates the ultimate thesis there is no chance of a promise of a solution.

But now, the central relevance of the ultimate thesis to understanding the stalemate has been *directly* provided by Durkheim himself. The earlier quo-tations from the end of Chapter 7 of *Moral Education* are exactly the place to go, for their telling content is repeated in the next chapter. In regard to the discussion that these quotations represent at the beginning of Chapter 8, Durkheim makes an observation in passing. It concerns the fact that mor-ality is a complex of such contradictory pairs of elements as good/obligatory, individual/group, and role/human nature (Durkheim Ibid: 111). Durkheim then asserts that

> It was this sort of thing that gave rise to the *new antithesis* that we encountered at the end of the last Chapter. On the one hand, *moral rules seem, from all the evidence, external to the will. They are not of our fashioning, consequently in conforming to them, we defer to a law not of our own making. On the other hand, it is certain that conscience protests such dependency. We do not regard an act as completely moral except when we perform it freely without coercion of any sort.*
>
> (Durkheim Ibid: 111–12, emphasis provided)

Apparently, Durkheim himself is, at the very least, consistent with my claim that his "twin theories" problem is a version of Kant's third antinomy. And he does more than that for us. From the quotations below on p. 251, consider carefully what is being declared.

> *Our whole nature* has the need to be *limited, contained, restricted* – our reason as well as our senses. For our reason is not a *transcendent* faculty; it is implicated in society and consequently conforms to the laws of society. *Everything in the world is limited, and all limitation presupposes forces which do the limiting.*

Two interconnected proposals are being presented:

- Things in the worlds of nature and culture are subject to laws of forces of limitation.
- Human beings as rational/sensational kinds of things in culture are subject to laws of social forces of limitation: external and internal forces of coercion for conformity.

In view of the simple and unsurprising fact that, as Jones has shown us, Durkheim accepted the traditional understanding that inertia entailed inertness, the import of the two proposals is unmistakable. With regard to the first proposal, a Newtonian social scientist who studies the laws of the social motion of human beings has given us his reading and thus his restatement of the first law of motion for his own theoretical purposes. The fraternal and twin theories together instantiate the ultimate thesis: since inertia means the relation of a thing to an external force, so the individual is a patient and the social is the agent, individuals in association are patients to the agency of the collective consciousness; any appeal to any idea of the agency of the individual then can only be an extra-natural theory of Kantian transcendent will; hence, the individual is passive, and, though active, there is no possible grounding in any such conception as an "autonomous causality" or "agent causality," that is causal power. This last point highlights the particular issue of the paradox of freedom: when the focus is the social, "autonomous causality" is assigned to the "social" as a "causal power"; but when the focus is the individual, "causal power" is assigned to the "individual" as "autonomous causality," and thus must be rejected as illegitimate under the rule of the ultimate thesis – the "agent causality" of human freedom can only be extra-natural.

This brings us to the question of Durkheim's introduction of the post-Sens Lecture's concept of human personality, or person, in counterbalance to the homo duplex conception of egoistic individualism. Even though it is introduced in order to give legitimacy to intellectuals and their real freedom, for example, not to bend their logic to generals as representatives of the laws of societal force, there is still the serious question of the location of agency. Since personality is constituted by a *super*-individual element, agency is ascribed to that "*super*-individual" element, not to the what? What's left? The homo duplex model provides nothing beyond the "social" external to the individual *and* its penetration as an internal "super-individual" element. With this point in mind, consider two major assertions from the homo duplex paper in relation to Pope's argument for seeing that naturalistic sociology is Durkheimian determinism. "The role of social being in our single selves" is to be that "something else in us besides ourselves [that] stimulates us to act" (Durkheim 1973 [1914]: 339, 328). To which Pope, in effect, responds.

> Durkheim (1960: 129–30) identified two consciences, one social and the other individual ... However, *the internalized component [spark] is an internal embodiment of an external social reality [current]. It remains exterior to, and exercises constraint on, the nonsocial individual and otherwise retains the characteristics of social phenomena generally ...* [Hence, Durkheim] uses the concept as one more way to explain how and why social phenomena control the individual.
>
> (Pope Ibid: 113, emphasis provided)

Pope's interpretation of the social fact is not at all illegitimate, and it allows us to use it to highlight its special import: the paradigm difference between the social fact and sociation is that Durkheim has effectively stayed within the Kantian subject (individual)–object (social) model. We saw that Durkheim objected to the fact that Simmel fundamentally shifted to a subject–subject model: *the third a priori is the central and key principle, the second then interprets the social as the interaction of personal agents, and then the force of the social is the force of individuals in their roles for social interaction.* As we move deeper into our analysis there a question to raise that will be important. What is it that Durkheim lacks that, if he had it, the Simmellian shift would be open to him? In Everett K. Wilson's introduction to *Moral Education*, we can take our point of departure from this comment on morality and its standard properties of the social fact.

Does this support the accusations of realism and hypostatization? [Not necessarily, for] there is his explicit rejection of a mystical brand of realism. Furthermore, there are several points at which the self-other dichotomy is resolved in a way that would be altogether be congenial to the symbolic interactionists – e.g. Charles Horton Cooley or George Herbert Mead. He says, for example, that society lives in, and expresses itself through, the individual. [Thus, although] it is infinitely greater than the individual [, that is] it is outside of us and envelops us, [yet,] we are fused with it.

(Durkheim Ibid: xxii–xxiii)

One thing is for sure, Simmel just barely had that "something" Durkheim needs; for another thing, George Herbert Mead definitely did have it (Varela 1973: 320–48). What Mead had, of course, in his theory of social association as the generative power of symbolically interacting personal agents, is a conception of role-taking. Specifically, taking the role of the significant other in reference to the primary/personal character of collective life, and, for us here, he had the conception of taking the role of the *generalized other* in reference to the secondary/impersonal character of collective life. The latter is certainly the interactional/associational dereified version of the social fact. This is one of Mead's great contributions that Leonard S. Cottrell Jr. has brought home to us in his classic paper "The Analysis of Situational Fields" (Cottrell 1942: 378–80).

The identification of Durkheim's subject–object framework leads us to the pertinence of Durkheim's new antithesis as the theme and problem of Chapter 8 (of *Moral Education*). How, he declares, can there be, on the one hand, social moral laws not of our own making, to which we are made to conform by their "natural" coercion, and, at the same time, how can there be individual moral action the freedom of which is the complete absence of any coercion whatsoever? While Durkheim's answer in the following quotation is an elucidation of the conception of "effective autonomy," our entire analysis to this point converges on and reaffirms an earlier negative conclusion: the upshot of the distortion of Kantian freedom is the fact that Durkheimian freedom is a conception of a "deceptive autonomy."

Such autonomy, then, leaves to moral principles all their distinctive qualities. ... The two antithetical terms are reconciled and rejoined. *We are still limited, for we are finite beings; and, in a sense, we are still passive with respect to the rule that commands. However, this passivity becomes at the same time activity, through the active part we take in deliberately desiring it.* We desire it because *we know the reason for its existence.* It is not *passive conformity* that, taken by itself, constitutes a reduction of our personality. It is a *passive obedience* to which we consent without full knowledge of the cause for it. When, on the contrary, we blindly carry out an order of whose meaning and import we are ignorant, but nonetheless *understanding why* we should lend ourselves to the role of *blind instrument*, we are as free as when we alone have all the initiative in our behavior.

(Durkheim Ibid: 118)

If only the social is a causal power, as it must be, the claim that "*passivity becomes at the same time activity*" can have no possible ontological purchase: deliberation may be "*the active part we take,*" but this is in fact the concept of the person of the third moral law, itself nothing more than Kant's free autonomous subject, minus the noumenal. As such, the person is passive and active, and completely empty of any ontological significance. Durkheim, I think, gives us a perfect articulation of this point when the above statement leads to this one:

Each of us is the point of convergence for a certain number of external forces, and our personalities result from the intersection of these influences. Should the forces no longer converge here, there would remain nothing more than a mathematical point, an empty place where conscience and personality could not be built up.

(Durkheim Ibid: 119)

Along with the ultimate thesis, this is a trace, and very significant at that, of a residual positivism: causality as intersecting events is reduced to force without power, without substance, and hence in the absence of agency. We have seen in an earlier chapter how an eminent Durkheimian, Levi-Strauss, has used the very same idea of intersecting forces converging on a given point to bring out the ultimate thrust of Durkheim's usage, the disappearance of the agency of the person in his idea of "personality." Agency, again, is given to the internalized "social," the super-individual element.

And right here, exactly, is the crucial relevance of the fact that Durkheim lacks Mead's idea of role-taking, specifically, taking the role of the generalized other. Durkheim's human person(ality) retains the fact of the reified super-individual element, the "social": *instead of the liberating insight of taking the role of the generalized other, what we have in Durkheim is the mysterious fact of social role-take over.* Without grounding role-take over in a joint act of taking the role of the generalized other, Durkheimian social realism lives. The assignment of causal power(s) to the "social" that takes over the individual outside and inside, only makes the problem of reification more intractable. And the fight over the freedom/determinism issue at the core of the structure and agency problem all the more bitter, as C. P. Snow has so elegantly suggested.

This is the ultimate fate of Durkheim's third antinomy, a stalemate without a ghost of a promise of the recovery of human agency. I do not see anywhere in the corpus of his entire work any indication what so ever that the ultimate thesis could have been identified, understood, and properly rejected. This would indeed have freed him to realize his impossible dream of so conceiving of society and the human being that the fact of the social would be identical to the fact of association. However, the above analysis encourages us to accept the conclusion that the dream that the social fact is sociation, properly grounded in scientific realism, was not Durkheim's promise to fulfill. But the same analysis has also encouraged us to understand that the fulfilling of that promise was, nevertheless, left for another day.

7 Weber

The noumenal freedom of the historical actor

Weber and Kant: noumenalism to nominalism?

Albrow has already informed us that Kantian philosophy grounds, suffuses, and thus thematically informs Max Weber's sociological enterprise. But Albrow's statement of the theme already encountered earlier, *the individual who is the bearer of reason is also the bearer of freedom*, no longer reveals to us the special importance of Kantian freedom for the sociologists of the second wave of The Sociological Tradition – especially Simmel, Durkheim, and of course, Weber. To advance our comprehension of the Kant–Weber relationship I begin with a claim that will be fully worked out in the course of this section: on the issue of human freedom in society and hence concerning the corresponding question of agency and structure, Weber was moving away from the conception of freedom grounded in a noumenal metaphysic to one grounded instead in a nominalistic metaphysic. Today, we can take this insight into Weber's relationship to Kant to be a sure way to take us through and beyond Reinhardt Bendix's classic understanding that Weber's radical departure from Durkheimian naturalistic sociology consists in the singular fact that he "was ... one of the great opponents of organic theories of community" (Liebersöhn 1987: 78). To develop this thesis I want to consider an unorthodox interpretation of the relationship of Simmel and Durkheim to the father of both the philosophy of science (the first *Critique and* the metaphysics of natural science) and the philosophy of social science (especially the last two *Critiques* and the metaphysics of natural science).

It is relevant, now, to mention the view of Kant as a social theorist that Stark, I believe, has so cogently convinced us is the interpretation to beat. In arguing that Kantian "social theory" is a normative variety of mechanistic nominalism, he particularly emphasized the fact that this meant that "Order will then be produced and perpetuated 'after the manner of an *automaton*'" (Stark 1963: 121–23, 122, emphasis provided). In one crucial respect, Stark's take is of course most unfortunate, for it is underwritten by the traditional automatonic understanding of Newtonian mechanics. And I think it is clear that, what that traditional understanding involves, that physical determinism is supposed to operate according to *rigid* laws that govern matter therefore conceived to be constituted by *material automatons*, expresses a belief that is underwritten by the doctrine of the *ultimate thesis*. Hence, the crucial way to challenge Stark's classification of Kantian "social theory" is of course to do so in terms of a scientific realist reading of Newtonian "determinism." Thus, Kant's preference for mechanistic nominalism rather than organic realism will then be seen quite differently. While from his reading of Newton's first and third laws of motion Kant saw nature as a community of active but *unfree* objects in law-like relations of reciprocity, human society, then, was to be seen as a subset community of active and *free* subjects in (potentially law-like) relations of reciprocity; freedom as self-determination is then a *peculiar* property of the subjects who together compose a given human community. The metaphysical character of that "peculiarity" was then *the* bone of contention in philosophy, science, and social science. From this insight into the metaphysical subtext of transcendental philosophy it should be apparent that Simmel's view that he was translating Kant's *individual* act of freedom into a *social* act is no longer acceptable. Kant's major interest was obviously *not* the nature of the social fact of such enlightened individuals, but rather the nature of what *constituted* that *enlightenment*. Hence, freedom referred to the determination of the self, to be sure, but of course this was a determinism that was to be an autonomy and not a heteronomy. (We've seen that Freud never understood this, since he in fact believed the reverse; and Holt has shown that, despite that, he returned to the Kantian ego in his Project for a scientific psychology: after that my analysis suggests it was the beginning of the end for the unconscious – that is the giving of agency to psychological structure and not the person.) It was this very idea of autonomy that Kant used to define "what is enlightenment" – daring to know – in the 1784 paper of that title. Now, we've seen that Simmel first of all took Kantian self-determination and tried to understand it as the real a priori of power, and so, in those terms, we could understand that it certainly was the center piece of the concept of sociation. Thus, *his* major interest was the nature of the community of *free and therefore active* subjects in (possibly law-like) relations of reciprocity, and in this perspective freedom as self-determination has the peculiarity of being a *relational* property of the subjects constituting a given community. In other words, comparing Kant and Simmel in this very different manner encourages us to declare that the Kantian theory of the subject is a theory of radical *agentism* and not, as Simmel representatively implies, a radical *individualism*. Thus, while Simmel's stated translation was certainly creatively insightful, it was not, to my mind, original. *His* genuine originality resided in translating Kant's bare outline *for* a theory of social life into a theory *of* social life.

With regard to Durkheim's the social fact, if indeed, as I have asserted, it is a *phoenix* that arose from the *ashes* of transcendental freedom, it nevertheless returned once again to the ashes that are composed, in fact, of *both* theories. The unorthodox dimension of this reading then is this: Durkheimian theory of social life is only as viable as the understanding of the Kantian theory of freedom that is its reason for being. But I have argued that the theory of the social fact fell far short of fully realizing a theory of sociation, and, in that sense, the nub of the problem was a failure, on the one hand, of understanding Kant's theory of freedom from the standpoint of Kant's *and* Durkheim's shared scientific realism, and thus on the other, of understanding that the robust realization of a theory of sociation required as a major condition the solution to Kant's theory of freedom in terms of its scientific realism. In other words, the fact of social structure should be a robust realization of the fact of human agency: structure is then not the theft of agency, for it is the way agency is lived, *"as"* various kinds of orders and their corresponding degrees of freedom. Here then, one now can understand that the natural disposition to agency is transformed into the structuralization of liberty; and so, to change that structure societal members must retreat to their natural disposition to agency, once again, and treat it as an infinite resource in order to seek new structures of liberty that will have expanded the degrees of freedom beyond those past structures. We arrive then at the doorstep of one last unorthodox view, given the above discussion: Weber's interpretative sociology of radical social change, I do believe, was grounded in that very standpoint.

Now, with this perspective on the relation of Simmel and Durkheim to Kant in mind, I am simply proposing that Kant's theory of freedom must have been a special problem for Weber as he was inventing interpretative sociology. In that case, perhaps Albrow did not have it quite right, for, in Weberian sociology the pessimistic, if not tragic, theme is that *the bearer of reason is not necessarily the bearer of freedom.* In locating the Kantian subject in history Weber no longer accepts Kant's proposition that freedom and reason are twin sides of a coin that is a metaphysics, and a noumenal metaphysics at that. For us then, in light of Weber's insight into the deeply problematic relation of freedom to reason in history, we must take up *this* major theme of Weber's interpretative sociology: *rationality in all of its historical forms, and particularly in that of the formal rationality of Western modernity, tragically compromises human freedom by the various ways in which reason orders social life.* Reification, from this standpoint, would then appear as the cunning and uncanny conspiracy of reason against freedom. Certainly, we have in this rendition of reification Weber's unique way of conceding to the traditional terms of the Science and Humanism debate: historical social structures at the hands of the various forms of rationality and of rationalized social action dominate and thereby virtually squelch individual agency. The consideration of Weber's historical depiction of freedom as being under this heavy burden of reason in reference to his dramatic image of the iron cage of modernity calls for, and indeed calls forth, a corresponding literary image that, I think, captures its dark existential power.

In the penultimate chapter of *The Trial*, Kafka presents a scene that takes place in a cathedral where K and a priest are to talk on the topic of, "Before the Law"; it is during K's wandering about the cathedral before the priest's arrival that, like a moth, he is drawn to a corner where there is a single candle in total encompassing darkness, except for the fact that it is lit. No longer a Prince, this commonplace(d) Hamlet feels his freedom not as freedom itself against the darkness, but rather he feels the immensity of the darkness itself, in which freedom is then barely noticed. After all, *freedom merely illuminates the darkness.* Thus, if, contrary to Durkheim, Weberian freedom is on the far side of agency (that is of autonomy, rather than of heteronomy as in Durkheim's case), in his theoretical vision of Western civilization, especially modern capitalism, reason winds up throughout its history being on the far side of structure. Here, intimately, Weber was, perhaps unintentionally, challenging Durkheim's claim that modern society was not a mechanical but an organic solidarity in which the unleashing of unprecedented freedom, amoral though it was, threatened the modern division of labor.

Weberian freedom: the problem of reason and charisma

A recent comment by Donald N. Levine about Weber will help us develop the above point that, for Weber, on the one hand, freedom is on the far side of agency, and, on the other, reason is on the far side of structure.

> By temperament a prophet, Weber could never refrain from insinuating his advocacy of what was in fact a heroic ethic of self-awareness and self-determination. He felt that the calling of scholars and scientists was best justified by the contributions their work makes to enhancing self-consciousness. He belittled the human tendency to submerge decisions about ultimate values under the surface of everyday routines, and urged that *"every important decision, indeed life as whole, if it is not to slip by like a merely natural process but to be lived consciously, is a series of ultimate decisions by means of which the soul, as in Plato, chooses its own destiny, in the sense of the meaning of what it does and is."*
>
> (Levine 1995: 208)

It will serve my discussion at this point to situate Levine's absolutely correct emphasis on the *heroic* ethic of *self-determination* in Harry Liebersöhn's elegant discussion of Weber in *Fate and Utopia in German Sociology, 1870–1923* (1987); since his discussion centers on exactly that heroism of the personal agent as a major theme of his entire corpus of work, we can spell out the full import of that rich reference to it. The italicized statement above indexes that richness, and the following comment of Gerth and Mills's concerning Weber's theoretical ideas points the way to its unpacking.

> *Charisma* ... serves as a *metaphysical* vehicle of man's freedom in history. ... He conceived of individual man as a composite of general characteristics derived from social institutions; *the individual as an actor*

of social roles. However, this holds only for men in so far as they do not *transcend* the routines of everyday institutions. The concept of charisma serves to underline Weber's view that all men everywhere are not to be comprehended merely as *social products.*

(Gerth and Mills 1958: 72–73, emphasis provided)

With Albrow's remark critically qualified by the major theme set out above that the bearer of reason is not necessarily the bearer of freedom, together with this index of Gerth and Mills's, it is clear now why we can say that Weber has shifted the conception of self-determination from the metaphysics of noumenal freedom to the metaphysics of nominalist freedom. But, Weber's nominalism must be carefully understood for being the complex metaphysical position that it actually is. The freedom of the subject, to be sure, is that of an *historical* actor (nominalism), but, while the actor is in history, the historical process itself is a natural deterministic process ("*to slip by like a merely natural process*": Kantian phenomenalism), in which freedom, only when it is an act of the "soul [choosing] its destiny," can thus "transcend" this determinism. Now, Gerth and Mills allow us to point out that, first, charisma is the exemplar of self-determination, second, that the historical trajectory of self-determination is to be understood in terms of the relation of *charisma* to (the historically changing forms of) *reason.* Thus, we can now see that Weber's new vocabulary in reference to the structure/agency debate is *charisma* (freedom) and *routinization* (reason). Or, as Liebersöhn's discussion encourages us to do, we can state this relation more fully as the charisma of the authentic person – persönlichkeit – and the routinization of social order (Liebersöhn 1989: 108–23).

Weber and Kant: charisma and transcendence

With respect to the discussions of Albrow, Gerth and Mills, and particularly Liebersöhn, in specifically bringing our attention to the intimate association of Kantian freedom and Weberian charisma, of course, *with religion*, what strongly stands out is the reference to "transcendence." Note here, that this special emphasis on the "transcendence" of determinism must be a reference to some metaphysical ground, no matter what Weber might say, and, if, as Weber saw it, it is not noumenalism, then which metaphysic is it? Since nominalism unfortunately presumes a Humean conception of empiricism, the answer to that question certainly cannot be nominalism; the positivist conception of empiricism is the basis for the very idea of the ultimate thesis. In other words, in that case Weberian freedom would then be conceived of as "nominalistic freedom," and that, obviously, is a self-contradiction. But of course, the upshot here is that, in fact, as we shall see, *that is, in effect, Weber's conception of freedom.* Furthermore, note what is also going on with Weber: even though noumenal freedom is, apparently, being abandoned for the oddity of "nominalistic freedom," nevertheless, it looks like the *framework* of the *noumenal/phenomenal* problematic has been clearly retained; but, retained in the historical setting of freedom as charisma, episodically transcending the determinism of the changing forms of routinized social order – "*Charisma* ... serves as a *metaphysical* vehicle of man's freedom in history," "[in so far as they do] ... *transcend* the routines of everyday institutions" and hence are not "merely ... *social products.*"

I want to be very clear here about the quite unexpected suggestion that the Weberian actor is "in" history but not "of" history: there is the *ahistorical* subject with his/her agency which is underwritten by the unchanging *Kantian framework*, and then there is the *historical* subject located in the dynamics of changing forms of rational order. This brings out the crucial theoretical question of the metaphysical or ontological status of the conception of freedom that Weber is torturously working out. And, in that question an irony is uncovered: in grounding freedom in the metaphysics of charisma, strictly speaking, while Weber may be suspending "noumenalism," at the same time he seems to be retreating to the idea that freedom is "transcendence"? If this is not to be judged simply incoherent, then, as I have suggested above, there must be an answer to this question: what metaphysic is to ground the real a priori of power that "transcendence" presupposes in Weber's sociological theory? Thus, "nominalistic freedom" is therefore better understood as referring to the forced juxtaposition of two incompatible ideas at the heart of Weber's thinking about freedom, that is nominalism as Humean empiricism and freedom as "transcendence." This somewhat takes the sting out of the oxymoronic character of the term, and it focuses attention on the fact that Weber, who was temperamentally ill-disposed to engage in philosophical thinking, wound up in this kind of philosophical muddle. In regard to this issue of "transcendence," the two-part definition of charismatic freedom must be examined. Given that definition, consider part one: charisma is

> A certain quality of an individual personality by virtue of which he is considered *extraordinary* and treated as endowed with *supernatural, superhuman, or at least specifically exceptional powers or qualities.* These are such as are not accessible to the ordinary person, but are regarded as of *divine* origin *or* as *exemplary,* and on the basis of them the individual concerned is treated as a leader.
>
> (Weber 1968: 241)

Part two is the principle incarnated in the legendary line, "It is written, but I say unto you."

> The charismatic individual disrupted the everyday world, creating a situation in which old customs or rules could end and new ones could begin.
>
> (paraphrased in Liebersöhn 1987: 121)

The first part of the definition is ambiguous: freedom refers to something *extraordinary*, that is powers that are either of an other-worldly status – *supernatural and thus divine*, or of a this-worldly status – *exceptional and natural and thus mundane* (Liebersöhn Ibid: 121). We must set aside the principle of the methodological usefulness of this ambiguity in empirical research where metaphysical matters should be suspended; in Weber's attempt to realize an allegedly post-Kantian conception of freedom, it is precisely the issue of metaphysical adequacy indicated above that is relevant, and hence should not be suspended. And to be sure about the understanding of this, I am using metaphysics in the strict scientific realist sense that a theory is a disguised ontology; thus, theory is a systematic metaphysic technically put to explanatory use. The second part of the definition is certainly not ambiguous, however, for, in the context of this discussion of Weber's apparent attempt to get away from Kantian philosophizing on the matter of human freedom, it is indicative of something quite important. I think that Weber has unself-consciously taken the philosophical argument of the third antinomy, that *human freedom is an ordinary rupture in the fabric of phenomenal determinism in which old actions end and new actions begin* ("you have been sitting in a chair, and then, you simply get up and leave" – Kant's actual example), and he has assimilated it to the historical argument that *human freedom is an extraordinary disruption in the fabric of social routines in which old customs or rules end and new customs or rules begin* ("It has been written, but I say unto you"). Let us be very clear about what I am asserting concerning this assimilation: *Weber has subsumed ordinary freedom under extraordinary freedom, and has consequently lost the idea of ordinary freedom; for all theoretical purposes that idea has no place in Weber's thinking.* But this is only one half of the significance of the suggestion under consideration. The other half has to do with Kant's, in effect, "reversal" of Weber's procedure: from the historical argument of charisma and its implied doctrine of transcendent freedom that, apart from Weber, is intrinsic to the history of religion, theology, and traditional philosophy in Western thought, Kant forged the philosophical argument for transcendental freedom. Again, let us be clear about this: *Kant was engaged in secular democratization, that is he transformed freedom as a revolutionary moment into freedom as an ordinary moment, highlighting its peculiar property of radical agency.* Note that, of course, radical did not mean revolutionary, and it did not mean extraordinary either, but rather, exceptionality. That he was trying to locate a suitable grounding site for the real a priori of freedom, the power of which was to be a genuine variety of a this-worldly *causality* of *nature*, will turn out to be important to mention right here. For, in the discussion to follow below we will discover that, in forging a conception of freedom for interpretative social research, Weber comes up with the *idea of freedom as a causal power without, however, a theory of causal powers with which to account for and to justify it.* Now, given this remark, my next point acquires an even greater importance for my discussion thus far.

On the issue of the third antinomy in relation to Weber's thinking about freedom, the special relevance of Kant's use of the argument to Weber's is this: there is the implication that Kant's move to the transcendental argument, and, that that argument was to be a superior advance over the transcendence argument was simply not taken seriously by Weber. For whatever reason either he never picked it out in what was most likely a standard reading that he gave of Kantianism, or, perhaps, given a standard reading, still, he may have had *some* intuitive sense of what Kant had done, and dismissed it in the then expected impatience with philosophy one was supposed to have if one were in fact involved in the more important business of forging the new field of sociology; this time, of course, in Germany under the auspices of the *Methodenstreit* dominating intellectual activity during the latter half of the nineteenth century (Turner *et al.* 1995: 179–83; Bryant 1985: 57–108). However, what is absolutely the case is that Weber generally gave no explicit, and certainly no systematic, indication in his methodological writings of having any understanding that science was a realist and not a positivist practice. In fact, again, the nominalist metaphysic that informs the practice of his research demands the conclusion that the empiricism it presupposes is Humean and not Newtonian. It is quite a shame that, although Weber and Durkheim had Simmel in common, as a colleague and friend in the former case and only as a known scholar in the latter, they never met; and there is no evidence that they even knew of each other's work. However, if they *had* known each other's work, could Weber ever have denied Durkheim's understanding that science was a realist practice? Such an encounter would surely have been a marvelous historical moment for the then burgeoning social sciences. But, despite all that, let us suppose, nevertheless, that they *did* read each other's work, especially the methodological discussions. This hypothetical allows me to set the stage for what is to follow: in that event, Weber would very likely have been confronted with the puzzling fact that, on the one hand, his nominalism and Durkheim's realism contradict each other, while, on the other, his appeal to the idea of causal powers in formulating his conception of social action presumes therefore a realist view of freedom, so that, from within his own position, the realist view of his contradicts his nominalism; but that is not all, for, in that realization, he would also have been returned to Kant, where he is dropped right back in the lap of the transcendental theory of the subject where freedom is a species of the causality of nature. The upshot would have been that, he would have come face to face with the fact that Kant's causality of freedom and his conception of individual social action would be, metaphysically speaking from the realist standpoint, impossible to distinguish. This is exactly to be expected from the fact that the noumenal/phenomenal schema is retained in what was supposed to be the alternative schema of charisma and routinization. This hypothetical realization brings into sharp relief the fact that Weber was obscure about the metaphysical status of the conception of freedom that he was very briefly working out in the theory of social action. We will see that

that obscurity has cost him dearly: the significance of the vocabulary of charisma (person) and routinization (society: system) in reference to the problem of recovering agency is that Weber's interpretative sociology is consequently a stalemate, rather than a promise, with regard to recovery. Does Weberian scholarship reveal anything about this question of the metaphysical status of Weber's conception of freedom?

Charismatic freedom and Weberian scholarship: disconnection and consequences

In *The Emergence of Sociological Theory* (1995) where Jonathan H. Turner and colleagues present Weber's four classificatory ideal types of social action, there is not a whisper of any question with regard to the metaphysical status of the conception of freedom that is presumed there (Turner *et al.* 1995: 196–99). Nevertheless, there is a place where Turner *could* have inserted the issue of freedom. He closes with a discussion of the noticeable impact of Weber's *methodological* as well as his substantive work on theoretical sociology today. Concerning the third strategy of causal analysis that is already presumed by the first two (ideal-type thinking and comparative analysis) Turner strangely focuses only on

> the general types of *historical* events that are necessary and sufficient *to bring about a* phenomenon (such as capitalism), which is usually described in terms of an ideal type, are isolated and described, again often in terms of an ideal type.
>
> (Turner *et al.* Ibid: 230, emphasis provided)

My point is clarified, and verified: the veiled allusion to causal powers – conditions "to bring about" – is then lost as it is assimilated and restricted to ideal types "of *historical* events," and therefore it completely erases the fact to be revealed below, that Weber explicitly formulates individual freedom as something that "brings about" phenomena, that is as a causal power. Hence, my initial statement concerning his presentation stands. However, since Turner does not discuss the classificatory ideal types of rationality we can very briefly consider Stephan Kalberg's comprehensive reconstruction of "Max Weber's Types of Rationality" (1980). And although the same conclusion follows for Kalberg as for Turner, nevertheless we can easily imagine exactly the moment where Kalberg too *could* have at least mentioned Weberian freedom and its relationship to the Kantian problem of the proper metaphysical grounding of freedom. In examining the integral connection of types of social action and types of rationality he asserts that they refer

> to universal *capacities* of *Homo sapiens*. Instead of depending for their existence on societal, cultural, or historical constellations, these types of action stand *"outside of history"* as anthropological traits of man.
>
> (Kalberg 1980: 1148)

What is presented here, I contend, is a statement that is actually a *conclusion*, and one that would have followed upon a systematic examination of the causal powers reading that Weber gives to the freedom of individuals in social action. Kalberg's assertion that the "anthropological traits" of such human action are "universal capacities" that "stand 'outside of history'" cries out for precisely that type of systematic examination and subsequent explication indicated above. After all, what we have here is the presupposition that human freedom as self-determination is grounded in a species-specific, *Homo sapiens*, set of causal powers – *capacities*. This is, essentially, the very idea that I suggested in Chapter 2 (agency as a problem of the stratified kinds of natural kinds of powerful particulars in the world of nature). Yet, there is an indication of the very problem that I have alluded to above (the ahistorical subject as agent) that is at the center of Weber's theory of freedom and individual social action. When Kalberg refers to those human traits that are the capacities of our species as being "outside of history," *there you have it*. The problem is the ambiguity of the first definition of charisma as extraordinary freedom: it refers to powers that are either supernatural/divine, or exceptional/mundane. In short, we have the traditional conception of *transcendent* freedom and, apparently, for want of a better word, Weber's version of a secular conception of *transcending* freedom, but what we don't have is any reference to Kant's *transcendental* freedom. Now, in view of Kalberg's reference, in effect, to the *powers* of freedom as being *"outside of history,"* which metaphysic in reference to "outside" is being indicated here? Clearly, the metaphysical content of this very question is defined by the issue of the charisma/routine version of the noumenal/phenomenal schema that grounds Weber's theory of freedom and historical reason. Consequently, I have certainly not only pointed out that *transcending* and *transcendence* are clearly interchangeable terms here, but also, that Weber, in effect, could never cogently justify the rejection of the implication that Kant's term *transcendental* is also interchangeable with either of the other two? In which case, *Weber's bid for the viable conception of "transcending" freedom is stranded between the metaphysics of "transcendence" and the metaphysics of "transcendental."*

To allow us now to move forward on this point, let us force the issue: how has Weber not failed to get beyond the traditional conflation of transcendent and transcendental freedom, so that, in being located "outside of history" the conception of "transcending" freedom is metaphysically muddled? In other words, taking *charisma* to be *the* constitution of freedom has led Weber back into the predicament in which self-determination and free-will are still not cleanly separated conceptions. Again, we are not and should not be talking about the empirical research context, but only the theoretical context where the metaphysical or ontological question is absolutely relevant, and therefore it is *the* question that *must* be the issue. Here then is the problem of Kantian freedom for Weberian freedom: in virtue of the fact that the metaphysical *grounds* of charismatic freedom are *"outside of history,"* while the *activity* of that freedom is *in history*, Weber therefore has not succeeded in abandoning noumenalism for nominalism in his conception of charismatic freedom.

Charisma and spontaneity: Kant to Weber?

Now, charismatic freedom becomes, in Kantian hands, the theoretical principle of freedom as an absolute spontaneity. And of course the relevant point then is that Weber's retreat from Kantian spontaneity and his return to charismatic spontaneity is realized in going back to the historical origins of that spontaneity in the Hebrew prophets of the Old Testament, and then tracing that origin to its culmination in the Puritans of the Calvinist reformation (Liebersöhn Ibid: 123). Spontaneity, itself, precisely, is incarnated in the prophet's cardinal virtues of *"inner autonomy" and a preference for "spiritual goods"* (Liebersöhn Ibid: 92, 120–23). But then, how is that an advance over Kant in metaphysical, that is ontological, adequacy? After all, since the purpose is no longer to rescue but to recover "inner autonomy" for the natural and cultural worlds, how has Weber contributed to that purpose in the location of its origins in the Jewish tradition, and, then, in the identification of its problematic end-point in the Christian puritan tradition? It is now quite clear that the problem of conflating transcendental and transcendent freedom of the will is certainly relevant to Weber's attempt to transform the former into his conception of transcending freedom; and, in view of that, I also want to insist that one is certainly entitled to suspect that the other problem of the conflation of inertia with inertness cannot be very far behind in its relevance to that alleged transformation of Kantian to Weberian spontaneity. We should remember that, for Simmel implicitly and Durkheim explicitly, it has been demonstrated that the ultimate thesis is of fundamental importance for an understanding of their relationship to the structure/agency problem and the promise of recovering human agency. Why then should Weber be the exception? If nothing else, his vision of the iron cage of modern formal social structures and institutions would seriously suggest that that's exactly why he is not an exception. Again, consider once more what we have uncovered here, namely, that the noumenal/phenomenal schema indeed underwrites the charisma/routinization schema, and, note carefully, that it does so in a special way: observe what Weber says – *either the soul makes ultimate decisions or the soul slips back into the natural process of routines.* This is exactly what the ultimate thesis prescribes: either the patiency of natural phenomena or the agency of extra-natural beings. For a crucial example of this insight let us carefully consider this quite relevant comment from Liebersöhn.

> Ascetic Protestantism's relationship to charisma became somewhat less consistent with the earlier argument. The aim of *The Protestant Ethic* was of course to define the *spirit* of capitalism. *Economy and Society* contrasted charisma and rationalization so sharply that such a spirit was

hardly thinkable. On the one hand Weber recognized a special relationship between ascetic Protestantism and authentic, personal charisma. ... On the other hand Weber virtually limited charisma to the original leader and his followers. By this definition, *the privileged moment of collective Puritan spirit was impossible;* ascetic discipline was already a substitute for the charisma of Calvin, an instance of rationalizing *Ungeist* succeeding the founders' spontaneous calling. *Either order or charisma: the schema did not allow them to mix.* In this respect Weber actually intensified the conflict between authentic individuality and social order to the point where brief charismatic outbursts turned society on its head only to be set aright by the cunning of *ratio*.

> (Liebersöhn Ibid: 122, emphasis provided for the second
> half of the comment)

In the light of the discussion to this point let us rearrange Liebersöhn's quite helpful comment in the following way in order to work out an import that advances the discussion. I am going to display the rearrangement as an array of three theses and their significance. In this regard, we should keep at the forefront of our minds the point that I have been insisting upon: the noumenal/phenomenal grid informs Weber's charisma/routinization schema.

- Thesis 1: since it is the case that "Either order [structure] *or* charisma" [agency]: hence "the schema does not allow them to mix"
- Thesis 2: it is therefore the case that "the privileged moment of charisma is impossible": "discipline [structure] was already a substitute for charisma"; so that the historical fact of the matter is that
- Thesis 3: "the [either/or] conflict between authentic individuality and social order [is such that, charisma is correspondingly restricted to] brief outbursts [which turn] society on its head only to be set aright by the cunning of *ratio*."

Significance

(1) Throughout history, routinization/order radically predominates over charisma; (2) hence, the metaphysical implication is that structure so dominates agency that human freedom is virtually swallowed up in determinism; (3) thus, the question that arises is that the status of absolute spontaneity, or autonomy, or agency, is seriously problematic, if not simply fatal; (4) perhaps Durkheim's assimilation of autonomy to heteronomy is the better understanding of freedom so conceived; or, perhaps, even Freud's more extreme decision to completely assimilate autonomy to heteronomy, so that freedom is the appearance behind which a theory of an unconscious would be the reality that explains that freedom; Schmaus's portrait of the scientific realism of Durkheim's naturalistic sociology is clearly absolutely consistent with the scientific realism of Freudian naturalistic psychology: their theories converge

on the principle of a deterministic collective/individual unconscious; (5) hence, *Weber's theoretical predicament*: the theory of freedom and individual social action is in danger of collapsing into the traditional format of the Science and Humanism debate: structure is the reality behind the appearance of agency; and worse, in (6) *Roscher and Knies*, the proposal to see self-determination as the agency of a powerful particular is to be thrown into the middle of this theoretical predicament; if we read this causal powers proposal as saving the conception of freedom from the fate of metaphysical incoherency, how is it not a *deus ex machina*; hence (7) Weber's shift away from noumenalism to nominalism is ultimately a failure; this forces upon us the consideration that Weber's conception of freedom certainly calls for a return to Kant.

Weber and Kant: unfinished metaphysical business

To get a further handle on this unfinished business, consider the implications of what Weber has actually done in transforming Kantian freedom into charismatically disposed historical actors in the manner discussed thus far. Martin Barker's discussion of "Kant as a Problem for Weber" (1980: 224) is most helpful in this regard.

> The distinction between noumenon and phenomenon, which is at the heart of the Kantian scheme of things, sets up the possibility of the kingdom of ends. It is *missing* in Weber. *Everything is phenomena*. All we have for purposes of understanding are useful fictions, and that is *all* we have for living. The best that we can do is to achieve some form of realization of our limitations. *In Kant, the noumenal world is a beacon inviting effort; in Weber, it isn't even worth trying*.
>
> (Barker 1980: 240, emphasis provided)

One implication here is simply Barker's point that the noumenal no longer inspires belief and therefore no longer invites effort as it did for Kant. I respectfully would like to suggest that Barker needs our help here to bring forth a fundamental part of the reason for the failure of the noumenal to "invite effort" in Weber's case. For, in Weber's vision the promise of the noumenal theory of freedom that human agency is a genuine species of the causality of nature has been virtually snuffed out. That reason is intimated by the vision of the iron cage, and is expressively illuminated by Kafka's image of the darkness engulfing the single lit candle. Hence, we can appreciate why one would suppose that the dead weight of the noumenal cannot invite Weber to forswear the vision of the iron cage. Now that strongly indicates, it seems to me, that the problem of deterministic structures and human agency was far more important in Weber's theoretical imagination than we have ever thought. And so it makes perfect sense that Barker suggests that Weber's theoretical pessimism dictates the premise that the structure of the social is such that "The power-relation is therefore the natural relation among men and women" (Martin Ibid). And the theme of this power-relation comes to this.

> My freedom is achieved not by developing the freedom of others, but by subverting their freedom, by making it appear that what I want is what they want.
>
> (Barker Ibid)

Given that Barker's brilliant insight that the resort to power is the natural relation in sociation, and that that resort is, allegedly, also an exercise of freedom, there is now good reason to suspect that the latter is now, on his own analysis, problematic. For, what Barker apparently does not see is another implication: the direct consequence of Weber having to abandon the human beings to the natural world – "everything is phenomena" – is that, in Kantian terms, human beings have hence been abandoned to the world of fate, that is the forces of determinism. Thus, the idea of the *natural force of determinism* is now open to the interpretation that the idea of the *natural relation of power in human relations* is to be construed in terms that favor determinism over freedom. That of course is the point of the problem of agency in a natural world of deterministic structures: human force – in relations of power – is going to be construed in terms of the category of a natural force; hence, the next temptation is to construe human natural force as the agency of energy and not the energy of agency. This reductionistic move is of course the prelude to reification. The paradigm case here would be, first, Freud, and then Durkheim: the former famously, but the latter, quietly, took a conception of the unconscious to be fundamental to explanation in psychology and sociology, respectively. Thus, the development of Barker's point that I have just worked out allows us to see how, in another way, the loss of the noumenal and the consequent abandonment of human beings to the phenomenal world must have pressed in upon Weber a deep challenge that intimately informed the formulation of his conception of interpretative sociology. In other words, *how is Weber going to overcome the belief that freedom is not the natural relation among human beings in the phenomenal world of culture in its historicity.* Indeed, we've seen that there is reason to think that Weber failed to avoid the belief that determinism overcomes freedom. That very failure is certainly suggested in the significance of the three theses spelled out from the Liebersöhn quote: the ultimate thesis dictates that the schema of "order or charisma" is virtually an absolute dichotomy.

The theoretical upshot of this disposition to believe that freedom is not the natural relation among human beings in lived culture constitutes evidence in support of what Stephen P. Turner and Regis A. Factor in *Max Weber: The Lawyer as Social Thinker* have persuasively argued, namely, that Weber was radically skeptical about the possibility of human freedom in the historical world of culture (Turner and Factor 1994: 156–65). To be sure, Weber does not resort to Dilthey's magic trick of salvaging human freedom by virtue of the distinction between the phenomenal and phenomenological. Up against the demand of his theoretical imagination for a strict rapprochement between the interpretative understanding of social action and its causal explanation, Dilthey's distinction apparently did not carry much weight for Weber (1968: 4). Yet, even though he took human beings to be existentially naked in the phenomenal world that calls for causal explanation, I have been repeatedly pointing out something odd in all that. First of all that his conception of freedom as a "transcending" act is interchangeable with both "transcendent" and "transcendental" freedom, and, then, that the "transcending" act is also connected to a causal powers reading. Thus, as I have suggested, Weber seems to be metaphysically stranded somewhere between free-will theory and noumenal freedom, and, in response, he seems to have come up with, in effect, what I have earlier referred to as "nominalistic" freedom. To further bring its oxymoronic character I now am going to call it *"phenomenal freedom."* Of course the point is that this oxymoronic move is the metaphysical business that demands a closure that Weber was not in a position realize. We must now enter into a careful examination of this paradox of "phenomenal freedom" in relation to Weber's contribution to the German debates on methodology.

Weber's solution to the *Methodenstreit*: phenomenal freedom?

Weber certainly *does* deal with the issue of free will in his first encounter with the *Methodenstreit* of German social science in his classic *Roscher and Knies: The Logical Problems of Historical Economics* (Weber 1975: 118, 93–209). *Roscher and Knies* may well be as laborious as Jonathan H. Turner and his colleagues believe, but, to be sure, there is more, much more, to this work than meets the positivistic eyes of these scholars. For example, as far as providing any insight into the question of the influence of Kant's theory of freedom on Weber's understanding of the prospect of causal analysis in sociological work, and, further, any insight into this influence and its relationship to the structure/agency problem, that very work turns out to be of special importance (Turner *et al.* 1995: 173; Kalberg 1994: 23–49; Oakes in Weber 1975: 16–39). At the center of the crisis is Knies's view that human beings have the mysterious power of a free will, the practical significance of which, according to Knies, is that in their economic conduct they are not subject to natural laws. In short, for Knies free will signifies the irrationality of human conduct. Thus, in not being predictable (orderly and stable conduct, hence calculable), human beings are not available to Weber's enterprise of interpretative understanding (of action as calculable conduct) (Weber Ibid: 95–97). His answer directly contradicts Knies's thesis with the counter-claim that "By using our own imagination, schooled in the experience of the everyday world, a genuinely positive *causal* interpretation in terms of 'motives' is produced" (Weber Ibid: 126). As we allow Weber to further speak to this point, at some length, two themes will be highlighted: Weber's uncompromising commitment to naturalism, *but not positivism*, and a sophisticated, but not unproblematic, sense of deterministic analysis.

> From a logical point of view, *the physical and chemical processes which produce a seam of coal or a diamond constitute a "creative synthesis" in the same sense as the chain of motives which links the intuitions of a prophet to the formation of a new religion.* The two sorts of "creative synthesis" can be substantively differentiated *only* by reference to differences in the predominant *values* in terms of which we conceive them. ... *If we represent [the latter production] anthropocentrically by ascribing to [it] the causal efficacy of "human action," then in such cases these actions may be said to be "creative."* However, as I have already said, *from a strictly logical point of view, the same status can be ascribed to purely "natural processes." This can happen whenever we abandon this anthropocentric conception.*
>
> (Weber 1975: 102–3, emphasis provided)

> Suppose that ... the degree of [an action's] "incalculability" increases. To that extent, we are inclined to *deny* that the actor has *"freedom of the will"* (in the sense of *"freedom of action"*). ... [And as regards] the interpretation of human "action," we are not satisfied by merely establishing a relation between action and a purely empirical generalization, regardless of how strict this generalization may be. ... [After all] ... such "laws" are *intrinsically* of *absolutely no "significance"* for the interpretation of "action." Suppose ... [such a law], showing that all men everywhere who have ever been placed in a certain situation have invariably reacted in the same way and to the same extent. Suppose. ... that this reaction is, in the most literal sense of the word, "calculable." ... By itself, such a demonstration would contribute *absolutely nothing* to the project of "understanding" "why" this reaction ever occurred and, moreover "why" it invariably occurs in the same way.
>
> (Weber Ibid: 128–29, emphasis provided along with Weber's)

> [Furthermore], consider an example like the conduct of Friedrich II during the year 1756, ... in a single, quite concrete situation. Such a case is not only nomologically "possible," like the splintering of the bolder. Not in the sense that we can establish, as a result of the ascription of causes, a statement of *necessity.* But rather in the sense that his conduct has an *"adequate cause."* I.e., given certain intentions and (true or false) beliefs of the monarch, and given also a rational action determined thereby, a "sufficient" motivation can be identified. In this case, the "possibility" of interpretation implies that *"interpretable" processes are "more calculable" than non-"interpretable" natural processes.*
>
> (Weber Ibid: 127, emphasis provided)

For Weber, in principle, the causal analysis of phenomena is as constitutive of the social sciences as it is of the natural sciences. To be sure, the focus on "meaning" and thus on "motives," constituted the very uniqueness that defined Weber's sociological enterprise as interpretative; but it was precisely that realization of an *interpretative* sociology that convinced him that he had resolved the *Methodenstreit* crisis (Oakes in Weber Ibid: 24). The doctrine of freedom that Knies embraced was definitively renounced in two ways. First of all the phrase *"freedom of action"* replaces the traditional phrase *"freedom of the will"*; clearly, what Weber has done here is to root out the metaphysics of "transcendence" by throwing out the idea of the "will," but also, Weber's cardinal emphasis on "persönlichkeit," the "person" of "inner autonomy," is now in place. Second, with the marriage of causal analysis and motivational analysis, Weber can then make the unique and totally unexpected claim that causal analysis is possible in the realm of human action, but that is precisely because *human action, itself, as a creative act, is a form of "causal efficacy."* It is right here, at this second reason, that the situation becomes interesting with regard to the Kant/Weber issue of unfinished metaphysical business. For, having made room for the person of autonomy, the business at issue is the metaphysical status of the location of agency: "inner" may refer to the "agency *of* the person" or *"in"* the person. But certainly, has not Weber, at least by implication, already eliminated that question by getting rid of the idea of the "will"? *The "freedom of action" is thus a "transcending" act but not an act of "transcendence."* The answer must be yes; but it is certainly no news to serious readers of Weber, that one has to say that the only question here concerns Weber's clarity and consistency with regard to his own thinking on this matter.

Even after the switch to "freedom of action," there is still the problem of "transcendental" freedom. But so far, it seems to have been simply ignored: Weber dismisses "freedom of the will" and, without any philosophical fanfare, directly substitutes "freedom of action." However, *is* the Kantian problematic out of sight here? Notice that the naturalist principle that "creative synthesis" is identical in the cases of the formation of a seam of coal, a diamond, and, *a new religion*, is plausible if, for Weber, *"Everything is phenomena."* Now, what does "From a logical point of view" have to do with the naturalist principle concerning Kant's phenomenal world – for all regions of nature all of its respective phenomena are, equally, constitutively deterministic? Nothing. Unless, it simply means this: if your value preference is naturalism (informed by Kantian transcendentalism), and you conduct your theoretical thinking from that standpoint, then and only then it will logically follow that natural and cultural phenomena are undifferentiated forms of "creative synthesis." But if your value preference is "anthropocentric" then the natural and the human are "substantively" differentiated by the implied difference between "behavior" and "action," respectively. How is this not quite simply an unsuccessfully washed down version of Kant's idea of the great gap between the causality of nature and the causality of freedom – from Kant and the noumenal/phenomenal distinction to Weber and the actional/phenomenal distinction? In other words, freedom as noumenal and freedom as action are equally problematic in the phenomenal world. Now here is the rub: in Weber's shift to axiology – values – away from metaphysics – ontology – we have the serious mistake discussed in an earlier chapter, namely, of translating the legitimate problem of ontology in realist theoretical science into a psychological problem of what Weber called the ontological fallacy. In other words, the questions of Kantian and Weberian dualism are the same theoretical questions of the ontology of natural and human agency. I simply do not see that Weber is anything other than a Kantian in his discussion thus far. It must be carefully noted that this is not the same thing as saying, according to the received view, that Weber is neo-Kantian, for that understanding, in this context, is simply no longer adequate. In short, what is missing in the received view, on the one hand, is that the Kantian problem of the noumenal in reference to the phenomenal still informs Weber's conjunction of human action and the phenomenal world, and, on the other, Kant's scientific realism is brought out of hiding precisely when Weber equates freedom and action by virtue of the fact that he treats freedom as genuine agency. In short, causal efficacy is causal power. The latter, particularly, is now to be confirmed as we get further into the critique of Knies.

Now we can note what Weber himself never brings out: the above idea of human freedom is an implicit expression of a confirmation of a scientific naturalism that is not conflated with positivism. And obviously it is not the traditional Humanist affirmation of freedom at the expense of science: freedom has not been rescued from the phenomenal world. Furthermore, and most important of all, it is a confirmation of the principle of *"freedom of action"* that is to be strictly understood as a *"causal efficacy of human action."* And what Weber means by "causal efficacy" is just that, as he himself declares: "[a] concept of causality ... as the idea of something as 'being produced.' ... " (Weber Ibid: 196). Weber is thus offering a naturalistic argument for what he himself refers to as "the real sanctuary of the personal," that is the concept of the "efficient causality of freedom." Now we have seen for ourselves that this *is* Kant's concept, and the foregoing certainly shows that what I earlier only proposed is indeed the case: Weber has, *despite himself*, argued, technically, for that very concept of human freedom as agency. Yet, ironically, and strangely, Weber not only does not see that he has indeed retrieved Kant's idea of the "causality of freedom," he actually renounces what he refers to as "a formulation which is, in its way, classical, Kant's conception of 'causality through freedom' (Weber Ibid: 118). And he does so because the concept is

> the philosophical archetype of all the metaphysical "culture" and "personality" theories [that posit] the agency of "sociopsychical development" [and] the mediation of the "personality" of genius [that]

objectively perpetuates the regeneration of the "progress" of the culture of humanity into the indefinite future.

(Weber Ibid: 118)

Thus, it is certainly the case that Weber renounces Knies's idea of free will, and does so ultimately as the offshoot of Kant's "grandiose" (Weber's word) metaphysical theory of noumenal freedom, which he sees as the basis for theories of progress that reify "culture" and "personality"(Weber Ibid: 118–19). We have thus returned full circle to the crucial question of what freedom is left in *Weber's muddled metaphysical situation*: on the one hand, in reference to the reciprocal principles that, while *the power-relation of domination is the natural relation among human beings, freedom thus is not the natural relation among human beings*, and, on the other, in reference to *the paradoxical concept of action as a powerful particular in a world of phenomenal particulars each without power*. We now can engage Turner and Factor's unorthodox view that Weber is radically skeptical of the reality of human freedom in the cultural historical world (Turner and Factor 1994: 161).

Weber's radical skepticism: the fate of the structure/agency problem

Educated in the law and its form of legal thinking, Turner and Factor argue that Weber effected a "transformation of the categories of legal science into the basic categories of his sociology" (Turner and Factor 1994: 1). His aim was to defeat nineteenth-century social scientific theory and its disposition to reify both collectivities as social forces and human nature as psychological forces, and then treat such forces as unconscious motives and purposes (Turner and Factor Ibid: 42–43). His cardinal theoretical achievement was to replace the natural scientific concept of "causal law" and the concept of "cause as a kind of real force" with the concept of "adequate cause" (Turner and Factor Ibid: 123). *According to Turner and Factor, Weber presumably believed that the idea of "cause as a kind of real force" was otiose.*

> "Probability," however, seemed to do the work of a notion of potency or efficacy [of causation] without its objectionable anthropomorphic and metaphysical overtones.
>
> (Turner and Factor 1994: 127)

His complementary methodological achievement was the use of ideal-type analysis of human activity which, on the one hand, functioned as a control for reifying the "social" and the "psychological," and on the other, promoted the causal analysis of human action. Thus, the two achievements together permitted Weber to declare that Marx was guilty of reification, that is treating an ideal-type as a real force (Turner and Factor Ibid: 119). In the realization of the transformation and replacement in the construction of his theoretical perspective, according to Turner and Factor, Weber comes to a "somewhat unusual" skepticism.

> Weber simply did not believe that any sort of sociological evidence or reasoning could overcome a fundamental question: whether the purposes we can attribute to people are the *real causes of their action.* "Real causes" is a peculiar phrase to use in connection with Weber. But it is nevertheless apt, for Weber's concern is that *"meaningful" explanations may often merely mask biological, psychophysical, and other causes, the "reality" of which he makes no attempt to deny.* ... In most cases of action, including charisma, *biological* causes play a large if not *predominate* role, and therefore the motives attributed to the agent are questionable and at best partial. In these cases *there is no question of whether the ideal-type of action entirely captures the real causes—it is freely admitted that it does not.*
>
> (Turner and Factor Ibid: 161–63, emphasis provided)

To make sure that the significance of Weber's radical skepticism is clearly understood, let us highlight the idea of the self-determinative freedom of reason and charisma in reference to his skepticism. They are forms of action which Weber concedes are, ideal typically, "free" actions, though empirically rare (Turner and Factor Ibid: 36–39). Even though Weber is convinced that "free actions," determined by the ideal-typical attribution of "clear and plausible intended purposes to people" (Turner and Factor Ibid: 162) can be empirically convincing, nevertheless, " ... what is difficult to show is that the intended purposes that are attributed are the real causes" (Turner and Factor ibid). Weber is, unsurprisingly, right in the middle of the structure/agency problem: he is wondering about whether the true causes are any of the traditional structural causes that are the reality behind the appearance of human agency. From the foregoing discussion of Turner and Factor, then, we can assert the following: *the freedom that is left in the human phenomenal world of culture where domination is natural, is the rare occurrence of freedom as rational and charismatic self-determination, and, furthermore, even this rarity is very likely not to be the "real cause" – domination is determined by causes other than human agency.* And if biology is the key to the real cause of charismatic leadership and practical reason, then it can also surely be said that

> From a psychoanalytic point of view, *charisma designates the force of the externalized unconscious,* that is, the unconscious tendencies which slip into awareness in the guise of an external force.
>
> (McIntosh 1975: 902, emphasis provided)

The import of this quote from McIntosh's "Weber and Freud: On The Nature and Sources of Authority," is that Weber's resort to the concept of "adequate cause" and his resort to the method of ideal-type, together, do not add up to even a relevant argument, let alone an effective one, against the positing of unconscious deterministic structures, of any kind, in the social sciences. The exemplary reason is found in the fact that Freud self-consciously fashioned a realist theory of unconscious psychological structure. He was presuming, because in fact he knew, and he was right, that the normal practice of natural science is to theorize genuine and plausible unobservable causal structures. And, most significantly, this realist practice of ascribing real causal forces, while certainly being metaphysical, it is neither anthropomorphic nor objectionable.

Weber, consequently, was quite wrong to regard, as he can be read to have done, such a realist practice in the social sciences as illegitimate, as if it were so in principle, even in the natural sciences. After all, Weber did believe, *in spite of himself*, that the idea of the "potency" or "efficacy" in reference to causation connotes "objectionable anthropomorphic and metaphysical overtones" (Turner and Factor 1994: 127). But if Turner and Factor were to argue, and it is reasonable to imagine that they might do so in light of Weber's fleeting realist treatment of causation, that he only believed that it was illegitimate in the social sciences, there is still a problem for Weber. Apart from his concept and method, Weber has to show that the concept of genuine causal power and the concept of plausible causal power, by the very nature of the concepts themselves as they are understood in the natural sciences, cannot be applied to human patterned activity. And that the only outcome of any contrary attempt to show that it *can* be so applied, will be nothing less than the theft of human agency. In other words, reification. As the result of *that* demonstration, *now*, Weber would be entitled to argue for the legitimacy of "adequate cause" and "ideal-type" as methodological alternatives. But, what is not clear is whether, and if so to what extent, Weber actually had any realization that he had in fact failed to solve the problem of the reification of human structures with the two ideas of "adequate cause" and ideal-type. Guy Oakes certainly suggests that Weber believed he had resolved the *Methodenstreit* crisis, and Turner and Factor lead one to believe that Weber might simply have regarded his skepticism as justified because it truly reflected the nature of the condition of the social sciences as practical sciences (Oakes in Weber 1975: 24; Turner and Factor Ibid: 163–65).

Whatever the answer may turn out to be in the future of Weberian scholarship in this regard, there is no doubt that Weber's magnificent attempt did fail, and the problem of structure and agency was going to continue to be a problem, and thus continue to be the root condition for a stalemate in the ongoing development of the social sciences. And to date, in this regard, nothing has changed. After all, I know of no one who has written about Weber's sociological theory who noticed the Kant/Weber connection on the issue of the efficient causality of freedom, on the one hand, and, on the other, has noticed that Weber has appealed to the idea of causal powers in arguing for a scientifically grounded conception of the "freedom of action." Furthermore, we have seen in an earlier chapter that in the paper of 1982 Marshall Sahlins insisted, against the general resistance of his colleagues across the generations, that Giddens's problem was a structural feature of anthropological thought; indeed, at a luncheon with Brenda Farnell, Tim Pauketat, and myself, around early 2000, Sahlins still took the structure/ agency question as seriously as he ever did. And in Chapter 2 I have pointed out that Michel Foucault, from the mid-1970s straight through to the last year of his life in 1984, returns to Kant to reinstate his *idea* of freedom without the metaphysics, and gingerly declares a commitment to nominalism, while he proceeds in his various writings to confront the very idea, oh yes, of the structure/agency problem. And finally, from the mid-1970s to the year 2007 the structure/agency problem is very much alive in the Bhaskar/ Archer continuation of Durkheim's social realism in the very terms of his scientific realism (consider my earlier reference to the June 2007 issue of *The Journal for the Theory of Social Behavior*).

Final words: Weber from Kant

But the significance of Weber's self-contradictory act of dismissing Kant's idea of *the efficient causation of freedom* and, in the same breath, his espousal of the idea of *the causal efficacy of human action*, must now be reckoned with. As we have already seen, since Weber argued for the very idea of the efficacy of causation in singling out "production" as the feature of causation that he accepted as *real*, this implied, of course, that human efficacy, in being causal, is an act of *real* causal production. It has thus been correct to assert that Weber is just wrong in his dismissal of Kant's "causation through freedom." Indeed, that dismissal was just that and nothing else, for Weber never returned to Kant's actual argument for noumenal freedom to deal with it, one way or the other. Consider his complaint of the "grandiosity" of Kantian metaphysics reveals that he simply took it to be a done deal that that argument was to be axiomatically set aside. And, given that he never read Durkheim, he was never in the position of discovering Durkheim's serious return to the problem of Kantian freedom (and then, of course Simmel's), and of discovering that *a direct answer to the noumenal argument was necessary in order to get the idea of human agency right in the light of Durkheim's mistaken reading,* which, perhaps, might have gotten him to reconsider his own. Furthermore, I have already regarded the fact that Weber did argue for the idea of the "efficacy of human action" and asserted its nature to be causal production, as a confirmation of the importance, at the very least, of Kant's identical idea. Once again, *this certainly means, contrary to Weber's belief, that the "potency" of causation is both metaphysical and unobjectionable.* And this also certainly means that, if only Weber could have returned to Kant with a clear understanding of the realism of science and the notion, in effect, of "agent causality" he in fact possessed, he would have fully realized that he was struggling to recover human agency in exactly the very spirit of Kant's transcendental theory of freedom.

But of course, such a return could never have occurred to him. This is exactly the point I have already made throughout this entire discussion. Since Weber could only hit on the *idea* of causal power without having the *theory* of causal powers that had been established by the mid-nineteenth century in physics, he simply was understandably at a loss to know how to negotiate the solution to the problem of biological, psychological, social, and cultural deterministic structures and human "agent causality." In reference to the reification problem of structure and agency, the theory of interpretative sociology was therefore left at a stalemate. The paradox of "phenomenal freedom," the muddled yet fruitful idea that human agency is a powerful particular in a phenomenal world of particulars without any powers, guaranteed that the promising idea of a *realist* conception of "adequate cause" could never even be *recognized* for what it was – the tip of the iceberg of a metaphysical theory of scientific realism.

And I do think that the decisive reason for Weber's predicament is that he too, like his contemporaries Simmel, Durkheim, and Freud, was similarly paralyzed by the ultimate thesis that so strongly informed and controlled their theoretical thinking. True, its influence may not have been as clear-cut as in the cases of the other three, nevertheless, it is, I think, cogently implied in Weber's theory of freedom and reason: *either charisma*, which is rare, or even, when it rarely does appear, it may well be chimerical, *or order*, which is virtually completely a constant property of nature at all levels. In that cognitive space between either/or, "transcending" and "transcendental" freedom are never clearly distinguished. And how could they have been: the "freedom of action" *is* "causality through freedom." While Kantian noumenalism haunts Weberian nominalism, the realism that they ultimately both shared, however dimly in Weber's case, lurks in the back of their minds and at the fringes of their respective theories.

8　Parsons, Dahrendorf, Berger
Rituals of return

The Sociological Tradition and twentieth-century sociology: Kantian connection

As I now move beyond Simmel, Durkheim, Weber and the close of the Sociological Tradition of the late nineteenth century by the 1920s to the twentieth-century sociology of Parsons, Dahrendorf, and Berger, the tradition of the return to Kant is of course not at its end. The grand programmatic gesture of *being a science*, as against *becoming a science*, that marked the Sociological Tradition of Comte, Marx, and Spencer seemed thus to have bypassed having to take up the problem of phenomenal determinism and transcendental freedom. This, we've seen, was not so for Nisbet's second half of the Sociological Tradition, for, precisely because at that historical moment Simmel, Durkheim, and Weber understood that modern sociology had to become a science before it could make the pronouncements of science, the Kantian challenge was indeed taken up. But with the end of that classical moment of sociology there came to an end, it appears, a fresh and original substance in their response to the problem of structure and agency tucked away in the conceptual thicket of Kant's transcendental idealism. Caught up as Parsons, Dahrendorf, and Berger were in the Science and Humanism debate that they themselves were participating in as important players, in order to retrieve some kind of a conception of freedom in the service of their variety of the sociological imagination they returned to Kant. Concerning the issue of a substantive return that was so clearly in evidence in Simmel, Durkheim, and Weber, I have come to think that Talcott Parsons is a transitional figure in this regard; although he indeed struggled with the spirit and somewhat with the letter of the "law" of Kant in a serious effort to forge a theory of freedom for his vision of sociology, yet I find him somewhere between substance and ritual in this regard. And perhaps that was exactly as it should have been, since at a time completely dominated by the history of positivism that culminated in the formidable forms of logical positivism and logical empiricism, there simply was no voice of the realism of science to be heard in the philosophy of science. And of course, what a shame: after Durkheim, Parsons himself made it modestly clear that he recognized the realism of science, although in his reference to it as a sociologist, "analytic realism," it did not stand out in relation to the problem of working out a theory of freedom before the structures of social life. For example, in the comment below, the realism of science is blandly presented, and it is not explicitly tied to either causality or to the ontological nature of theory. And, unfortunately, but understandably, Parsons's emphasis on the match-up between human logic and natural order, ends there.

> As opposed to the *fiction* view, it is maintained that at least some of the general concepts of science are not fictional but adequately "grasp" aspects of the objective external world. This is true of the concepts here called analytical elements. Hence the position here taken is, in an epistemological sense, *realistic*. ... [Hence], *scientific theory implies that empirical reality ... is a factual order*. Furthermore its order must be of a character which is, in some sense, congruent with the order of human logic. For a common feature of all scientific theory is the logicality of the relations between propositions.
>
> (Parsons 1949 [1937]: 730, 753–54)

In the 9 years I spent in the department of sociology working closely with my doctoral committee members, Robert Bierstedt, then chairman of the department, Leonard S. Cottrell, and Dennis Wrong, "analytic realism" was never mentioned, let alone the fact of its reference to scientific realism. Even my fortunate encounter with Alvin W. Gouldner, the great Parsons critic in *The Coming Crisis of Western Sociology* (1970), in discussions in his office and as one of my oral examiners, Parsons's "philosophy of science" was completely absent as a topic. Indeed, I do not recall in the entire literature of Parsonian scholarship that I have read, for that matter, that the revolt against positivism was ever examined from the specific standpoint of the "analytic realism" of the author of *a voluntaristic theory of human action* (the Parsonian literature is referenced below; for a minor exception see Savage 1981: 62–90, 87–90). That possible connection I have only discovered in the writing of this book.

Parsons's transitional status, I will argue, is revealed in my reading of the traditional understanding of his connection to Kant with special regard to *The Structure of Social Action*. This foundational work to all his theorizing, it is well known, is an attempt to salvage a theory of human action in the face of the varieties of reductionism in the behaviorism of positivism, the idealism of historicism, and the radical individualism of utilitarianism; with Dahrendorf's analysis of the theoretical importance of the concept of social role in "Homo Sociologicus" (1958) and its postscript "Sociology and Human Nature" (1962), we have an honoring of the Humanist belief in freedom in the face of the absolute sovereignty of phenomenal determinism in nature and society; Berger's discussion of freedom and sociological determinism in "Sociological Perspective – Society as Drama" (1963) and its continuation in "Sociological Interpretation and the Problem of Freedom (1981) leaves us, I believe, with the last voice of social scientific Humanism on the question of the human ontology of freedom (on Parsons: Devereux 1961: 3–28; Williams 1961: 64–99; Bershady 1973: 26–50; Savage 1981: 91–127; Levine 1995: 35–58; Turner 1999: 164–84; Shilling *et al.* 2001: 91–107). In their own manner, all three return to Kant under the heavy burden of the tradition of rescue, and, the rather dim and quite shaky prospect of recovery. Thus there are significant differences in their resort to that tradition: Parsons's eventual response to critics of his voluntaristic theory of social action with a "cautious naturalism" is the occasion to discover surprising connections to Kantian noumenalism and to scientific realism in the wavering but ongoing theory of voluntarism right to the end of his life; in Dahrendorf's seemingly unwavering acceptance of Kantian freedom in response to what he believed to be the natural determinism of social structure, there is more than a hint that the return is not much more than a ritual; a brief look at Gouldner's Weberian defiance of this alleged "natural" determinism of social structure will bring into the sharpest relief the emptiness of Dahrendorf's ritual. In accepting rather than rejecting science in Berger's defense of freedom as a Humanist, oddly, Kant is needed to buttress the philosophical anthropological speculations of Helmut Plessner and Arnold Ghelen on the phenomenology of human freedom. Of the three returns, Berger's reaching for Kant for the sake of the Plessner/Ghelen position seems more like an afterthought, and, I think, finally inexplicable. What particularly stands out, with the advantage of looking back, to be sure, is that they are all absolutely independent of each other: Parsons gives no indication of being aware of the return to Kantian freedom on the part of Simmel, Durkheim, or Weber. In the case of the last one, Parsons's complete lack of understanding of Weber's deep connection to Kant in working out his conception of freedom as "agent causality" I will show comes back to haunt him; Dahrendorf proceeds as if Parsons's Kantian encounter, and all of the others never existed, and, the same is true for Berger. In other words, the wheel is being reinvented with each return, but therefore, most unfortunately, without the benefit of learning from the history of each of the footnotes to Kant.

Parsons from Kant: three theses and the ultimate thesis

Today, it is well understood that the 1935 paper, "The Place of Ultimate Values in Sociological Theory," provides the framework for *The Structure of Social Action* of 1937 (Scott 1963: 721, footnote 21).

> The positivistic reaction against philosophy has, in its effect on the social sciences, manifested a strong tendency to obscure the fact that man is essentially an *active, creative, evaluating creature.* Any attempt to explain his behavior in terms of ends, purposes, ideals, has been under suspicion as a form of teleology which was thought to be incompatible

with the methodological requirements of positive science. One must, on the contrary, explain in terms of "causes" and "conditions," not ends.

(Parsons 1991 [1935]: 231)

However free of philosophy and hence straightforward Parsons's explication may appear to be, what comes through here is the fact that his conception of the actor is directly informed by Kantian idealism; the comment that a human being is "an active, creative, evaluating creature" is a reduction of Kant's conception of the subject to a simple set of ideas that have become commonplace in the discourses of the social sciences and of the educated public (Parsons 1991 [1935]: 237). Now, the Bershady/Hinkle debate with regard to the latter's thesis that Parsons was "thoroughly Kantian", that is that voluntarism and functionalism were a product of German Idealism, once again there is the mistake of assuming that Kantian Idealism is German Idealism (Bershady 1973: 84–85). The idea that "man" is "active" is of course a central theme of the theory of the transcendental ego, and it is that theme which is directly relevant to Parsons's formulation of the theory of the voluntaristic ego. To spell out the significance of that relevance we again take up Munch's claim that

we have to read *The Structure of Social Action* as the sociological equivalent of Kant's moral philosophy.

(Munch 1981: 713)

In the context of my entire discussion of Kant in this work thus far, Munch's thesis that *The Structure of Social Action* is the second *Critique* in disguise is quite fruitful, and thus points to two others. For instance, I am proposing that the key to the relevance at issue is the second thesis: the *voluntarism* of the Parsonian ego is the sociological equivalent of the *noumenalism* of the Kantian ego. Now, it is not the normative component – ultimate ends – of voluntarism that is singled out here, but rather voluntarism itself. And precisely because of the internal relation between noumenalism and voluntarism there is the third thesis: the direct consequence of that relation is that the Parsonian theory of action is going to be involved with the issue of transcendence and the transcendental. The particular importance of this point that voluntarism will be mistakenly confused with the transcendent theory of free will is the assumption that Parsons necessarily needs transcendence for the rescue of his voluntarism from the three reductionisms that he was up against in the 1937 work. Right from the start, then, the three theses are informing us that Parsons was "up to his neck" with the entire problem of structure and agency. In using the three theses together as a fruitful way to understand Parsonian action theory in its intimate involvement with Kantian freedom on the issue of structure and agency, an examination of Stephen S. Savage's *The Theories of Talcott Parsons* (1981) will be of great value in this regard. Since in this study of Parsons's work the Kant/Parsons connection is a central question, the second thesis will be of particular importance in my examination.

Savage on Parsons: ultimate values or voluntarism?

We should keep it in mind that Savage takes it for granted that transcendental freedom is free-will theory, as we pay careful attention to his highlighting the role of the noumenon in the theory of action.

> While we may disagree with Scott's attempt to *reduce action as a whole* to the status of a *Kantian noumenon*, it is not unreasonable to make a parallel between Parsons's presentation of the *value component* of action and *Kant's ethical stance on human action*.
>
> (Savage 1981: 111, emphasis added)

Of special interest here is Savage's implication that Parsons's reference to *ultimate values* as the ground of freedom is a *sociological* translation of Kant's conception of the noumenon as the ground of freedom. In other words, Savage declares, "[Although] human will is a *mechanism* in between the normative and the conditional, [yet] it does *not* itself *constitute* the *norms* and the *conditions* of action" (Savage Ibid: 103, emphasis provided). In all fairness to Savage, I am going to set to one side the fact that he makes this statement in reference to the ultra-humanist proposal of ethnomethodology, phenomenology, symbolic interactionism that "action is ... [a] totally unstructured and indeterminate process," which he wishes to radically differentiate from Parsonian action theory (Savage Ibid: 93). With that acknowledgment in mind and for the purposes of development of this discussion, we must note the implicit Durkheimian theme here that the agency of the *individual* actor is not the source of norms and conditions. Consequently, this theme brings out the fact that two important issues are not identified and differentiated by Savage: *the issue of the nature of human nature*, that is "*individualism*" (individuals *and* social relations) or *socialism* (individuals in social relations), and *the issue of the nature of the mechanism of human action*, that is the location of agency at the site of *persons* or the *social*. Now, his conclusion is that, for the very reason of such a translation of the *noumenal* into the *normative*, Parsons's theory of voluntaristic action theory is a *failure*. And, furthermore, the Kant/Parsons failure resides in this crucial fact.

> If the value sphere of action is not to be determinately conceptualized and is to remain as a transcendental and symbolic realm, then any investigation into its *effectivity* must of necessity contain an element of *ambiguity* and a degree of *speculation*. The contradictory co-existence of an indeterminate realm of values [noumenal] and a determinate sphere of action [phenomenal] requires that the theoretical specification of the effectivity of any given set of values can never be rigorously achieved. It

is impossible to relate coherently a level that cannot be known and a level that can be, and any attempt to do so will inevitably be characterized by speculation. That is, *it is not possible to determine in any particular case that some particular value has determined the action* [freedom, hence, is ambiguous]. This is the case in either direction. [Action cannot be deduced from value, nor can concrete action be derived from symbolic objects] To attempt any such derivation would be to fall into an "idealist emanationism." ... And since [value cannot be deduced from action] this would imply that value is purely solipsist, whereas Parsons insists that the most important feature of values is their relation to symbolic systems. ... So we have it: the mode of achieving the autonomy and effectivity of normative orientation in relation to the other elements of action involves the apparent intervention of a reality which is *inaccessible to science.*

> (Savage Ibid: 102–3, emphasis provided)

This then drives Savage to the crowning feature of his conclusion:

> In his insistence on the unique and primary characteristics of values in relation to the action complex, Parsons is forced to rely upon a *sophisticated yet arbitrary idealism.*
>
> (Savage Ibid: 127, emphasis provided)

From these comments, but without due consideration, one is able to agree with Savage when he asserts that the Parsonian theory of voluntarism will be distorted if it is construed to be "a metaphysical polemic for the assertion of free will" (Savage Ibid: 103). Savage is here alluding to Robert Bierstedt's and John Finley Scott's discussions of Parsons's voluntaristic theory of action. Examine first Bierstedt's critique in "The Means-End Schema in Sociological Theory" (1974) and then Scott's in "The Changing Foundations of the Parsonian Action Scheme" (1963) with regard to Savage's above statement.

Bierstedt

Sociology as a natural science can have no commerce with an "ego" or "self" which is not *identical* with the living *biological organism*, or at least which is not a *symbol* derived from sense experience of such an organism. *To construct such a non-temporal, non-spatial, non-sensory "self" for the purposes of analytical abstraction is to remove its social action from the sphere of science.* When subjective categories refer to this kind of an actor, they cannot evade the charge of invalidity because of ... the empirical impossibility of dealing objectively with phenomena as they appear from the point of view of an actor who is not an organism and who is not in space. The attempt to know the mind of such an actor and to delineate its *power* [?] is an *epistemological* venture, not a *sociological* one. The social action of an individual can be dissociated from his social behavior only on *metaphysical* grounds and at the price of playing dialectical dominoes with concepts which died a natural and not unwelcome death with the demise of *faculty* psychology.

(Bierstedt 1974 [1938]: 39, emphasis provided)

Scott

Parsons' exposition of voluntarism. ... never answers the one question on which so much of its discussion turns: what is the nature of valuation? To get an answer to that question it is necessary to extrapolate from the discussion in the "The Place of Ultimate Values in Sociological Theory," where valuation involves a *will independent in critical ways from the world of nature.*

(Scott 1963: 732, emphasis provided)

From the standpoint of this book, Savage can now be understood to be, in effect, dismissing the Bierstedt/Scott tradition of assimilating voluntarism to the standard tendency of conflating Kantian transcendentalism and Rousseauan transcendence, and then on that basis, renouncing voluntarism (Bierstedt 1974 [1938]: 39; Scott 1963: 732). But, upon due consideration, I cannot *fully* agree with that assertion, and for the very important reason that Savage only sees the free-will thesis in reference to the systematic idealist neglect of the complex of structures for and of action – cultural, social, psychological – that is the focus of Parsons's theoretical attention. But, what Savage does not (bother to?) see, and this is of major importance for his argument from the standpoint taken here, is that, nevertheless, he traces both free-will and Parsonian human will back to the same metaphysical ground – "the mode of achieving the autonomy and effectivity ... involves the apparent intervention of *a reality which is inaccessible to science.*" And in that specific sense, Savage *too* consigns Parsonian human will to the free will metaphysic of transcendence, *as well as* to the metaphysic of noumenalism. Of course, this was the critical complaint he implicitly aimed at Bierstedt and Scott. However, in, "A Paradigm of the Human Condition (1978)," where we have Parsons's last major effort to keep the pre-World War II voluntaristic thesis and the post-World War II social system thesis together in some systematic order, he not only refers to himself as "an reconstructed Kantian," but he actually uses "transcendental" as if it is a synonym for "transcendence," repeatedly (Parsons 1978: 355, 352–433, 413). In fact, the "transcendental" realm, which Parsons labels the Telic System, is one of four foundational systems of the entire Paradigm (Parsons Ibid: 361, 382). And not only has the fact of conflation been true of his work since the pre-World War II period, it has been a *deliberate* truth on his part. But again I must remind us, that while the conflation is Parsons's position, it is not Kant's, and Parsons himself acknowledges just that (Parsons Ibid: 371).

Now, it is for the reason of the conflation at issue that Savage's under-standable conclusion must be relocated in the context of my thesis here of the return to Kant in reference to the old tradition of rescue and the new one of recovery. To begin with, doing so allows me to pinpoint the bone of contention between us: *Savage's claim* is that the Parsonian (and therefore Kantian) theory of freedom is an *idealism* after all, *the Varela claim* is that, despite Parsons's deliberate conflation, *since the Kantian theory of freedom is an idealism that in fact is grounded in scientific realism, this is absolutely relevant to Parsons's theory because, we will shortly see, Kantian scientific realism is in principle – but not fully in substance, of course – Parsons's "analytic realism" (re-examine the above Parsons quotes on his "realism").* This crucial fact of clarification radically changes the other and final feature of Savage's conclusion concerning Parsons's alleged sophisticated but arbi-trary idealism. His interest here, and correctly so, is the obvious problem of conceptualizing

> the determinate intervention of the value-sphere [noumenal realm of ultimate values] of action: "the way is cleared for value standards to be effective whenever the plasticity of the organism *leaves a realm of freedom* in the relation between the situation and the organism." The human organism is provided with a *pre-given capacity* to respond to value orientations. The basic motivational elements of the personality, "drives" and "dispositions," are in every significant respects already compatible with the existence of value standards. Although the organism has its own prerequisites and is by no means born a well-adjusted citizen, *there is already in its constitution an endemic capacity* to respond to the culture in *which it appears. It is for this reason that Parsons prefers the term "motivation" to that of "instinct"* for there is apparently a point at which human *organism* and human *subject* merge. ... In other words, the organism *is already a subject*, and what is considered to be the process by which the "ego" is constituted is, in fact, merely the realization of that which is already in every significant respect present in the organism. *Parsons does not provide a theory of the mechanism by which the ego is formed but operates with an ambiguous circularity* – the process of learning is not a mechanism by which the personality is formed but is a process of *realization* of an immanent capacity. ... This is the point of the paradox, for Parsons appears to have returned inadvertently to the idealism which the theory of action explicitly attempted to avoid. ... [Thus] the human organism is char-acterized by a "plasticity" *because* such a capacity allows the determi-nate intervention of values. Nature has a purpose to realize ideas, and while this may not be the simple idealist *emanationism* as criticized in SSA, it certainly does involve the subordination of natural processes to the exigencies of the ideational realm. This subordination takes the form of an apparent teleological relation in which the natural organism is

already a human subject [an arbitrary assumption] in compliance with the requirements of action.

(Savage Ibid: 124, 126 emphasis added)

However, there is a significant point to be added to the major fact that the commitment to scientific realism and analytic realism is presupposed by Kant and is relevant to Parsonian voluntarism, so that, for that special reason, Savage's treatment of them as if they are transcendent theories because they reference a realm outside of science must be carefully reconsidered. To be sure, in the complex case of Parsons's deliberate conflation in the service of his Paradigm of the Human condition, he would probably not agree with the point I am now going to make. Once scientific realism is fully acknowledged, and Giddens's Call is considered as it is understood in the context of this book, *the conflation, deliberate or not, is no longer a necessary strategy for Parsons in the attempt to forge a theory of freedom, and especially so since, on the one hand, Parsons never abandons his intent to formulate a naturalistic theory of voluntarism, and, on the other, in that regard, the strategy of recovery is now available* (Parsons 1978: 383). On the question of the attack on Parsons's conflation, I now want to argue that Savage's claim that the Parsonian "organism is already a subject" is not the primary issue, indeed, it is not the issue at all. For, *that* issue is the internal relation between the "subject and the organism," that is between *noumenalism: "a realm of freedom,"* and *voluntarism: "the plasticity of the organism."* The plasticity of the human organism has to do with a theory of autonomy and rationality: the realm of freedom is thus the metaphysical foundations of the autonomy and rationality of the human subject. In being the problem of Kantian freedom in disguise, the problem of Parsonian voluntarism is therefore not the dead-end problem of an idealism, once more, but rather the open-ended problem of connecting "analytic realism" to the theory of voluntarism. *This,* however, demands a return to Kant, no longer for the old traditional reason, but the new reason of returning in order to discover a way to connect his realism to his transcendental idealism. Now I am claiming that the primary issue is the second thesis and its refinement for two good reasons: it *is* the issue for Parsons, and it must be so, in view of Parsons's commitment to the realism of science. The substance of this argument will be a central concern in the ensuing discussion.

The second thesis, and particularly in light of the Savage critique, has certainly shown us that the third is a virtual twin. Nevertheless, I do want to treat it on its own for the purposes of the following point. That is, what I am particularly interested in is the consequence of the above insight that, in view of Parsons's commitment to realist science, the critique of Parsonian voluntarism in terms of its assimilation to transcendence/transcendentalism is no longer a relevant reading of Parsons's predicament. After all, Scott's theme of Parsons's post-World War II "cautious naturalism" certainly suggests just that: Parsons began to see in Tolman's cognitive behaviorism some kind of light at the end of the naturalistic tunnel for his theory of voluntaristic action (Scott Ibid: 724–31). But Scott was at the very least as limited as Parsons was with regard to the philosophy of science, both of them being imprisoned by the complete dominance of positivist varieties of naturalism in the philosophy of science. And my point is that, ultimately, Parsons did not know what to do with whatever that light was – and its realist grounding simply was not available to him to be of any help. In the discovery that Savage's critique of the Kant/Parsons theory of freedom too is guilty of the same special sense of the conflation, the more important discovery there will be that that very conflation is the specific reason why Savage's critique, itself, is a failure (Savage Ibid: 96–97). And the conception of that failure, I believe, I have just provided: *since the problem of the voluntarism of the actor is the problem of the noumenalism of the subject, hence, voluntarism is the problem of Kantian freedom.* In short, Savage has not understood this at all in his otherwise absorbing analysis of *The Structure of Social Action.*

The Parsons/Lundberg connection: voluntarism and the ultimate thesis

Furthermore, the three theses that systematically connect Parsons to Kant cannot be understood for this book without suspecting that the ultimate thesis must be implicated in this connection. Later, the discussion will show that that turns out to be quite right. Under the shadow of George A. Lundberg's celebration of Parsons converging toward positivism by way of proposing four sociological laws, three of which "are identical with those of classical mechanics, and the fourth is definitely of the *same type*," it is not surprising that we find that Alvin Gouldner's critique of Parsons's Newtonian-centered theory of bureaucratic order, the natural-system model, is indeed the site of the ultimate thesis (Lundberg 1955: 24; Gouldner in Merton, Broom and Cottrell 1959: 423–26). And that very insight leads us back to the above thesis that Parsons is theoretically paralyzed in his attempt to forge a scientifically grounded theory of voluntarism. Certainly then, the 1935 paper on Ultimate Values strongly encourages us to surmise that Parsons had been thinking about this relationship between the structure of freedom in *individual* life and the structure of action in *social* life for some time before the breakthrough to his renowned treatise. Thus, with the second thesis and its refinement in mind we can enter Parsons's 1937 major work with this crucial question: how is Parsons going to handle the internal connection between the problem of the *noumenal* ego and the problem of the voluntaristic ego? I cannot seriously doubt that, with such serious attention that Parsons must have given to something like that question, surely he cannot have missed the traditional understanding of the problem of the atemporal argument for the justification of human freedom located thus in the noumenal realm. And what is most surprising, in view of the excellent Parsons scholarship that one must consider in this regard, is that no one has noticed that *Parsons's voluntaristic theory of freedom is a variety of Kant's noumenal argument for freedom*. In fact, he is closer to Kant than Dilthey on this issue. And therefore, since voluntarism is a variety of the noumenal argument, I contend that it is the root of the paralysis that plagues Parsons's attempt to resolve his "cautious naturalism."

Giddens on Parsons: limits of criticism

In this light, it is not possible to *fully* accept Giddens's tendency to assimilate Parsons to the Durkheimian side of the structure/agency problem.

> "*Voluntarism*" here thus becomes largely *reduced to* making space in social theory for an account of *motivation, connected via norms to the characteristics of social systems*. The *conduct of actors* in society is treated as *the outcome of a conjunction of social and psychological determinants*, in which the former dominate the latter through the key influence attributed to normative elements.
>
> (Giddens 1990 [1979]: 52, emphasis provided)

If anyone should be subject to Giddens's critique that voluntarism is lost to the joint determinants of social-normative and motive-psychological factors, it is certainly not Parsons, but, rather, it is John Finley Scott. He is the source of just that kind of positivist sociological theory in *Internalization of Norms: A Sociological Theory of Moral Commitment* (1971). In first declaring that

> While a wide variety of hypotheses about social behavior may be expressed in terms of this "action scheme," one that cannot be expressed is the hypothesis that normative elements have natural causes which sociology, or any other science, can study.
>
> (Scott 1971: 9)

Scott then gives us his naturalistic theory of causation:

> Moral commitment has traditionally been accounted for in terms of psychical and often voluntary processes. Our object has been to try to explain it in terms of social reinforcement [Skinnerian theory]: in short, *to replace psyche with sanction whenever there is the opportunity to do so.*
>
> (Scott 1971: 216, 18–19, 41, emphasis provided)

The ultimate thesis is directly in evidence in Scott's presentation of scientific and social scientific study: natural causation is external – social sanction – and any other causation is extra-natural – voluntary processes of the psyche. Parsons, on the other hand, did not give agency *outright* to the "social" at the expense of the "individual," as I have shown how Durkheim actually did, even though, admittedly, in the post-World War II treatment of the structure of action the incorporation of the Durkheim/Freud convergence thesis certainly threatened the voluntarism of the foundational work of 1937. Indeed, Scott does believe that in the second period of his writings Parsons has crossed the line from Tolmanian *cognitive* behaviorism to a behaviorism more in line with the Skinnerian variety that underwrites Scott's theory of moral commitment (Scott Ibid: 8). But no matter how incautious Parsons's naturalism can be, his theoretical heart is where Kant's was on the matter of freedom, that is the noumenal argument; it's just that he could not bring it to its proper realization, and I dare say that the commanding influence of the ultimate thesis in Scott's theory of moral commitment is a heavy reminder of that same influence on Parsons when he theorizes about the structuralization of the action systems surrounding the voluntarism of actors. This influence of the ultimate thesis, indeed, is *the* point about Parsons's paralysis.

Now Scott has seen this very idea about the voluntaristic theory and Freud with admirable clarity, and, indeed, with some welcomed humor. In commenting on Parsons's truly astonishing comment that the *Structure* book would have been better if it had included Freud's work (!), he then remarks.

> Yet the daring involved in making a voluntarist out of Pareto would be as nothing compared to that involved in making one out of Freud.
> (Scott Ibid: 725)

From my earlier discussions of Freud and Durkheim, the following can now be said: Freud fully realized, in effect, Durkheim's theory of the social fact as a force from without and from within the individual that controlled both the body and the mind, in his deterministic structural theory of the superego (the social fact dominant), the ego (over the mind), and the id (and over the body of the individual). Since Parsons never seriously confronted the special problem of the determinism of the unconscious, and particularly as one of the structure/agency problems under the auspices of scientific realism, he was never in the right position to see the point of Scott's humor, the blatant theoretical danger of Freudian theory to his voluntaristic theory of social action.

And as we now go to Parsons and the Savage/Varela debate on agency and values in the action schema, we should make a timely note. It is certainly no surprise that not only were Freud and Parsons bedeviled in their respective theories by the ultimate thesis, but as a direct consequence of its fatal impact, they both wind up right back in Kant's philosophical lap, mightily struggling with the demands of Newtonian determinism and Kantian freedom. And at the center of their work is the realism of their science and therefore the idea of the *power* of causality that insinuates itself in the *force* of the individual in action: in Freudian theory there is the conflict between the "agency of *energy*" – determinism at the expense of freedom – and the "energy of *agency*" – freedom as the human form of determinism; in

Parsonian theory there is the conflict between the voluntarism of the actor – freedom at the expense of determinism – and the conduct of the actor as the joint outcome of social and psychological determinants – determinism at the expense of freedom. The latter conflict is rooted in a *predicament: Parsons's sense that the agency of the actor as a causal efficacy is compromised by his Kantian sense that the freedom of the actor is a variety of the noumenal argument.* And though his "analytic realism" is in principle the realism of the Kantian metaphysics of science, the critical substance of that realism, the theory of causal powers, is simply unavailable to Parsons's understanding. He dies in 1978, 2 years after Giddens's Call and 1 year before its transformation from the problem of deterministic social systems and individual voluntarism into the problem of deterministic social structure and human agency.

A Kant/Parsons theory of action: values or agency?

As I now move into the inner sanctum of Parsonian voluntarism in order to examine the Savage/Varela debate on the place of values and agency in Parsons's Voluntaristic theory of action, it will be important to remember Weber's relation to Kant on the issue of a conception of freedom: Weber's the "freedom of action" *is* Kant's "causality through freedom." I am thus suggesting that there is a parallel to the Kant/Weber connection in the relation of Kant and Parsons via the second thesis. Hence, particularly from the standpoint of that thesis, it can no longer be a surprise then that Parsons begins the formulation of his theory of the means-end schema in *The Structure of Social Action* in true Kantian fashion with the principle of the human ego as an *active* individual, that is as an "actor" (Parsons 1940: 44). And, right to the point, since "actor" means that the individual's presence or absence makes all the difference in any given situation, it is thus, Parsons avers, "determinative." Hence, the human actor is an *efficacy* of some kind (Parsons Ibid: 49).

> Within the area of control of the actor, the means employed cannot, in general, be conceived either as chosen at random or as dependent exclusively on the conditions of action, but must *in some sense* be subject to the influence of *an independent, determinate selective* factor, a knowledge of which is necessary to the understanding of the concrete course of action.
>
> (Parsons 1949 [1937]: 44–45, emphasis provided)

The phrase "course of action" and its property of "determinateness" here refers to the human realization of ultimate ends, that is ends that are not reducible to and explainable by the natural world of the environment – human and non-human. The determinate property of realization has the character of duty, the necessity of moral obligation as an end in itself that is certainly involved with physical and biological necessity, but just as certainly is not reducible to those natural kinds of necessity (Parsons 1991 [1935: 237]). And, furthermore, the nature of this moral necessity

> cannot be derived from the empirical properties of "human nature" as revealed by scientific psychology—for this part of the same external world as the environment—the subjective point of view is that of *the ego not of the body, or even the "mind."* ... Moreover, this [scientific] explanation would violate *the inner sense of freedom, which is just as ultimate a fact of human life as any other*, and its consequent moral responsibility.
>
> (Parsons Ibid: 237, emphasis provided)

The "ultimate fact" that the "inner sense of freedom" of the ego is not of the *body or mind* is obviously one kind of clear evidence from Parsons himself that confirms the second thesis. Furthermore, the assertion that the character of the "inner sense of freedom" is "determinative" implies that it is some kind of *causal* efficacy. We've seen that this is strictly in line with both *Critiques* and the *Opus Postumum* where Kant declares that freedom is "a principle of causality" (Kant 1995: 230). But since the Kant/Weber equivalence on the matter of freedom and causality is based on Weber's explicit reference to "causal power," the absence of the latter reference in the writings of Parsons means of course that Kant and Parsons do not share any such equivalence.

It is of course exactly at this theoretic point – an efficacy of some kind of causality – that the issue of the traditional conflation of transcendence and transcendental arises, and hence the question of the noumenalism of Parsonian voluntarism. And this of course brings us directly to the question of whether Savage's emphasis on values or mine on agency is confirmed by Parsons's presentation of the action schema.

Parsons never, to my knowledge, explicitly and directly ties his voluntarism to Kantian transcendental freedom, although in the Human Condition paradigm mentioned earlier he casually reasserts the barest essentials of the voluntarist schema of action, "selection and choice," while all three of the Kantian critiques are systematically being used to construct the paradigm at issue (Parsons 1978: 412). Nevertheless, such a tie can certainly be identified if we examine certain select details of the conceptual structure of voluntarism in the 1937 work. The key factor is the understanding of Parsons's reference to the "independent determinate selective factor." The key question is whether the primacy of emphasis is on the "*selective*" or the "*selecting*" factor. If the former, "selective," then it is the normative element – ends in themselves; if the latter, "selecting," then it is the agentive element – actors in and by virtue of their "activeness" as causal efficacy (Parsons 1949 [1937]: 44). Keep in mind this statement tucked away in Note A on the normative element before we examine a select few of Parsons's relevant assertions on the matter: "In terms of the given conceptual scheme [of voluntarism] *there is no such thing as action except as an effort to conform to values and their corresponding normative ends*" (Parsons Ibid: 76). The telling reference, we will see, is the reference to "effort." In the first two, Parsons intends to sharply distinguish between two kinds of theories of action.

Idealistic

While [this type] involves a process of interaction between normative and conditional elements, at the idealistic pole the role of the [latter disappear]. In idealistic theory "action" becomes a process of "emanation," of self-expression of ideal or normative factors. Spatiotemporal phenomena become related to action only as ... "embodiments" of meanings. The scientific standard of rationality becomes irrelevant to the subjective aspect of action. The means-end schema gives way to a meaning-expression schema. Non-normative elements cannot "condition" action, they can only be more or less "integrated" with a meaningful system.

(Parsons Ibid: 82)

Voluntaristic

As opposed to all types of positivistic theory [this is not a reference to any variety of *scientific* positivism, from Hume to logical positivism pitted against *scientific* realism], the basic tenet of voluntarism is that neither positively or negatively does the methodological schema of scientifically valid knowledge exhaust the significant subjective elements of action. In so far as subjective elements fail to fit as elements of valid knowledge, the matter is not exhausted by the categories of ignorance and error, nor by the functional dependence of the elements on those capable of formulation in non-subjective terms, nor by the elements random relative to these. Positively, a voluntaristic system involves elements of a normative character.

(Parsons Ibid: 81)

Thus, the cardinal features separating idealism and voluntarism: for the former in reference to science, we have the *meaning–expression schema* whose normative character cannot be assimilated to the ontological and epistemological demands of science (scientific rationality is irrelevant to the subjective aspect of action); in reference to the latter, although the *means–end schema* cannot, according to Parsons, and against Savage, be equated with the meaning–expression schema, nevertheless, it too cannot be assimilated to the ontological and epistemological demands of science (scientific knowledge does not exhaust subjective elements for action); especially in this difference of schemas, again, according to Parsons, voluntaristic action is not action that is an "emanation," that is action that *is an expression from the self of the actor.* Instead there is action that depends directly on the "independent determinate selective factor." Of course, contra Parsons, why can we then not simply say *action is a direct expression from the self of the actor?* Hence the only alleged difference hangs on the difference between the two phrases: *idealism and "indirect expression"* and *voluntarism and "direct expression."* Parsons is absolutely of no help here, for one can see that he never explains "emanationism" very well. But does he have to, when he says at one point in his discussion of the positivistic theory of action (behavior, actually, for Parsons) that, "In conformity with the voluntarism of the Christian background the reality of the agency of the actor was never doubted" (Parsons Ibid: 63). In other words, what else could "emanationism" be but a code for the transcendent theory of freedom. Hence, on the question of the possible theoretical meaning of "direct expression," we have to go back to Parsons's further discussion of voluntarism, specifically concerning the thesis of action as effort. Now observe how Parsons presents the action schema, and then how he uses it in presenting the utilitarian dilemma.

Action schema
    First, there is the minimum differentiation of structural elements, end, means, conditions and norms. ... Second, there is implied in the relations of these elements a normative orientation of action. ... *Action must always be thought of as involving a state of tension between two very different orders of elements, the normative and conditional.* Elimination of the normative aspect altogether eliminates the concept of action itself. ... Elimination of conditions ... equally eliminates action and results in idealistic emanationism. *Thus the conditions may be conceived at one pole, ends and normative rules at the other, means and effort as the connecting links between them.*

(Parsons Ibid: 735)

Utilitarian dilemma
    Either the *active agency of the actor in the choice of ends is an independent factor in action*, and the end element must be random; or the objectionable implication of the randomness of ends is denied, but then their independence disappears and they are assimilated to the conditions of the situation.

(Parsons Ibid: 64)

The critical foci and theme here are, on the one hand, *"effort" and "means" link "conditions" and "ends,"* and, on the other, *"the active agency of the actor in the choice of an independent factor in action."* The point here regarding the question of the theoretical meaning of action as "direct expression" then is this: the "direct expression" of action is action from the actor, that is that "effort" of choosing ends (and means) for action that are independent of the "conditions" of action; *the "expression" of action from the "effort" of the actor is a "direct" expression of the "active agency" of the actor.* In the 1935 paper Parsons makes all this quite clear that it is "ends as a factor in action ... *through the agency of the actor*" that is primary in the voluntaristic thesis of 1937 (Parsons 1991 [1935]: 253). And for Parsons, in light of his deliberate conflation of transcendence and transcendentalism and the theoretical use of the latter term for the former, the metaphysical status of "active agency" is not clear? But any final consideration of an answer to that question should await the discussion of Parsons's noumenalist argument with regard to his voluntaristic thesis. Now, I take the above discussion of Parsonian action theory in his own words to be a confirmation of the thesis that *the agency of the actor* is primary to the action schema. At the heart of Parsonian action theory, then, is the problematic status of freedom as the "effort" of "personal agency": the determinate character of "the inner sense of freedom" that must be identified with some kind of a conception of causal efficacy. And in the last major statement, the Human Condition Paradigm, it is science that Parsons is committed to in all this (Parsons 1978: 383). *Thus, one can say that this problematic status of the "effort" of freedom in Heidegger's terms is the problem of reconciling the two causalities; in Parsons's terms, the twin faces of "conditions" (causality of nature) and the "actor' (causality of freedom).* While this is certainly substantive, and Parsons is certainly involved in all this, more or less, yet, is it not, still, nothing more than the substance of Kant's theory of transcendental freedom? However much Parsons is trying to rework it, is he not, when all is said and done, simply *restating* it? *"Restatement" is the ritualistic dimension of Parsons's venture: nothing new, yet, is being discovered in the Kantian theory.* And I think that is exactly right, since, it seems to be clear that, in constructing the Human Condition Paradigm Parsons makes a passing reference to the cardinal question of Kant's theory of freedom, to which question the noumenal argument was his best answer, but to which, in effect, Parsons confesses that he has not a clue as to what answer can be offered at the end of his life (Parsons died in 1978). With strict reference to this point, consider Parsons's remark concerning the problem that voluntarism as "motivation"

> enters into more complex courses of action, organized in *symbolic* terms and subject to *"voluntary" selection and choice* [voluntarism reaffirmed]. A line of distinction must, however, be drawn between this level and that possible for organisms as differentiated from actors. Presumably, *human experience of motivational drives rooted in the organism is filtered through symbolic structures of action and is no more immediately accessible to socialized humans than is direct cognition of the external world.* There is thus a sense in which *human attitudes toward such drives are partly projected from an action point of view; whereas the problem of how directly they can be felt, uncomplicated by modifications from action sources, remains moot.*
>
> (Parsons 1978: 412–13, emphasis provided)

It seems to me that this is a remarkable statement, and is so because it is as Kantian as Parsons can get, without not just using the great man's own words to pose the problem of the absolute spontaneity of mind and action; the autonomy that is a freedom from causes other than the agentic subject – "[That the] human experience of motivational drives [are] uncomplicated by modifications from action sources" and "how directly they can be felt ... " "remains moot." Frankly, I find it hard not to understand here that Parsons is encouraging us to take seriously the above thesis that, *in so far as the problem of the noumenalism of the transcendental ego becomes the problem of the voluntarism of the actor, the problem of Kantian freedom is the problem of Parsonian voluntarism.* And at the end of his life, that is why it was agency and not values that remained a problem. That problem was of course the problem of *a naturalistic* account of human agenc*y*, and certainly no longer John Finley Scott's implied thesis that Parsons never gave us a naturalistic account of human valuation exactly because voluntarism was "an [idealist] argument for the causal efficacy of valuation" (Scott 1962: 60, 1963). And thus, in not being an account of the natural causes of valuation, it was a reaching for an account of the natural agency of the actor as a causal power; and that, most certainly, Scott's commitment to Humean causation cannot possibly imagine (Scott 1971: 18–19). Hence, in the realization of that possibility, not only is Weberian action Kantian freedom, but Parsonian action would be Weberian freedom. But of course it wasn't, and for two reasons: one was the fact that Parsons's voluntarism was a version of Kantian noumenalism, and the other, that Parsons did succumb to the ultimate thesis.

Kantian and Parsonian freedom: varieties of noumenalism

Since voluntarism is the equivalent of noumenalism, the problem of Parsonian freedom can no more be solved than the problem of Kantian freedom, and for the same reason: *they are complementary forms of noumenal argument.* We know full well that Kantian freedom is based on the noumenal argument of atemporality or extra-temporality, so let us now see how Parsons can be judged to have presented a complementary noumenal argument, that is that action is in time, but it is not in space.

First, there is the minimum differentiation of structural elements, end, means, conditions and norms. ... Second, there is implied, in the relations of these elements, a normative orientation of action, a teleological character. ... As a process, action, in fact, the process of alteration of the conditional elements in the direction of conformity with norms. ... *Thus conditions may be conceived at one pole, ends and normative rules at the other, means and effort as the connecting links between them.* Third, there is inherently a temporal reference. *Action is a process in time.* The correlate of the teleological reference is a time coordinate. ... [that is] the concept of end always implies a future reference ... but will not necessarily exist without the intervention of the actor.

(Parsons 1949 [1937]: vol. 2, 732–33, emphasis provided)

On an analytical basis it is possible to see emerging out of this study as a whole a division into three great classes of theoretical systems. They may be spoken of as the systems of nature, action, and culture. ... *Only the first two are systems of empirical scientific theory in the usual sense; the third occupies a special status.* This is because empirical science is concerned with *processes in time.* The problematical data of the theories of both the nature systems and the action systems concern such processes; *those of culture systems do not.* The line of distinction which may be drawn between the first two is that *the nature systems involve systems in relation to space in the frame of reference, the action systems in relation to the means-end schema.* Physical time is a mode of relationship of events in space, *action time a mode of relation of means and ends and other action elements. ... Action is non-spatial but temporal.*

(Parsons Ibid: 762–63, emphasis provided)

Let us be reminded of the basic issue that unifies this book on agency and the two other proposed books on reification and embodiment, respectively. And that is the general problem of deterministic structures and dynamically embodied agency. Now, at this juncture in the overall discussion of the interplay of rescue and recovery in the return to Kant, that Parsonian action is conceived of as being in *time but not in space* indicates that Parsons's place in that interplay cannot be properly identified unless we pay attention to the particular dimension of *dynamic* embodiment. Dilthey is the obvious and outstanding reason: in conceiving of human freedom as being both in time *and* in space, nevertheless, freedom of action is "in" the *phenomenal* world of nature only in a secondary sense, and that is because its primary reality was *existential and therefore its primary location was phenomenological.* This was the astonishment of Dilthey's new and original contribution to the Kantian problem of freedom, but there was a striking dimension to this theory as well. Not only was the body fundamental to action, but Dilthey emphasized the moving body (Chapter 1). There is no question that the basic idea that freedom is dynamically embodied action originated with Kant. In 1784 in *What is Enlightenment* Kant gave the primary principle for the paradigm of dynamic embodiment in his comment that human freedom is a "kind of free motion" (Kant 1997 [1784]: 84). As I have already pointed out, in *The Metaphysical Foundations of Natural Science* (1985b) Kant himself made a major contribution to the development of the causal powers theory of moving things in the history of physics. Something, then, is seriously amiss in the case of the Parsonian theory of action: where Kant's theory of agency as human free movement is therefore continuous with the theory of the dynamic embodiment of human agency, Parsons's theory of voluntaristic actors realizing normative ends turns out to be discontinuous with the theory. In other words, *Parsons's actors are not moving, though they are supposed to be "men in action."* The unavoidable conclusion then must be that in its very logic, Parsonian action theory is not a theory of dynamically embodied human agents.

Parsons's noumenalism: disembodied voluntarism

However, the conclusion is actually stronger than that: exactly because Parsonian action is in time but not in space, in principle, the theory of social action cannot get to human movement. Specifically, the Williams/Farnell thesis of dynamic embodiment that social activity is the cultural practice of signifying moving persons is a proposition that cannot be generated from the action scheme. And the deep upshot is that, though Parsonian actors should be signifying when they are in action, since they cannot move – the theory makes no such conceptual provision for that possibility – *they cannot be signifying either*. But, if Parsonian actors cannot be signifying because they cannot be moving, how can they even be *in action?* After all, how is any causal action in the physical, biological, and cultural worlds possible if agentic particulars cannot move? This is precisely to say that the "efficacy" that makes an agent "causal" resides in the principle that the power to be a force is the power to be moving in order to be a "forceful particular at work." Is this not the ever so utterly simple ontological presumption of Newton's second law in its otherwise equational form? Otherwise, it would be as if dynamite, when ignited, will explode, though there simply will not be any pieces that are involved flying around in any and all directions according to their lawfully expected corresponding measures of force. In this event, the power of a causal agent would certainly be a ghost in the machine. In the real world that realist science envisions, that is just not the way it is. The formula, then, $F = ma$, (in this context of discourse) means that force is a thing in motion. And so causal activity is nothing, absolutely nothing, if it is not "forceful particulars at work." *Power*, and thus *force* and *movement* are, together, *the holy trinity of theoretical physics*. Social scientific theories of human action cannot afford to violate that understanding, for then their theories will be seriously wanting.

Parsons's theory of action then is a spectacular case in point. On this question, consider Richard Munch's succinct interpretation of Parsonian action theory.

> If we do not want to miss the point of Parsons's solution to the [Hobbesian] problem of [social] order, ... to read him from the Kantian perspective ... means first of all recognizing that Parsons's solution can be neither normative nor utilitarian. Parsons presents a voluntaristic solution to the problem of social order.
>
> (Munch Ibid: 722)

Let us state this in propositional form: Parsonian action theory is normative because it is voluntaristic. Munch, I believe, has given us the substance of the second Kant to Parsons's thesis and its refinement right there: if voluntarism is logically prior to normativity, that's because agency is primary and values are secondary. Thus, it certainly becomes important now to realize once more that the problem of noumenal freedom is the problem of Parsonian voluntarism. Hence, freedom from determinism is the primary solution that makes a theory of action, and then, of social system, possible. Parsons's noumenal argument is the logic of that primary solution: action is free from determinism in so far as it is in time but not in space, and that is because "Physical time is a mode of relationship of events in space." In other words, events in space are Kant's phenomenal world of that determinism in which freedom is banished. *That* is why the sentence following is *"Action is non-spatial but temporal."* Now, what is the difficulty? It is the contradiction between Kantian and Parsonian freedom: *while Parsons's conception of action in his theory of voluntarism is Kantian, yet, it is not dynamically embodied.*

The clue that indicates this feature is in the quote above that asserts that conforming with norms is only possible if human action is possible, and action is only possible if human effort is possible. Freedom, then, must be exactly the element of "effort" that defines what is the active factor, that is the "act," in the fact of act-ion. Hence, what is this factor of the "act"? Well, don't we have that when Parsons asserts that a social or psychological determinism violates the ultimate fact of our sense of freedom? Of course we do. But now Parsons gets tricky, for, that which is the source of the effort, the act, is an ego which itself, Parsons says, is not either "the body or even the mind." Here then we cannot escape the fact that Parsons's voluntarism is up against a central and very serious incoherency. If "effort" is to be an intelligible notion, the effort of conforming with norms must be "the action of a body which is the body of a person." It is absolutely not clear that Parson's ego or actor is meant to reference "the embodied person." And when one now considers the principle that action is in time but not in space, it is even clearer that not only is the body of the actor not theoretically referenced, but the moving and gesturing body as well. After all, given that action must be in time it takes place at "some-when." But then if action must be "some-when" that is because it must be "somewhere." *For, how can effort, if we take it to be the action of a moving body, which is the moving body of a person, mediate conditions and ends in the realization of those ends, if it is non-spatial?* If a "when" of an action is indifferent to space, then "what" is this "who" that can be at some point in time while being anywhere in space or no where in space? The implication of the idea of non-spatiality is that the natural place of action is in the dark. But if you cannot "see" the action how does one know that action is "going on." And if there is talking going on in the dark, is that the only talk that is or could be going on? Supposing the "talking" stops, is there any action, apart from thinking about it before it is done? Of course there is – sign-talking. Perhaps Parsons has in mind the limiting case of a human actor who is not acting *as yet*, but *can*, and is *about to*, or, *may or may not do so*, at some point. For example, we seem to have here Rodin's the thinker, in particular, the stereotype of the academic: thinking, itself, so that action is not the main point. Action thus is, presumably, unproblematic, and thus so is space. No wonder Parsons provides a footnote to his noumenal argument.

> Of course every concrete event occurs in space, *too*. But this fact is an unproblematical datum to analytical sciences of action.
>
> (Parsons Ibid: 763)

Parsons of course is simply wrong: if action is in time but not in space, even if the latter is amended accordingly, the theory of action is not about human beings in action, because it is not about human beings moving or gesturing – neither with their lips and tongue, nor with the rest of the body in any of the media for meaning-making (Farnell and Varela 2008, in press). That Parsonian action theory in principle cannot get to dynamic embodiment is the ultimate proof that Parsons was paralyzed in his return to Kant: he could neither rescue nor recover human agency – "the "effort" of the actor as the "direct" expression of the "active agency" of the actor."

Parsons and Gouldner: voluntarism and the ultimate thesis

One would have to think that one of the strangest features of the Parsonian effort to forge a conception of voluntarism at the center of a theory of the social system, is that Alvin W. Gouldner *had to remind Parsons* that the conception and the theory together constituted an enterprise that self-destructs. The strangeness consisted in this: Gouldner demonstrated that, on the one hand, the Newtonian law of inertia that informed Parsons's theory of the social system eliminated voluntarism, and, on the other, that Gouldner's conception of the reciprocity-multiplier restored voluntarism to the theory of the social system (Gouldner 1959: 423–27). Note that the reciprocity-multiplier restores voluntarism *from outside* Parsonian theory! Thus, at a certain theoretical moment "action" vanishes as the "system" takes over. I want to call this the Scottian moment: he indeed suggests that in the post-World War II period of social system building, in the treatment of the pre-World War II voluntaristic schema Parsons's Tolmanian behaviorism drifted close to the Skinnerian behaviorism of his theory of moral commitment (Scott 1971: 8). We have then a devastating parallel between Scott and Parsons: the aim of the former's theory to eliminate voluntarism turns up in the absence of voluntarism in what Gouldner called Parsons's "natural-system model" (Gouldner Ibid: 423).

By the end of the next decade in *The Coming Crisis of Western Sociology* (1970) Gouldner was to campaign against the Durkheim/Parsons "substantive domain assumption" central to sociology.

In Peter Blau's contribution to Parsons's *American Sociology*, there is the conventional and unexamined assumption that, "once firmly organized, an organization tends to assume an identity of its own which makes it independent of the people who have founded it or of those who constitute its membership." Although flatly asserted as fact, Blau's statement is a characterization of *all* formal organizations, clearly a domain assumption. ... But there is nothing uncommon in this; it is the common way of men with domain assumptions. [However] whether Blau's statement is actually a fact or only a domain assumption parading as one, there is still a consequential choice of how to view it. It makes a substantial difference whether one views the autonomy or alienation of social structures from people as a normal [and natural] condition to be accepted or as an endemic and recurrent disease to be opposed. It is inherent in the very occupational ideology of many modern sociologists ... not only to stress the potency and autonomy of social structures – and therefore the dependence of people – but also to accept this as normal, rather than asking: under what conditions does it occur? ... In short, then, from the substantive domain assumptions that human beings are raw materials of independent social structures, to the methodological domain assumption that men may be treated and studied like other "things", there is a repressive technocratic current in sociology and the other social sciences as well as in the general society.

(Goebbels 1970: 51–52)

It is this campaign against an ideologically driven substantive domain assumption of the Parsonian enterprise that properly frames the earlier paper on the "natural-system-model." It underwrites the key feature of the latter, that is the implicit assumption of social equilibrium that "the complementarity of role-expectations, once established, is not problematical. ... No special mechanisms are required for the explanation of the maintenance of complementary interaction-orientation" (Gouldner in Merton, Broom and Cottrell 1959: 423–24).

The Achilles heel of the equilibrium model is the principle that the *autonomy of the actors* is transformed into the *automaticity of their social interaction* in the social system, hence Gouldner asserts that "both impressionistic observations and theoretical considerations ... would lead one to doubt [that] rewarding responses to a series of identical conforming actions will either remain the same or increase" (Gouldner Ibid: 424). There are major critical points that Gouldner is making to fundamentally ground his skepticism concerning the "natural-system-model":

- Problem: "the longer the sequence of Ego's conforming actions, the more likely is Alter to take ego's conformity for granted; the more Alter takes Ego's conformity for granted, the less appreciative Alter will feel and the less propensity he will have to reward and reciprocate Ego's conforming actions" (Gouldner Ibid: 424).

- Solution: "the more Ego's conforming action is defined by Alter as voluntary, the greater is Alter's tendency to appreciate and reward it" (Gouldner Ibid: 425).
- Theoretical statement: reciprocity-multiplier
  - assumption: "if Alter feels that a given conforming act has been imposed upon Ego ['sheer repetition,' 'situational constraint,' moral obligation'], we would expect Alter to value and reciprocate it less than if he defined Ego's conformity as 'voluntary' (Gouldner Ibid).
  - formulation: "reciprocity is a function of the degree to which a given act is desired, multiplied by the degree to which the act is perceived as voluntary" (Gouldner Ibid).

Now, taken together, of course what is of special interest in these three points is that Gouldner is contradicting the ultimate thesis that tacitly informs Parsons's use of the law of inertia in his theory of the social system. In bringing voluntarism back into the social system, this is being done specifically by implying that not only is "Alter" voluntaristic, but Ego, too, must be voluntaristic as well, otherwise dis-equilibrium will be the result, "at some point repeated acts of conformity [automaticity] may induce a strain toward anomic instability and group instability" (Gouldner Ibid: 424). Note clearly the precise point right here: the misreading of the first law, that entities in interaction are patients not agents, by implication, is now being supplanted by a realist reading of the first law, that interacting entities are agents; that social equilibrium may be a system, but it is not a machine, since entities are not in the service of external forces, themselves in the service of external forces, and so on.

But certainly, one should like to examine Parsons's own actual statement of Newton's law of inertia to confirm the expectation simply implied by the previous points, that is that Parsons's statement of inertia should match the point of the critique. Let us see what Lundberg, the arch positivist, so approved of in presenting his position that Parsonian sociology is converging on "the framework of physics," and so "Parsons and his associates are returning to the cradle of positivism" (Lundberg 1956: 24, 25). But, we will see, that Lundberg was more right than he realized: for Parsons the idea of action in the social system was being constructed *in* the "framework of physics" with the cardinal assumption that the basic structural unit of the social system, "status role," is analogous to the particle of mechanics (Bershady 1971: 198). Here is the Parsons/Bales/Shills formulation of The Principle of Inertia:

A given process of action will continue unchanged in rate and direction unless impeded or deflected by opposing motivational forces.

(Parsons *et al.* 1953: 102–3)

Since this statement is given with no comment at all, it can be taken as an example of the mistake concerning the first law that has been institutionalized since the eighteenth century. However, Lundberg does make a comment, and in doing, pays Parsons the supreme compliment by applauding the "striking similarity between Dodd's formulation and that by Parsons and his associates [of Newton's laws for sociological theory]" (Lundberg Ibid: 25). And consider that, in Lundberg's discussion of Dodd's own formulation of the laws at issue, he particularly applauds the latter's treatment of the concept of *force*.

> Force thus is not a *thing* nor an *active agent* as it is in the popular view. Scientifically it is *that which* produces a measured effect. It is a pure invented concept justified by its usefulness in dealing with phenomena. If this is understood, forces may be spoken of as ... convenient designations of agencies producing forces, i.e. stimulating people to respond.
>
> (Lundberg Ibid)

Of course, one cannot help but notice that Lundberg gives us the standard positivist line that causation is neither an entity nor agency, being a passive event, and then proceeds to contradict himself, once, and then a second time, by finally declaring that as an agentic force of production, it is nevertheless a mechanical s-r behavior unit. However, his positivism triumphs: the ultimate thesis shines through. And so, there we have it for Parsons: while Weberian action is Kantian freedom, Parsonian action reaches toward Weberian freedom, but does not actually reach it. Although, I have argued, Parsons's voluntarism was a version of Kantian noumenalism, in succumbing to the ultimate thesis he left his theory of voluntarism stranded on this side of the tradition of rescue, with no prospect of getting to the other side of the tradition of recovery. Both he and Kant could not use the resources of the scientific realism and analytic realism, respectfully, that they were committed to, so that they could transcend being stranded at the level of their complementary noumenal arguments.

Dahrendorf

Homo Sociologicus (1968 [1958]: 19–87) and the response to its critics, *Sociology and Human Nature* (1968 [1963]: 88–106), give us Dahrendorf's intriguing version of the Science and Humanism debate, and especially his most peculiar use of the traditional Kantian solution to the problem of structure and agency. To begin with, he presents himself, paradoxically, to be both a scientist *and* a humanist. As a telling contrast, for example, Kroeber expresses a diluted mutation of a Kantian attitude in his assertion that "I am myself a determinist. ... And ... I am aware that in living my practical life I must necessarily, if I am to act at all, do so as if I enjoy freedom of will, even though intellectually and impersonally I choose to remain a determinist" (Kroeber 1948: 413). Note that in the case of Kroeber the stance of determinism and the belief in free will refer to the public versus the private spheres of life, respectively. In other words, his "Humanism" has nothing to do with his anthropology. And the Kantian attitude seems so neutered, that it could just as well reflect the free-will tradition of the Cambridge Platonists, Rousseau, and the Romantics, or perhaps nothing more than a formulaic philosophical commonsense that has informed a reflective human being, who just happens to be a social scientist. As we will see now, Dahrendorf's humanism has everything to do with his sociology.

Self-consciously, that is reflexively, Dahrendorf is bringing Kantian freedom back to sociology, in part, in the name of the moral responsibility of the human being who is a sociologist. And this is done, however, not because naturalistic sociology, in its deterministic treatment of "society" and the "social," is guilty of the fallacy of reification and the consequent theft of human agency. It is instead done because, outside of the natural sciences and sociology, "the wider public sees homo sociologicus as the scientific truth about man ... [and thus is engaging in] the massive reification of the basic assumptions of sociological theories. ... " (Dahrendorf 1968 [1963]: 97, 101). What separates the social scientist from the "general public" here is that only scientists understand the difference between methodologically intended "unrealistic postulates" and ontologically intended "realistic" statements (Dahrendorf Ibid: 97). Emerging here is the theme of Dahrendorf's philosophy of science: a "nominalist epistemology" and its "associated logic of science" (Dahrendorf Ibid: 96).

Let's get the full picture from Dahrendorf himself, now, so we can nail all this down.

> Sociology has paid for the exactness of its propositions with the humanity of its intentions, and has become a thoroughly inhuman, amoral science. ... *This development was inevitable from the moment that sociology emerged as a science.* ... The two intentions with which sociology began [scientific explanation and promoting freedom] are [hence] incompatible. [Thus], as long as sociologists interpret their task in moral terms, they must renounce the analysis of social reality; as soon as they strive for scientific insight, they must forgo their moral concern with the individual and his liberty. *What makes the paradox of moral and alienated man [homo sociologicus] so urgent is not that sociology has strayed from its proper task, but that it has become a true science*
> (Dahrendorf 1968 [1958]: 77, emphasis provided)

> ... Now, the assumption [of this true science] that man behaves as *homo sociologicus* makes possible a general explanatory proposition: that a person in a situation of role conflict will *always choose* the role with which the stronger sanctions are associated
> (Dahrendorf 1968 [1963]: 93, emphasis provided)

> ... [But this must be properly understood]: even if sociology asks questions about man, it is in substance concerned not with man, but with ways of reducing man's actions to rational terms. ... sociology ... is

fundamentally indifferent to man as such, since it can reach much further with homo sociologicus than with statements that aim at an accurate description of man's nature

(Dahrendorf Ibid: 94–95)

[In other words]. ... the idea of inventing homo sociologicus as a deliberately
"unrealistic" fiction [is] for the sole purpose of formulating powerful
explanatory theories (Dahrendorf Ibid: 96). [The basis for this position
is this:] extreme advocates of the *modern deductive-logic of science –
notably its founder, Karl Popper* – at times go as far as to say that the *less
realistic the assumptions, the better the theory. ... By reification [then,
for instance, of homo sociologicus] is meant the reinterpretation or mis-
interpretation of a deliberately unrealistic assumption, made in the interests
of good scientific theory, as a realistic description of the nature of man.*

(Dahrendorf Ibid: 92, 95, emphasis provided)

Dahrendorf reveals in the above that he is buttressing his nominalism by the
Popper/Hempel *et al.* D-N model of explanation, and hence he is judging the
reification of human structures from a positivist standpoint of logicism and
empirical realism. Thus, of course, from the Harréan realist standpoint, he is *not*
engaging in such judgment simply from the standpoint of "sociology defined as
an *empirical science* [doing 'good scientific theory'], [so that] homo sociologicus has no implications for the nature of man" (Dahrendorf Ibid: 95–96).

We have here, as expected, another unfortunate instance of the conflation
of science with positivism (and logicism), which, as a direct result, derails and
renders ineffective Dahrendorf's otherwise unique handling of the problem
of the reification of deterministic structures and human agency. Thus, we can
immediately note this ineffectiveness in Dahrendorf's disconnecting the
ideal-type strategy from Weber's use of it as the means of promoting interpretative analyses of "the efficacy of human action." Dahrendorf, in effect,
has taken the "efficacy" out of human action in having fully accepted the
idea that freedom is not the natural relation between human beings in the
exclusively phenomenal character of their sociocultural world. This is
clearly recognized in the above role-theory proposition that in any role conflict a person "will *always choose* the role with which the stronger sanctions
are associated." Let us remember that Weber argued that this kind of proposition leaves out the whole point of interpretative analyses:

Suppose ... [such a law], showing that all men everywhere who have ever
been placed in a certain situation have invariably reacted in the same
way and to the same extent. Suppose. ... that this reaction is, in the most
literal sense of the word, "calculable.". ... By itself, such a demonstration
would contribute *absolutely nothing* to the project of "understanding"
"why" this reaction ever occurred and, moreover, "why" it invariably
occurs in the same way.

Now, certainly, it must be said that the anti-realist stance is at the heart of what we take to be the fatal difficulty of Dahrendorf's handling of the issue of reification in the social sciences. For, clearly, he believes that the determinism of science warrants the reification of human structures as a purely methodological procedure. This very strange move indeed has permitted him to displace the problem of the fallacy of reification, on the one hand, onto the scientifically unsophisticated general public, and on the other, onto those many sociologists for whom the "idea of inventing homo sociologicus as a deliberately 'unrealistic' fiction ... [is] meaningless, or at best incomprehensible" (Dahrendorf Ibid: 96). The former move is a "red herring," speaking theoretically, while the latter instantiates the mistake of the conflation of science with positivism. Today, scientific realists in the social sciences will justifiably regard the idea of the conversion of theoretical causal constructs (implicitly under the authority of the Humean rejection of causal powers) into shear formal exercises of predictive intent as positivistically comprehensible, and therefore meaningless. Dahrendorf, to be sure, was not in a position then, in the late 1950s and 1960s, to have been able to appreciate the philosophy of scientific realism that Bunge and Harré were articulating during the same period.

Dahrendorf's return to Kant: empty ritual

With these conclusive critiques in hand, the final issue of Dahrendorf's odd handling of the problem of reifying structures has to do with his return to Kant. Why is it, I am contending, that it can be judged a merely sterile ritual? Let us examine this question from the following standpoint. When Dahrendorf declares that the person in a role conflict will "always choose" according to the directive of the explanatory proposition in question, he cannot, technically, mean that. After all, Hull explained away "choice" with his explanatory proposition that "making one response rather than another" was determined by the law of differential reinforcement! The point is, then, that Dahrendorf's proposition can be correctly seen as an instance of Hull's behavioristic more general proposition. In view of the fact that it can be assumed that Dahrendorf would not necessarily disagree with this point, then we may suppose that the return to Kant is already implicated in his phrase "always choose." But if so, he has to presume that the return to Kant allows him to bring "efficacy" back into "human action." And surely that will have to be his answer to his own question regarding the incredulity of social scientists concerning Kantian freedom.

> Why do so many find it so hard to discover freedom in the antinomic existence of man?
>
> (Dahrendorf Ibid: 105)

But how can it be the answer? Dahrendorf was not in a position then to appreciate why anybody in philosophy and the social sciences, outside of positivists, should find Kantian freedom incredulous.

To appreciate why Dahrendorf's return to Kant is problematic we should keep in mind this view of his project from the standpoint of what we have learned here from Simmel, Durkheim, and Weber in their respective encounters with the challenge of Kantian freedom. Given Dahrendorf's dual identity of being a scientist and a humanist in the traditional social scientific sense: he cannot abandon Simmel's strategy of preserving Kantian freedom by treating it as a given feature of social interaction, and he cannot accept Durkheim's strategy of losing Kantian freedom in social role structure. After all, the two strategies are internally connected: as soon as Simmel treats freedom as somehow given in the *empirical fact* of the human interaction of persons, Durkheim's losing freedom in the social role behavior of persons is inevitable. It is Weber's fate according to Kant's rule: once the noumenal is abandoned and "all is phenomena," freedom is not the natural relation of persons in interaction. Thus, we have a predicament: contra Simmel, freedom cannot be a sociological a priori without the noumenal argument, and contra Durkheim, there cannot be freedom as individual power when it is abandoned to the deterministic force of social structure. And so, Dahrendorf's return to the noumenal argument to counter Durkheim's sociologism must fail, for, how, after Simmel, Durkheim, and Weber, is it to be substantive? If we now enrich our understanding of this predicament with the Parsonian variety of noumenalism tucked away in the voluntaristic theory of action, the gravity of the question is enhanced.

Here is Dahrendorf revealing his location in this predicament as he is about to enter the return to the Kantian theory of freedom for the traditional Humanistic purposes of rescue.

> The assumptions and theories of sociology refer not to *man* but to homo sociologicus, man in the *alienated* aspect of an incumbent of positions and a *player of roles.* It is not Schmidt the man but Schmidt the grammar school teacher ... the party official ... the driver ... the husband and father. ... And Schmidt the man? What does he do? What can he do without being robbed of his individuality and converted into ... a player of roles? *Does Schmidt the man begin where his roles end? [Simmel] Does he live in his roles? [Durkheim] Or is his a world in which roles and positions exist as little as neutrons and protons in the world of the housewife who sets the table for dinner?* This is the insistent *paradox of homo sociologicus.* Our discussion of it will take us next to the region where sociology and philosophy meet ...
>
> (Dahrendorf 1968 [1963]: 74, emphasis provided)

> ... [And that meeting brings forth a new consideration] So far we have referred to the paradox of the two human beings as if it were beyond theoretical or practical resolution ... Is there a necessary contradiction between the *moral image of man as an integral, unique, and free creature and his scientific image as a differentiated, exemplary aggregate of*

predetermined roles? ... At least one aspect of this question, that of the free or conditioned character of human action, has been dealt with extensively by Kant in his third antinomy of pure reason; and since Kant was concerned with the same paradox that concerns us, we may do well to follow his argument.

(Dahrendorf 1968 [1958]: 78)

And indeed Dahrendorf does follow out Kant's argument, but not completely. And there's the rub: missing the major key to Kant's whole argument, the logic of it, in thus being lost, any chance of its theoretical promise is hence lost as well. First of all Dahrendorf quotes Kant in order to identify his important point that "the deceptive glitter of freedom promises calm to the searching mind in the chain of causation by leading it to an *uncaused first cause that acts of itself; but this first cause, being blind, shrugs off the guiding light of rules, by which a completely coherent experience is possible*" (Dahrendorf Ibid: 79, emphasis provided). Note that from the very beginning of Kant's discussion of freedom in the first critique, human agency implies that it is a species of agent causality. In other words, a significant difference in the kind of agency: an "uncaused" kind of "first cause" in the sense of "agency." This is one of the crucial problems of Kant's theory, that is the deeper problem of the metaphysical location of freedom as a kind-difference. The position I have here taken and argued for is that the best reading of kind-difference is the metaphysic of naturalism and realism, and not supernaturalism or any such functional equivalent. Thus, again, we have a difference in the natural kind of agency in the case of human freedom. Now, Dahrendorf never enters into this kind of analytic discussion, and, in all fairness to him, it is not expected. But it must be noted, certainly, in view of my purpose here to recover rather than merely rescue human agency. This of course clearly highlights Dahrendorf's traditional usage of Kant, and he shows this further as he goes on to reveal the precise relevance, in his view, of that usage.

In the language of Kant, homo sociologicus is under the spell of natural "laws"; his every move is merely a link in a chain of recognizable relations. The integral individual ... cannot be linked to such a chain; he is free. Each of these two versions of man can be justified by a logically conclusive argument; they are thesis and antithesis of an argument. ... [But], if and only if we assume ... that outside our experience but accessible to it there is a being in itself, *Ding an sich*, the contradiction between two theses is indeed an unresolvable antinomy. But there is no evidence to support such an assumption. Rather, the transcendental critique shows that thesis and antithesis ... do not contradict each other, but are simply different ways of comprehending the same subject, ways that derive from different sources of knowledge.

(Dahrendorf Ibid: 79)

Dahrendorf rounds out his resort to Kantian freedom with quotes that identify the renowned vocabulary of "phenomenal," that is the empirical character of things experienced, and the "thing in itself," that is the intelligible character of things not experienced (Dahrendorf Ibid: 80). In these quotes Dahrendorf passes over the fact that has been pointed out repeatedly here, namely, that Kant explicitly uses the term "efficient cause" for both "nature" and "freedom," thus anticipating *The Critique of Practical Reason* in which he then refers to the "efficient causality of nature" and the "efficient causality of freedom." Again, Kant's naturalism, as mentioned above, is clear from the first critique. That Dahrendorf never gives those quotes where Kant does use the term "noumenal" for the thing in itself is significant, for it is indicative of the fact that the critical argument for freedom is simply missing: that is the argument that the act of human agency is "not in time." *So, freedom as the fact that human agency is "an uncaused cause" has no rational justification, that is no metaphysical grounding.* Therefore, speaking technically, Dahrendorf cannot be taken seriously in his intellectual contentment when he states that,

> The antinomy of human knowledge is thus revealed as merely apparent: there is no *plausible* reason to reject Kant's conclusion that the two characters [empirical for phenomena and intelligible for noumena] "may exist independently of each other and undisturbed by each other."
>
> (Dahrendorf Ibid: 81, emphasis provided)

Sadly, there *is* plausible reason to reject Dahrendorf's conviction about Kant's conclusion – he has omitted Kant's metaphysical reason for the thesis that freedom is an uncaused cause.

Furthermore, even if we pretend that Dahrendorf did include the metaphysical grounding of the rational argument with regard to time, Dahrendorf is not, as they say, "out of the woods." His resort to Kant must be judged to be a resort that comes from "out of the blue," at least with respect to the already reconstructed history presented here of the sociological theory of Simmel, Durkheim, and Weber, and now as we've seen, Parsons. The point is this: from the variegated failures of Simmel, Durkheim, Weber, and Parsons, taken together, I have demonstrated that there is good reason to be against the significance of a Dahrendorf ritual of return, and therefore it can be declared, contra Dahrendorf, that it *is* "hard to discover freedom in the antimomic existence of man." The key word is "discover," and it should be replaced with the words "rescue" and "recover'; in that difference, we now know why it is all the difference that matters here. It is no longer the purpose to rescue freedom from antinomic existence of human beings, for that is an absolute stalemate and thus impossible, and so, once again, it is now the purpose to recover freedom with reference to the two causal realities of natural and cultural existence, for that is now quite possible. Dahrendorf has unfortunately been misled by the mistaken view of the realism of science:

theoretical constructs are not methodological fictions, rather they are ontological proposals concerning the nature and conditions of the causal agents
that may be found throughout the physical, the biological, and the cultural
realms of the natural world. Instead of having taken seriously the Popper/
Hempel standpoint on realism and explanation, Dahrendorf should have
taken seriously Robert MacIver's position in *Social Causation* (1942) on
causation and freedom and William Catton's correlative standpoint in *From
Animistic to Naturalistic Sociology* (1966) on freedom and Newton's first law.

MacIver

> The world of experience is a world. ... in which *causation* reigns over
> experience. ... Our experience has the finality that belongs not to mere
> change, but irrevocable change. ... Hence our *experience must always
> assume the character of a causal nexus.*
>
> (MacIver 1942: 7, emphasis provided)

> The crux of my case is the assumption that there is at least the possibi-
> lity of *causal power in nature.* ... The only alternative to the hypothesis
> that causal power exists is the hypothesis that nature's laws are stu-
> pendous runs of luck.
>
> (MacIver Ibid: 62, emphasis provided)

> *To live ... is itself a special causal activity,* and *to be aware is also to be
> aware of this causal activity of ourselves.* In being aware there is at least
> implicit the concept of causation.
>
> (MacIver Ibid: 8, emphasis provided)

> The environment calls the tune and the organism plays it. Such language does
> not concede to the *conscious agency* any initiative, any *efficacy.* It mis-
> apprehends the *interactivity of the factors within the causal complex.*
> Moreover, in this interactivity, the role of the conscious agent is a distinctive
> one, to express which the *"response"* is wholly inadequate. As we have
> seen he envisages a total situation ... so as to turn its intrinsic dynamism
> into his own. ... comprehension and his control. ... [Thus, it is the case
> that] the onus of *responsibility* lies here, it is his particular being that
> thus meshes with the total situation. *Being what he is, he acts as he does,
> and so becomes an agent of change* within a larger system of change.
>
> (MacIver Ibid: 236–37, emphasis provided)

Catton

> And, as noted earlier, *naturalism* cannot be defined simply as the com-
> posite of *physicalism, mechanism, determinism, monism, behaviorism,*

materialism, positivism, and empiricism. There are no affinities between each of these and naturalism. *Naturalism* would not be adequately defined, either, by the negation of all the following [dimensions of animism]: *vitalism, idealism, voluntarism, spiritualism, supernaturalism, transcendentalism, rationalism, indeterminism, and historicism.*

(Catton 1966: 42–43, emphasis provided)

To deny unmoved movers, as naturalists do, is not to assert that all forces are physical. Nonphysical accelerations will be produced by nonphysical forces; but they will not occur apart from the operation of *forces of some sort.* Nonphysical actions will happen, but they will not happen without equal and opposite reactions of a similarly nonphysical sort. ... *nonphysical forces are not entelechies of which men only make mysteries.* To avoid entelechies, *the sociologist does not have to reduce sociology to physics; to avoid reductionism, he does not have to deal in entelechies.*

(Catton Ibid: xiii–xiv, emphasis provided)

[Proclaiming] the *efficacy of effort*, provided it is guided by intelligence. It would remove the embargo laid upon human activity by a false interpretation of *scientific determinism*, and, without having recourse to the equally false conception of a *power of will*, it insists on the *power to act.* ... [For, the deep error of free-will theory is its assumption that] a will ... does *not* conform to the principle of *inertia*, and now and then does act as an unmoved mover.

(Catton Ibid: 37–38, 57, emphasis provided)

The theoretical lesson of the stalemates of Simmel, Durkheim, Weber, and Parsons of the return to Kant with regard to the impossibility of rescue and the possibility of recovery is contained in the MacIver and Catton commentaries. The proper answer to Giddens's Call is a realist theory of causal powers and a realist reading of the law of inertia: the possibility of freedom resides in a conception of agent causality that is consistent with an agentic causal understanding of inertia. That possibility under the auspices of that conception is theoretically implied by Gouldner's correction of Parsons's equilibrium model of social organization with the idea of the reciprocity-multiplier. Dahrendorf's return to Kant was unfortunately uninformed by that history lesson.

The problem of sociology: science and reification

There is one final critical observation that must be made with regard to Dahrendorf's grand effort to come to terms with the problem of deterministic structures and the fate of human agency. It has to do with the problem of sociology as a science and reification, especially in reference to role theory. Dahrendorf can guide us here.

Analogies to natural science are objectionable to many social scientists, but one seems worth proposing here. Even in physics by no means all problems directly involve the atom. Entire branches of physics – e.g., classical mechanics – have been developed without a single reference to atoms. Nevertheless, it would be correct to describe the atom as a fundamental element of the physical sciences. *Possibly, role sociology, i.e. the scientific concern with roles as such, will one day be a special field like nuclear physics.*

(Dahrendorf 1968 [1958]: 75, emphasis provided)

Looking back at this fantastic suggestion in italics, its incredible implausibility is quickly exposed by the knowledge that within the next two decades, as the (old) Science and Humanism connection implodes and fades out, virtually to be extinguished, for some of us in sociology there is the fundamental conceptual shift away from social structure and social role to social action as discursive and embodied practices with their processes of positioning. The implication of that profound theoretical change for a critical appreciation of Dahrendorf's conviction is this: apart from his return to Kant, something must be radically wrong with the very substance of the argument of homo sociologicus. Remember my criticism of the role-conformity proposition, namely, that the factor, "always choose," can be read as a Hullian derivative. We can now go further. Note carefully that that has to be right, since, Dahrendorf never said that such persons in that situation will "choose always." The crucial difference is that "always choose" presumes human "patiency" and "choose always" presumes instead "human agency." It is clear that Dahrendorf is absolutely consistent in his choice of phrase with his absolute conviction that science means the causal determinism that Giddens renounces because it rules out his preference for the idea of agent causality. But now consider that Dahrendorf betrays a serious inconsistency that shows up in reference to a very different theoretical implication in his discussion of social structural/role theory. What is going on with Dahrendorf, I believe, is that, in that discussion, he is actually hovering between the idea of persons "always choosing" and the idea of persons "choosing always," in his nominalistic argument against the sociologism and its intrinsic disposition to reification.

Dahrendorf identifies the problem of the freedom of man as a social being as a balance between the determinism of role-behavior *and* the autonomy of the individual behaving in that role. Consequently, for Dahrendorf, the sociology of homo sociologicus presumably illustrates the dialectical paradox of freedom and necessity (Dahrendorf Ibid: 44). Supposing that the role behavior of social structure, defined as a system of normative expectations for those roles, is illustrative of that philosophical paradox, hence, individuals are either "always choosing" or "choosing always" (Dahrendorf Ibid: 37). Or, mysteriously, they are, at one time the former, and, somehow, at another, the latter? This clarification of this implicit problem suggests that the paradox of freedom and necessity in his theoretical hands is a muddle and a mystification. Now, let's see God and the devil in their details.

> Society is a *fact*, one that can *cause* people to stumble like a stone or a tree stump … [And yet], society consists of individuals and is in this sense *created* by individuals … On the other hand, experience suggests that in some sense *society is not only more than the sum of its individual members, but something significantly different in kind. Society* is the alienated persona of the individual, homo sociologicus, *a shadow that has escaped the man to return as his master.* [Nevertheless] *society is patently not a person, and any personification of it obscures its nature and weakens what is said about it.* … [However] even if we renounce for the moment the attempt to sound the depth of this paradoxical condition, as sociologists, *we must still seek some way, not only of identifying the agency responsible for social rules, but of describing this agency with operational precision.* In the literature, this problem has rarely been considered and never been solved; yet *modern sociology has assembled all the tools for its solution.*
>
> (Dahrendorf Ibid: 44, emphasis provided)

We can reduce the above assertions that comprise Dahrendorf's sociological theory to two propositions that contradict each other.

The *Scientific* thesis of society as an object: society is the fact of an agency apart from persons that is responsible for determining the role behavior of persons so that they will *"always choose"* role-conformity to normative expectations.

The *Humanistic* thesis of society as a subject: society is the activity of persons who are reciprocally the agents responsible for determining that they will *"choose always"* role-conformity to normative expectations.

The import of these fatal twin propositions is in two parts: the first has to do with Dahrendorf's return to Kant; the other involves Gouldner's humanist response, in effect, to Dahrendorf's first thesis in terms of his view of the sociological presumption that it is normal, natural, and indeed a subject for naturalistic sociology. In the first case, Dahrendorf's return to Kant is *irrelevant*: aside from the realization that human freedom cannot be found in the antinomic existence of man, homo sociologicus theoretically specifies for itself the need for both human patiency *and* human agency. In other words, Dahrendorf is already presuming that sociological determinism cannot make sense unless its social role players are the agents that create society and make themselves live it. It is simply no longer scientifically credible, à la Popper/ Hempel, to regard the conceptions of human being as an object and as a subject as "unrealistic fictions." His return, then, to Kant is thus an empty ritual in proving itself to be a futile one. A return to Kant must leave the traditional positivist and Humanist versions behind without abandoning Kant. Without the traditional terms of the Science and Humanism debate and its theme of return for rescue, however, Dahrendorf is absolutely at a complete loss: the very idea of recovery cannot be imagined. He is thus waiting for Giddens's Call as if it is a waiting for Godot.

Dahrendorf and Gouldner: Pirandellian predicament

This is even clearer in the second case of Gouldner's rejection of the modern sociological tradition's thesis of the natural fact of sociological determinism (Gouldner 1970: 51–54). Specifically, Gouldner's dismissal of this thesis is not based on any critical question of the adequacy of positivism's view of science; in fact, that issue is, effectively, nowhere in sight. It seems that science as positivism is taken for granted: the critique of conflation is not understood. Thus, the natural fact thesis is rejected because the resort to natural science is a kind of professional defense mechanism against the early birth trauma of the social sciences, particularly sociology.

> Academic Sociology's emphasis on the potency of society and subordination of men to it is itself an historical product that contains an historical truth. The modern concepts of society and culture arose in a social world that, following the French Revolution, men could believe they themselves had made. ... Yet, at the same time men could also see that this was a world out of control, not amenable to men's designs. It was therefore ... a world made by men but, despite this, not *their* world. ... The concepts of culture and society tacitly predicate that men have created a social world from which they have been alienated. ... [Thus], the emerging academic social sciences ... come to conceive of society and culture as ... things that are independent and exist for themselves. ... In other words *sociology emerged as a "natural science" when certain domain assumptions and sentiments became prevalent: when men felt alienated from a society that they thought they had made but could not control.*
>
> (Gouldner Ibid: 52, 53)

Now *Dahrendorf's problem here with Gouldner's position is this*: from the standpoint of the philosophy of science he cannot show that Gouldner's dismissal of the determinism which Dahrendorf accepts as being the ontology of the natural world, is not valid; so that determinism is the point to his return to Kant. *Gouldner's problem with Dahrendorf's position is this*: from the standpoint of the philosophy of science he cannot show him that determinism is not the ontology of the natural world, so that there is a point to his analysis that the resort to science is a rationalization against the birth trauma of the emerging modern social world (Gouldner Ibid: 53). And as Dahrendorf and Gouldner are lock-stitched in a Pirandellian predicament, the problem of system and voluntarism that hangs in the balance is about to be transformed into the structure and agency problem of Giddens's Call. The

Dahrendorf/Gouldner predicament thus simply fades away, and is forgotten in the silent paradigmatic shift from positivism to realism at the metaphysical foundations of the determinism/freedom issue that grounds both sets of vocabulary.

Berger

While Parsons's return to Kant was found to be transitional and hence substantively problematic with respect to his location between the poles of rescue and recovery, and Dahrendorf's return was deemed to be a sterile ritual in that same regard, the example of the last Humanist voice of return is a ritual, to be sure, but one that I found to be particularly puzzling. That puzzlement is to be gleaned from Peter L. Berger's two works, *Invitation to Sociology* (1963) and, with H. Kellner, *Sociology Reinterpreted: An Essay on Method and Vocation* (1981). In *Invitation*, Kant's theory of freedom is implicit, where it is highly muted and reduced to a minimalist rendering. There it is claimed that science is a closed causal system whose deterministic logic in principle rules out the human "subjective inner certainty" of a freedom believed to be "an event that is its own cause" (Berger 1963: 122–24). In insisting that "as its own cause," freedom nevertheless is not uncaused, Berger, in effect, is dismissing the "uncaused cause" argument which Dahrendorf approvingly quoted from Kant. Ultimately, then, the claim to freedom as " a very special category of causality" reveals that Humanism must "step outside the narrowly scientific frame of reference and *postulate* the reality of freedom" (Berger Ibid: 123–24). Thus, I contend, Berger forgoes any talk of the noumenal and phenomenal worlds of freedom and determinism, respectively, favoring instead talk of the incommensurable frames of reference of Science and Humanism, and the fact that freedom and determinism are both categories of causality, and making it pointedly clear that freedom, particularly, is "a very special category of causality" (Berger Ibid: 123). Presumably, rather than any reference to the metaphysical argument of atemporality in defense of freedom, Berger reduces Kant's entire discussion to the act of postulation, and where the issue of causality is never discussed, thereafter to be left hanging in metaphysical mid-air. But, now, just shy of 20 years later, in *Sociology Reinterpreted*, Berger's insecure Kantianism comes out into the open.

In the later work at issue, as expected, Berger repeats his view in *Invitation* of the deterministic perspective of positivist science. This time, however, his Humanist stand for freedom is enriched, for it now depends on the argument from the philosophical anthropology of Helmut Plessner and Arnold Gehlen, and then, partly, on Kant's own argument. And, in that occasion, it is my contention that there is an unmistakable dissonance between the Plessner/Gehlen interpretation of human biology as an argument for freedom and the argument for freedom from Kant (Berger 1981: 95). *The dissonance comes to this: either, on the one hand, the move to Kant is redundant, or, on the other, it is inconsistent.* The theme of that interpretation of biology is

A minimal philosophical concept of freedom ... [that] propose[s] that the human will can, essentially transcend the systems of determination in which man finds himself. In an older philosophical language, ... human acts are their own cause, therefore cannot be explained by antecedent causal chains. ... If there is merit to [this proposal], then we would assume that this has been so ever since *homo sapiens* appeared in the evolutionary process. That is, *this capacity for freedom is an inherent and universal human trait.*

(Berger Ibid, the last emphasis is mine)

In other words, the Plessner/Gehlen interpretation of biology is an anti-instinctivist thesis of human freedom. To make sure that the particular significance of this argument for my analysis of Berger's discussion is unmistakably clear, let me use the theoretical substance of Donald O. Hebb's robust conception of instinctive behavior that permits him to compare instinctive behavior (exemplar: ants) and intelligent behavior (exemplar: homo sapiens) (Varela 2003: 105–15).

Berger and Hebb: the relevance of the intelligence/instinct distinction

Hebb's concept finally allows social scientists to assert a proposition that is derived from the neural systems of instinctive animals, for example, ants, and human beings, that are radically opposite in structure and therefore in function (behavior): to believe that human beings are instinctive is to believe in a proposition that is a theoretical self-contradiction (Varela Ibid: 113–15). This proposition is unique because it is definitive: it is not simply the case that, as a matter of empirical fact, up till now (the past and present), scientists have not been able to discover even one confirmed instance of such behavior on the human level; the necessary implication of the neurological evidence of the brain structure of instinctive and human animals is that it is impossible that there could be instinctive behavior produced from human brain structure; thus, there is every theoretical reason not to look any further. Now, this is the basis for the claim that Hebb's theory of instinctive behavior is *robust*. And so it can be declared that "It just isn't human nature to be instinctive," and, correlatively, that "It is human nature to be intelligent." *In other words, the respective behavior of instinctive animals and human beings exemplifies the traditional meaning of the concepts of determinism and freedom.* But one more point can be made here, and it is of major importance. Hebb's scientific work on the problem of "instinct" and intelligence is a straightforward example of the practice of science as a realist practice. Thus, such a practice presumes the concept of natural kind entities as powerful (causal) particulars: their "character" and "behavior" follow the general law or principle of structure underwriting function.

The understanding that instinctive species and especially human intelligent species are exemplars of the realist idea of natural kinds of powerful particulars, bears directly on the issue of agency as human autonomy in relation to John P. Seward's naturalization of Gordon W. Allport's theory of functional autonomy (Allport 1937: 141–56; Seward 1963: 703–10). In that realist light, I read Seward's naturalization thesis accordingly: the autonomy of such motives as curiosity, exploration, manipulation, play, meaning-making (understanding, controlling, predicting the environment) are internally related functions stemming from the brain structure of, for example, human "intelligent" species. We can refer to these motives as motives of intelligence (and for its utilization). As such, Seward avers, "In a literal sense exogenous motive [motives of intelligence] *are* functionally autonomous; since they began that way, a *theory* of functional autonomy becomes superfluous" (Seward 1963: 709). Thus, such motives are species-specific causal powers and individual species-member personal tendencies (Bhaskar 1979: 229–38). But now, Hebb's concept of instinct must be used to correct Seward's predilection to regard what we are calling motives of intelligence (exogenous motives) "instincts," opening up, as he claims, "a new and exciting area to investigation" (Seward Ibid). Instinct is no longer the scientifically proper word to use: motives of intelligence are genuine powers, causal properties of the human species.

Now, uncovering the scientific realist theoretical framework of Hebb's work on instinct permits me to claim that the Plessner/Gehlen anti-instinctivist argument for human freedom assumes a very different significance from that suggested by Berger. And that is that *their argument for freedom does not require any further philosophical clarification and justification.* Humans and ants represent disjunctive ontological kinds of causal agents, which, in Kantian language would be referred to, respectively, as the "causality of freedom" and the "causality of nature." In other words, in discarding philosophical anthropology and replacing it with Hebb's realist theory of instinct and intelligence, it can be seen that the metaphysical conception of "powers" underwrites the theoretical conception of "capacity." And so, "the capacity for freedom [as] an inherent and universal human trait" is now a theoretical proposition concerning the ontology of human behavior. In this new light, what is to be made of Berger's turn to Kant immediately after his presentation of the Plessner/Gehlen argument for human freedom (Berger Ibid: 96–97)?

Berger's resort to Kant reveals that he seems to think that, in some unexplained way, the Plessner/Gehlen argument is deficient, and the resort to his understanding of Kantian freedom will make up for that deficiency. Let's find out.

> Now, one exceedingly important point must be made here (philosophically, it is a point rooted in the insights of Immanuel Kant): *Man's freedom is not some sort of hole in the fabric of causality.* Put differently, *the same act that may be perceived as free [a phenomenological relevance structure of everyday lived-life] may also and at the same time be perceived as causally bound [a theoretical relevance structure of science].* ...

Therefore: Freedom cannot be disclosed by the methods of any empirical science; sociology ... included. For this reason, it would be an impossible undertaking to devise a type of sociology that would include within itself the category of freedom even in its minimal philosophical sense. What *is* possible is to insist ... that the perspective of sociology and of any other empirical science is always partial, and that other perspectives are possible – including the perspective of human beings as acting freely.

(Berger Ibid: 96–97)

I am at this juncture ready to declare that Berger's use of Kant here is a pointless redundancy, and that is because the Plessner/Gehlen reading of human freedom as grounded in a biological capacity contradicts the use of the Kantian distinction at issue. Note that Berger has accepted the phenomenological tradition that Dilthey bequeathed to Husserl, Sartre, and Merleau-Ponty. And the heart of the problem of this new tradition consisted in the suspect conviction that the noumenal can be categorically discarded without further argument, and the determinism of the phenomenal can be set aside by merely asserting the new mysterious ontology of the phenomenological – the human experience that "grounds" and therefore justifies an "inner subjective certainty" of freedom. The "certainty" of which, however, cannot be derived from that "experience" presupposed by "inner subjective" consciousness, and so can only be postulated. Furthermore, that the act of postulation covers over the fact that Dilthey's shift from the phenomenal to the phenomenological is an argument that amounts to nothing more than a mystification. In other words, Berger's act of postulation is actually a confession that no account of the ground of human freedom is possible. This is the heart of Dilthey's legacy. For the Humanist, freedom therefore is a belief in the belief that we are free in the phenomenal world of determinism. And, incidentally, that William James could declare that his first act of free will was to believe in free will is no longer relevant for us today, thus it cannot save Humanism from its tradition of affirmation. For, the way out of this trap of believing in a belief, I contend, is found in the systematic significance of Hebb's realist conception of instinct and human intelligence: the metaphysical conception of the "human causal power to act" has become the theoretical proposition that human freedom is species-specific human biological capacity of human intelligence. The great significance of the phenomenological radical suggestion from Dilthey to Husserl to Merleau-Ponty that human will is an "agent causality" is brought home to us in the appreciation, in effect, of Hebb's realization of that very suggestion in the realist achievement of his theory of instinctive and intelligent behavior.

Concluding commentary

Looking back at Parsons, Dahrendorf, and Berger, the persistent and unavoidable historical lesson is that any return to Kant in search of a way to save freedom from determinism is doomed to constitute an absolute stalemate. Any return, if there is to be one, must be for the purpose of recovering agency from nature in order to recover human agency from cultural life. The spelling out of the metaphysical achievement of that promise is the subject of the next two chapters: the recovery of agency in nature is realized in the triumph of the dynamic theory of matter in the history of physics, the recovery of agency from cultural life is realized in a new way to integrate Kant's conception of the "causality of freedom" with scientific realism of the "causality of nature."

Part III

Returning to Kant and to Giddens's Call

9 The dynamical theory of matter
Natural agency

Immanuel Kant's early interests were in the field of mathematical physics, and his philosophical training was under the inspiration of Leibniz, particularly as interpreted by Christian Wolff. These two early influences largely determined the development of his distinctive philosophy, *which probably has as much claim to being a philosophy of science as any other philosopher.*

Wallace (1974: 60–62, emphasis provided)

Introduction

In this chapter and the next, the view of Kant that centers the business of recovering natural and human agency is this: Kant is a philosopher of science who was involved in the integral problems of knowledge and mind (transcendental idealism) and of matter and causal powers (metaphysics of realism). On the one hand, Kant is interested in understanding how knowledge of an objective world of nature is possible for the mind of the human subject, and, on the other, how the objective world of nature is possible as material matter grounded in immaterial powers. Kant is ultimately interested in uniting the idea of the subject knowing nature as a material world of powers and the idea of the subject being free by virtue of its being one of those powers of and thus in the material world of powers. But Kant's having only been able to *discover* that that idea is a *problem*, the task which he left to the future is to discover how to *solve* it. In taking up that challenge, I am going to proceed in two stages: in this chapter I take up the recovery of agency in the natural world of matter, in the next, I pursue the recovery of human agency in the world of culture.

The enlightenment of Kant's realism: Newton's first law redeemed

It is my contention that the scientific realism that is the substance of Kant's *Metaphysical Foundations of Natural Science* (1786 in Kant 1985b) can be profitably used to reread his essay "What is Enlightenment." Let me first establish a reading of this essay itself by identifying certain important implications apart from his scientific realism. Consider the declaration that he opens with.

> Enlightenment is man's release from his *self-incurred* tutelage. *Tutelage* is man's inability to make use of his understanding without the *direction from another*.
>
> (Kant 1997: 83, emphasis provided)

Now examine the closing declaration.

> As *nature* has uncovered from under this *hard shell* the seed for which she most tenderly cares – the propensity and vocation to *free thinking* this gradually works back upon the character of a people, who thereby stepwise become capable of managing freedom; finally, it affects the principles of government, which find it to its advantage to treat men, *who are now more than machines, in accordance with their dignity.*
>
> (Kant Ibid: 89–90)

Note Kant's point that connects these two declarations, and, moreover, one that would not have delighted Rousseau's demand for a Cartesian dichotomy between nature (machine) and human agency (dignity). Kant is asserting that within the "hard shell" of nature's machinery one also finds human nature and its dignity. To avoid any suspicion of Cartesianism here, it must be quickly indicated that for Kant human nature as it is lived out societally involves communal machinery as well as individual dignity.

> Many affairs which are conducted in the interest of the community require a certain mechanism through which some members of the community must passively conduct themselves with an artificial unanimity, so that the government may direct them to public ends. ...
>
> (Kant Ibid: 85)

For the moment, we are going to accept what seems to have been then, and for many still is, the acceptable view that the idea of mechanism necessarily requires the idea that nature is a machine. Just one, but very telling, exemplar of this fact will do. The great Max Weber's Kantianism shows itself in his idea that the social mechanism of bureaucracy reveals the machinery of the iron cage of modernity.

> An inanimate machine is mind objectified. Only this provides it with the power to force men into its service and to dominate their everyday life as completely as is actually the case in the factory. Objectified intelligence is also that animated machine. ... Together with the inanimate machine it is busy fabricating the shell of bondage which men perhaps will be forced to inhabit some day. ...
>
> (Weber 1978: 1402)

This aside, Kant here certainly expresses his primary and firm commitment to naturalism. Now, the theme of enlightenment follows with the twin ideas of maturity and immaturity. Consider Kant's view of the latter: a human being who is immature is a human being who is only a machine, and as such is without freedom, and hence is devoid of dignity. The implication is that the conception of mechanistic naturalism (the machine/mechanism nexus) presupposes the classic principle of determinism (nature's hard shell). Thus, the link between mechanism and determinism is the principle of passivity: it is in the nature of material things to behave reactively (not re-actively), that is as a result of being constitutively without an internal driving force they must be under the direction of a determinism whose source lies external to a given material thing. As I have especially emphasized from Chapter 3, what we have here is the ultimate thesis and its technical definition of activity in the natural world at all levels of being: behavior, not action, in accordance with external direction is the principle that has been institutionalized as the cardinal thrust of Newton's first law of matter in motion. Since for the Cambridge Platonists, Descartes, and Rousseau, only God is an active principle, that is a causal power, matter is thus solely constituted by the principle of passivity. As John Wisdom would have it, nature is a machine by virtue of the fact that matter is inert (Wisdom 1971: 123, 127, 132–33). And in so far as human nature is originally a natural fact and so solely constituted by the deterministic nature of the physical world, the complement would be the rule of Kantian heteronomy in human communal affairs. *However, defiantly, this, Kant never accepted.* His deep loyalty to Western culture's traditional belief in what Trilling has referred to as our *ancient potency* and in what Liebersöhn has called *persönlichkeit* – inner autonomy (Trilling 1968: 145–78) – is transformed into his *primordial spontaneity of freedom*; along with his rational commitment to naturalism as a scientific realism, we have virtually the entire substantive basis for this defiance. That substance and that defiance is the quintessence of Kant's "What is Enlightenment."

Observe now how Kant continues the opening statements of his essay and introduces the substance underwriting his defiance.

> Self-incurred is this tutelage when its cause lies *not* in the lack of reason but in the *lack of resolution and courage to use it without the direction from another.* Sapere aude! "Have courage to use your own reason!" – that is the motto of the enlightenment.
>
> (Kant 1997: 83, my emphasis)

According to Kant's idea of enlightenment, human nature also has the capacity for a maturity that stems from the dignity of courageous reason. Clearly, *maturity is the rational defiance of the machinery of passivity.* In other words, in the early part of the decade of the three *Critiques* during which his realist metaphysics was at least being thought through, Kant explicitly broke the back of the ultimate thesis. The courage of reason is an act of spontaneity expressed by the exercise of a daring to think for oneself. Here, spontaneity is an active principle, and thus the presumption of a

primary independence of external direction. Spontaneity therefore is a genuine "act" (action), and so human agency is the primacy of autonomy. But,
now note carefully what, to our knowledge, has not been highlighted in
scholarly discussions of "What is Enlightenment" from the essay itself. Kant,
it seems in passing, simply says that this act has the special character of
being a *"kind of free motion"* (Kant Ibid: 84, emphasis provided). Hence
courageous reason is action, to be sure, but action according to the understanding that, although human beings are not only not machines because
they are free, dignity in action is a human *kind* of *motion* that is, itself, *free*.
This idea of freedom as human motion that thus internally connects freedom, physical being, and motion should be no surprise for recent readers of
the Kantian corpus from the beginning of his philosophical career. I have
already pointed out that from the start Kant presumed that nature is a
commercium, that is a community of physical beings interacting and in
motion, and that human beings are also among the physical beings of this
world. Harré has certainly articulated this idea as the very principle of scientific realism: "To be is to have a place among the beings of a world, not to
be the value of a variable." With the first critique the idea of commercium is
transformed into the third analogy of experience, reciprocity. Freedom as
human motion involves an important implication that Kant himself does not
explicitly make, though it is, I contend, internal to his position. The
"motion" of free subjects is not the mechanical kind of "bodies in motion"
of ordinary matter, that is sheer physical being, but rather, the kind of
"moving bodies" that is natural to being human. In passing, let me simply
say that Kant's idea of enlightenment harbors only the initial principle *for* a
theory of dynamic embodiment (Farnell and Varela 2008: 215–40).

At this point, consider the implications of Kant's position outlined thus
far, and in doing so, remember Durkheim's declaration that he is a Newtonian scientist of motion: while Kant's social fact – the commercium of
human agents as "a kind free motion" – is a realization of the Newtonian
thesis of inertia, Durkheim's social fact is a realization of the bogus ultimate
thesis of inertia. Clearly, Kant is laying the groundwork for honoring Catton's
rule that a theory of human agency must be consistent with the law of inertia.

Kant's breakthrough: beyond traditional religion

Kant's idea of courageous reason means then that the human world is under
the rule of both a primary autonomy (agency: spontaneity) and a secondary
autonomy (culture: formal normativism), as well as being under the rule of
heteronomy. This reveals a fundamental tension between the disposition to
autonomy and the disposition to heteronomy in Kant's theory of reason,
freedom, and morality. And so it is not surprising that he affirms that the
denial or the prevention of the human exercise of courageous reason "would
be a crime against human nature" (Kant 1997: 87). And even if any such
denial or prevention in the form of, let us say, a religious edict, be found in

the affairs of human beings, this would be the greatest crime against humanity (Kant 1997: 89). And that is because, "religious immaturity is not only the most harmful but also the most degrading of all" (Kant Ibid: 89). It must be noticed here that this passage reveals, with the simple power of ordinary expression, the seriousness of Kant's commitment to naturalism against the seriousness of his undoubted deep religiosity. It seems quite clear to me, though certainly it is arguable, that this seriously religious human being would never compromise, to the best of his rational ability and courage, his commitment to naturalism and science in his thinking about human reason, freedom, and culture. He would prefer to err on the side of mystery in his formulations, for instance, of freedom, rather than risk descending to the level of dogmatism in order to keep faith with faith (Bieser 1987).

The ultimate, and perhaps, the most profound benefit of enlightenment is that "he who [is] himself enlightened [is one who] is not afraid of *shadows*" (Kant Ibid: 89, emphasis provided). The implication of this benefit is truly stunning: only human beings determine and rule human beings in the affairs that they live together, and any such appeal to determination and rule other than human is an appeal to a mere "shadow." It is, thus, an artifact of humanity's self-incurred tutelage. In regard to this theme, I will bring to the fore the deeper significance of Kant's realism for a proper interpretation of his reference to "shadows," or Giddens's "chimera," those bogus structures that spook our agency.

Kantian realism: beyond the machine and beyond reification

What I wish now to particularly stress is that, from the standpoint of Kant's scientific realism, nature is *not* to be understood as a machine, though reactive passivity, that is liability, can be understood to be a property of material things. After all, Kant's realist metaphysics gives us a conception of the variety of matter that "[is] not from matters as *machines,* that is, as mere *tools of external moving forces*" (Harré and Madden 1975: 170, emphasis provided). And so it must now be entertained that our best metaphysical bet is that nature is *not* a machine. There is therefore a surprising consequence from this very different Kantian view of nature for our reading of Kant's idea of enlightenment. For, it must now be claimed that precisely in virtue of the fact that, if nature is not a machine, hence it is the case that human beings also are not machines.

What is involved here is an enriched rather than an impoverished metaphysical conception of naturalism. Nature still is certainly determinate, and nature is certainly some kind of order according to laws, but, the determinateness and the law-like order of nature and human nature, though metaphysically identical in principle, are different in kind. *The principle, provisionally, is this: nature in all of its material variety is a situated activity of the moving forces of various kinds of powerful particulars interacting with each other; and any laws that may or may not be involved are laws that are peculiar to the "kinds" of powerful particulars in their respective situated frameworks of activity.* This enriched conception of nature that dismisses the idea that nature, and hence human nature, is a machine, encourages me to suggest that Kant is anticipating the very idea of reification; the basis for the understanding that deterministic structures cannot be the theft of human agency. After all, that agentic forces (culture, society, personality, biology, language) other than the forces of human agency are "shadows" that are of our own making is the meaning of reification. In this regard, can it be any surprise at all that not long after Kant's death in 1804, a mere teenager will be writing *Frankenstein,* or the *Modern Prometheus*? This great piece of science fiction promotes the interpretation that with the tool of modern promethean rationality, human beings are not only capable of *discovering* structures in nature, but they (Dr. Frankenstein) are also capable of *creating* structures (Frankenstein's creature) for their shared social and individual life, and then treating them as if they are natural structures (reifications or discoveries). The dangerous result of course is that these created lived structures are now open to becoming veritable Frankenstein monsters. And they do so at that very point where, following Dr. Frankenstein's example, they renounce their promethean creativity in an act of the failure of courageous reason. As such monsters, these structures are now Kantian shadows or Giddensian chimera.

Transcendental freedom: prelude to Kant's place in the history of the dynamic theory of matter

Kant's defiance of the traditional belief that nature is passive because God alone is a causal power, was certainly constituted by his commitment to naturalism and realism. To be sure, that was not all. There was certainly Kant's pietism and thus the implied duality of our "ancient potency": that "inner religion" which intimates that God's supreme power of freedom is *mysteriously paralleled* in the freedom that is the primordial spontaneity of humanity. But now we should recall Kant's statement in an earlier quote above that the "seed of free thinking" is found "under nature's hard shell." Here of course we have the general idea that the human mind is a natural fact, but specifically, its power and form originate, somehow, from within the process of nature. In the *Creation of Adam*, Michelangelo has both the forefinger of God and the forefinger of Adam mutually, though differently, extended toward each other, *but they do not touch.* The idea of the mysterious parallelism of the two agencies in "What is Enlightenment" and in the *Creation of Adam* fit together. Human agency originally is a natural fact, and therefore the embodiment of the human agencies of "mind" and "body" implies their strict continuity. This seems to be the very point of Kant's thesis of nature's reciprocity in reference to humanity: that human beings as physical beings are located in nature's and therefore their own community, raises the question as to how mind is possible from the fact of human physical being? But of course, this *was* Kant's initial question (Shell 1996: 10–80). *At the heart of Kant's work then there is more than the suggestion of a disjunction, not between mind and body, but between spiritual being and human being.* In other words, Kant came up against the understanding that God's agency and the agency of humanity are discontinuous. Partly, this can be recognized in the fact that, in breaking with the dogmatism of (religious) metaphysics, Kant not only separated himself from the tradition of transcendence and its doctrine of God's power and nature's passivity, but he also separated himself from the idea that the power of human freedom had to be in some way continuous with God's power. Historically, the reason is clear. Henry More's spiritualization of natural causal power of course presented a challenging version of such a continuity that haunts us to this very day. For, in such a case, human freedom would have remained within the supernaturalist paradigm, and therefore some kind of Malebranchean occasionalism, rather than Berkeleyan subjective idealism, would have been necessary for Kant in theorizing about freedom. But instead, thoroughly consistent with his scientific realism, a theory of freedom as spontaneity was the compromise that Kant came up with: on the one hand, freedom as an *act* has a noumenal character, and, on the other, freedom as an *efficient cause* also has a phenomenal character. The metaphysical challenge is to work out an interpretation that at least honors the "methodological" intent of the noumenal status of human freedom, while nevertheless pursuing the idea that a metaphysic of scientific realism requires that freedom must be constitutively natural through and through. Thus, since human agency is a kind of free motion of embodied persons, it must be a non-mechanical variety of efficient causality. In other words, Kant was identifying a problem and suggesting its formulation: the *regulative status* of noumenal freedom is transformed into the status of a *sensitizing concept* that is awaiting the metaphysical possibility of becoming a *new definitive concept*. This helpful reconfiguration unloosens Kantian freedom from the makeshift confinement of its noumenal conceptualization. This is one way of making sense of some critic's recent complaint that Kant's two-realm solution to the problem of freedom is nothing more than gerrymandering. Well, it is certainly not, because it is more than that. Kant's philosophy of mind and his philosophy of matter are twin topics in his overarching philosophy of scientific realism. To see how Kant's philosophy of scientific realism can give us a concept of human agency as the free motion of embodied persons, his contribution to the historical development of the concept of causation in relation to the machine theory of nature and matter that took place between the seventeenth and the early twentieth centuries must be understood.

Kant and the dynamic theory of matter

During this period the problem of causation was subsumed under the general problem of two conflicting theories of matter, namely, the material versus the dynamical. The central bone of contention was this: material particulars are either *particles of material stuff* or material particulars are *activities of immaterial forces*. Kant was at the very center of that rich complex history as one of the major contributors to the modern scientific view of causation as an activity of immaterial forces. There is a telling indicator of Kant's contribution to this new view of causation that can be seen in the fact of a historical step that had to be taken beyond the dynamical theories of Boscovich and Kant in the eighteenth century, and Priestley in the early nineteenth century. Their theories were a converging influence on the great work of Faraday in the mid-nineteenth century that led to the culmination of causal powers thinking into that of field theory in modern physics (Harré and Madden 1975: 166). The heart of this concept is the idea of a field as a spatial distribution of potentials (dispositions), and thus correlatively, a distribution of active beings that are centers of influence. Specifically, nature was now to be seen as an active realm of material particulars that are constituted by immaterial forces of two kinds: the dispositional properties of powers (the potential to act upon) and liabilities (the tendency to be acted upon). As such, these immaterial forces or active beings are localized charges (Harré and Madden 1975: 161; Harré 1995a: 289). The key metaphysical criterion of the field concept is that *potentials or dispositions are in principle not directly perceivable by the human senses. Indeed, they are as unobservable as are the social relations and meanings that constitute cultural life* (Harré and Madden Ibid: 176). This in fact represents a fundamental principle of realism, namely, that while the ultimates of scientific explanation are unperceivable and yet, nonetheless, they are definitely conceivable (Harré 1995b: 2). Disposition as potential is a fruitful concept precisely for the very reason that it satisfies the most fundamental requirement in the natural sciences that goes back to the scientific realism of the father of Western science, Aristotle (Wallace 1974: 11–18; 1996: xi). Three or more decades ago Wallace reinstated Aristotle's scientific credentials, and that achievement is captured in a quote that summarizes the relevance of Aristotle's Posterior Analytics to the metaphysical center of the scientific revolution.

> We know the cause and nature of a thing when we understand either the material or formal factor in its generation and destruction, or best of all if we know both, and also its efficient cause.
>
> (Wallace 1974: 18)

Today, there is the same understanding of the requirements of a science: it is the search for causes that are *real and agentic*. Thus the concept of field potential as a dispositional place of influence satisfies both of these criteria (Harré and Madden Ibid: 179). And so, with regard to Kant's contribution to causal powers theory,

> It is worth noticing that though Kant speaks of "forces," both his attractive and repulsive force systems are what we now call "fields of potentials."
>
> (Harré and Madden 1975: 171)

The interconnection of dynamical theory of nature and human nature: a proposal and the history of social science

That Kant's force systems are today called "fields of potentials" is an indication of an important moment in the history of the triumph of the dynamical theory of matter over the static corpuscularian theory of matter. The significance of this moment resides in the fact that the dynamical theory argues for causal power being a constitutive property of matter. In short, *the dynamical theory of matter is the recovery of natural agency in the world of material things.* The force of causation is effective, that is efficient or efficacious, by virtue of its being a power of causation (dispositional property); a power that is not Platonic and thus transcendent to a given particular nature, but rather a power that is immanent in a given particular nature; and as such it is structured to act thus and so when it *is stimulated,* that is *released* or *unblocked* in circumstances involving other particular powerful beings. It is therefore not simply that material things act, it is rather that material things act, when they do, because they *can.* The possibility that is provided by the potential of "can" is the dispositional property of a power to become a force in a world of other such powerful possibilities of particulars that are so natured. But now we can recognize that there is a complementary triumph implicated in the history of the conflicting theories of matter in the following proposal. *The dynamical theory of the nature of matter paves the way toward a dynamical theory of human nature: the recovery of agency in the natural world of things is internally connected to and is therefore the occasion for the recovery of agency in the world of persons.*

We can now recall that, for instance, Dilthey, Bidney, and Catton are certainly correct in their common claim that a viable conception of human agency is only possible if we get past the idea of a "power of will"; and embrace instead, not only the idea of a "power to act," but with a step beyond Dilthey, that it is a "natural power." And this step to the idea of a "natural power" is clearly relevant to the fate of that idea in the work of Simmel, Durkheim, and Weber. The variable promise of the recovery of agency in the seminal conception of sociation for all three sociologists in their theories of the individual(s) in social relations is now possible. And of course it is exactly the realization of Parsons's hope (with respect to his noumenal version of voluntarism) and Giddens's Call for the grounding of human agent causation in an appropriate metaphysic of the natural power of causation in nature. And Catton, alone, is deeply correct in the suggestion that, presumably, the idea of a power of action can only be viable if it is comprehended, somehow, under Newton's first law. For, in that achievement, the human power of action would indeed be a natural power. This is indeed a moment of considerable significance: the marginal promise of recovery in Simmel, Durkheim, and Weber was blocked by the fact that their theories were fatally infected by the ultimate thesis. Simmel, by the acceptance of a concept of scientific law that implicitly instantiated the idea of inertness of matter thereby compromising his reaching for causal biological power; Durkheim, in the paradoxical acceptance of human individual patiency while granting agency to the social element; and Weber, in the restriction of agency to a fleeting moment of charismatic implosion that vanishes in the seemingly inevitable take-over of the determinism of the iron cage of order, leaves his ascription of causal efficacy to individual action unnoticed and dangling in metaphysical mid-air. In my encounters as a scholar *and* a graduate student with Robert Bierstedt and Dennis Wrong, members of my doctoral committee, and Alvin W. Gouldner, as one of my oral examiners in social theory, I have never read nor heard any of these eminent students of Max Weber ever even so much as mention his work on the problem of agency, particularly in reference to Kant.

Now, knowing that Catton is absolutely right I can offer this clarification. To see human agency fit the rule of inertia first of all requires that we comprehend agency as a natural property of matter, generally. In that case we certainly cannot take seriously Toulmin's attempt to eliminate the concept of force in the understanding of causality, since that effort makes the recovery of natural agency impossible. After all, the dismissal of force is the elimination of power. As a consequence, once again, we are taken back to the joint conviction of the sacred positivism of Berkeley and the secular positivism of Hume, Smith, and the rest of the positivists to come from then on, that nature is constituted only by events and not also agents (Manicas 1987: 18–23). Fortunately, given the metaphysical failure of Toulmin's strategy, we also have the fact that Wisdom has contradicted it further by at least recognizing the necessity of changing our fundamental conception that matter is inert to the conception that it is active (Wisdom Ibid: 135–35). Both the ordinary experience of "bodies in motion" and "persons moving," for instance, are to be understood in the terms of the metaphysic of immaterial forces. Physical motion and human movement are hence actions that, as centers of influence, are forces in virtue of their powers. But Wisdom could only give us the idea that matter is active, and that is because he only seems to have had the idea of forces without its necessary complement, the concept of causal power. His rehearsal of the history of physics is clearly revealing in that regard (Wisdom Ibid). But, without the dynamical theory of matter and its concept of causal powers in hand, ironically, the outcome of Wisdom's legacy is fatally similar to Toulmin's. Not having a powers concept makes all the difference. Whether we have the idea of force, that is that things get work done and so they must be active (Wisdom), or whether we get rid of the idea of force, presumably because of its necessary involvement with the principle of determinism (Toulmin), the outcome, ultimately, amounts to the same thing. The idea of force, itself, is not enough for the recovery of human agency as a natural property of human being. Indeed, as it is very clear in the example of Toulmin and especially so in the case of Wisdom, the idea of force is not enough even for the recovery of the natural agency of matter. This certainly goes some way in accounting for the fact that Wisdom's important paper fell on deaf ears at the time, and as far as I know, ever since then as well.

The proposal and recent social science: Catton and Turner

But we are left with a most intriguing observation with regard to two historical facts concerning the recovery of natural agency. The first fact is simply that the triumph of the dynamical theory of matter was of course the recovery of natural agency at the very center of the scientific revolution and the development of science thereafter. The second fact is that, parallel to this history, there was of course the foundation of modern positivism that crystallized out of the history of modern empirical philosophy that developed after John Locke, Bishop Berkeley, and Hume (Manicas 1987: 12–15; Harré 2000). The highlighting of these two facts in relation to each other is not what one expects to find in the standard texts in the history of philosophy, particularly on the topics of explanation and causality. An excellent reason for that omission is that it is the case that the recovery of natural agency in physics was not only overshadowed by the emergence of positivism, but with the institutionalization of the positivist paradigm of science by the end of the nineteenth century and its culmination in logical positivism in the 1930s, the recovery was, for all intents and purposes, eclipsed. An important indication of this is found in the fact that, even Kuhn, who is not a positivist, in a paper on the history of causation in physics since the seventeenth century does not make it at all evident, at least not to me, that efficient causation becomes causal powers and that this has developed into modern field theory (Kuhn 1977: 21–30). The consequences of this eclipse in terms of its impact on the social sciences is astonishing.

After all, for the most part, to be trained in the social sciences, to date, is to realize that it is as if there was no such historical development that took us from efficient causality to causal powers to field theory in physics. It is only with the 1970s that we begin to receive such insight and knowledge. And, furthermore, what was also eclipsed was the proposed understanding that, from the recovery of natural agency there is the implication that the recovery of human agency is actually a correlative part of that story. Catton's case is a paradigm example of the impact of the eclipse in the social sciences: having discovered causal powers, nevertheless, he wound up regressing to the assimilation of causal powers to "matrices of multiple correlations" (Catton Ibid: 41–42). Thus, his link-up of agency as the power of action to its consistency with inertia failed to be recognized for what it could have been, the recovery of natural and human agency.

But after the 1970s when knowledge of the history in question was available there are, not unexpectedly, other examples of the continued effect of the eclipse. In effect, in earlier chapters, many of the various philosophers and social scientists carefully examined are exactly such cases. In my judgment, Stephen Turner's work is a contemporary excellent and complex paradigm case. This is to be found in three special publications: an important discussion of the problem of causation, explanation, and agency in the history of the social sciences in 1986, with an update in a 2003 volume of papers on the contemporary philosophy of social science, and also in the same 2003 volume, there is a report on the contemporary status of the philosophy of social science (Turner 1986, 2003: 21–38; Turner and Roth 2003: 1–17). The effect is located in the fact that Turner entitles one to think that there is an internal connection between two major themes of his, one from each of the second and third publications just referred to (Turner and Roth 2003: 1–17; Turner 2003: 21–38). The first theme is that Turner doesn't quite *accept* the fact that scientific practice in, let us say, physics, is realist and that causal powers or its assimilation into field theory is the unproblematic central concept and interest of that practice; and yet there are grounds to also believe that he does seem to *understand* that in fact science is a realist practice (Turner 2003: 21–27, 28, 37–38). There is thus a tension between his apparent lack of acceptance and the suggestion of his understanding of the realist practice of physics that speaks to an ambiguity or uncertainty in his thinking on the matter. And this to me is deepened by what appears to be underwriting this first theme. Turner seems to regard science and its relation to realism strictly from the perspective of the history of the positivist critique of realism in science; and there is every indication that the positivist perspective is taken to be unproblematically viable, and its critical view of realism the right one to take (Turner Ibid: 25–29). Presumably, this is believed to be the case for natural scientists and not just philosophers generally, and philosophers of science specifically.

The second theme concerns an implication that stems from the idea that, generally, philosophy and science are inextricably intertwined, and that in the social sciences that characteristic revolves around their scientific intentions. Thus, Turner's implication, namely, that

> Today, the challenges typically relate to "normativity", which is understood to be that which stands beyond the reach of naturalistic explanation. And behind many of the issues are questions that arise with naturalism generally ... Is there something normative beyond the naturalistic that interacts with the causal world? Or is normativity in the "philosophical" sense another ghost in the machine? With questions such as these the issues at the core of philosophy of social science once again move to philosophical center stage. For it is in competing conceptions of social science – is what we value simply part of the *explanans*, or is it an *explandum* – that such debates are played out. Perhaps. ... with normativity we reach an incompatibility as profound as mind and body.
>
> (Turner and Roth 2003: 13)

There is little doubt then, from my reading of Turner's quote in the context of his entire discussion in the two papers in question, that the issue of naturalism and normativity is still being cast, either in terms of Kant's transcendental freedom – noumenal/phenomenal – or in terms of the Cartesian/ Cambridge theory of transcendent freedom – spirit/mind versus matter/body.

Indeed, he certainly seems to run them, "philosophical" and "ghost," together – "Or is normativity in the 'philosophical' sense another ghost in the machine?" And this I insist is not unrelated to the first theme of his relationship to positivism. That relationship, I have suggested above, is odd. Let me examine exactly that oddness.

Note how Turner's presentation of positivism is fatal to the coherency of his discussion. To rehearse Comte's dismissive conviction that both efficient and final causation are "spooky " because their efficacy is unobservable in principle, and, after just mentioning that there are merely objections to this view, for instance, by citing Durkheim's realist commitment which he himself supported by a reference to chemistry's acceptance of the explanatory force of an unobservable chemical reality, to then leave it at that as if it is all equally a matter of preference, simply won't do (Turner 2003: 28). But it doesn't get better: in the remainder of his discussion, to make a reference to what are clearly examples of the success and the legitimacy of the scientific practice of explanation in terms of real, causal, and unobservable mechanisms, and not to bring such reference to bear on his seemingly favorable discussion of positivism, is just unacceptable (Turner Ibid: 28, 37–38). For, it must be said that, if Turner did in fact definitively understand that science is a realist practice, he simply would have to make it clear that positivism, *in any of its instantiations*, Humean, Comtean, Millsian, Machian, and the rest, is irrelevant. After all, since it is wrong about the status of causal explanatory unobservables, positivist empiricism is inimical too because it cannot account for the understanding of the scientific practice of explanation and experimentation (Bhaskar 1978; Aronson *et al.* 1995; Mumford 1998; Manicas 2006). How, then, is it not the point to make, in reference to Turner's presumption that positivism is still relevant to the social sciences as a philosophy of science, that the acceptance of that presumption decisively blocks the possibility of naturalism in the social sciences, and blocks any genuine understanding of scientific realist practice? Now, the significance of highlighting the serious limitations of Turner's discussion of the philosophy of social science and the themes of explanation, causation, and agency in the social sciences here is this: the history of the triumph of the dynamical theory of matter, and especially Kant's major contribution to that triumph, is exactly the standpoint that argues against Turner's presentation of the issue of naturalism and normativity, and in favor of the alternative that I have formulated. Thus, to assert, even as a question, that the status of normativity may well be noumenal and so a Cartesian ghost in the machinery of nature, as if this is still a viable formulation of the problem, is just no longer adequate. We can say today that this point of view, with all due respect to Turner, is not even wrong.

Now then, the significance of the Catton and Turner examples of the eclipse of the history of causal powers thinking in physics in the social sciences for my work here is this: we in the social sciences must truly understand what exactly it was about the conception of causal powers that captured the minds of the philosophers and scientists involved in its discovery and articulation. And this has to do with the metaphysical and genetic question of "when" it happened that the very idea of material particles had to give way to the very idea of immaterial forces, and hence powers, in the minds of philosophers and scientists? One effective way to show how the "penny dropped" in that genetic sense is to understand both *Boyle's Principle and Boscovich's successful resolution of the Maclaurin paradox in the history of the two contending theories of matter that covers the period of the seventeenth to the eighteenth centuries.*

Recovering natural agency: efficient causes become causal powers

It will serve us well to discuss Boyle's principle that "*much that cannot be observed yet can be manipulated*" in conjunction with More's misappropriation of the results of Boyle's use of it (Aronson *et al.* 1995: 191–203, 200). The Cambridge Platonists engaged both religion and science in their dedication to the defense of the nature of human being as it was defined in terms of reason, freedom, and the soul (Mintz 1996: 80–109). Specifically, particularly Henry More and Ralph Cudworth, they defended this Trinitarian constitution of human being against both the sacred determinism of Calvinism and the secular determinism of Hobbism. The fatalism of Calvinism in virtue of its virulent anti-rationalism, and the consequent denigration of the critical relevance of the practice of Christian virtue both to its perfection and to the presupposition of its freedom to practice, was roundly condemned. And well it should have been. Its more serious challenge, however, was the secular determinism of Hobbesian materialism.

The challenge of materialism to the Cambridge Platonists was actually a metaphysical family quarrel among contending realist theoreticians. What implicitly united them in their realism was the outright dismissal of the positivist form of realism. The quarrel that separated them is the expression of the deepest and the most important Judeo-Greco-Christian principle that an *invisible generative power is the mysterious yet intelligible source of all that is visible.* And it was precisely this Western tradition in its three varieties of realism in the seventeenth and eighteenth centuries, namely the spiritist (Cambridge Platonists), the materialist (Hobbesian and Cartesian), and the immaterialist (Boscovich, Kant, Priestly), that was totally shelved in Comte's law of the three stages of the human mind's historical development. As we are now looking back at Comte's law in relation to these three varieties of Western realism, ironically, it is Comte's positivist law that in effect is being definitively shelved as the outcome of the competing realisms in the triumph of the dynamical theory of matter. It was, of course, Comte's misfortune not to know and not to have understood this history of the triumph that enabled him to present his renowned anti-realist thesis. From the Western supernaturalist idea of an invisible generative power the scientific realist idea is a clear derivation: *unobservable ultimates of some kind explain all of the observable material things and our perceptual experiences of them in nature.*

The basic premise of Cambridge Platonism was that the real presence of God in man was man's reason: it is an imperfect copy of God's reason. The perfectibility of Christian virtue through Christian practice is the perfectibility of sacred as against secular reason. The consequence of this premise is that it is man's sacred or religious reason that permits him to have a perception of the supernatural, that is an inward illumination of the soul. It was this faculty of the mind to perceive the soul that revealed its essence to be freedom, *that is the power of self-moving activity* (Mintz 1996 [1962]: 80–109, 95). Hence the bone of contention between the Cambridge Platonists and the Hobbists concerning the question of what is real, and the consequence of the answer for the fate of human freedom, was the materialist law of inertia and its premise that only bodies are real and only motion externally determined is possible (Mintz Ibid: 111–12). The singular *uniqueness* of More's response to this problem lay not in his claim that we know by our sacred reason that we are free in virtue of the truth that God and man are self-moving, nor that freedom is a power, or even that this power is the spirit of God's power. In this Cudworth concurred. It was, rather, his daring genius to think from *within the paradigm of materialism and boldly use the results of its own methods to defeat, he believed, materialism.* The boldness consisted in the claim that *Boyle's experimental demonstration of the reality of causal power was indeed the demonstration of the reality of spirit.*

> There was yet another way in which More deduced the existence of the spirit – from the evidence of natural science. More had read with interest Boyle's *New Experiments Physico-Mechanical touching the Air* when that work appeared in 1660; because he was persuaded that Boyle had provided fresh evidence for the existence of spirit, More interpolated an account of three of Boyle's experiments on the vacuum into the third edition of *An Antidote Against Atheism* (1662). In More's opinion Boyle's experiments exhibited more than the mere power of the vacuum pump. They demonstrated the presence of an immaterial force which can only be equated with spirit.
> "The ascending of the Sucker of the Air-pump with above an hundred pound weight at it" proves "that there is a Principle transcending the nature and power of Matter."
>
> (Minz Ibid: 86)

More clarified his principle that natural agency is spiritual agency in disguise with the declaration that mechanical effects in nature,

> [Certainly are the] Effects [of] ... [an] immaterial Principle (call it the *Spirit of Nature,* or *what you will*) which is the Vicarious Power of God upon this great Automoton, the world.
>
> (Linz Ibid, my emphasis in the second case)

Now, the metaphysical heart of the matter concerning the issue of the invisible or unobservable substructures of material things is the question of the relationship of experimentation to the induction of a reality beyond the positivist reality of material things. Evidently, More *interpreted* the experimentally demonstrated intelligibility of inferring that the air-pump was an efficient cause because its causal force was a causal *power*. Even more precisely, what he did was to question the metaphysical sufficiency of the causal powers interpretation of experimental fracta, deciding that another metaphysical interpretation was required. Recognizing that both power and spirit are forces in potentia, and as such they must be real because of their efficacy, and they are so when it is not actual, the implication is that More presumed that power and spirit, themselves, needed to be grounded. This seems connected to his deeper belief that nature's inertia condemns it to be inert. Thus, if power means that inert matter can be active, the latter property must be grounded elsewhere other than in nature itself. For, Aristotle's law of the excluded middle to the rescue, how can activeness and passiveness mutually come from each other? What is involved here are the two issues of what More did, and, what else he could have done, but chose not to. In the former case the *rationality of Newton's experimental philosophy* is relevant; in the latter, *Boyle's principle* "brings home the bacon."

Newton's experimental philosophy: three rules of reasoning

The use of Newton's three rules of reasoning are of course those of experimental reasoning, from which only the following decision is legitimate.

> that all *bodies are movable, and endowed with certain powers* (*which we call the inertia*) of preserving in their motion, or in their rest, we only infer from the properties observed in the bodies which we have seen.
> (Newton in Cohen and Westfall 1995: 117, emphasis provided)

Note first the devastating refutation of More's deep belief that inertia means that matter is passive, that is, instead, that *inertia has to do with the causal powers of bodies*, whatever their current state. The next refutation is fatal: rule one is the key.

> We are to admit no more causes of natural things than such as are both true and sufficient to explain their appearances. To this purpose the philosophers claim that Nature does nothing in vain, and more is in vain when less will serve; *for Nature is pleased with simplicity, and affects not the pomp of superfluous causes.*
> (Newton Ibid: 116, emphasis provided)

If we subtract who has said this, the relevant authority stands out, namely, Ockham's razor. It would seem, though, that, nevertheless, the true force of the rule of Ockham really stems, not from that rule itself, but that rule in conjunction with the seemingly contradictory belief that inertia is the reverse of inertness. In short, that efficient causes are causal powers. It must be remembered that both More and Newton introduce God into the activity of nature, but under different metaphysical decisions. And Newton's decision that the powers of causal forces are natural and never supernatural is maintained in the history of physics. Maintained by all of the prominent contributors to the eventual triumph of the dynamical theory, even though Newton himself was a corpuscularian theorist. Kant of course followed Newton's decision regarding the status of efficient causes, but did so as the challenger of his corpuscularianism. Thus, there seems to be some leeway in the determination of the metaphysical status of the naturalist purification of the realist thesis that efficient causes are causal forces. It is here at this juncture that Boyle's principle becomes relevant.

Boyle's principle: power not spirit

What More did not do was evaluate his interpretation of the effectiveness of the air-pump in light of the import of Boyle's experimental observation that "A green emerald, reduced to powder, is white" (Harré 2000a: 205). In his *Origins of Forms and Qualities* (1666) Boyle presented the principle that one can indirectly manipulate what cannot be observed (material corpuscles of the green emerald at the molecular level) by directly manipulating what can be observed (the emerald at the level of a material thing). Based on this idea he was not only able to challenge Locke's pessimism that one can only conjecture about unseen or unseeable substructures (Harré 2002). He, in effect, *defeated the Humean transformation of Locke's pessimism into the lethal skepticism that became the positivist doctrine of the denial of their reality, from which came as well Comte's third law that unobservable powers are replaced by observable regularities.*

> Boyle argued for the *reality of corpuscles* on the grounds that the techniques of chemistry, when closely analyzed, turned out to be intelligible only as ways of manipulating the unobservable corpuscularian substructures of material stuff.
>
> (Aronson *et al.* 1995: 199)

That Boyle's method of manipulation has become common practice in modern physics is readily seen in the example of Stern and Gerlach manipulating magnetic fields in order to manipulate atomic nuclei (Aronson *et al.* 1995: 200). But Boyle's method, beyond its being *the commonsense practice of physics*, is actually such *a commonsense practice in our everyday lives* that it is largely unnoticed. For example, "Every time we *turn on the shower and stand underneath it* we are, in effect, using the unobservable gravitational field to manipulate the water" (Aronson *et al.* 1995: 200).

The understanding of the full substance and argument of Boyle's principle proves to be categorically fatal to any attempt to slide from the fact that power and spirit share in the properties of being immaterial and hence unobservable generative forces, to the equation of their status under a supernaturalist or, in Kant's version, a dogmatic metaphysic. For, the above discussion and commentary of the success, not only of Boyle's principle in his own work, but of its increasingly sophisticated use in the development of realism in modern physics, indicate that therein lies a robust argument in favor of the dynamical thesis that causal forces are forces because, as powers, they are real (Aronson *et al.* 1995: 199–203). If certain effects can be produced by the method of the manipulation of their causes, and these same causes are unobservable in fact, and especially in some cases in principle, then the causal powers of such forces at issue must be real. *The point at issue is that, if the causal powers of material things were entirely unmanipulable, they could never assume a place in our accepted ontology of beliefs that indicate to us what is real* (Aronson *et al.* 1995: 200). The upshot, once again, for religion and dogmatic metaphysics is final: unless we take the standpoint of magic, and assume that God can be indirectly manipulated by the direct experimental manipulation of objects, or animals, or persons, to serve our epistemological intentions, only natural causes can be natural agents. *The recovery of natural agency is the recovery of the genuinely active character of nature, itself.* This may well be the crucial reason why the idea that eventually won the day in modern science was that the concept of God was only necessary, if at all, to account for the fact that the world existed. Given its creation, or simply, its existence, scientific interest is defined by the circumstance that the world is a Kantian community of different natural kinds of beings that work on their own causal grounds.

It must then be the case that science cannot take seriously the deep metaphysical question, haunting as it may well be, as to why there is being rather than non-being. Yet, regardless, science is the practice of metaphysics: its root question is the nature of being (of things) and the variety of natural kinds of beings (of things) that there are. And the issue of being is the question of the nature of real things as generative sources of appearances. Hence, again, the method of science presupposes that metaphysics is its normal business: the latter is the source of ontological questions and the former is to be the test of the ontological answers proposed by such questions. Perhaps this is precisely why Max Born declared that theoretical physics is actual philosophy. To be sure, the special and necessary feature of "real things" responsible for appearances is of course that generativity is likely to be hidden, that is unseen (unexaminable in fact) and unseeable (unexaminable in principle). And as we have now appreciated, the beauty of Boyle's method of manipulation is that it provides us with as definitive a fundamental answer as we are likely to get to the question of whether knowing such real things is possible. The foregoing presentation can be encapsulated as follows: the logic of Boyle's method has two dimensions, namely, the necessity of human action and the principle of epistemic invariance. The logic of the former: *dynamically embodied human action is methodologically required to verify the natural agency of real things.* The logic of the latter:

> When it comes to gathering evidence for our beliefs, *the epistemological situation remains the same for* observables and unobservables alike, no matter whether we are dealing with *observables, possible observables or unobservables.*
>
> (Aronson *et al.* 1995: 195, emphasis provided)

In other words, if the results of two identical experiments on test objects of the same type are the same, and the only difference is that in one of the experiments the object is not open to observation, why would the fact of unobservability be relevant to the reliability of the inference under that condition (Aronson *et al.* 1995: 196–203)?

Particles and forces: two stories

From our position today, looking back, clearly, the "penny dropped" in the matter of the thesis that causal powers are real, certainly with the help of Newton's rules of reasoning, but definitively as a direct consequence of Boyle's methodological argument. Yet, there is still the question of how the other "penny dropped," that is why should it be believed that the ultimates of explanation must be the powers of forces and not the fact of (material) particles? As it turns out, since Boyle wound up on the side of particles and not powers, his argument should have, but did not, yet, settle the matter. *The first part of the story concerning the "other penny" is about the transition to the triumph of the concept of powers over the concept of particles. The second part is the triumph itself signaled by Boscovich's resolution of the Maclaurin paradox.*

From particles to forces

The crucial issue of the story of transition was the problem of *how to conceive of a "real thing": how is substance to be understood as an adequate conception of causation.* Historically, how is it that Boyle and Locke, who were seriously involved in thinking about causal powers as an explanatory concept, yet finally they could not get a sure handle on it? Indeed, although the reasons in each case were different, for both of them, ultimately, the idea of causal powers in fact vanishes in virtue of its being an unavailable conception (Harré 2000b: 6). As the under-laborer for Newtonian science the thrust of Locke's philosophy of knowledge was to provide a mechanistic view of the material world with a rational foundation (Harré 2000a: 204). The basic thesis of his epistemology is that the active powers of clusters of primary qualities that constitute material things determine our knowledge or the ideas of them that we experience as sensations in our minds (Harré 2000a: 229). While the relationship between a primary idea of the primary quality of a thing, for instance shape, is a relation of resemblance, the relationship between a secondary idea of a secondary quality of a thing, for instance warmth and the vibrations of the minute parts, respectively, is not (Harré 2000a 203; 2000b: 2–4). However, the resemblance doctrine could not save his theory of knowledge from the deadly consequences of its solipsism: primary qualities must be passive since our knowledge of them can only be an idea, and, as Berkeley claimed, ideas are inert (Harré 2000b: 4). Hence, the subtle implication of Locke's predicament is that his pessimism about being able to know the powers of invisible corpuscles reveals that Locke simply was not in the relevant metaphysical position to conceive of pure powers. Consider that complementary to his pessimism is the fact that an unobservable corpuscular entity is not a power precisely because it is a cluster of primary qualities that incarnate the power of a material thing (Harré 2000b: 3). Technically, then, "power" can have no explanatory purchase because that power has been handed over to only those properties that are *occurrent* in being primary (Harré 2000b: 4). And of course, as we've just seen, thanks to Berkeley, they cannot be generative. What you have here then is the mistake (or fallacy) of *actualism: though occurrent, primary qualities are supposed to be "forces," but, without "powers," they are mere events and not forces.*

This leads us to consider that Locke (and others in this situation) was entangled in a web of certain compelling ideas: at the center was the enthrallment to empiricism, then, on one side you had the enormous prestige of Newtonian mechanical science, and, on the other, of course, there was the electrifying ideology of radical individualism. Now Locke's corpuscularianism can be accounted for by the fact that his primary commitment to empiricism and radical individualism jointly determined the way he misappropriated Newtonianism. This misappropriation was exactly what Galileo and Boyle were *not* guilty of. True to his commitments, Locke regarded the *qualities of material things* from the standpoint of the philosophy of *perception*, and so, disastrously, he shifted to the *false* distinction between *ideas* (as mental representations) *of sensations* and the *qualities they are to represent* (Harré 2000b: 4). Galileo and Boyle regarded the qualities of material things in terms of *material things themselves*, thus they focused on the distinction between those qualities that are *observable and those that are unobservable*. Locke's position is an exemplification of the fact that the fatal consequence of the enthrallment to empiricism has been the general failure of empiricists to understand the import of the fact that, no doubt, "substance" is not an empirical concept. The point, however, was not to dismiss it but instead to realize that in science metaphysics and methodology are necessarily reciprocals of each other, and therefore, "substance" is a vitally important metaphysical problem in science. More accurately, it is *the* problem to solve for the success of scientific method to be genuinely scientific. And so *what was needed was a better conception of what individual things must be in order to understand how real things are responsible for appearances* (Harré and Madden 1975: 173). Now, Boyle suffered the fate of being faithful to the end to the corpuscularian theory of matter. Hence, the ultimates of explanation for Boyle are not *powers*, but *particles* that occupy space by filling it with matter (Harré and Madden 1975: 165). This concession to matter in the cases of both Locke and Boyle sharpened the problem of how to tilt the balance, finally, in favor of powers. This brings out the cardinal issue in this conflict of the metaphysical interpretations of nature.

The reality of forces? Limits of perception

What is involved is the role that human sensibility is to be given in the description and explanation of material things. In other words, *why should nature as it is in its real workings resemble the way it is experienced and perceived by human subjects?* Consider two seemingly abstract complementary theses that, however, are in fact directly relevant to this question. Since human sensibility is an *evolutionary accident*, why should it be taken as having any resemblance to nature's real causal activity? After all, the human species just happened, and the point of that is survival: it took some time to discover that in order to hang on the world has to be known and not only mythologized, and then a longer time to realize that one can, and should, know the world independent of hanging on and independent of mythology, and longer still, to know how to do that scientifically and not any other way. And further, as such an accident, of course human sensibility has in fact appeared long after the big bang and the evolution of the physical world into its fundamental causal multileveled structural constitution. Thus, again, why would one expect human sensibility to informatively resemble that structural constitution? A crucial thesis of (a sophisticated) realism is clearly given here: since the physical world is independent of human beings, there is no necessary connection between the nature of the world and human perception. *The structure of nature and the function of perception were not interdependently evolving, though they were related.* The relevant insight that the import of the two theses suggest can now be expressed.

> The cause of our perceiving colors is not color, or to put it less paradoxically, color in a thing is a different sort of quality from color as we perceive it. It is *electrical* in things and to our eyes it appears as a *hue* of a surface.
>
> (Harré 2000a: 159, emphasis provided)

This insight strongly encourages the adoption of the following principle that aims to accurately capture the relevant connection of human sensibility and material things. *Generally speaking, in many cases human perceptions simply do not, because they cannot, resemble the material qualities causing them.* This principle is validated by the dynamical concept of causal powers that underwrites it. From this deep recognition that perception is not critically decisive in knowing real causal forces, we can appreciate why both the materialist and phenomenalist theories of matter must be, and are, dismissed.

Materialism and phenomenalism: realism preferred

It is of the utmost importance to be clear about the deep dissatisfaction with the materialist theory, for instance, of Descartes, and with the phenomenalist theory of, for instance, Berkeley, that decisively motivates some philosophers and eventually all scientists to favor the dynamical theory. Again, the critical focus here is the status of the concept of "substance" in reference to the fundamental issue of forging a theory of substance that is adequate to *the cardinal thesis that "real things are responsible for appearances."* The traditional idea of substance/quality (or form) in materialist theory thus must be rejected wholesale: *"substance" is viewed as a quality-less material substratum, and reciprocally, "quality" is viewed as a substance-less phenomenon.* The upshot is a mysterious dualism: commonsense can only recognize but cannot cognize two dichotomized features of sensible reactivity, *raw material stuff* and the *phenomenal* forms of *immediate experience.* The *phenomenalist* alternative to materialism must also be dismissed: while correctly rejecting the materialist substance/quality model in toto, we are then left with the other glaring mystery of substance-less qualities free-floating in nature and in human experience.

We must remember, however, that in the exemplary case of Berkeley it is only in the phenomenology of appearances that qualities are free-floating. He is obviously a theological realist, and so the realism of nature is preserved in the reality of God, *for a price.* The coerciveness of material things that is the mark of the objectivity of their natural laws is distinguished by Berkeley from the arbitrariness of our imaginative sensibility, to be sure, but, his solipsism is not to be defeated. The causal powers that are the forces that work nature's laws are kept completely within the mystery of God's omnipotence and omniscience. But at this point, exactly, it must be recognized that it is a positivist mistake to think that we are left with the bare regularity of such laws, for, the truth of the matter is that Berkeley's solution must be relocated within the history of the particles/powers debate that was going on. In that proper light, Berkeley's ultimately very traditional solution of keeping causal powers out of nature and back with God is not a serious challenge to, for instance, the Newton/Boyle argument. The real challenge was for someone to accept the Newton/Boyle demonstration that nature's work is the work of the powers of causal forces, and then argue that natural powers are proof that, since matter is inert in being inertial and therefore matter cannot be the ground, it can only be active if God, however vicariously, is the metaphysical reason why powers are real. *When Berkeley's philosophy is appreciated in this manner, its value is that it is one sign post along the way, and a minor one at that, toward recognizing the triumph of the dynamical theory of matter.* That his radical empiricism was the occasion, along with Hume, of the emergence of positivism can now be seen as of an importance that was and is misleading. He was a closet deep realist: God is *the* exemplar of the explanatory power of causal powers that are in principle unobservable. Thus, the mistake that made him a positivist – empirical realism – is the reason why positivism was and is a mistake.

In these respects then, materialism and phenomenalism violate the cardinal twin theses of realism: on the one hand, no conception of genuine causation is possible without a viable conception of substance, and, on the other, without a conception of substance no account of human qualities is imaginable.

Transition to forces: Leibniz, Reid, and Green

Leibniz's defeat of Descartes's idea that matter is res extensa was indicative of a major contribution that must be included with that of Newton's rules and Boyle's method to the achievement of significantly advancing the concept of natural causal powers.

> The "concept of corporeal substance" involves "force of action" and resistance rather than extension, the latter being merely a repetition or diffusion of something prior to it, namely, this force.
>
> (Leibniz 1956: 752 in Harré 2000b: 4)

The singular spectacular insight of Leibniz resides, precisely, in the realization that "extension" is a *secondary* feature of matter, being itself a direct result of the fact that matter is "force." To be clear, the concept is one of force as a primary or primitive property, that is a disposition or potential that is a striving or effort constitutive of real things (Harré and Madden 1975: 168). Note that, as in Galileo and in Newton, Leibniz contradicts that idea that the inertia of matter means that it is inert. Leibniz, however, is only on the verge of cleanly identifying the concept of powers, for he uses "force" to indicate both actual force and potential force (Harré and Madden Ibid). With Thomas Reid and J. Green, however, there was a genuine breakthrough to a formulation which cleanly distinguishes power from its presence as an actual force in the interaction of material things (Harré 2000b: 6–7). Both philosophers then arrive at a pure dispositional concept, so that power is a property in principle not perceivable by the external senses, but is conceivable by our ontological sense (Harré 2000b Ibid). In Green's radical generalization of dispositionalist thinking the doctrine of resemblance is totally denounced and material things are regarded as possessing a variety of dispositional properties that can produce the entire range of experienced qualities (Harré 2000b Ibid). For Reid his remarkably subtle understanding of causal powers is revealed in his specification that *a power not only can exist when not being exercised*, but *a given power may be capable of a greater degree of power, even when only a lesser degree has been thus far identified* (Harré 2000b: 7). The one limitation of Reid's achievement is that he stops at the clear specification of *causality as a disposition to act upon.* What is thus required is the idea of *liability*, that is *the reciprocal disposition to be acted upon.* Note, in this regard, that Green failed to honor the *metaphysical* principle of Newton's third law of action and re-action: if nature is a community of entities, and thus this entails a reciprocity between entities, then the property of causation that they all possess must be composed of powers *and* liabilities.

There can be little doubt but that Green and Reid realized the ideal of a fundamental conceptualization of causation that transcended the metaphysical achievement of Locke and that of Boyle. Nevertheless, in light of the telling fact that Boyle's method of manipulation literally proves *only* that some kind of ultimate particular is real, neither Green's nor Reid's imaginative and remarkable achievement is an argument proving the thesis that forces and not particles must be that kind of particular. *That* penny was about to drop.

Forces to powers: Boscovich and the definitive argument

There is a more serious reason to believe that corpuscularian theory leads to the loss of natural agency than that which is found in the examples of Locke and Boyle. Berkeley's observation that Locke's idea of powers must be wrong simply because ideas are passive, and thus matter too must be passive, certainly has some sense. But actually, in Locke's case, how compelling could it have been? Let us set to one side the obvious fact that, intuitively speaking, no natural scientist worth his or her salt would take Berkeley's argument seriously and give up powers (Ernst Mach of course is the formidable exception). As perfect exemplars of this fact we have of course the Newton and Boyle achievement and its institutionalization in the culture of physics. Now, that said, is it not true that the Bishop was being decidedly disingenuous in that clever argument against Locke's pessimistic belief in powers? On the one hand, and of *only* secondary importance, he is a *subjective idealist* and thus he is tacitly but illicitly assimilating Lockean thinking to his own on the issue of the rejection of the reality of matter. But, *Locke, himself,* cannot be so easily counterpunched, for his epistemological pessimism suggests to us that he *is a realist in spite of Berkeleyan empiricism.* And on the other hand, as I have already indicated, Berkeley is an out and out realist; the realism is just not secular and naturalistic. He is a deep but sacred realist, rather than being a deep and secular realist. The upshot surely is that Locke and Berkeley, ultimately, are realist brothers under the skin. No, the *deep* problem that corpuscularian theory is connected to the loss of the powers concept is not to be found simply in Berkeley's idealism, for his empiricism, as Green understood, is not British (Harré 2000a: 5). *The key to the core of the problem is to be found in connection to Locke's handing over powers to the cluster of primary qualities of material things. This is the mistake of actualism.*

What is it about the fact that those properties that are occurrent in being primary cannot therefore be genuine "forces," since, to say it now slightly differently, *in being events they cannot be powers*? "Events" in this context are made up of material corpuscles, that is bodies that *occupy space, fully,* are *perfectly rigid and perfectly solid*, and are of *definitive shape* (the basis for the following discussion: Harré 1970: 259–60, 285–93; Harré and Madden 1975: 161–75). The corpuscle's four features are unified around the substance/quality model of matter. Bodies conceived of in this manner necessarily imply that they are extraordinary in that they are not compressible. Thus, as a direct consequence of the fact that in mechanical interaction, or action by (impulsive) contact, since no energy can be stored up in them, the only form of energy that is available for dissipation between corpuscles is transfer of motion. And that's the key: *no storage, no potential, hence, no potential no powers*. Corpuscularian theory is the paradigm of the fallacy of actualism: there is the violation of the principle that as a *force* causation is *realized* but not *exhausted* by any one of its occurrent moments; as a *power* causation is not to be *identified* with any one of its occurrent moments. Strictly then, *powers and forces are not ontologically identical but ontologically reciprocal*. This principle is the defeat of actualism at its very root in corpuscularian theory. And, of course, the very idea of positivism, that is its Humean doctrine of empirical realism, is an impossible idea in science. Traditional philosophy is another matter. And as for social science, well, that's something else altogether.

Let us put this differently. Boscovich discovered that action by contact for the mechanical interactions of material corpuscles is impossible. Hence, explanatory ultimate particulars cannot be particles, and thus they can only be powers. The deep and general reason for this is that action by corpuscular contact violates the universal truth that all actual actions, which actions can only occur in space and time, must be seen and understood according to the law of continuity. Since actions in space and time exemplify the law of continuity they are genuinely possible actions and hence determinate. In being determinate, the forces which the actions are, are grounded in the type of generative mechanism that a given natural kind of particular is built to be. And, this is crucial, the forces of the mechanism must be finite because of the structure of the natural kind that it is. This is central to the proof that the law of the continuity of space and time is exemplified by the actions of moving particulars. *And now, here in a nutshell is the problem of the impossibility of mechanical action by contact: it implies that the forces of such actions are infinite (in-finite or not finite).* Now this means that all actions of bodies are indeterminate and thus unintelligible. After all, force signifies a generative mechanism of some kind, and the kind that it is requires that a finite mechanism can only generate finite forces. An infinite or non-finite force therefore signifies a generative mechanism that cannot be imagined. This means of course that there is no such mechanism, hence there can be no new particular state of action for a given body. In other words, an unimaginable generative mechanism means the absence of a possible reason that any new state can be any particular state. "A possible reason" is obviously a reference to a structural moment of potential generativity of a given natural kind of powerful particular that would be responsible for a new particular state.

There is one other cardinal feature of the problem of infinite force that tells the story of the impossibility of corpuscular action by contact. This has exactly to do with the fact that interactions that presume an infinite force thus also presume that such a force is acting *"for no time."* In short, such interactional forces occur *instantaneously*. And it is at this point that the violation of the law of continuous time and space is exposed. For, *in the alleged mechanical action by contact, what is happening instantaneously is the discontinuity of the transfer of motion*. In the conception of non-corpuscular bodies such bodies are mutually compressible (they can interpenetrate) in that they are imperfectly rigid and imperfectly solid, and thus have a shape that is less than definitive. Such bodies, so to speak, are a specified set of properties ordered into a dynamic of structural possibility(ies). Thus, they can interact by contact because by mutual compression they can slow down and accelerate in a finite time. Ordinary interaction then is not instantaneous, it takes place in some time, not "for no time." But then the interaction is continuous, not discontinuous, that is the change in velocity takes place with a passage through intermediate stages. The law of continuity is preserved. The definitive consequence is that the action by contact of material corpuscles cannot take place. In violating the law that the actions of bodies must occur continuously at some time and at some space, in effect, there is, in my judgment, a complementary and deeper law that is being violated. That is what I will call the law of intelligible causation: a generative mechanism must be conceivable in order for an action to be conceivable as an effect. *The law of continuity preserves, because it metaphysically presumes, the law of intelligible causation.* Boscovich thus demonstrated that the incoherency of the corpuscular theory of particles as the ultimate form of explanation in physics therefore fails to preserve both laws. The triumph of the dynamical theory of forces by virtue of that demonstration was secured in the history of physics. *That was the penny that dropped: no continuity and hence no causal powers, no causal powers and hence no modern physical field theory.*

10 Kantian realism

Human agency

There are human powers and there are natural powers.
All kinds of questions emerge around the distinction.

Rom Harré

Introduction: the noumenal impasse to recovery

With its culmination in Faraday's physical field theory, the history of the triumph of the dynamical theory of matter shows itself to be the recovery of natural agency in the world of physical objects. Wisdom's rejection of the thesis that efficient causation is passive can now be understood to have been, actually, unnecessary for the natural science of physics. The reason is eminently available: his proposal of an active conception of causation had already been presumed by the meaning of the dynamical theory, and its triumph finalized the establishment of that very meaning, and much more, in physics (Wisdom 1971: 123–27, 135–36). The central theme of field theory then is that material particulars are *active because of their efficacy*: while potentially efficacious in virtue of their powers, they are actually efficacious by virtue of the forces they become when their powers are released or unblocked in interaction with other powerful particulars. This theme can be enriched with a metaphysical principle that, I suggest, is implied by Newton's three laws. But it can be seen with particular clarity, however, in the second law ($F = ma$), and that is exactly because the law defines force as the product of the mass of an object multiplied by its acceleration. If we peal away the mathematical concepts of weight (m) and speed (a), what is revealed is the relevance of the metaphysical relationship unifying the concepts of power, motion, force according to this principle: *the power to be a force is the power to be moving.*

I now propose that we have in this principle the first part of Giddens's Call answered: natural agency is the concept of "agent causality."

That nature is constituted by powerful moving particulars promotes the thesis that the recovery of the agency of physical objects is the necessary but not the sufficient basis for the recovery of the agency of cultural subjects. This thesis is underwritten by Kant's suggestion that human freedom is a "kind of free motion." The above metaphysical principle can be developed to express exactly this thesis, with Kant's contribution: *if the power to be a thing is the power to be a moving thing, (an object), the power to be a human thing is the power to be a signifying moving thing (a subject).* Thus moving physical objects and thence moving cultural subjects are, equally, to be seen as constituted by powers of agency, though, as Kant magnificently intimated, they are of quite different natural kinds. Hence the question to be raised, which is Kantian through and through, is that, although natural agents are to be conceived of as being dynamically embodied efficient causes, how can human dynamically embodied agency be conceivable as a special case? This is the cardinal question at issue in the recovery of human agency, but only because, in our time, it is finally and fully recognized to be ontological.

The intimation here is that, metaphysically speaking, it is another and very different matter to realize the recovery of human agency, and that is because it requires that we come to terms with the difficult treatment of time in Kant's theory of transcendental or noumenal freedom. In *The Cambridge Edition Of The Works Of Emmanuel Kant* Wood clearly reveals that the question of time is the heart of the matter in Kant's noumenal theory (also, see Harré 2000: 8–9).

> By the resolution of the third antinomy, the supposed contradiction between natural necessity and a causal activity not determined by temporal conditions, the *Critique of Pure Reason* had established the logical possibility of a free causality.
>
> (Gregor and Wood in Kant 1999: introduction, 135)

The importance of Wood's explicitly stating exactly the Heideggerian issue of atemporality in the thesis of free causality is that it firmly counters a long standing tendency in the history of philosophy and the social sciences concerning this issue of Kant's thesis. And of course that has been the tendency to omit it, to forget it, to focus on some other feature of the thesis, or even to treat it as if there is no genuine and serious issue in considering Kant's thesis because it is an inexplicable mystery. For some, this has been the occasion to simply dismiss the very idea of free causality. Ironically enough, in her review of Michael S. Gazzaniga's *The Ethical Brain*, Patricia S. Churchland is a perfect contemporary example of this dismissive and quite muddled stance.

> Some philosophers – usually called libertarians – resolutely believe that voluntary decisions *actually are* created by the will, free of causal antecedents. Like flat-earthers and creationists, libertarians glorify their scientific naiveté by labeling it transcendental.
>
> (Churchland 2005: 356–57)

It has been amply demonstrated in this book that such a critical view is simply irrelevant. Reading Churchland in the terms of the discussion of freedom in this work, I must assert that she has thrown out the baby with the bathwater: conflating, in effect, Kantian freedom (transcendental) with Rousseauan freedom (transcendent), she has properly thrown out free-will theory while at the same time improperly throwing out the freedom of the Kantian subject. The death blow to this kind of position, in this case enunciated by Churchland's uninformed rejection of the idea of "will free of causal antecedents," is this quote of Mario Bunge's on precisely the issue of human autonomy and causality in 1959 on the eve of the neo-romantic revolt in the social sciences.

> *Self-movement* is by now a solid philosophical acquisition of the *sciences*. In no department of science are scholastic *patients* recognized. On the contrary, *material objects at all levels of organization are* more and more *regarded as entities having an activity of their own, conditioned but not entirely determined by their surroundings*.
>
> (Bunge 1979: 176–78, emphasis provided)

Ultimately then, the deep reason why we are grateful to Wood for (unintentionally) following Heidegger in correctly presenting Kant's thesis of free causality with the intellectual respect it deserves is that it thus opens it up to being finally treated as a legitimate problem concerning the metaphysical principles of scientific thinking on the questions of causality, agency, and freedom.

Kant's noumenal problem: philosophy and the social sciences

As I have emphasized throughout this book, the history of the challenge of the structure/agency problem to date, while it has often been formulated in terms of the noumenal/phenomenal dualism dividing physical objects and cultural subjects, has never been accurately conceptualized in the very terms of that central issue of the treatment of time. And more germane, conceptualized in strict reference to a realist understanding of causality and human agency. Chapter by chapter we have seen what a difference that failure of conceptualization has made in the history of philosophy and the social sciences to the fate of that central debate. In philosophy and the social sciences we have seen this in the principal examples of Bidney, Dahrendorf, Benton, and Berger. In philosophy, Dilthey of course is the brilliant exception, and in the social sciences, we've seen that Parsons, surprisingly, is the other exception. But, even then, while Dilthey's conception of the temporality of phenomenological freedom was certainly an alternative to Kant's conception of the atemporality of noumenal freedom, yet, he never directly confronts that issue of time itself in Kant's theory of freedom; and in the example of Parsons, it seems that his space–time reversal, where action is in time but not in space, was certainly not deliberately formulated with the Kantian problem in mind. The most important point here in these two cases is that both alternatives were not earned by directly encountering Kant's theory in its proper intellectual context. Thus, Kant's atemporality argument was not confronted, Heidegger's two-causalities reading of the argument was not identified, and these internally related problems were not systematically traced to Kant's realist metaphysics of science, and done so with the understanding that knowledge/mind and matter/causal power were the integrally connected sets of problems in the mind of a philosopher of science who was one of the architects of the dynamical theory of matter. Hence, it is clear why it can be claimed that a good reason why Dilthey's phenomenological conception of freedom and Parsons's noumenal variety of voluntarism failed to be seriously noticed, for instance even by Giddens, was exactly because, though clearly a notion of "agent causality" in the former case, and reaching for such a notion in the other, such a notion was cut off from its only proper metaphysical grounding in the theory of dynamical matter. Now we can present the deeper reason for the failure of Dilthey's attempt to side step the problem of the phenomenal world: "phenomenology" is without proper metaphysical grounding, in principle, since it is the unwitting reinstatement of the "phenominalist" alternative to the substance/quality model of matter. *Without, therefore, a suitable alternative conception of "substance," Diltheyean freedom is therefore a phenomenological quality without a "subject" that would be the agent of that freedom.* This certainly must be judged to be an astounding consequence in view of the fact that Dilthey actually formulated a conception of dynamically embodied action: the embodiment of action is without a conception of "substance" to ground both agency and the moving body. No wonder the phenomenological tradition comes to grief because its conception of the power of action is power-less: the conception of causal power entails the ideas of "power" *and* "substance." And so that "cutting off," I contend, results from not taking seriously the problem of Kant's intellectual context, and then tracing that mistake, and the opportunity of its correction, back to that context, particularly, to the realist metaphysics of nature where a suitable conception of "substance" as the agent of nature and freedom is forthcoming. Although he too sidestepped the problem of the phenomenal world, but did so without being a phenomenologist, nevertheless, Parsons is even more definitely in Dilthey's predicament: since action that is in time but not in space cannot be action, Parsons is in need of a conception of "substance" with which to ground the actor to the body in order for action to actually be action.

Kant: rescue to recovery?

Now then, when the noumenal/phenomenal division and its justification in atemporality are examined in relationship to Kant's realist metaphysics of nature, it is not immediately clear that, for him, human freedom is recoverable on the basis of the realist nature of the causal activity of physical objects. Since I have not been able to find that Kant explicitly considered the relationship in the texts of any of the three *Critiques*, could it be that such a question of recovery simply never recommended itself to him? And, in view of the fact that I also have not found any such consideration of that relationship between freedom and scientific realism in any of the eminent discussions of Kantian freedom, and that is also true of Henry E. Allison's definitive reconstruction of *Kant's Theory of Freedom* (1990, 1995), Kantian scholarship to date has not recognized the possibility of recovering human agency from Kant's scientific realism (Allison 1983; Ameriks 2000; Beiser 1987; Guyer 1993; Shell 1996; Taylor 1989: 355–91). However, from the shorter version of the first *Critique*, the *Prolegomena to Any Future Metaphysics* (1985a [1783]), in a footnote (39) to his discussion of the third antinomy we find Kant declaring that,

> The idea of freedom occurs only in the relation of the intellectual, as cause, to the appearance, as effect. Hence we *cannot* attribute freedom to matter in regard to the *incessant action by which it fills space*, though *this action takes place from an internal principle.*
>
> (Kant 1985b: 85, my emphasis)

Before I comment on this passage, we should remind ourselves of the fact that *the Prolegomena* was published 3 years before the *Metaphysical Foundations of Natural Science* was itself published (1985b [1786]), the content of which, we have seen, was his contribution to the dynamic theory of matter. It is hence reasonable to suppose that Kant had his realist treatise in mind, so to speak, either because he was writing it around the time of the *Prolegomena*'s publication in 1783, or he was to begin writing it just afterward. So, it is to be expected that the last sentence of the above quote captures the metaphysical theme of the dynamic theory of matter – matter is agent causality, and therefore is naturally active (force) by virtue of an "internal principle" (power). Does the above quote necessarily require the inference that Kant discounted the plausibility of such a recovery? *After all, perhaps that is simply the obvious implication of the noumenal/atemporal argument in the first place?* So then, Kant *did* indeed discount the conceivability of recovery, so that, as a consequence, he did not need to discuss it in the critiques.

Certainly, that consideration is impressive, and yet I am not fully persuaded. Let us entertain two facts and their implications (which the quote presumes) that define my reason against the acceptance of that inference: (fact 1) once again, as the quote reminds us, Kant was indeed one of the principal architects of causal powers theory; (fact 2) from the thesis of the third antinomy, Kant not only refers to freedom as "another *causality* through freedom" that anticipates what in his next *Critique* will be understood to be the *efficient* causality of freedom, but he also refers to freedom as "a *power* of spontaneously beginning a series", which power is "an *absolute* spontaneity of the cause" (Kant 1999: 484; Kant 1985a: 412, 411; 1996: 178–79); *first implication*, the *template* for his theory of human freedom is the theory of causal powers; *second implication*, the efficient causality of freedom is clearly "agent causality." In view of all this, I am convinced even more, that, although Kant was keenly torn between the intimately connected themes of recovery (his scientific realism) and rescue (his religious faith), this ambivalence was located, as I have contended from the beginning, within a predominant commitment to naturalism. And so it is especially important to take very seriously, again, the fact that, for Kant, freedom in being transcendental is thus never transcendent. With this declaration in mind, consider the following pieces of evidence, the first of which is the line that follows the famous reference to "the starry heavens above me and the moral law within me" that opens Kant's conclusion to the *Critique of Practical Reason* (Kant 1996: 269).

> I do not need to search for them and merely conjecture them as though they were veiled in obscurity or in the transcendent region beyond my horizon; I see them before me and connect them immediately with the consciousness of my existence.
>
> (Kant Ibid)

And now consider the next piece of evidence that clinches the matter from the second *Critique*. Kant is here stating the new, that is positive, definition of freedom as the immediate determination of the will by the employment, from pure reason itself, of the legislative form of maxims of action. This new definition

> ... is able thus to give objective though only practical reality to reason, which always became extravagant ["transcendent", another translation] when it wanted to proceed speculatively with its ideas, and changes its *transcendent* use into an *immanent* use (in which reason is by means of ideas itself an efficient cause in the field of experience).
>
> (Kant Ibid: 178; the emphasis is Kant's)

In other words, just as natural science established natural agency divorced from any conception of divine agency, Kant was moving modern philosophy in the direction of establishing natural but human agency divorced from any conception of divine agency. And so, if matter is agent causality, then so is human freedom. Although, in keeping with Kant's correct understanding, the reverse is not true – matter is not freedom. This means, of course, as I have maintained, that freedom is not being located in some "transcendent region beyond [Kant's] horizon" because it is divorced from divine agency, and implies that the inner sense of free will must be a secondary feature of human being. Consider, along with the above quote as well, Kant's comment in the second critique that is relevant to this issue.

This Analytic shows that pure reason can be practical – that is, can of itself, independently of anything empirical, determine the will – and it does so by a fact in which pure reason in us proves itself actually practical, namely the autonomy in the principle of morality by which reason determines the will to deeds. At the same time it shows that this fact is inseparably connected with, and indeed identical with, consciousness of freedom of the will.

(Kant 1999: 173)

Note here, that free will is identical with the autonomy of reason as the ground of the agency of practical action, and is identical with efficient causality. In short, free will is logically subordinate to moral autonomy: we are conscious of the former because of its groundedness in the latter. Yet, despite all this, by virtue of his ambivalence concerning his journey along the slippery slope of naturalism, Kant stopped half way. And thus, ultimately, that has to be understood in order for us to know that Kant was on a journey toward recovery, and that it has to be completed for him.

The attempt here to complete that recovery can be understood as being *complementary* to two of three major discussions of Kantian freedom in relation to scientific realism: (1) Rom Harré's similar attempt in, "Active Powers and Powerful Agents" (2008); (2) John D. Greenwood's attempt in "Kant's Third Antinomy: Agency and Causal Explanation" (1990). The recovery of agency is *supplementary* to the third discussion, Alasdair MacIntyre's "The Antecedents of Action" (1966). I will be offering a fifth step to the four which Harré has identified in Kant's "account to postulate a transcendental ego as a powerful particular" (Harré Ibid). To be shown below, the fifth step is my discovery of Kant's unrecognized argument concerning time that challenges the atemporal argument at the center of the classic statement in the first *Critique* and its variations thereafter (to be discussed below). In the case of Greenwood, I will be filling in the conceptual space that, in effect, he has provided for the recovery of human agency that this chapter is unfolding, in his crucial distinction between "ontologically sufficient conditions" – for prediction – and ontologically "necessary enabling conditions" – of causal production – in the business of realist explanation in science (Greenwood 1990: 43–57, 54–57). MacIntyre's important paper is special in that, although he in no way is discussing the problem of freedom and scientific determinism from the standpoint of a scientific realism, his attempt to preserve freedom in the face of determinism exactly requires that it be read from that very standpoint (1966: 205–25, 209–11, 223–24). And this is true, I contend, precisely because of this observation: not only is preservation not recovery, indeed, MacIntyre cannot, strictly speaking, preserve freedom before "the fear of [mechanical] determinism" without the recovery of freedom or agency that is being realized in this chapter (MacIntyre Ibid: 223). Let us examine this briefly.

He insists that human action is not a mechanical happening, which, in being subsumable under a universal generalization, thus the event is now outside of human control and alteration. His deep point here for this chapter is that the "causal verb" "produce" is necessary to any discussion of human "action" as against the Hullian/Skinnerian sense of human "behavior" (MacIntyre Ibid: 220). All this is quite clear to us when we consider MacIntyre's following comments.

> ... the fear of determinism. ... springs from accepting a determinist view of the Hume/Mill concept of causality. But to show that an action is caused is not necessarily to show that it must have happened, that the *agent* could not alter what he did. For to assign a cause to a happening is to go some way to informing us both *how to produce and how to inhibit the happening in question.* It follows from this that to assign causal explanations to actions is not to show that the actions in question are inevitable and unalterable. Nor does it even follow that if the explanations are explanations of my actions, I cannot alter them. But it certainly does follow that the more I know about possible and actual causal explanations of my behavior the more likely I am *able to intervene* successively and control what I do.
>
> (MacIntyre Ibid: 223, emphasis provided)

I am convinced that, of course, MacIntyre knows full well that Humean causality as regularity, laws as universal generalizations ("whenever I am losing at cards, and so long as I do not know what is going to happen to my behavior as a result, I shortly become angry," MacIntyre Ibid: 222), presumes his dismissal of causal powers, forces, and entities; nevertheless, his call for the necessity of "causal verbs" in any conception of human freedom as agency I take to mean that MacIntyre simply ignores that famous Humean dismissal of causal powers of production. But, this means, in the context of this book, that MacIntyre's Call entails that the preservation of human freedom against determinism is not its recovery. And since his theory of agency is an interventionist theory taken from Kant, his project of preserving agency requires, as I've declared above, that Kant's journey toward recovery has to be completed for him (MacIntyre Ibid: 205–6). After all, that is exactly what MacIntyre did not do.

In this regard, it has been said that, in the matter of his theory of freedom, Kant needed Darwin. Of course he did, but that can only be right if Darwinian evolutionary theory is successfully dislodged from the paradigm that has been predominate since Harvey and Descartes for the mechanization of all living phenomena and relocated in the metaphysic of scientific realism (Lewontin 1995: 117–18). Thus, biological entities are conjoined with physical entities in being conceptualized according to the principle of agent causality, as this is being done explicitly by Goodwin; and in effect is being done by Lewontin when he calls for the concept of adaptation to be redefined as the act of construction (Goodwin 1994; Lewontin 1995). What we have in this development is that the necessity of natural selection is no longer to imply a determinism whose metaphysical import is the passivity of the organism. Hence, an open invitation to agentify genes and/or populations at the expense of the agency of organisms is blocked off. Note here the parallel problem of structure and the proper location of agency in biology and the social sciences: genes/organisms/populations and genes/persons/collectivities. One may suggest that, just as the attempt here is to recover the agency of persons from the metaphysical error of the agentification of biology and collectivities, Lewontin and Goodwin may well be similarly engaged in the recovery of organismic agency from the problematic ascription of agency to genes (Dawkins) and populations (Gould).

That Kant's half-way journey to recovery needs completion of course means that I can now go beyond the other important fact I have also stressed throughout this book: the theme of recovery has been and still is deeply overshadowed by the standard social scientific misunderstanding that Kant's theory of freedom exclusively aims to rescue cultural subjects from the realm of physical objects, and thus is virtually buried by the institutionalized conviction that natural agency cannot be the basis of the recovery of human agency because of the very philosophical terms of the rescue. I can do so by formulating the problem of recovery from Kant's theory of freedom in terms of the plausible idea that the freedom of the noumenal subject hinges on its reconciliation with the determinism of the phenomenal subject: *the heart of the problem is that the noumenal/atemporality argument is an impasse to reconciliation.* It is right here that my position is in open opposition to the center of Kant's theory of freedom: *the noumenal thesis of atemporality has to be wrong. That it now has to be proven is a major burden of this chapter.*

Kant and Harré: noumenality or continuity?

If the noumenal thesis of human freedom is wrong, the important implication is that the efficient causalities of nature and freedom are both metaphysically constituted by the causal powers principle of efficacy. This of course means that the deep issue of human freedom *is* ontological after all, and that the fact that the noumenal argument for freedom at least does not violate the question of logic is no longer of any importance. In fact, Kant's resort to the justification of his theory of freedom in terms of logic and not ontology can, *now, not then,* be appreciated to be something akin to a dodge. There is a strong reason for taking this implication seriously, and it can be articulated if we locate Kant's noumenal/atemporality argument in the context of Boscovich's demonstration that the motion of real bodies is impossible if any account of their motion contradicts the law of temporal and spatial continuity. The reason in question is in two interconnected parts and can be stated in the following way: (1) given a Boscovichean reconfiguration of Kant's noumenal/atemporal argument we have the proposition that, as a noumenal subject (freedom) human being is temporally discontinuous, but as a phenomenal subject (determinism) human being is spatially continuous, and so in view of the fact that (2) the free motion of real embodied subjects is impossible if any account of their free motion contradicts the law of temporal and spatial continuity, it follows that (3) the above proposition is a self-contradiction: discontinuous action in continuous space has to be impossible, and not only for physical moving objects, but for cultural moving subjects.

With this in mind, we can go to Harré's superb demonstration that two propositions are false regarding the possible identification of the motion of real bodies with respect to space and time: (a) space is continuous, but time is discontinuous; (b) time is continuous, but space is discontinuous. Now, part (a) provides the condition under which Kant's noumenal/atemporality argument can be judged to be an impossible truth. Thus, that argument for the freedom of agency either can have no proper metaphysical ground in the noumenal, and so the theory of freedom self-destructs, or, it can only be salvaged by the occasion that Kant's scientific realism can provide that ground in the dynamic theory of matter. And so, again, Kant must be, at least partly, wrong. Hence, while the principle of power that is internal to material particulars of matter is not freedom, obviously in any human sense, nevertheless, the efficient causalities of freedom and nature are both grounded in that same metaphysical principle of natural agency. This, as I have been insisting, is an insufficient basis for the recovery of human agency. But it *is* necessary.

To move into the reconstruction of Harré's propositions (a) and (b), I will begin with the conclusion to Chapter 9: the doctrine of mechanical action by contact leads to the fatal proposition of the impossibility of discontinuous action in continuous time (Harré 1970: 289). As I have shown there, the implication that the forces of such action are infinite is contradicted by the fact that an infinite force cannot be imagined as a generative mechanism. And the self-destructive consequences of the contradiction go deeper, and do so by bringing us full circle: since an infinite force must be an instantaneous force, what is thus revealed is the impossibility of the discontinuity of a transfer of motion, and the ultimate downfall of this feature of the doctrine is that it violates the law that the actions of bodies must occur continuously at some time and in some place. Now, the reciprocal to the violation of the law of continuity is its twin violation: only if a generative mechanism is conceivable can an action be understood to be an effect. The crucial idea here is the impeccable metaphysical logic that underwrites the twin relationship of these two laws, and this is expressed by Harré when he says, "The successive occupation of the spatial positions *is itself time,* and the occupancies are *its events*" (Harré Ibid: 291, my emphasis). This comment is the occasion for us to realize that Kant's intuitions of time and space do much more than enable us to pick out the diverse kinds of the event of dynamically embodied agency in the natural world. For, to restate Harré somewhat differently in order to magnify his insight: since the way of the world is the way of agency, *position is the time of agency*. Now we can especially appreciate why Harré gives us the following rationale for his contribution of the above two proofs of the law of continuity.

> For the general outlines of the proof of the law of continuity, I follow Boscovich, supplementing his argument at some important points. For a principle of the degree of importance Boscovich argues that two different kinds of proof ought to be offered. There should be an *inductive* proof, to show that the Principle [the Law of Continuity] in fact is operative in all known actions, but there should also be a *metaphysical* proof. *This* has the aim of showing that the *Principle is necessary, in the sense that it is a principle which could not be abandoned without abandoning the whole scientific enterprise.* Such a proof proceeds by showing how the Principle is related to very fundamental features of space and time. In his proof Boscovich simply *assumes* the continuity of time. I shall try to *supplement* his proof by advancing what I believe are powerful reasons for that assumption.
>
> (Harré Ibid: 287, emphasis provided)

Indeed, since "position is the time of agency" (the Law of Continuity and its substantive content the Law of Intelligible Causation) it is the case then that science is possible. But this reason underwriting Harré's proofs also involves one other.

Harré's supplement: two metaphysical proofs

According to Harré, it is impossible to show the following: either that time is not discontinuous in virtue of the fact that a genuinely continuous process cannot empirically be picked out, or that time is not continuous in virtue of the possibility that empirical discontinuity only apparently results from the "eigenstates" of processes which in reality may be continuous (Harré Ibid: 289). With these two reasons for the necessity of the metaphysical proofs at issue in place, the analysis then is to focus on space and time in reference to the possibility of motion. The phrase the "possibility of motion" presumes the principle of definite demonstrative reference: in principle, a real particle must be able to be referred to *at all times* so that it is *at some place at all times*. Since the analysis is so important, and it is short, let's see it fully in Harré's own words.

> Proposition #1: the motion of a real particle [particular] in continuous space but in discontinuous time.
>   Again a destructive dilemma can be formulated, on the supposition that motion must be possible. A moving real particle [particular] in transition from s1 to s2 must necessarily be at every intermediate point in the course of the motion, and being a real particle must be capable, at

least in principle, of being the subject of demonstrative reference at any one of those points. But if time is discontinuous there must be fewer instants in the temporal interval t1 to t2, where t1 is the instant the particle was at s1 and t2 the instant it is at s2, than there are points in the spatial interval s1 to s2. *Either there is more than one spatial point at which the particle is at any given instant, or there are sequences of spatial positions, traversed by the particle in no time at all.* The proposal set out in *the first horn of the dilemma is objectionable because it violates the condition that no one real thing can be in more than one location at a time.* Two spatial positions allow two simultaneous acts of demonstrative reference, which would be enough to prove that there were two real particles, and not just one at two places, contrary to hypothesis. *The second horn effectively proposes that the motion of a particle be reduced to a sequence of spatial leaps at infinite velocity, since they take no time at all, though all intermediate points must be traversed. This would require infinite acceleration and deceleration, and this in turn would require infinite forces. And there are no infinite forces.* It follows that motion is impossible in a world in which space is continuous and time discontinuous.

(Harré Ibid: 290–91, my emphasis)

Proposition #2: the motion of a real particle [particular] in continuous time but in discontinuous space.

A real particle [particular] exists at all times from t1 to t2. But if space is discontinuous it occupies successively what may be an infinite number of positions, during the t1 to t2, but there will be more instants in the continuous time interval t1 to t2 than there are points in discontinuous spatial interval s1 to s2. So the supposition of the possibility of motion in a continuous time, but discontinuous space, is subject to a *destructive dilemma*: either there are some times when the real particle is at *no place*; or it is at *some place* at every time.

The first horn of the dilemma would require the real particle to go in and out of existence, contrary to the hypothesis of its reality. A real particle must be able, in principle, to be demonstratively referred to at all times, and so must be at *some* place at all times. *The second horn requires* further analysis. Consider two sequential spatial positions, s1 and s2. If the particle is somewhere at all times, and time is continuous, then at the Boscovichean point Q, defining and distinguishing the temporal intervals at which it is at s1 and at which it is at s2, the particle must be able to be considered indifferently and arbitrarily at either s1 or s2. But since it is *a real particle it must be demonstratively at s1 or s2, actually, and it cannot be arbitrarily set at either.* So, the second horn of the dilemma is just as unacceptable. *Really both horns hinge on the same feature of a real particle, since the requirement that a real particle be always capable in principle of definite demonstrative reference is equivalent to the condition that a real particle must exist continuously in space, that is must always be at some point.* Discontinuous space and continuous time define a world in which motion is impossible for a continuously existing thing.

(Harré Ibid: 289–90, my emphasis)

Kant and Dilthey: two metaphysical errors

The metaphysical analysis of propositions 1 and 2 is informed by two requirements. If the motion of a real particular, be it physical, biological, or human, is to be possible in the real world of nature (one requirement) then we must be able to refer to that real particular at all times so that it is at some place at all times (second requirement). The two requirements of course are bound by the principle that "position is the time of agency'; the metaphysical point of which is that, for agency to be possible in nature, time and space must be understood to be conceptually interdependent (inseparability). And so, to violate the inseparability of space and time generates propositions 1 and 2.

I am now going to suggest that the two propositions at issue correspond to the two classic kinds of theory of human freedom of Kant and Dilthey that have been fundamental to the Science and Humanism debate on the problem of structure and agency. While I have already declared that *Kant's theory of freedom is an exemplar of proposition 1*, I am now going to declare that *Dilthey's theory of freedom is an exemplar of proposition 2*. In other words, in violating the inseparability of time and space in their respective theories of freedom the metaphysical errors of Kant and Dilthey are reciprocals of each other. In *Kant's case, for one and the same person, we have the noumenal subject where human being is free in discontinuous time, and the phenomenal subject where human being is unfree in continuous space*. In *Dilthey's case* we have a rather *special difficulty*. First of all, this much is clear, that, for one and the same person, we have Dilthey's subject where human being is free in continuous time. However, with the implicit rejection of Kant's atemporal argument in the very fact of Dilthey's locating freedom in temporality, the role of space, hence, is a problem. For, consider that the dismissal of the atemporal at the same time is the dismissal of both the noumenal realm *and* the phenomenal realm because of the latter's determinism. And with the positing of the realm of the phenomenological for the location of the subject and its freedom "in time," *"where" is "space" in reference to freedom? Is it the "where" of the "phenomenal" or of the "phenomenological"?* It would seem that that means that the two "spaces" are disconnected, or, it means that the space of determinism and the time of freedom are disconnected. Disconnected "spaces" is a metaphysical mystification, and the disconnection of time and space is a metaphysical error of the proposition 2 type. The full force of the principle that *"position is the time of agency"* here becomes quite evident in its reciprocal, *time is the position of agency*. Freedom as a Kantian "kind of motion" cannot be a human motion that goes in and out of existence, as Harré declares in the second quote above, since it must be demonstratively at some place, s1 or s2. Now, in Parsons's placement of the actor in time but not in space, we do not have Dilthey's special difficulty of the two "spaces"; we do, however, have the clear difficulty of denying space altogether. And that would mean that Parsonian voluntarism cannot be a theory of action precisely because it is a virtually pure example of a metaphysical error of the proposition 2 type.

What now can be made of Kant's metaphysically fashioning an argument for freedom that seems to quite properly be identified as a proposition 1 type of error? The *key issue* here for Kant is that *the human kind of free motion must traverse a sequence of positions at no time at all, that is instantaneously, and thus the force of human agency must be infinite.* In other words, *Kantian freedom as spontaneity is instantaneity. Hence as a mechanism that allegedly must correspond to the production of infinite force, such a mechanism cannot be conceived.* Thus, *and this is of major significance for Kant, noumenal freedom is in principle an idea that can have no intelligible purchase.* This question of the intelligibility of the mechanism of human agency is an ontological problem, and the Harréan/Boscovichean reconfiguration of Kantian freedom provided here establishes just that. Now it is definitively clear that the conviction that Kantian freedom is an idea that doesn't violate logic is suspect. And not only, as I have already suggested, as a dodge. For, in view of the judgment that the theory is a proposition 1-type error, Kant's noumenal theory of freedom may well be logically safe, but it is self-deception to believe in its intelligibility. Now it can be said that it was unfortunate for Kant, especially as a scientific realist, to have believed that logical safety protected his claim that noumenal freedom was at least intelligible; and hence regulative and never constitutive. In committing the metaphysical error of violating the principle that "position is the time of agency" Kant's theory of noumenal freedom is in a difficulty that proves to be fatal. At best, the theory is a sensitizing notion: it alerts and directs us to the need for a definitive conception of human agency as agent causation. *The new key in philosophy that is suggested here is this: under the jurisdiction of the metaphysical proof of continuity, as a noumenal power Kantian freedom is sentenced to be an infinite force for which no mechanism is conceivable.* There are thus two consequences for which there can be no serious doubt: if it is to be a viable idea ever again, *spontaneity cannot be "instantaneity,"* and therefore it must be conceived anew. Hence, if spontaneity is to presume an intelligible mechanism, in honoring its name, freedom must be temporal in being spatial.

Kant: idealism to realism

How is one to make the transition from Transcendental Idealism to the Metaphysics of nature, as I have contended, in order to recover human agency? It is evident from the above discussion that the former, but not the latter of course, has already been realized. The self-destruction of the noumenal theory of freedom by virtue of the fact that it is an instance of a Harréan propositional type 1 metaphysical error has thus revealed that Kant's Idealism through the theory of freedom must be and is rooted in his scientific realism. That understanding can be deepened by a consideration that Kant gives us a very different argument from the standard, in that he gives an argument that is *different in kind* from the first (the standard); in keeping with this strict sense of a different kind of argument, I will call this his *second argument* for the alleged noumenal grounding of freedom, which we will see is to be found in *The Critique of Practical Reason* (Kant 1996a: 121; Kant 1996b: 219). Thus as a kind-difference, it is *not* Kant's first and standard argument from *The Critique of Pure Reason* that freedom is "*not a beginning in time but in causality*" (1985a: 413–14). However, it is important to notice that it is certainly related to the variation of the standard argument that is found in the *Prolegomena to Any Future Metaphysics*: freedom is "*not under time-determinations of its state*" (1985b: 84). However, clearly, within the logical space of the first (including the briefer version) and second *Critiques* the general contour of the argument for freedom in its relation to time involves a tension. The tension shows up in these two statements in terms of a critical difference in meaning that can be brought out by an examination of the second (different in kind) argument. In my judgment the import of this argument comes to this: condensing Kant's various characterizations of freedom into the definition that it is "an absolute power of spontaneity," the suggestion is that freedom is a primary autonomy. Thus the freedom of legislating moral laws for ourselves would then be a secondary autonomy. Indeed, I should like to maintain that, although Kant's language is understandably philosophical overkill, the very idea of an absolute power of spontaneity *is* the definition of primary autonomy. And in the constitution of that freedom in light of the second argument it is presumed that the relation of freedom to "time" has a very different significance. *Freedom has a beginning in causality, to be sure, but it's relationship to time is that of a relative independence; and so the implication is that freedom would still be under the time-determinations of its state, but of course, not absolutely.* Observe then the different kind arguments at issue here: (1) first argument and variation, time is of *central* importance; "in time" is the rule of determinism in the phenomenal realm; "not in time" is the rule of freedom in the noumenal realm; (2) second argument, time is of *peripheral* importance; determinism and freedom are in principle in time; *determinism is absolutely* under time-determination, *freedom is relatively* under time-determination. And finally, this observation of the systematic kind difference in the two arguments isolates the fact that (2) contradicts (1).

Kant and Schneewind: conflicting arguments for freedom

In Kant's examination of reason in the practice of human life he returns to the unsolved problem that freedom can only be a regulative and not a constitutive idea, and in revisiting the earlier argument on time he now presents, at least by implication, a *refinement* of the argument. In doing so, Kant continues his discussion from the *Prolegomena* in taking up the question of freedom as a principle of power internal to a particular. He indicates this principle in, for instance, such examples as a projectile and a clock in their "free motion" (Kant 1996a: 118). But this reductionism that assimilates human freedom to the "free motion" of physical particulars is for Kant "a wretched subterfuge," and his well-known objection comes to this (Kant Ibid): as long as the principles determining causality may be within the subject as either instincts or reasons, it is of no matter, for

> ... they are still determining principles of the causality of a being whose existence is determinable in time, and therefore under the necessitation of conditions of *past time,* which therefore, when the subject has to act, are *no longer in his power.*
>
> (Kant Ibid: 118–19, also my emphasis)

Now, the refinement is the implication that, given that one's reasons as determining principles of causality of a being whose existence is not under time determination of its state of spontaneity, the significance of this is that *that state is therefore always in the power of the agent.* Thus *Kant's final word on the question of freedom is that it is a state of spontaneity that is in the power of the agent directly because it is not in time, and therefore freedom is not under the determinations of time.* With this final thesis we are, I suggest, up against a conflict of interpretations concerning its meaning and theoretical status.

Reconsidering the earlier demonstration of the impossibility of atemporal freedom and the consequent declaration that the power of spontaneity presumes that there is a mechanism underwriting a primary autonomy (this is Kant's Willkur, not Wille), there is a new import to be noted. And that import is simply that Kantian freedom is *The Discovery of Autonomy.* But then in that case, in J. B. Schneewind's history of modern moral philosophy, that thesis is contradicted and the conflicting thesis proclaimed is that Kantian freedom is *The Invention of Autonomy* (Schneewind 1998). Kant is the central figure in this history precisely because he is the cardinal reason for the writing of it. That reason, however, is quite revealing of the radical difference between traditional philosophy and realist social science in the understanding of the relevance of Kant's theory of freedom to the problem of deterministic structures and the recovery of agency – natural and human.

> Autonomy, as Kant saw it, requires contracausal freedom; and he believed that in the unique experience of the moral ought we are "given" a "fact of reason" that unquestionably shows us that we possess such freedom as members of a noumenal realm. *Readers who hold, as I do, that our experience of the moral ought shows no such thing will think of*

his version of autonomy as an invention rather than an explanation. Those with different views on freedom and morality may wish that I had called this book *The Discovery of Autonomy.* We can probably agree that Kant's moral thought is as hard to understand as it is original and profound. Systematic studies from Paton and Beck to the present have greatly improved our critical grasp of his position. In this book *I try to broaden our historical comprehension of Kant's moral philosophy by relating it to the earlier work to which it was a response.*

(Schneewind 1998: 3, emphasis provided)

The key to Schneewind's position on Kantian freedom is his reference to "historical comprehension" as the *only* critical approach to the problem of the noumenal character of Kantian freedom. But how does Schneewind specifically read that problem? Well, his account is that the failure to discover autonomy presumably is the ground from which, Phoenix-like, Kant arises, to call a spade a spade, and *fabricates* autonomy. Only in passing does Schneewind mention, and at that almost as an afterthought, that the noumenal character of both freedom (spontaneity) and reason (autonomy) "cannot be bound in the network of time and change." But then his real point, as I see it, is not the genuine and central problem of the atemporality of freedom and reason from the standpoint of Kant's scientific realism, of course, but rather the genuine but peripheral problem of "what explanation can be given of it?" from the standpoint of Kant's response to the earlier work of moral philosophers" (Schneewind Ibid: 505). While the expected answer is that, "As noumenal, it (the willkur that grounds our autonomy) is ultimately inexplicable," the reason for this answer is found in his interpretation of one of Kant's pre-critical writings, the *Dreams of a Spirit-Seer* (Schneewind Ibid: 515, 505–7). The upshot of the interpretation is unsurprising.

Much more clearly than the earlier writings, it shows that although Kant thinks, as Hutcheson did, in terms of a moral world, he refuses to accept Hutcheson's deterministic naturalism about it (see chapter 16.iii). Where Hutcheson saw self-love and benevolence as the forces that, like Newtonian attraction and repulsion, keep the human world in order, *Kant now* puts in their place the moral force of a *free spiritual world* controlling the self-interested powers of those in the natural world.

(Schneewind Ibid: 507, my emphasis)

Clearly then, Schneewind sees Kantian freedom as inexplicable because it is a religious mystery – "a free spiritual world." But, for now, aside from my earlier discussions of this matter, is this traditional reading the best one to make in this case of the problem of noumenal freedom? Consider a comment make by Kant that is actually quoted by Schneewind in the context of the discussion in which that very quote is to be found.

Inner sense, if it is adduced as a logical principle of judgment of moral law, is an *occult* quality; if as a *power* of the soul whose ground is unknown, a *phenomenon*.

(Schneewind Ibid: 506, my emphasis)

Now I am going to declare that the crucial metaphysical point that Schneewind is, in effect, claiming is that Kantian freedom as a spiritual quality is an occult power. And of course that could be correct, but only if one supposes that Kant is not committed to naturalism as a scientific realist; and only if one also supposes that he was not subordinating his religiosity, that is his piety, to his metaphysics of nature. Note, in this regard, what Schneewind presents about Kant and the morality–religion connection.

Morality is identified with objective necessity, which cannot rest on any advantages the act brings about. *Neither can it rest on the will of God.* Kant asks whether we can make moral distinctions only if we know the will of God who is the creator, and he is ready with a *negative* answer. "Piety is only a kind of virtue", he says, and he claims that *to subordinate morality to religion is to engender hypocrisy and idolatry,* but *to control religion by morality makes people "good-hearted, well-meaning, and just."*

(Schneewind Ibid: 486, my emphasis)

And so it is clear, to me, that Schneewind does not connect the dots here – the systematic relationship I have argued for Kant between freedom as spontaneity/autonomy and scientific realism and to the relation between morality and religion. Thus, although he consequently acknowledges that for Kant "morality ... is ... not ... obedience to the divine will. ... [but to the] the 'laws of freedom,' nevertheless, he does not claim that Willkur as power enabling us to choose between desire and morality is to be naturalistically located among phenomena, as Kant himself suggests in the quote above concerning the "inner sense" (Schneewind Ibid: 486). Throughout his long career we have reminded ourselves that Kant was forever engaged in trying to negotiate a way to ground Willkur in the idea of an efficient causality of nature that yet does not compromise freedom. In the *Dreams* essay Kant can be seen struggling with the difficulty of this very negotiation. In that struggle he has adumbrated what will become the noumenal/phenomenal schema in his sketchy distinction between "*occult* quality" and "*phenomenon*"; with the "*power* of the soul whose ground is unknown" as the deep problematic of his emerging theory of freedom already vaguely indicated.

Kant and Weldon: negotiating freedom in nature

But it is T. D. Weldon, not Schneewind, who brings this out in the examination of the pre-critical writings in his *Kant's Critique of Pure Reason*

(Weldon 1958: 64, 65). Now, the relevance of Weldon's citing of Kant's difficulty with negotiating freedom in nature can be carefully spelled out. It will lead us back to the first *Critique* and its deep connection to, on the one hand, the *Metaphysical Foundations of Natural Science* and the victory of the dynamical theory of matter, and, on the other, *The Critique of Practical Reason* and Kant's second argument on the question of time and freedom. What we will come to is that, given the above point that the second argument for freedom contradicts the first argument, that eventuality is prepared for in Kant's discussion of the analogies of experience concerning the peripheral status of time in relation to the causal property of substances. As we are now going to see, the theme of the second argument can itself be refined: *freedom is only relatively under the time determinations of its state because freedom is an act that is in time generally but not specifically.*

Weldon asserts that in the *Dreams* essay Kant goes far beyond his ostensible interest in the spiritualist theory of Swedenborg to take up the topic of soul/body relations and the possibility of rationally understanding soul apart from the body beyond "mere conjecture and hypothesis" (Weldon 1958: 64). After this point in his discussion let us consider the two examples he presents that exemplify Kant's interest in the problem of negotiating freedom. Note that, ironically, the exemplification is clearly in evidence in Schneewind's emphasizing Kant's claim in *Dreams* that life has the principle of spirit and thus the capacity of the power of choice to determine itself (Schneewind Ibid: 505). However, he does not pick out the two examples that Weldon has.

> He [Kant] begins by pointing out that the concept of spirits as immaterial entities which none the less are spatially located in bodies is itself extremely difficult. When carefully considered, however, it may be seen *not* to differ in principle from the similar problem dealt with in the Monadologia Physica of *the spatial location of forces which also must be regarded as pervading space without being themselves extended.* Such an account has the advantage of rendering *unnecessary* all discussions as the seat of the soul in the body and also of making possible a distinction in kind between souls and material substances.
>
> (Weldon Ibid, my emphasis)

In this first example consider carefully that, here, Weldon reveals that Kant is quite clear about the integral connection between spirits as immaterial forces (powers of choice) located in human bodies pervading space, and immaterial forces located in nonhuman bodies pervading space. It should in particular be observed that Kant seems to mention "forces" and "powers" in the same breath, so to speak, without, however, metaphysically making a systematic distinction between them. Related to the question of the powers/forces fusion is Weldon's mentioning the fact that Kant believes that the very difficult problem of understanding the interaction of soul and body can be overcome, so long as a difference in kind is not imputed to them (Weldon

Ibid: 65). In other words, so long as Cartesian Dualism is not taken seriously. And in the first *Critique*, as Sir Peter Strawson has especially demonstrated, Kant doesn't take it seriously since he in fact dismisses Cartesian Dualism by reducing it to a fallacious inference in his discussion of the Paralogisms of pure reason (Strawson 1978). Now examine the second example. It emerges as Weldon continues his discussion of spirits and Kant's developing interest in their possible relations with one another, not as the bodies they pervade are related to each other in space, but immediately in a spirit world of life and choice Kant calls mundus intelligibilis (Weldon Ibid).

> The phenomenon which most favors our belief in [a spirit world] is the existence of a general will, or rather of *a moral or social sense shared by a number of individuals.* For this readily *admits of being regarded as the empirical manifestation of a real connection between spirits just as the laws of gravitation are a manifestation of the real though inaccessible vis viva which is the essence of material things.*
>
> (Weldon Ibid)

So, we have Kant's driving toward a virtual identification of two very different natural activities: the general will empirically manifesting spirit as the power of human agency located in human bodies and laws of gravitation manifesting the vis viva of nonhuman bodies. The mode of this identification is an implied metaphysical standpoint that has not been articulated. To simplify this parallel of general will and gravitational laws we can say that we have two natural but radically different kinds of immaterial forces – human agency and nonhuman agency – that are manifested in their corresponding material bodies. And now we must remember the point made before that the idea of "forces" also involves the idea of "powers" in Kant's presentation. Clearly, he does use the latter explicitly and consistently in reference to human beings, in keeping with the free will tradition, but when the context is the discussion of matter, "forces" are mentioned and "powers" are implied (for instance, the first example: forces pervade space but are not extended). This failure to distinguish powers and forces is consistent with his contribution to the dynamical theory of matter in the *Metaphysical Foundations of Natural Science*. Its import must now be examined in light of a question emerging from the two examples of Kant's apparent move toward the identification, at some metaphysical level, of the agency of embodied persons and the agency of impersonal bodies.

Kantian freedom: substance and the powers/forces distinction

On the question of metaphysical level, are Guyer and Wood right when, in make the following observation concerning the discussion in Kant's first *Critique* of the paralogisms, they take Kant at his word?

In the second edition, the entire chapter on the paralogisms was rewritten and simplified (B 406–22) to fill the place of the superseded fourth paralogism, Kant adds an argument that his dualism of appearance and reality undercuts the traditional dualism of mind and body, with its problem about the interaction of two fundamentally distinct kinds of substances, by opening up the possibility that both mind and body are different appearances of *some single unknown kind of substance.*

(Guyer and Wood in Kant 1999: 15–16, my emphasis)

I am not here concerned with the fact that taking Kant at his word means that Kant will go on to introduce the noumenal/phenomenal distinction in reference to this "single unknown kind of substance" where he will "locate" God, freedom, immortality, and causation. For this begs the question: what is this "substance that underwrites freedom and causation"? Must we continue to accept the historical fact that Kant's answer is the noumenal/phenomenal distinction? Certainly not after it has been shown that the idea of the noumenal in reference to its atemporal argument for freedom has self-destructed when it is properly relocated in the context of my development of the Boscovich/Harré arguments for powers over particles. Thus, since, I contend, we must suppose that a possible answer lies elsewhere, my suggestion is that the analogies of experience provide the answer. To show that, I will use the following strategy: in taking as given Kant's conclusions in the first and third analogies, that is that *substance underlies all change in the phenomenal world* (A182–86) and that *substances necessarily coexist in a dynamical community of reciprocal interaction* (A213–14), the analytic focus is on the second analogy on the question of causation, specifically the discussion between sections A204 and A206. Here Kant is interested in the precise conceptual connections between *"action," "force," and "substance."* Kant's cardinal declaration on this matter is the critical moment of a key change in our understanding of this discussion.

Wherever there is action – and therefore activity and force – there is also substance, and *it is in substance alone that the seat of this fruitful source of appearances must be sought.* ... [In other words], causality leads to the concept of action, this in turn to the concept of force, and thereby to the concept of substance.

(A204–5, my emphasis)

The theme here is starkly clear: *the permanence of the appearance of things is the action of the substance of things* (A205–6). Note very carefully the exact way Kant expresses this theme when he asks how we are to derive directly from the action of that which acts, the permanence of that which acts (A205).

Action signifies the relation of the subject of causality to effect. Since, now, every effect consists in that which happens, and therefore in the transitory ... its ultimate subject, as the substratum of everything that changes, is the permanent, that is substance. *For, according to the principle of causality actions are always the first ground of all change of appearances, and cannot therefore be found in a subject which itself changes, because in that case other actions and another subject would be required to determine this change.* For this reason action is a sufficient empirical criterion to establish the substantiality of a subject, without my requiring first to go in quest of its permanence through the comparison of perceptions.

(A205–6)

What precisely is Kant after here? *Is he not, as one of the major contributors to the victory of the concept of powers over the concept of particles, trying to get at a new and suitable conception of substance?* After all, I have pointed out that what drives the history of the powers/particles debate and outcome is the central realist question of how substance is to be understood as an adequate conception of causation. And so the proper subtext for a fruitful understanding of Kant's discussion of causation and substance must be, first of all, that very question, and, second of all, the reminder that materialism and phenomenalism violate the cardinal thesis of realism: on the one hand no conception of genuine causation is possible without a viable conception of substance; and on the other, without a conception of substance no account of human qualities is imaginable. Hence, it now can be suggested that the twin concepts of action and force that Kant is trying to formulate in reference to substance is in fact an attempt to get at a new and suitable conception of substance in order to work out an adequate conception of causation. Seen in this light, *the problem of Hume in Kant's discussion of causality is certainly the tip of the metaphysical iceberg, but it must now be judged to be a distracting tip at that.*

Now, consider the following from the two Kantian quotes above: if action is the activity of force and force is the appearance of action, and the principle of causality insures that the *first* ground of all changes of appearance are actions, then, to avoid the self-contradiction that force is both action and its appearance, as if it is something else, *Kant needs to differentiate the concept of force and the concept of power.* Thus it is power that is a disposition and therefore the possibility that there can be action as the activity of forces and forces as the appearance of action. *The idea of the power of a particular then allows us to correct Kant: while action is indeed the activity of force, that is precisely because power is the possibility of force as the appearance of action.* And hence, the (causal) *power* of action (not action by itself) is that first "ground of all change of appearances, and cannot therefore be found in a subject which itself changes, because in that case other actions and another subject would be required to determine this change." In other words, *it is the powers of subjects as agents, rather than those powers not being in time, that have that "permanence."* And thus it is the fact of the "permanence" of powers that define subjects as distinct particulars, so that when they function as actual forceful entities of influence (generation) there is that dynamic community of reciprocal interaction that is the ontological constitution of the natural world. Now, not only is it the case that *actions as forces are grounded in the powers of particulars*, but, it must also be the case that *no other argument is needed to establish the agency of physical and personal particulars*. This, I contend, is one of the most persuasive reasons for regarding "time" as not being of central importance in Kant's theory of freedom; it does supreme justice to the demonstration that Kantian freedom is definitively refuted as an example of Harré's metaphysical error of the proposition 1 type.

Kantian freedom and time: a new view

With this new appreciation that Kant's examination of the concepts of action, force and substance can be understood as his attempt to answer the realist question as to how substance is to be construed as an adequate conception of causation, what then is Kant's view on the issue of time in this discussion? As a matter of fact, preceding the taking up of the question of substance and causality that view is found in the presentation of the idea that "The *sequence in time* is ... the sole empirical criterion of an effect in its relation to the causality of the cause which precedes it" (A204, my emphasis). Here, first of all, the main business is the definitive establishment of the absolute distinction between "causation" and "correlation." To take only one of several of his examples, this is done with the elegant observation that, if one lays a ball on a cushion, the cushion now suffers a depression; but if there is a depression of the cushion, the ball does not then follow (A203–4). And now, in reference to this example, note Kant's comment concerning what it is about the "sequence of time" that is relevant to the cause and effect relation?

> Now, we must not fail to note that it is *the order of time, not the lapse of time*, with which we have to reckon; the relation remains the same if no time has elapsed. The time between the causality of the cause and its immediate effect may be a vanishing quantity, and they may thus be simultaneous; but the relation of the one to the other will always still remain determinable in time.
>
> (A203–4)

Yet, given, as Kant says, that determinability can only be possible in time, or more precisely now, *position is the time of agency and time is the position of agency*, hence the crucial question concerning causal activity, Kant insists, is the order of time. But is it? *Is it not in fact the case that it is causal activity that gives time and space their importance, not the reverse.* Thus time and space are important linguistic devices that an agentic interest in causal activity requires for the location of causal activity in the business of effective human action, whether in the home or in the lab. The realist significance of the order of time then is that the cause and effect connection is not just a relation of order, after all that would be something akin to correlation, rather, it is a relation of order that is produced in the reciprocal interaction of a commercium of powerful particulars. And so while Kant is right in asserting that it is not the lapse of time, he must now be judged to be wrong to have *said* that it is the order of time, for as a scientific realist he must be taken to *mean* instead that *causal actions in space are the content of the ordering in time.* Now, stepping back in order to once again relocate Kant in the history of dynamical theory, this cleaning up his language so that it now presents the understanding that space and time preserve causal activity, honors the Boscovichian insight that *the law of continuity preserves the law of intelligible causation.* Kant then must not only make explicit, as I have demonstrated above, the concept of power, but now it is clear that he must also make explicit the concept of production or generation. For, to take Kant literally in terms of the letter but not the spirit of the law of the ontology of causal powers, one is forced to believe that it is the empirical fact of the relation of time itself that determines the depression of the cushion, and not the empirical fact of the ball forcing the depression of the cushion. And of course Kant doesn't believe *that.*

The second argument: the recovery of human agency

The entire foregoing analysis of this chapter has demonstrated the truth of the claim in Chapter 2 that the noumenal thesis of atemporality is wrong. And it is upon the defeat of the thesis of the noumenal as atemporality that the recovery of human agency is possible from both the natural worlds of physical objects and the cultural worlds of subjects. For it was the recovery of agency in the natural world of objects that promoted the possibility that human agency could also be recovered. Indeed, the recovery of the natural agency of physical objects already is the *general* recovery of human agency. As we have seen, this was always the deep thrust of Kantian thinking from the very first *Critique* and on to the second: the idea that both subjects (freedom) and objects (nature) are efficient causes grounded in laws having to do with the powers of things to be moving signifying things and the powers of things to be only moving things, respectively. And it is at this point that I can now declare that the defeat of the atemporal argument opens up a simple way to correct the mistake of the terminology of the noumenal and the phenomenal. What unites both kinds of things is the idea that it is power that is the disposition and hence the possibility that there can be action as the activity of forces and forces as the appearance of action, be they human or not. *Thus, the relation of the noumenal to the phenomenal is best understood as being the relation of the reality of powers to the appearance of forces. Since we now understand that the idea of "not being in time" is actually the impossibility that there can be genuine powers of agency, then the only metaphysical significance of the idea of "not being in time" must be that it is the demand that powers not be reduced and therefore lost to forces.* In short, that we avoid the fallacy of actualism in our metaphysics of natural and therefore human agency. And in Kant's second argument, we have another and final way to get rid of the argument for freedom that demands that the powers to act for objects and subjects must not be in time and hence not under the determinations of time conditions.

All of Kant's arguments are presented together within a few pages of each other in the *Critique of Practical Reason* in Book 2, Chapter 3 entitled, *Critical Examination of the Analytic of Pure Practical Reason* (Kant 1996a: 111–30, 116–21; Kant 1999: 211–25, 215–19): The *standard* argument of *atemporality* (not in time), with its *refinement* (past time no longer in the power of the agent), and the *variation* argument from the *Prolegomena* (not under time determinations). Conservatively considered, the variation argument is, in my judgment, of indeterminate or ambiguous meaning. In the discussion of the analytic of pure practical reason the argument of the *Prolegomena* is stated differently, thus, instead of "not under time-determinations" we now have "not subject to time conditions." This difference quite obviously does not constitute any significant difference in meaning, so that I would assert that it is not at all clear, in and of itself as stated, that the variation argument points to the standard thesis. For, "not under time etc. or not subject to time etc." could just as well mean that the agent is free in virtue of the fact that he/she is in the noumenal realm and so is "not in time," or, is free in that he/she is generally in time but not necessarily tied to specific conditions of time, and hence by implication is in the phenomenal realm. And it is in the latter sense of being in time generally but not specifically that there is the indication of being relatively and thus never absolutely independent of time. This amounts to inferential proof that human beings in a state of such freedom have a capacity for a fundamental or primary autonomy. It is this thesis of primary autonomy which, I contend, is the most plausible reading of Kant's statement in the second critique that, when our conscience induces the moral pain of recognizing that we have failed to act in the past the way we morally ought to have acted, that that is as it should be.

[The point is that the] pain is quite legitimate, [and is so] because when the law of our intelligible ... existence (the moral law) is in question, *reason recognizes no distinction of time, and only asks whether the event belongs to me, as my act, and then always morally connects the same feeling with it, whether it has happened just now or long ago.* For in reference to the supersensible consciousness of its existence (i.e., freedom) the life of sense is but a single phenomenon, which. ... must be judged. ... according to the absolute spontaneity of freedom.

(Kant 1996a: 121; 1999: 211)

In view of the fact that the order of time is produced in the reciprocal inter-action of a commercium of powerful human and nonhuman particulars, in the former case, the requirements of practical normative action are the use of the linguistic devices of time and space for the location and the organization of those relevant causal activities whose utilization will promote effective human action. Thus there is a "time" for considerations of "time distinc-tions" when action is to be taken, and there is a "time" for an indifference to "time distinctions" when action must be prepared for, from Kant's stand-point, according to the criterion of normatively effective action. The unique powers of human primary autonomy constitute the conditions of human nature that enable human beings to be able to take action and to be able to refrain from taking any such action, in order to do what *Kant has been tacitly trying to understand and articulate all his life, the pausing in between "stimulus and response," for the possibility of "reflection" or "deliberation."* This means that the primary autonomy of human subjects refers to the fact that subjects are generally in time, but they are not necessarily tied to having to act at any specific time. *With the final breakthrough beyond the mistaken understanding of the relevance of time to action, and then beyond the vocabulary of the noumenal and the phenomenal, human agency has been recovered from within the auspices of Kant's normative theory of human freedom.*

Kant to Hebb: neurology of autonomy and intelligence

As a self-proclaimed " pseudo-behaviorist" who saw himself carrying for-ward the second wave of "The American Revolution in Psychology," D. O. Hebb would probably not admit to being a Kantian in his work on the understanding of the conceptual nervous system for a theory of mind that was suitable to the reality of human beings in their everyday life (Hebb 1960: 735). In such work Hebb was moving toward a cognitive S-O-R model of human behavior that was closer to John Dewey's "organic circuit" model than to Ivan Pavlov's "reflex" model of behavior (Dewey 1896). The loss of human agency in the model of the latter is cancelled by its preservation in the model of the former: "O" is the source of "S" as well as being the source of "R." In Hebb's S-O-R model, there is a conception of "O" as the rela-tively autonomous function of intelligence that mediates and so can be the source of both the external and internal environmental forms of "S," that is stimulation, and of "R" as the responses (actions and reactions) of human beings. Historically, living and working during the decades from the 1940s to the 1980s Hebb was philosophically situated in between the determinism of both behaviorism and psychoanalysis (Hebb Ibid).

Thus, on the one hand, Hebb was up against the S-R model of behavior-ism with its explicit commitment to either eliminating the category of the mind in psychology ("O") or to the setting to one side of any reference to mind and its autonomy in psychology; and on the other, Hebb had to con-tend with the subtle and deceptive S-O-R model of psychoanalysis with its commitment to a variety of biological instinctivism and a correlative conception of mind as an unconscious process that undermined the implicit autonomy of human intelligence. Hebb's predicament can be appreciated by a reminder of the earlier discussions of Hull and Skinner and of Freud, where I have shown so clearly that the project of classic behaviorism and of classic psychoanalysis failed. To be specific, Hull's automaticity of the s-r machine and the "instantaneity" of its reflex mechanism that replaces the autonomy of a person and the spontaneity of his/her mind is a mirror reflection of the two sides of the ultimate thesis, natural patiency and extra-natural agency, respectively; Skinner's astounding blindness to the fact that emitted behavior is personal agency is certainly made possible by the correlative blind faith in the ultimate thesis that explicitly dominated his work. And Freud's understandable but fatal acceptance of the *Solemn Oath* directly led him to produce a psychoanalytic model of mind that, in magnificently realizing the ultimate thesis, thereby imploded; not knowing what to do with a reluctant return to the Kantian ego, both Freud and Holt leave psychoanalytic theory stranded, unable to understand that "directly experienced psychological energy" must be translated into Giddens's "directly experienced personal agency." Of course what was required here to get beyond the two scientific projects for psychology was the shift away from positivistic naturalism to the realist naturalism of natural science and its taken for granted correct understanding of Newton's first law. The simple upshot would have been the simple acceptance of natural agency in the physical and biological worlds, hence the easy acceptance of human agency in the cultural world. In effect, I maintain, that that in fact is the case with D. O. Hebb. In his *Essay on Mind* (1980) then, it is no surprise that the theme of agency as a natural and evolutionary fact that underwrites what is actually his cognitive psychology is straightforwardly stated.

> There are those who deny the existence of free will in man because it would be inconsistent with natural law, and those who reject law, or determinism, for the same reason. Both are wrong. Free will exists, and it is fully compatible with, and indeed a product of, the operation of natural law: in an effect known as evolution. ... If it is predetermined that I take the left-hand turning at a fork in my path, it is also predetermined that this will be preceded by a certain activity in my brain, causally related to my behavior, and that activity is *choice*. Even in a deterministic universe, the living higher animal is not in any sense an automaton, for an automaton's mechanism remains the same from one time to the next and in the same situation does the same thing. Though the *cells* that compose the human body, and especially the human brain, *can plausibly be regarded as automata, the whole organism can not, for the brain is never the same twice running*. It is modified by experience, an effect we call memory. The pattern of its activity is continually changing, deterministically or not, and saying that if there is predetermination

there are no new patterns – the essential meaning of creativity – is to use the word *new* in a very peculiar sense. ... [Hence], the biological evident phenomenon of free will, the control of behavior at least some of the time by thought process, thus provides no more evidence in support of indeterminism than Heisenberg's uncertainty principle. ... I can see no way in which determinism lowers the worth and dignity of human beings.

(Hebb Ibid: 139–40)

Hebb may or may not be a closet Kantian, but they were certainly on the complementary sides of the same page. He and Kant were working on the identical fundamental problems of providing a realist metaphysical and theoretical grounding, respectively, for the possibility of autonomy and reflection in the functioning of human intelligence in the everyday world of cultural life. Consider the point that Hebb's denial of the idea that the cognition of human beings, their "autonomy [Kantian spontaneity] and intelligence [Kantian normativity]" (control of behavior by thought process), could plausibly be set to one side to favor a deterministic model of an automaton. At the center of his entire work on cognition has been his neurological (as well as empirical) demonstration that, on the one hand, *the concept of instinctive behavior cannot apply to us*, and on the other, the conception of cognition is grounded in the research discoveries that *cortical cells can* fire *spontaneously and can retain stimulation* (Varela 2003: 103–15; Hebb Ibid: 7–10). Indeed, it is eminently clear in the *Critique of Practical Reason* that Kant was metaphysically fighting against the determinism of the "practically conditioned" (natural wants and inclinations – Kant 1996b: 132). Thus, he was combating three theories of human automata, two of which he called "automaton materiale ... mechanical being moved by matter," for instance, instinctivism (natural wants) and S-R theory (inclinations), and one variety of what he called "Leibnitzian spiritulae ... the [subject] is impelled by [unconscious] ideas ... [being] nothing better than [the psychological] freedom of a turnspit" (Kant Ibid: 119). In reference to the first two automata, we see Kant, in effect, addressing these possibilities in *The Cannon of Pure Reason* of the first *Critique*.

For the human will is not determined by that alone which stimulates, that is, immediately affects the senses; we have the power to overcome the impressions on our faculty of sensuous desire, by calling up representations of what, in a more indirect manner, is useful or injurious. But these considerations ... as to what is good and useful, are based on reason.

(A802, B830)

And with regard to the latter problem of the Leibnitzian unconscious, Allison points out that Kant was ever mindful that that conception of foreign internal causes posed a threat to the principle of reason's independence from pathological necessitation (Allison 1990: 59). In view of these considerations, we can certainly declare that in Kant's problems of spontaneity and normativity he was metaphysically anticipating what would become Hebb's problems of autonomy and intelligence that he, Hebb, would be confronting between the 1940s and the 1970s in both behaviorism and psychoanalysis. And that is what it should be, since theory is a disguised metaphysic.

Concluding remarks

The recovery of human agency that has now been demonstrated from within the intellectual context of Kant's work has given Giddens the answer to his Call, and has provided Hebb's breakthrough to the victory of the autonomy of human intelligence over the automaticity of instinctive behavior with the proper realist metaphysic that his scientific practice richly deserves. The idea of human agency can thus be conceptually given, the formulation of which captures the variety of such an idea that this study has revealed in the work of not only Kant, but Dilthey, Sartre, Merleau-Ponty, Weber, Parsons, Bidney, Catton, Sahlins, and, of course, Giddens (see, in this regard, Manicas's concept of dominant causal agents – persons. 2006: 75). The principle of the conception is the correction of the Sartrean principle that existence precedes essence. The principle and conceptual formulation are as follows:

Principle
(1) *The essence of human existence is freedom: voluntarism is personal agency.*

Conceptual formulation
(2) *Personal agency is an emergent case of agent causality – self-movement – in nature.*
(3) The agency (potentials: possibilities) of the person (agent: thing: substance) is the (causal) power(s) of action.

References

Albrow, Martin. 1990. *Max Weber's Construction of Social Theory*. New York: St. Martins Press.

Alexander, Jeffrey. C. 1978. Formal and Substantive Voluntarism in the Work of Talcott Parsons: A Theoretical and Ideological Reinterpretation. *American Sociological Review* 43 (April): 177–98.

—— 1983. *The Modern Reconstruction of Classical Thought: Talcott Parsons*. Berkeley, CA: University of California Press.

Allison, Henry E. 1983. *Kant's Trascendental Idealism. An Interpretation and Defense*. New Haven, CT: Yale University Press.

—— 1990. *Kant's Theory of Freedom*. Cambridge: Cambridge University Press.

—— 1995. Spontaneity and Autonomy in Kant's Conception of the Self. In *The Modern Subject*. Karl Ameriks and Dieter Sturma, eds. Albany, NY: State University of New York Press.

Allport, Gordon G. 1937. The Functional Autonomy of Motives. *American Journal of Psychology* 50: 41–156.

Alpert, Harry. 1961. *Emile Durkheim and his Sociology*. New York: Russell and Russell.

Althusser, Louis. 1995. Ideology and Ideological Apparatuses (Notes Toward an Investigation). In *Mapping Ideology*. Slavoj Zizek, ed. London: Verso, pp. 100–40.

—— 1996. *For Marx*. London: Verso.

Ameriks, Karl. 2000. *German Idealism*. Karl Ameriks ed. Cambridge: Cambridge University Press.

Antonio, Robert J. 1998. Mapping Postmodern Social Theory. In *What is Social Theory: The Philosophical Debates*. Alan Sica, ed. Oxford: Basil Blackwell, pp. 22–75.

Archer, Margaret S. 1995. *Realist Social Theory: the Morphogenetic Approach*. Cambridge: Cambridge University Press.

—— 1996. *Culture and Agency. The Place of Culture in Social Theory*. Cambridge: Cambridge University Press.

—— 2000. *Being Human. The Problem of Agency*. Cambridge: Cambridge University Press.

Aronson, Jerrold. L. 1984. *A Realist Philosophy of Science*. New York: St. Martins Press.

Aronson, Jerrold L., Rom Harré and E. C. Way. 1995. *Realism Rescued*. Chicago, IL: Open Court.

Barker, Martin. 1980. Kant as a Problem for Weber. *British Journal of Sociology* 31 (1): 224–43.

Barnes, Barry, David Bloor and John Henry. 1995. *Scientific Knowledge: A Sociological Analysis.* Chicago: Chicago University Press.

Baudrillard, Jean. 1983. *In the Shadow of the Silent Majorities or the End of the Social and Other Essays.* New York: Semiotexte; New York: Macmillan Publishing; London: Collier Macmillan Publishers.

—— 2007. Forget Foucault. introduction and Interview by Sylvere Lotringer. Los Angeles, CA: Semio Text(e).

Bauman, Zygmunt. 1976. *Towards A Critical Sociology: An Essay on Commonsense and Emancipation.* London: Routledge and Kegan Paul.

—— 1992. *Intimations of Postmodernity.* London and New York: Routledge.

Baumer, Franklin L. 1977. *Modern European Thought: Continuity and Change in Ideas, 1600–1950.* New York: Macmillan.

Beiser, Frederick C. 1987. *The Fate of Reason: German Philosophy from Kant to Fichte.* Cambridge, MA: Harvard University Press.

Bellah, Robert. 1973. *Emile Durkheim on Morality and Society.* Chicago, IL: University of Chicago Press.

Bendix, Reinhard and Guenther Roth. 1971. *Scholarship and Partisanship: Essays on Max Weber.* Berkeley, CA: University of California Press.

Benton, Ted. 1977. *Philosophical Foundations of the Three Sociologies.* London: Routledge & Kegan Paul.

Berger, Peter. 1963. *Invitation to Sociology.* Garden City, NY: Doubleday & Company, Inc.

Berger, Peter with Thomas Luckmann. 1966. *The Social Construction of Reality.* Garden City, NY: Doubleday, & Company, Inc.

Berger, Peter with Hansfried Kellner. 1981. *Sociology Reinterpreted.* Garden City, NY: Anchor Press/Doubleday.

Berlin, Isaiah. 1992. *The Crooked Timber of Humanity.* Chapters in the History of Ideas. New York: Vintage Books.

Bershady, Harold J. 1973. *Ideology and Social Knowledge.* New York: John Wiley & Sons.

Bertens, Hans. 1995. *The Idea of Postmodernism.* London: Routledge.

Best, Steven and Douglas Kellner. 1997. *The Postmodern Turn.* London: Routledge.

—— 2003. "Postmodernism. " In *Continental Philosophy.* Robert C. Solomon and David Sherman, eds. Oxford: Blackwell, pp. 285–308.

Bhaskar, Roy. 1975. *A Realist Philosophy of Science*, 2nd edn. Atlantic Highlands, NJ: Humanities Press.

—— 1979. *The Possibility of Naturalism.* Atlantic Highlands, NJ: Humanities Press.

—— 1991. *Philosophy and the Idea of Freedom.* Oxford: Basil Blackwell.

Bidney, David. 1996. *Theoretical Anthropology*, 2nd edn. With a new introduction by Martin Bidney. New Brunswick, NJ: Transaction Publishers.

Bierstedt, Robert. 1966. *Emile Durkheim.* New York: Dell.

—— 1974. *Power and Progress: Essays on Sociological Theory.* New York: McGraw-Hill Book Company.

Bock, Kenneth. 1994. *Human Nature Mythology.* Champaign-Urbana, IL: University of Illinois Press.

Bogard, William. 1990. *Closing Down the Social: Baudrillard's Challenge to Contemporary Sociology.* Vol. 8 No.1 (spring), pp. 1–15.

Borenstein, Audrey. 1978. *Redeeming the Sin: Social Science and Literature.* New York: Columbia University Press.

Boring, Edward G. 1950. *A History of Experimental Psychology*. New York: Appleton-Century-Crofts.

Bourdieu, Pierre. 1997. *Outline of a Theory of Practice*. Cambridge: Cambridge University Press.

Brown, James Robert. 2001. *Who Rules Science: An Opinionated Guide to the Science Wars*. Cambridge, MA: Harvard University Press.

Bryant, Christopher. 1985. *Positivism in Social Theory and Research*. New York: St. Martin's Press.

Bunge, Mario. 1979 [1959]. *Causality and Modern Science*. New York: Dover.

—— 1996. *Finding Philosophy in Social Science*. New Haven, CT: Yale University Press.

Carnap, Rudolf. 1995. *Introduction to the Philosophy of Science*. New York: Dover Publications.

Cassirer, Ernst. 1946. *Myth of the State*. New Haven, CT: Yale University Press.

—— 1953. *Substance and Function*. New York: Dover Publications.

—— 1961. *The Logic of the Humanities*. New Haven, CT: Yale University Press.

—— 1964. *Essay on Man*. New Haven, CT: Yale University Press.

Catton, William. 1966. *From Animistic to Naturalistic Sociology*. New York: McGraw-Hill.

Chein, Isidor. 1972. *The Science of Behavior and the Image of Man*. New York: Basic Books.

Ceri, Paolo. 1993. Durkheim on Social Action. In *Emile Durkheim: Sociologist and Moralist*. Stephen P. Turner, ed. London: Routledge, pp. 139–68.

Churchland, Patricia S. 2005. Review of Michael S. Gazzaniga's *The Ethical Brain*. *American Scientist*, 93 (4): 356–57.

Cohen, Bernard I. and Richard S. Westfall. 1995. *Newton*. New York: W. W. Norton & Company.

Collins, Finn. 1997. *Social Reality*. London: Routledge.

Cottrell, Leonard S. Jr. 1942. The Analysis of Situational Fields. *American Sociological Review*. 7 (3): 370–82.

Dahrendorf, Ralf. 1968. *Essays in the Theory of Society*. Stanford, CA: Stanford University Press.

Dawe, Alan. 1978. Theories of Social Action. In *A History of Sociological Analysis*. Tom Bottomore and Robert Nisbet, eds. New York: Basic Books, pp. 362–417.

Delbruck, Max. 1986. *Mind from Matter*. Oxford: Blackwell Scientific Publicatioins, Inc.

Devereux, Edward C. 1961. Parsons' Sociological Theory. In *The Social Theories of Talcott Parsons*. Max Black, ed. Englewood Cliffs, NJ: Prentice-Hall, Inc.

Dewey, John. 1896. The Reflex-Arc Concept In Psychology. *Psychological Review* 3: 357–70.

Dilthey, Wilhelm. 1989. *Introduction to the Human Sciences. Wilhelm Dilthey,* vol. 1. Rudolf A. Makkreel and Frithjof Rodi, eds. Princeton, NJ: Princeton University Press.

Dreyfus, Herbert L. and Rabinow, Paul. 1983. *Beyond Structuralism and Hermeneutics,* 2nd edn with an Afterword by and an Interview with Michel Foucault. Chicago, IL: University of Chicago Press.

Durkheim, Emile. 1951. *Suicide. A Study in Sociology*. New York: The Free Press.

—— 1961. *Moral Education. A Study in the Theory of the Sociology of Education*. New York: The Free Press of Glencoe.

—— 1964a. *The Division of Labor.* Translated by George Simpson. London: The Free Press.

—— 1964b. *Essays on Sociology and Philosophy.* K. H. Wolf, ed. New York: Harper Torchbooks, pp. 325–40.

—— 1964c. The Rules of Sociological Method. Eighth edn. Traslated by Sarhah A. Solvay and John H. Mueller and edited by George E. G. Catlin. London: The Free Press of Glencoe, Collier-Macmillan Limited.

—— 1965. *Montesquieu and Rousseau. Forerunners of Sociology.* Foreword by Henri Peyre. Note by A. Cuvillier. Ann Arbor, MI: University of Michigan Press.

—— 1972. *Emile Durkheim: Selected Writings.* Edited, translated, and with an Introduction by Anthony Giddens. Cambridge: Cambridge University Press.

—— 1973. *Emile Durkheim on Morality and Society.* Edited and with an Introduction by Robert N. Bellah. Chicago, IL and London: University of Chicago Press.

—— 1978. *Emile Durkheim on Istitutional Analysis.* Edited, traslated and with and Introduction by Mark Traugott. Chicago, IL: University of Chicago Press.

—— 1982. *The Rules of Sociological Method and Selected Texts on the Sociology of Method.* Edited with an introduction by Steven Lukes. Translated by W. D. Wallis. New York: The Free Press.

—— 1995. *The Elementary Forms of Religious Life.* Translated and with an Introduction by Karen E. Fields. New York: The Free Press.

Edelson, M. 1988. *Psychoanalysis: A Theory in Crisis.* Chicago, IL: University of Chicago Press.

Elder-Vass, David. 2007. For Emergence: Refining Archer's Account of Social Structure. *Theory of Social Behaviour* 37 (1): 25–44.

Farnell, Brenda M. 1994. Ethno-Graphics and the Moving Body. *MAN. Journal of the Royal Anthropological Society* 29 (4): 929–73.

—— 1999. Moving Being, Acting Selves. *Annual Review of Anthropology* 28: 341–73.

Farnell, Brenda M. and Charles R. Varela. 2008. The Second Somatic Revolution. *Journal for the Theory of Social Behavior* 38 (3): 215–40.

Feynman, Richard P. 1999. *The Pleasure of Finding Things Out.* Foreword by Freeman Dyson. Cambridge, MA: Helix Books, Perseus Publishing.

Foucault, Michel. 1994. *Michel Foucault: Ethics, Subjectivity and Truth.* Paul Rabinow, ed. New York: New York Press.

Frank, Philip. 1957. *Philosophy of Science: The Link Between Science and Philosophy.* Englewood Cliffs, NJ: Prentice-Hall.

Freud, Sigmund. 1954. *Project for a Scientific Psychology: Letters to Wilhelm Fleiss, Drafts, and Notes, 1887–1902.* M. Bonapart, A. Freud and E. Kris, eds. New York: Basics Books, Inc., Publishers.

—— 1998. *The Interpretation of Dreams.* Edited and translated by J. Strachey. New York: Avon Books, Harper Collins Publishers.

Freundlieb, Dieter. 1994. Foucault's Theory of Discourse and Human Agency. In *Reassessing Foucault. Power, Medicine, and the Body.* Colin Jones and Roy Porter, eds. London: Routledge, pp. 152–80.

Gardner, S. 1991. The Unconscious. In *The Cambridge Companion to Freud.* Jerome Neu, ed. Cambridge: Cambridge University Press, pp. 136–60.

Garrett, Richard. 1996. Skinner's Case for Radical Behaviorism. In *The Philosophy of Psychology.* William O. Donohue and Richard E. Kitchner, eds. London: Sage Publishers, pp. 141–48.

Geertz, Clifford. 1983. *Local Knowledge.* New York: Basic Books.

—— 2003. *Available Light.* Princeton, NJ: Princeton University Press.

Gellner, Ernest. 1986. *Relativism and the Social Sciences.* Cambridge: Cambridge University Press.

Giddens, Anthony. 1972. *Emile Durkehim: Selected Writings.* Edited, traslated and with an Introduction by Anthony Giddens. Cambridge, new Yourk and Melbourne: Cambridge University Press.

—— 1978. *Emile Durkheim.* New York: Penguin Books.

—— 1979. *Central Problems of Sociological Theory.* London: Macmillan.

—— 1984. *The Constitution of Society.* Berkeley, CA: University of California Press.

—— 1993[1976]. *New Rules of Sociological Method.* Stanford, CA: Stanford University Press.

—— 1996. *In Defense of Sociology.* Cambridge: Polity Press, with Blackwell Publishers Ltd.

Giddens, Anthony and Christopher Pierson. 1998. *Conversations with Anthony Giddens.* Stanford, CA: Stanford University Press.

Gilbert, Margaret. 1992. *On Social Facts.* Princeton, NJ: Princeton University Press.

Goodwin, Brian. 1994. *How the Leopard Changed its Spots.* Princeton, NJ: Princeton University Press.

Gouldner, Alvin W. 1970. *The Coming Crisis of Western Sociology.* New York and London: Basic Book, Inc.

Greenwood, John D. 1990. Kant's Third Antinomy: Agency and Causal Explanation. *International Philosophical Quarterly* 30: 43–57.

Grene, Marjorie. 1976. *Philosophy In and Out of Europe.* Berkeley, CA: University of California Press.

Guyer, Paul. 1993. *Kant and the Experience of Freedom.* New York: Cambridge University Press.

Habermas, Jurgen. 1989. *On the Logic of the Social Sciences.* Cambridge, MA: The MIT Press.

Hall, Calvin S. 1964. *The Roots of Consciousness.* Princeton, NJ: D. Van Nostrand Company, Inc.

Halperin, John. 1983. *C. P. Snow: an Oral Biography.* Together with a Conversation with Lady Snow. New York: St. Martin's Press. p. 62.

Harré, Rom. 1970. *The Principles of Scientific Thinking.* Chicago: University of Chicago Press

—— 1979. *Social Being.* Oxford: Basil Blackwell.

—— 1984. *Personal Being.* Oxford: Basil Blackwell.

—— 1985. *The Philosophies of Science.* Oxford: Oxford University Press.

—— 1986. *Varieties of Realism.* Oxford: Basil Blackwell.

—— 1991. *Physical Being.* Oxford: Basil Blackwell.

—— 1993. *Laws of Nature.* London: Duckworth & Co.

—— 1995a. Agentive Discourse. In *Discursive Psychology.* Rom Harré and Peter Stearns, eds. London: Sage, pp. 120–36.

—— 1998. Recovering the Experiment. *Philosophy*, 73: 353–77.

—— 2000a. *One Thousand Years of Philosophy.* Oxford: Blackwell Publishers.

—— 2000b. *A Discussion of Causal Powers.* Unpublished manuscript 2.

—— 2005 Causal Mechanism and Social Practices: What can Social Science Contribute to Social Practice. Unpublished manuscript.

—— 2007. Extended Semantic Field of Dispositions and the Grounding Role of Causal Powers. In *Dispositions and Causal Powers,* Max Kistler and Bruno Gnassounou, eds. Aldershot: Ashgate.

—— 2008. *Active Powers and Powerful Agents.* London: Sage.

Harré, Rom and Paul Secord. 1973. *The Explanation of Social Behavior.* Totowa, NJ: Littlefield, Adams.

Harré, Rom and E. H. Madden. 1975. *Causal Powers.* Oxford: Basil Blackwell.

Harré, Rom and Grant Gillet. 1994. *Discursive Mind.* London: Sage.

Hebb, Donald O. 1960. The American Revolution. *American Psychologist* 15 (12): 735–45.

—— 1980. *Essay On Mind.* Hillsdale, NJ: Lawrence Erlbaum Associates.

Heidegger, Martin. 1962. *Being and Time.* Oxford: Basil Blackwell.

—— 1993. *Basic Writings.* David Farrell Krell, ed. With introductions. New York: Harper Collins.

—— 2000. *Introduction to Metaphysics.* New Haven, CT and London: Yale University Press.

—— 2002. The *Essence of Human Freedom.* London: Continuum.

Herzfeld, Michael. 1997. *Cultural Intimacy: Social Poetics in the Nation-State.* New York: Routledge.

—— 2001. *Anthropology: Theoretical Practice in Culture and Society.* Oxford: Blackwell Publishers.

Hirst, Paul Q. 1975. *Durkheim, Bernard and Epistemology.* London and Boston: Routledge and Kegan Paul.

Hobbes, Thomas. 1957. *Leviathan.* Edited with an introduction by Michael Oakeshott. Oxford: Basil Blackwell.

Hocutt, Max. 1996. Behaviorism as Opposition to Cartesianism. In *The Philosophy of Psychology.* William O. Donohue and Richard F. Kitchner, eds. London: Sage Publishers, pp. 81–95.

Holt, Robert. 1989. *Freud Reappraised: A Fresh Look at Psychoanalytic Theory.* New York and London: Guilford Press.

Homans, George C. 1964. Bringing Men Back. In: *American Sociological Review* 29 (5): 809–18.

—— 1967. *The Nature of Social Science.* New York: Harcourt, Brace & World, Inc.

—— 1986. Fifty Years of Sociology. *Annual Review of Sociology* 12: xiii–xxx.

Hoy, Cyrus. 1963. *Hamlet: William Shakespeare.* New York: W. W. Norton and Company.

Hoy, David. 1990. Jacques Derrida. In *The Return of Grand Theory in the Human Sciences,* Quentin Skinner, ed. New York: Cambridge University Press, pp. 43–64.

Hughes, H. Stuart. 1964. *Consciousness and Society.* New York: Alfred A. Knop.

Hull, Clark L. 1937. Mind, Mechanism, and Adaptive Behavior. *American Psychological Association* 44 (1): 1–32.

Husserl, Edmund. 1970. *The Crisis of European Sciences and Transcendental Philosophy.* David Carr, introduction. Evanston, IL: Northwestern University Press.

James, Susan. 1990. Louis Althusser. In *The Return of Grand Theory in the Social Sciences.* Quentin Skinner, ed. Cambridge: Cambridge University Press, pp. 141–57

Joas, Hans. 1985. *G. H. Mead: A Contemporary Examination of his Thought.* Translated by Raymond Meyer. Cambridge, MA: MIT Press.

—— 1993. *Pragmatism and Social Theory.* London: Cambridge University Press.

—— 1996. *The Creativity of Action.* Chicago, IL: Chicago University Press.

Jones, Alun. 1999. *The Development of Durkheim's Realism.* Cambridge: Cambridge University Press.

Jones, Ernest. 1949. *Hamlet and Oedipus.* Garden City, NY: Doubleday & Company.

Kalberg, Stephen. 1980. Max Weber's Types of Rationality: Cornerstones for the Analysis of Rationalization Processes in History. *American Journal of Sociology* 85 (3): 1145–79.

—— 1994. *Max Weber's Comparative Historical Sociology.* Chicago, IL: University of Chicago Press.

Kant, Immanuel. 1985a. *Immanuel Kant's Critique of Pure Reason.* Translated by Norman Kemp Smith. London: Macmillan Publishers.

—— 1985b. *Philosophy of Material Nature.* Indianapolis, IN: Hackett Publishing Company.

—— 1993. *Opus Postumum.* Edited, with an Introduction and Notes, by Eckart Forster. Translated by Eckart Forster and Michael Rosen. Cambridge: Cambridge University Press.

—— 1996a. *Critique of Practical Reason.* Translated by T. K. Abbott. Amherst, NY: Prometheus Books.

—— 1996b. *Practical Philosophy.* Translated and edited by Mary J. Gregor and Allen Wood. Cambridge: Cambridge University Press.

—— 1997. What is Enlightenment. In *Foundations of the Metaphysic of Morals.* Upper Saddle River, NJ: Prentice Hall, pp. 83–90.

—— 1998. *Critique of Pure Reason.* Translated and edited by Paul Guyer and Allen Wood. Cambridge: Cambridge University Press.

Kaufman, Walter. 1975. *Existentialism From Dostoyevsky to Sartre.* New York and Scarborough, Ontario: The New American Library.

Keat, Russell. 1971. Positivism, Naturalism, and Anti-Naturalism in the Social Sciences. *Journal for the Theory of Social Behavior* 1: 3–16.

Keat, Russell with John Urry. 1975. *Social Theory as Science.* London: Routledge.

Kellner, Douglas. 1989. *Jean Baudrillard: From Marxism to Postmodernism and Beyond.* Cambridge: Polity Press and Stanford University Press.

Kerr, R. 1993. *A Most Dangerous Method.* New York: Alfred A. Knopf.

Kitchener, Richard F. 1996. Skinner's Theory of Theories. In *The Philosophy of Psychology.* William O. Donohue and Richard F. Kitchner, eds. London: Sage Publishers, pp. 108–25.

Klein, George S. 1976. *Psychoanalytic Theory: An Exploration of Essentials.* New York: International University Press.

Kroeber, A. L. 1948. White's View of Culture. *American Anthropologist.* Vol. 50, no. 3, Part I: 405–15.

Kuhn, Thomas S. 1977. *The Essential Tension. Selected Studies in Scientific Tradition and Change.* Chicago, IL and London: University of Chicago Press.

LaCapra, Dominic. 1972. *Emile Durkheim. Sociologist and Philosopher.* Ithaca, NY: Cornell University Press.

Lamont, Corliss. 1990. *The Philosophy of Humanism.* New York: Continuum Publishing Co.

Lehman, David. 1991. *Signs of the Times.* New York: Poseidon Press.

Lehmann, Jennifer M. 1993. *Deconstructing Durkheim. A Post-Post Structuralist Critique.* London: Routledge.

Lemert, Charles. 1995. *Sociology After the Crisis.* Boulder, CO: Westview Press.

—— 1997. *Postmodernism is not What you Think.* Oxford: Blackwell Publishers.

Levi-Strauss. 1966. *Savage Mind.* Chicago, IL: University of Chicago Press.

—— 1979. *Myth and Meaning.* New York: Schocken Books.

Levine, Donald N. 1995. *Visions of the Sociological Traditions.* Chicago: University of Chicago Press.

Lewis, Paul. 2000. Realism, Causality, and the Problem of Social Structure. *Journal for the Theory of Social Behavior* 30 (3): 249–68.

Lewontin, Richard C. 1995. Genes, Environment, and Organisms. In *Hidden Histories of Science.* Robert B. Silvers, ed. New York: New York Review Book, pp. 115–40.

Liebersöhn, Harry. 1987. *Fate and Utopia in German Sociology, 1870–1923.* Cambridge, MA: The MIT Press.

Lopez, Jose and Garry Potter. 2001. *After Postmodernism: An Introduction to Critical Realism.* London: The Atholine Press.

Loyal, Steven and Barry Barnes. 2000. "Agency" as a Red Herring in Social Theory. *Philosophy of the Social Sciences* 31 (4): 507–24.

Lukes, Steven. 1972. *Emile Durkheim. His Life and Work.* New York: Harper & Row.

McClelland, David. 1964. *The Roots of Consciousness.* Princeton, NJ: D. Van Nostrand Company.

McIntosh, Donald. 1975. Weber and Freud: On the Nature and Sources of Authority. *American Sociological Review* 40 (4): 910–11.

MacIntyre, Alasdair. 1966. The Antecedents of Action. In *British Analytical Philosophy.* B. Williams and A. Montefiore, eds. London: Routledge and Kegan Paul, pp. 205–25.

MacIver, Robert M. 1942. *Social Causation.* Boston, MA: Ginn and Company.

Mackenzie, Brian D. 1977. *Behaviorism and Scientific Method.* Atlantic Highlands, NJ: Humanities Press.

Malcolm, Norman. 1964. Behaviorism as a Philosophy of Psychology. In *Behaviorism and Phenomenology. Contrasting Bases for Modern Psychology.* T. W. Wann, ed. Chicago, IL: University of Chicago Press, pp. 141–62.

Manicas, Peter. T. 1986. *A History and Philosophy of the Social Sciences.* Oxford: Basil Blackwell.

—— 2006. *A Realist Philosophy of Social Science. Explanation and Understanding.* Cambridge: Cambridge University Press.

Mayr, Ernst. 1985. How Biology Differs from the Physical Sciences. In *Evolution at the Crossroads: The New Biology and the New Philosophy of Science.* D. J. Depew and B. H. Weber, eds. Cambridge, MA: MIT Press, pp. 43–63.

—— 1997. *This is Biology. The Science of the Living World.* Cambridge, MA: Harvard University Press.

Mead, George H. 1900. Suggestions Toward a Theory of the Philosophical Disciplines. In *Selected Writings: George Herbert Mead.* Andrew J. Reck, ed. Chicago, IL: University of Chicago Press, pp. 6–24.

Merleau-Ponty, Maurice. 1964. *The Visible and the Invisible.* Translated by A. Lingis. Evanston, IL: Northwestern University Press.

—— 1989. *Phenomenology of Perception.* Translated by Colin Smith. London: Routledge.

Merton, Robert K., Leonard Broom and Leonard S. Cottrell, Jr. 1959. *Sociology Today: Problems and Prospects.* New York: Basic Books, Inc.

Mestrovic, Stjepan G. 1993. *Emile Durkheim and the Reformation of Sociology.* Boston, MA: Rowman and Littlefield.

—— 1998. *Anthony Giddens: The Last Modernist.* London: Routledge.

330   *References*

Milbank, John. 1993. *Theology & Social Theory: Beyond Secular Reason.* Oxford: Blackwell Publishers Ltd.

Mintz, Samuel I. 1996. *The Hunting of Leviathan.* Bristol: Thoemmes Press.

Moore, Henrietta L. 1999. Anthropological Theory at the Turn of the Century. In *Anthropological Theory Today.* Henrietta Moore, ed. Malden, MA: Blackwell Publishers, pp. 1–23.

Moran, Dermot. 2000. *Introduction to Phenomenology.* London: Routledge.

Mumford, Stephen. 1998. *Dispositions.* Oxford: Oxford University Press.

Munch, Richard. 1981. Talcott Parsons and the Theory of Action. I. The Structure of the Kantian Core. *American Journal of Sociology* 86 (4): 709–39.

—— 1982. Talcott Parsons and the Theory of Action. II. The Continuity of the Development. *American Journal of Sociology* 87 (4): 771–826.

Nagel, Ernst. 1979. *The Structure of Science: Problems in the Logic of Scientific Explanation.* Indianapolis, IN: Hackett Publishing Company.

Natanson, Maurice. 1973. *Phenomenology and the Social Sciences.* Evanston, IL: Northwestern University Press.

Newton, Roger G. 1997. *The Truth of Science.* Cambridge, MA: Harvard University Press.

Nisbet, Robert. 1974. *The Sociology of Emile Durkheim.* New York: Oxford University Press.

Norris, Christopher. 2000. *Deconstruction and the "Unfinished Project of Modernity".* New York: Routledge.

Ortner, Sherry. 1984. Theory in Anthropology Since the Sixties. *Comparative Studies in Society and History* 26 (1): 126–66.

Parsons, Talcott. 1949. *The Structure of Social Action,* vols I and II. New York: The Free Press, Collier Macmillan Publishers.

—— 1978. *Action Theory and The Human Condition.* New York: The Free Press, Collier Macmillan Publishers.

—— 1991. *Talcott Parsons. Early Essays.* Edited and with an Introduction by Charles Camic. Chicago, IL: University of Chicago Press.

Parsons, Talcott, Robert F. Bales and Edward A. Shills. 1953. *Working Paper in the Theory of Action.* New York: Free Press.

Pawson, Ray. 1989. *A Measure for Measures. A Manifesto for Empirical Sociology.* London: Routledge.

Poole, Steven. 2007. Jean Baudrillard [Obituary]. *Guardian Weekly* March 16–22: 26.

Pope, Whitney. 1973. Classic on a Classic: Parsons's Interpretation of Durkheim. *American Sociological Review* 38 (August): 399–414.

—— 1973. Parsons on Durkheim, Revisited. *American Sociological Review* 38: 111–14.

—— 1976. *Durkheim's Suicide.* Chicago, IL: University of Chicago Press.

Porpora, Douglas. 1993. Cultural Rules and Material Relations. *Sociological Theory* 11: 212–29.

—— 2001. Do Realists Run Regressions? In *After Postmodernism: An Introduction to Critical Realism.* Jose Lopez and Garry Potter, eds. London: Atholine Press.

Poster, Mark. 1988. *Jean Baudrillard. Selected Writings.* Mark Poster, ed. Stanford, CA: Stanford University Press.

Rabinow, Paul and William M. Sullivan 1987. *Interpretative Social Science. A Second Look.* Berkeley, CA: University of California Press.

Rapaport, David. 1959. The Structure of Psychoanalytic Theory: A Systematizing Attempt. In *Psychology Issues, Monograph* 6. New York: International Universities Press.

Richmond, Sarah. 2005. Politics and Paradox in Sartre's Life and Work. *Times Literary Supplement* November 4: 3.

Roche, Maurice. 1975. *Phenomenology, Language and the Social Sciences.* London: Routledge and Kegan Paul.

Rosenau, Pauline Marie. 1992. *Post-Modernism and the Social Sciences: Insights, Inroads, and Intrusions.* Princeton, NJ: Princeton University Press.

Rossi, Ino. 1974. *The Unconscious in Culture.* New York: E. P. Dutton & Co.

Rousseau, Jean J. 1996. *Emile.* London: J. M. Dent & Sons.

Ryan, Alan. 1974. The Nature of Human Nature in Hobbes and Rousseau. In *The Limits of Human Nature.* Jonathan Benthall, ed. New York: E. P. Dutton & Co., pp. 3–19.

Sahlins, Marshall. 1976a. *Culture and Practical Reason.* Chicago, IL: University of Chicago Press.

——1976b. *The Use and Abuse of Biology: An Anthropological Critique of Sociobiology.* Ann Arbor, MI: University of Michigan Press.

—— 1998. Two or Three Things I Know About Culture. *Journal of the Anthropological Institute* 5: 399–421.

—— 2000. *Culture in Practice.* New York: Zone Books.

Sartre, Jean-Paul. 1957. *The Transcendence of the Ego.* New York: The Noonday Press.

—— 1965. *The Philosophy of Jean-Paul Sartre.* Edited and introduced by Robert Denoon Cumming. New York: Vintage Books.

—— 2007. *Existentialism is a Humanism.* New Haven, CT: Yale University Press.

Savage, Stephen P. 1981. *The Theories of Talcott Parsons: The Social Relations of Action.* New York: St. Martins Press.

Sayer, Andrew. 1984. *Method in Social Science. A Realist Approach.* London: Routledge.

Schaffer, Roy. 1976, *A New Language for Psychoanalysis.* New Haven, CT: Yale University Press.

Schmaus, Warren. 1994. *Durkheim's Philosophy of Science and the Sociology of Knowledge: Creating an Intellectual Niche.* Chicago, IL: The University of Chicago Press.

Schneewind, J. B. 1998. *The Invention of Autonomy. A History of Modern Philosophy.* Cambridge: Cambridge University Press.

Schopenhauer, Arthur. 1969. *The World as Will and Representation*, vol. 1. Translated by Eric F. J. Payne, New York: Dover Press.

—— 2004. *Prize Essay on the Freedom of the Will.* Edited by Gunter Zoller and translated by Eric F. J. Payne. Cambridge: Cambridge University Press.

Scott, John F. 1962. The Impossible Theory of Action: Some Questions on Parsons's Prewar Classification of Action Theories. *Berkeley Journal of Sociology* 7: 51–62.

—— 1963 The Changing Foundations of the Parsonian Action Scheme. *American Sociological Review* 28 (5): 719–31.

Seward, John. 1963. The Structure of Functional Autonomy. *American Psychologist* 33 (4): 703–10.

Shell, Susan Meld. 1996. *The Embodiment of Reason. Kant on Spirit, Generation, and Community.* Chicago, IL: The University of Chicago Press.

Shilling, Chris and Philip A. Mellor. 2001. *The Sociological Ambition.* London: Sage Publications, Ltd.

Shotter, John. 1975. *Images of Man in Psychological Research.* London: Methuen.

—— 1984. *Social Accountability and Self Hood.* Oxford: Basil Blackwell.

—— 1993. *Conversational Realities.* London: Sage Publications.

Simmel, Georg. 1964. How is Society Possible. In *Essays On Sociology, Philosophy, and Aesthetics.* Kurt H. Wolff, ed. New York: Harper & Row Publishers, pp. 337–56.

—— 1968. *The Conflict in Modern Culture and Other Essays.* K. Peter Etzkorn, translation and Introduction. Teacher's College Press, Columbia University.

—— 1991. *Schopenhauer and Nietzsche.* Translated by Helmut Loiskandl, Deena Weinstein, and Michael Weinstein. Urbana, IL: University Illinois Press.

Skinner, B. F. 1938. *The Behavior of Organisms.* New York: Appleton-Century Crofts.

—— 1953. *Science and Human Behavior.* New York: The Free Press; London: Collier-Macmillan, Ltd.

—— 1971. *Beyond Freedom and Dignity.* New York: Knopf.

—— 1976. *About Behaviorism.* New York: Vintage Books.

—— 1990. Can Psychology be a Science of Mind? *American Psychologist* 45 (11):1206–10.

Skinner, Quentin. 1990. *The Return of Grand Theory in the Human Sciences.* New York: Cambridge University Press.

Smart, Barry. 1993. *Modern Conditions, Postmodern Controversies.* London: Routledge.

Sokal, Alan. 2000. Why I wrote My Parody. In *The Sokal Hoax. The Sham that Shook the Academy.* Edited by the editors of *Lingua Franca.* Lincoln, NB: University of Nebraska Press.

Stark, Werner. 1963. *The Fundamental Forms of Social Thought.* New York: Fordham University Press.

Steinmetz, George. 2005. Introduction. Positivism and its Others in Twentieth-Century Social Science. In *The Politics of Method in the Social Sciences: Positivism and it Epistemological Others.* George Steinmetz, ed. Durham/London: Duke University Press, pp. 1–58.

Strawson, Peter. 1966. *Bounds of Sense.* London: Methuen.

Taylor, Charles. 1964. *The Explanation of Behavior.* London: Routledge and Kegan Paul.

—— 1989. *Sources of the Self. The Making of Modern Identity.* Cambridge, MA: Harvard University Press.

Thomas, William I. 1972 [1931]. The Definition of the Situation. In *Symbolic Interaction. A Reader in Social Psychology,* 2nd edn. Jerome G. Manis and Bernard N. Meltzer, eds. Boston, MA: Allyn and Bacon, pp. 331–36.

Tiryakian, Edward A. 1962. *Sociologism and Existentialism.* Englewood Cliffs, NJ: Prentice Hall, Inc.

—— 1978. Emile Durkheim. In *A History of Sociological Analysis.* Tom Bottomore and Robert Nisbet, eds. New York: Basic Books, pp. 187–236.

Todorov, Tzvetan. 2002. *Imperfect Garden.* Princeton, NJ: Princeton University Press.

Toulmin, Steven. 1990. *Cosmopolis.* New York: Free Press.

—— *Philosophy of Science.* New York: Harper & Row.

Traugott, Mark. 1978. *Emile Durkheim on Institutional Analysis.* Chicago, IL: University of Chicago Press.

Trilling, Lionel. 1968. *Beyond Culture: Essays on Literature a Learning.* New York: Viking Press.

Tudor, Andrew. 1982. *Beyond Empiricism. Philosophy of Science in Sociology.* London: Routledge.

Turner, Bryan. 1999. *Classical Sociology.* London: Sage Publications Ltd.

Turner, Jonathan. 1988. *A Theory of Social Interaction.* Stanford, CA: Stanford University Press.

—— 1992. The Promise of Positivism. In *Postmodernism and Social Theory.* Steven Seidman and David G. Wagner, eds. Cambridge, MA: Blackwell, pp. 156–78.

Turner, Jonathan, with Leonard Beeghley and Charles H. Powers. 1995. *The Emergence of Sociological Theory.* Belmont, CA: Wadsworth Publishing Company.

Turner, Stephen P. 1986. *The Search for a Methodology of Social Science: Durkheim, Weber, and the Nineteenth-Century Problem of Cause, Probability, and Action.* Dordrecht: D. Reidel Publishing Company.

—— 1994. *Max Weber: The Lawyer as Social Thinker.* London: Routledge.

—— 2003. Cause, the Persistence of Teleology, and the Origins of the Philosophy of Science. In *The Blackwell Guide to the Philosophy of the Social Sciences.* Stephen P. Turner and Paul A. Roth, eds. Oxford: Blackwell Publishing, pp. 21–41.

Turner, Stephen P. and Regis A. Factor. 1993. *Emile Durkheim: Sociologist and Moralist.* Stephen P. Turner, ed. London: Routledge.

Turner, Stephen P. and Paul A. Roth. 2003. Introduction. Ghosts and the Machine: Issues of Agency, Rationality, and Scientific Methodology in Contemporary Philosophy of Social Science. In *The Blackwell Guide to the Philosophy of the Social Sciences.* Stephen Turner and Paul A. Roth, eds. Oxford: Blackwell Publishing, pp. 1–18.

Twain, Mark. 2000. *What is Man?* Kobenhavn: Green Integer.

Varela, Charles R. 1973. The Crisis of Western Sociology: The Problem of Social Interaction, the Self, and Unawareness for Social Theory. Unpublished PhD Dissertation. New York University, New York, NY.

—— 1993. *Freud and Mead: The Third Psychologist's Fallacy and the Social Nature of Unawareness.* Unpublished manuscript.

—— 1994. Harré and Merleau-Ponty: Beyond the Absent Moving Body in Embodied Social Theory. *Journal for the Theory of Social Behavior* 24 (2): 163–85.

—— 1995a. Cartesianism Revisited: The Ghost in the Machine and in the Lived Body. In *Human Action Signs in Cultural Context: The Visible and Invisible in Movement and Dance.* Brenda Farnell, ed. Metuchen, NJ: Scarecrow Press, pp. 216–93.

—— 1995b. Ethogenic Theory and Psychoanalysis: The Unconscious as a Social Construction and a Failed Explanatory Concept. *Journal for the Theory of Social Behavior* 25 (4) 263–385.

—— 1999. Determinism and the Recovery of Human Agency: The Embodying of Persons. *Journal for the Theory of Social Behavior* 29 (4): 385–402.

—— 2001. The Ethogenics of Agency and Structure: A Metaphysical Problem. In *After PostModernism: An Introduction to Critical Realism.* Jose Lopez and Garry Potter, eds. London: The Atholine Press, pp. 63–74.

—— 2002. The Impossibility of Which Naturalism? A Response and a Reply. *Journal for the Theory of Social Behavior* 32 (1): 105–11.

—— 2003. Biological Structure and Embodied Human Agency: The Problem of Instinctivism. *Journal for the Theory of Social Behavior* 33 (1): 95–122.

—— 2005. Parsonian Action Theory and Dynamic Embodiment. *Journal for the Anthropological Study of Human Movement* 14 (4): 1–15.

—— 2007. Elder-Vass's Move and Giddens' Call. *Journal for the Theory of Social Behavior* 37 (2): 201–10.

Varela, Charles R. with Brenda M. Farnell. 2008. The Second Somatic Revolution. In press *Journal for the Theory of Social Behavior.*

Varela, Charles R. with Rom Harré. 1996. Conflicting Varieties of Realism: Causal Powers and the Problem of Social Structure. *Journal for the Theory of Social Behavior* 26 (3): 313–25.

Wallace, William. 1974. *Causality and Scientific Explanation,* vol. 2. Ann Arbor, MI: The University of Michigan Press.

—— 1996. *The Modeling of Nature.* Washington: The Catholic University of America Press.

Weber, Max. 1958. *From Max Weber: Essays in Sociology.* Translated, edited, and with an Introduction by H. H. Gerth and C. Wright Mills. New York: Oxford University Press.

—— 1968. *Economy and Society.* Gunther Roth and Claus Wittich, eds. Berkeley, CA: University of California Press.

—— 1975. *Roscher and Knies: The Logical Problems of Historical Economics.* Translated with an introduction by Guy Oakes. New York: The Free Press.

—— 1978. *Economy and Society.* Edited by Gunther Roth and Claus Wittich. Berkley, CA: University of California Press.

Weingartner, Rudolph H. 1960. *Experience and Culture. The Philosophy of Georg Simmel.* Middletown, CT: Wesleyan University Press.

Weinstein, Deena and Michael Weinstein. 1993. *Postmodern(ized) Simmel.* London and New York: Routledge.

Weldon, T. D. 1958. *Kant's Critique of Pure Reason.* Oxford: Clarendon Press.

Whyte, Lancelot, Law. 1960. *The Unconscious Before Freud.* New York: Basic Books.

Williams, Drid. 1982. Semasiology: A Semantic Anthropologist's View of Human Movements and Actions. In *Semantic Anthropology.* David Parkin, ed. London: Academic Press, pp. 161–82.

—— 2003. Signifying Bodies, Signifying Acts. (manuscript available from JASHM).

Williams, Robin Jr. 1961. The Sociological Theory of Talcott Parsons. Max Black, ed. Englewood Cliffs, NJ: Prentice-Hall, Inc.

Wisdom, John O. 1971. Science versus the Scientific Revolution. *Philosophy of Science* 1: 123–144.

Wolff, Kurt H. 1950. *The Sociology of Georg Simmel.* Translated, edited and with an introduction by Kurt H. Wolff. London: The Free Press of Glencoe, Collier-Macmillan, Ltd.

—— 1960. Essays On Sociology and Philosophy by Emile Durkheim *et al.* With appraisals of his life and thought. Kurt H. Wolff, ed. Harper Torchbooks: The Academy Library.

—— 1978. Phenomenology and Sociology. In *A History of Sociological Analysis.* Tom Bottomore and Robert Nisbet, eds. New York: Basic Books.

Wood, Allen. 2005. *Kant.* Oxford: Blackwell Publishing.

Woolgar, Steve. 1993. *Science: The Very Idea.* London and New York: Routledge.

Index